Reforming Early Retirement in Europe, Japan and the USA

Reforming Early Retirement in Europe, Japan and the USA

Bernhard Ebbinghaus

OXFORD
UNIVERSITY PRESS

Great Clarendon Street, Oxford OX2 6DP

Oxford University Press is a department of the University of Oxford.
It furthers the University's objective of excellence in research, scholarship,
and education by publishing worldwide in

Oxford New York

Auckland Cape Town Dar es Salaam Hong Kong Karachi
Kuala Lumpur Madrid Melbourne Mexico City Nairobi
New Delhi Shanghai Taipei Toronto

With offices in

Argentina Austria Brazil Chile Czech Republic France Greece
Guatemala Hungary Italy Japan Poland Portugal Singapore
South Korea Switzerland Thailand Turkey Ukraine Vietnam

Oxford is a registered trade mark of Oxford University Press
in the UK and in certain other countries

Published in the United States
by Oxford University Press Inc., New York

© Bernhard Ebbinghaus, 2006

British Library Cataloguing in Publication Data
Data available

Library of Congress Cataloging in Publication Data
Data available

Typeset by SPI Publisher Services, Pondicherry, India.
Printed in Great Britain
on acid-free paper by
Biddles Ltd., King's Lynn,
Norfolk

ISBN 978-0-19-928611-9

Acknowledgments

*Books, like proverbs, receive their chief value from the stamp and esteem of
ages through which they passed.*

(William Temple, 1881–1944, Archbishop of Canterbury,
who coined the term 'welfare state')

This book had all but an early exit. The first step toward a study of the
interaction between labor relations and welfare states dates back to my
arrival at the Max Planck Institute for the Study of Societies (MPIfG) in
1997. Conducting this study would not have been possible without
having had the many opportunities provided by a senior research fellowship at the MPIfG under the directorship of Wolfgang Streeck and Fritz W.
Scharpf. Cologne was the right place to undertake research that joins
comparative perspectives on welfare regimes, corporatism, and varieties
of capitalism. The MPIfG workshop 'Comparing Welfare Capitalism',
which I organized with Philip Manow, brought together European and
American scholars working on welfare states, labor relations, and political
economy. My paper on the elective affinities between production, protection, and partnership was the genesis of the project that developed into
this book. Another MPIfG project, 'Work and Welfare in an Open Economy', organized by Fritz W. Scharpf and Vivien Schmidt, was a further
catalyst in studying the potentials for policy reversal of early retirement
practices.

A John F. Kennedy Memorial Fellowship, funded by the DAAD (German
Academic Exchange Service), at Harvard's Center for European Studies in
1999/2000 provided time in an ideal environment to explore the political
economy of early retirement and the role of social partners in negotiated
welfare reforms. Discussions with Peter A. Hall, Jytte Klausen, Andy Martin, Cathie Jo Martin, and Paul Pierson stimulated my considerations of
political economy and welfare reform. A semester at the University of
Wisconsin-Madison, as International Institute Visiting Professor in fall
2001 allowed me to discuss the results of the *Comparing Welfare Capitalism*
book in a workshop at the European Union Center and to teach American

students European labor relations at the Industrial Relations Research Institute. For their support, my thanks go to Orfeo Fioretos, Crister Garrett, David M. Trubek, and especially to Jonathan Zeitlin for inviting me to Madison in the first place. For their helpful comments as the project evolved, colleagues and students at Chapel Hill, Duke, Harvard, Northwestern, and Wisconsin-Madison—as well as at the European University Institute in Florence—deserve acknowledgment.

This book is based on a manuscript submitted as the 'second thesis' (*Habilitation*) to the University of Cologne's Economic and Social Science Faculty. My gratitude to Wolfgang Streeck, Jürgen Friedrichs, and Frank Schulz-Nieswandt for their support and commentary as readers, and to my Cologne colleagues for bestowing the *venia legendi* in sociology, although my thesis crossed cherished disciplinary boundaries between macrosociology, comparative politics, and political economy.

After a *Wanderjahr* as visiting professor in the Sociology Department at the University of Jena, a professorship in Mannheim provided the home base needed to complete this book. The Mannheim Center for European Social Research will be a well-suited research environment to conduct further comparative studies on social governance in modern welfare states. Thanks also to my MPIfG research assistants over the years who gathered materials: Annette von Alemann, Tine Bredo, Gudrun Schlöpker, Stefanie Schramm, Volker Stander, and Silke Vagt. Marisa Cid read the proofs of the *Habilitation* manuscript. During the final stage of manuscript production at Mannheim, Thomas Biegert, Julian Brückner, Sebastian Koos, Nadine Reibling, and André Schaffrin helped update graphs and tables.

Completion of this project would not have been possible without friends and colleagues in Germany and elsewhere who provided support and comments. Intellectual exchange with a stimulating mix of colleagues and visitors of the MPIfG in Cologne was crucial for developing the larger questions and for learning from country case studies. In particular, I am grateful for the collegial encouragement and friendship of Anke Hassel, Anton Hemerjick, Bernhard Kittel, Christine Trampusch, Gerda Falkner, Gregory Jackson, Jelle Visser, Lane Kenworthy, Michael Nentwich, Philip Manow, and Steffen Ganghof.

Justin Powell reduced Germanisms in the manuscript, enhanced its American style, and helped throughout the project. The long journey through the German academic system would have been far more difficult without the enthusiastic, encouraging, and caring support of my life partner who also filled our transatlantic life with the excitement of joining two worlds. Finally, thanks to my parents, Hans and Susanne Ebbinghaus, who continue to be active well beyond their retirement age.

Bernhard Ebbinghaus
Mannheim, September 2005

Contents

Contents

Contents

List of Figures

List of Tables

Abbreviations

AAW	*Algemene Arbeidsongeschiktheidswet* (General Disablement Act, the Netherlands)
ABPW	*Algemene Burgelijke Pensionenwet* (General Civil Service Pension Act, the Netherlands)
ACA	*Allocation chômeur âgé* (compensation for older unemployed, France)
ACS	*Allocation conventionnelle de solidarité* (solidarity contract for preretirement compensation with job replacement condition, France)
AGIRC	*Association Générale des Institutions de Retraite des Cadres* (supplementary pension fund for managerial and technical personnel, France)
ALG II	*Arbeitslosengeld II* (means-tested unemployment and social assistance benefit, Germany)
ARPE	*Allocation de remplacement pour l'emploi* (French job substitution allowance scheme)
ARRCO	*Association des Régimes de Retraite Complémentaires* (supplementary pension fund for employees, France)
ASF	*Allocation de soutien familial* (French transitional fund)
ATP	*Allmän tilläggspension* (earnings-related second-tier pension, Sweden)
CA	collective agreement
CES	*Contrat emploie solidarité* (French wage subsidies for the employment of problem groups)
CGIL	*Confederazione Generale Italiana del Lavoro* (General Confederation of Italian Labor)
CIGS	*Cassa Integrazione Guadagni Straordinaria* (special wage guarantee fund, Italy)
CME	coordinated market economy
DB	defined benefit
DC	defined contribution
DRE	*Dispense de recherché d'emploi* (unemployment benefits for older workers without job-seeking requirment, France)
ERIP	early Retirement Incentive Plan (United States)
EP	employee pension
ERISA	Employee Retirement Income Security Act (United States)
Eurostat	Statistical Office of the European Communities
FNE	*Fond National pour l'Emploi* (national employment fund, France)

FNE–AS	*FNE allocation spéciale* (special allocation for preretirement, France)
GDP	gross domestic product
GRD	*Garantie de ressources démission* (guaranteed-income scheme after dismissal, France)
GRL	*Garantie de ressources licenciement* (guaranteed-income scheme after plant closure, France)
ILO	International Labour Organization
IMF	International Monetary Fund
ITP	*Industrins och handelns tilläggspension* (occupational pension for industry, Sweden)
JRS	Job Release Scheme (United Kingdom)
KPA	*Kommunernas pensionsanstalt* (occupational pension for local government, Sweden)
LME	liberal market economy
LO	*Landsorganisation* (trade union confederation, Sweden)
LR	labor relations
OECD	Organization for Economic Cooperation and Development
OMC	Open Method of Coordination (European Union)
OP	occupational pension
PARE	*Plan d'aide au retour à l'emploi* (reintegration of unemployed, France)
PAYG	pay-as-you-go
PP	public pension
PRP	*Préretraite progressive* (progressive early retirement, France)
SAF	*Svenska Arbetsgivareföreningen* (Swedish confederation of employer associations)
SERPS	State Earnings-Related Pension Scheme (United Kingdom)
SiD	*Specialarbejdersforbundet i Danmark* (Danish general worker union)
SPV	*Statens personalpensionsverk* (occupational pension for state employees, Sweden)
SSDI	Social Security Disability Insurance (United States)
SSI	Supplemental Security Income (United States)
STP	*Särskild tilläggspension* (occupational pension for private sector, Sweden)
UI	unemployment insurance
UNEDIC	*Union Nationale pour l'Emploi dans l'Industrie et le Commerce* (National Union for Employment in Industry and Commerce, France)
UR	unemployment rate
VUT	*Vervroegde Uittreding* (voluntary preretirement scheme, Netherlands)
WS	welfare-state regime

Part I

Exploring Interests and Institutions

Chapter 1

Introduction: The Paradox of Early Exit from Work

Today, people live longer, yet they also tend to retire earlier. This paradox concerns not only the student of modern societies but also current political debates around the world. Since the 1970s, older working people have been withdrawing from employment prior to statutory pension age (commonly around age 65) at increasingly higher rates across all advanced industrialized economies, including the member states of the European Union, Japan, and the United States. In response to powerful social demands and economic challenges, the extension of social policies and increased labor shedding by firms have fostered early exit from work or premature withdrawal from employment. For workers and their representatives, early retirement is a deferred social wage for a long working life and a way to bring younger people into work; for employers, it provides a means to restructure their workforces in a socially acceptable way, avoiding industrial conflicts.

In this book, I will argue that early exit from work emerged as a social practice for two main reasons: (*a*) as an unintended consequence of the expansion of social rights and (*b*) as a deliberate policy to facilitate economic restructuring and reduce unemployment. And I will show that early retirement is not only a case of politics *against* markets (Esping-Andersen 1985) or the expansion of social rights in response to market vagaries but also that it functions as politics *for* markets, facilitating the restructuring of production systems. I will argue that the social partners—employer associations and trade unions in the political and economic arenas, and management and worker representatives at firm level—play an important role in facilitating and using early exit from work, advancing their interests.

Because of its considerable consequences for individual life courses, labor markets, and welfare states, early retirement has become a pressing policy issue and the subject of considerable debate in public and academic circles. In addition to declines in average retirement age, all modern industrialized societies are aging due to increased life expectancy and declining birth rates (Bosworth and Burtless 1998*a*). The resulting demographic 'time bomb' and the trend toward earlier exit have thus led to rising social expenditures for inactive older people, a burden shouldered by fewer and fewer employed people. No policy report on aging fails to forecast soaring old-age-dependency ratios, with ever fewer employed people paying for the retirement of ever more older people. The Organization for Economic Cooperation and Development (OECD) has advocated a reversal in early retirement as part of its *Reforms for an Ageing Society* (2000). Similarly, the European Union, in its European Employment Strategy, has set the goal for its member states to raise employment rates among older women and men (aged 55–64) to 50 percent by 2010, a considerable challenge to Continental European countries with significant inactivity rates in this age group. In addition to such supranational political coordination and the influence of 'epistemic communities' (Haas 1992) of international policy experts, a gradual paradigm shift occurred in most national policy communities due to social learning (Hall 1993) about the adverse effects of widespread early retirement on welfare-state financing, nonwage labor costs, and employment levels. Under the common pressure of fiscal austerity, demographic shifts, and persistent unemployment, national governments are now hard pressed to seek ways of reversing early exit from work.

Many critics claim to know the 'culprits' supporting widespread early exit from work: the 'social partners', both organized capital and labor. Indeed, employers and unions often 'collude' in using early retirement as a socially acceptable labor-shedding strategy, externalizing the costs of economic restructuring onto the public at large. Initially, governments were not opposed to this practice or were reluctant to intervene. They began to change course only when they could no longer ignore the fiscal limits to welfare-state expansion and the persistence of high unemployment. However, reversal of early exit proves difficult. The social partners are singled out as the social forces that are generally against a policy reversal; indeed, both unions and employers have vested interests in the current practice. Especially in welfare states with strong partnership traditions in labor relations and social policy governance, the social partners have considerable veto power in the policymaking and implementation stages. If this is the case, reform-minded governments might seek to negotiate reforms with the social partners, instead of unsuccessfully trying to impose changes from above. The social partners thus play an ambiguous role: as defenders of early exit from work and as potential partners in negotiated reversal of early exit trends. Which of the two actor-orientations becomes dominant is largely an empirical question: Under which institutional conditions are the social partners more likely to impede or facilitate a policy reversal? In this book, I unravel the roles the social partners play in bringing about the widespread practice of early exit from work and their involvement in the current reform process to reverse this trend.

By analyzing the social partners, I complement and integrate in this study the two dominant but divergent social science approaches to the study of early retirement. These perspectives have focused either on the impact of welfare-state arrangements on individual workers' decisions to retire early or on the economic forces that lead firms to shed older workers. I emphasize the crucial role of the social partners at national and firm levels in mediating between the 'pull' and 'push' factors of policies and institutions. In response to the exigencies of their production system, employers, workers, and their representatives develop their own strategies in drawing on available opportunities for early retirement that are provided by the public protection system and are often supplemented by the social partners. The shared expectations and social norms held by the social actors themselves are crucial in explaining the self-reinforcing process of early exit trajectories. Workers and their representatives see early retirement as a preferable way around economic exigencies but also as an earned social right. Employers expect older workers to be less productive and see in early retirement a peaceful means to restructure their workforces. Therefore, we would expect differences in partnership traditions to influence the ways in which the social partners 'collude' in using early exit from work and their varying abilities to impede or facilitate a reversal of early exit policies.

The main objective of this study is thus twofold. First, I aim to achieve a better understanding of long-term trends toward early exit from work since the mid-1960s. I provide an institutional explanation of the cross-national variations in early retirement patterns across ten theoretically selected OECD countries. In contrast to explanations that focus merely on the micro level—the decision by an individual to retire early or the age-related personnel policy of a firm—my analysis focuses on the macro-institutional configurations that structure the opportunities and alternatives for early exit from work at both national and firm levels. Adopting a comparative-historical approach, I single out the welfare regimes, production systems, and labor relations as institutional arrangements that are most prone to facilitate and utilize early exit from work. Second, in order to avoid a deterministic view of path dependence (for a critique of this concept, see Ebbinghaus 2005a), I explore the issue of policy reversal: the conditions under which the social partners impede or facilitate efforts to turn around this entrenched social practice. How can governments reverse the course of early exit, given the vested interests and potential veto power of the social partners at national and firm levels? If governments cannot intervene unilaterally, will it be possible to negotiate reforms or will it be necessary to change partnership institutions in order to reform early exit policies? Here I address two fundamental issues with relevance to policymaking: (*a*) the reasons why the social partners in some countries are more likely to use early exit from work and (*b*) the conditions under which it has become feasible to induce the social partners to reverse this social practice.

In the remainder of this introduction, I present the study's main concepts and approaches. My first research question asks why there are cross-national differences in early exit trajectories. In addition to explanations that focus on the incentives provided by preretirement benefits, which strongly induce workers to choose early exit and on the production-related forces that push older workers out of work, I also consider the role of social partners in fostering this practice. My second research concern is the current process of reform. Facing the negative consequences of the expansion of early retirement, governments seek to reverse the early exit trend, although they face multiple obstacles, including resistance by the social partners.

First I describe the phenomena to be explained: the cross-national trends and variations in early exit from work. I then sketch the study's explanatory model. Encompassing both pull and push perspectives, it also highlights the social partners' crucial involvement at both national and firm levels in policymaking and in the everyday practice of early exit from work. In a further step, I explain the rationale for comparing ten countries in a long-term historical analysis. Central to my approach is the regime perspective, combining insights from cross-national analyses of welfare regimes, production systems, and labor relations. While the following two chapters provide detailed discussions of the theoretical approaches used to analyze the (individual and corporate) actors' interests (Chapter 2) and regime constellations (Chapter 3), this introduction provides a brief overview of the study's overall conceptual foundation.

1.1 Common Trends, Diverse Trajectories

Early retirement commonly has two meanings: (*a*) withdrawal from employment prior to age 65 (*early exit from work*) and (*b*) the drawing of *preretirement benefits* until a statutory pension becomes available. It is thus a social practice that is related to and entails consequences for both social security programs and the labor market. During the first three postwar decades, retirement at statutory pension age (in most countries at age 65, albeit with some significant exceptions) became a social institution of modern welfare states that regulated the later part of the life course (Atchley 1982; Kohli 1985; Mayer and Müller 1986; Mayer and Schoepflin 1989). However, since the 1970s, early withdrawal from work before age 65 has become increasingly widespread. Consequently, the transition from work to retirement has been considerably altered, its timing even 'deinstitutionalized' (Guillemard 2003; Guillemard and van Gunsteren 1991; Kohli and Rein 1991): increasing numbers of older people expect to leave work early, while the age at exit is becoming less predictable.

An important task for an empirical study is 'establishing the phenomena that form the explananda' (Goldthorpe 2001). In Chapter 4, I use quantitative longitudinal data on employment changes as indicators of early exit from work—the dependent variables. Aggregate labor force data were collected mainly from the OECD, European Union, ILO, and national sources to compare *early exit patterns* over time (1965–2004) and across the selected ten OECD countries. In contrast to most other comparative empirical studies that use labor force participation rates of older *men* (age 55–64) as a proxy measure for early retirement (Clark and Anker 1993; Clark, York, and Anker 1999; Pampel and Weiss 1983), this study applies *cohort-adjusted* early exit rates for both men and women (see Appendix Note) which are informed by the life course approach (Settersten and Mayer 1997). Especially regarding women, exit indicators that are not cohort-adjusted would be quite misleading due to the often substantial increases in female labor force participation from cohort to cohort. With cohort-adjusted exit rates, we can see that not only among older men but also among their female peers, early withdrawals from work before age 65 have increased over time.

Although there has been a general tendency toward early retirement, these data show significant cross-national variations in its timing, frequency, and form. A first glance at the long-term trend in early exit from work (see Figure 1.1) reveals considerable differences across welfare regimes in the propensity of employed men or women to depart from

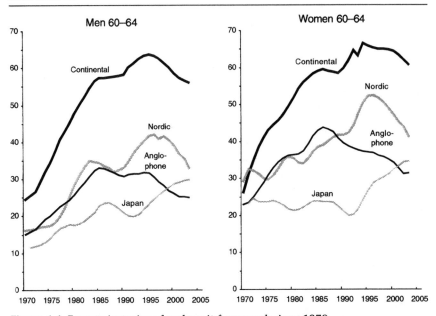

Figure 1.1 Four trajectories of early exit from work since 1970

Notes: Cohort-specific exit rates for men and women aged 60–64 (five-year moving average); multiple country averages—Continental trajectory: (West) Germany, the Netherlands, France, Italy; Nordic: Denmark, Sweden; Anglophone: United Kingdom, Ireland, United States.

Sources: OECD, *Labour Force Statistics 1965–2004*; and own calculations (see Appendix Note).

work between ages 60 and 64. The Continental welfare states (France, Germany, Italy, and the Netherlands) reached the highest level of inactivity in the group aged 55–64, in comparison with the other countries, which have slower expansion and lower levels of early exit from work, though early retirement was more common among women, especially in Denmark and Britain. In contrast to the Anglophone cases, the Scandinavian welfare states (Denmark and Sweden) saw further increases in early exit in the 1990s. Japan stands out with the slowest growth and the lowest overall level but with a recent upward trend. More detailed cross-national and longitudinal analysis of the macro-indicators follows in Chapter 4. This study focuses on a macro-level data analysis due to the scarcity of cross-nationally comparable micro-level data and on longitudinal developments across a larger set of OECD countries.[1]

---

[1] For recent efforts to analyze early retirement with the help of micro-level data, see the country-by-country analyses in Gruber and Wise (1999*a*) and Blossfeld, Buchholz, and Hofäcker (2006) as well as the first results from new survey data of the SHARE-Project (Börsch-Supan et al. 2005). A problem of micro-level analysis continues to be the limitation in data availability for many countries, comparability across countries, and limitations in time (recent surveys only or retrospective data only for older cohorts).

These cross-national differences in trend and level suggest the first set of research questions. We need to explain the general trends of early exit, and the timing in particular. When did early exit from work take off and what are the forces that led to its expansion and fluctuation? In particular, why did the trend toward early retirement more or less universally accelerate during the late 1970s and early 1980s? Moreover, we need to account for substantial cross-national differences in exit trajectories. Why do some countries manifest higher rates of early retirement than others? For instance, why do we find lower exit rates among older workers in Japan, Scandinavia, and Anglophone societies, while on average their counterparts in Continental European welfare states tend to leave work earlier and in larger numbers? In this study, I explain these significantly different trajectories of early exit from work by cross-national institutional variations in welfare regimes, production systems, and labor relations (the *explanans*).

1.2 Reform Efforts to Reverse Early Exit

The widespread diffusion of early exit from work has had major consequences for today's welfare states. As people tend to retire earlier but live longer, the proportion of their lives spent in employment has shortened, with corresponding increases in the length of retirement. Early exit from work has considerable repercussions on the financing of social insurance. First, early retirement increases overall social expenditure (Boeri, Brugiavini, and Maignan 2001). Second, early withdrawal from work lowers income and payroll tax receipts owing to reduced employment (OECD 1998c). Finally, premature withdrawal from work represents losses of human resources (Herberttson and Orszag 2001), while the hopes of replacing older retiring workers with younger workers or unemployed persons remain only partially fulfilled. Reversing early retirement thus represents a major issue in current reform debates at national and international levels such as the OECD's proposal *Reforms for an Ageing Society* (2000).

Reversing the course of early retirement occurs in the context of more general efforts to reform social security and labor markets under conditions of fiscal austerity, demographic changes, and persistent unemployment (Pierson 2001a). Since the late 1970s, governments have increasingly sought to retrench welfare programs, that is cut back on benefits and close down expensive programs. However, welfare retrenchment has met with considerable resistance, particularly in the area of pension policy and labor market reform (Pierson 2001b; Samek Lodovici 2000a; Taylor-Gooby

1999). Obstacles to reform seem particularly high in the case of early retirement. Governments were rather slow in realizing the direct and indirect costs of early exit and in taking appropriate action once they recognized its scope. Often, they were afraid of negative consequences for already aggravated labor markets. Furthermore, the social partners have considerable vested interests in maintaining early retirement. Although trade unions have come under pressure due to membership losses, bargaining decentralization, and flexible employment relations, they still have significant political and industrial power to block large-scale reforms (Brugiavini et al. 2001; Scarbrough 2000). Also, the social partners are involved in social policymaking and implementation, this provides them with additional veto power, though this may vary according to the modes of *social governance* (see Ebbinghaus 2004). Finally, even if retrenchment measures are enacted, they often fail to produce the hoped-for effects, as workers and firms replace them with second best alternatives. For instance, the social partners sometimes fill the gaps left by public benefit cuts, undermining the reform's intended effect of enhancing work incentives. On the other hand, firms may continue labor shedding despite closed exit pathways, further swelling the ranks of jobless older workers.

Grappling with these contentious issues, the second set of research questions focuses on failed but also successful efforts to reverse early exit from work. Why have governments found it difficult to reform early exit policies? What are the obstacles to enacting and implementing reforms in the area of early retirement? Do the social partners have enough veto power to block reform? In cases when reform measures are undertaken, why are the results often mixed? In Chapter 7, I review governments' various reform efforts to reverse early exit by raising the retirement age, applying stricter rules for disability pensions, closing down special preretirement schemes, promoting more active labor market policies, and fostering prolonged transitions to retirement via gradual pensions. Several countries were able to stabilize or even partially reverse the trend of early retirement, though it remains to be seen whether these were only temporary successes during the improved labor market situation of the late 1990s. Changes in both early exit rates and social expenditure over the last two decades are analyzed here as indicators to evaluate these reforms' effects. Why have many policy measures failed to bring the hoped-for reversal in early exit from work?

In this study, I argue that it is difficult to reform early exit policies because they constitute a complex multitude of exit opportunities across diverse public programs and private welfare arrangements (see Chapter 7).

Both of the social partners—unions and employers—have interests in continuing the early exit practice, thus playing a crucial role in hindering the reform process. To the degree that the social partners have (partial) veto power in policymaking and implementation, they will be capable of blocking or watering down retrenchment efforts. Therefore, governments that want to circumvent reform blockage and implementation problems will have to seek concerted reforms by bringing the social partners into reform coalitions (see Ebbinghaus and Hassel 2000). In order to do so, governments may need to begin reforming governance structures in the social policy arena: to instill social responsibility and to reduce the social partners' opportunities for collusion and externalization of costs onto the public.

1.3 Combining Pull and Push Perspectives

Early exit from work has thus far been studied in the social sciences from two main perspectives. These are either protection-oriented analyses of *pull* factors that impact labor supply or production-oriented studies of *push* factors that affect labor demand (for an overview, see Casey 1996; Guillemard and Rein 1993; Kohli and Rein 1991). Arguments about the role of social partners or labor relations in both perspectives remain implicit, whereas I delineate a third, encompassing perspective. I argue that the social partners play a crucial role in *mediating* between welfare incentives (pull) and economic contingencies (push). Involved in the arena of social policy and collective bargaining, the social partners and management–labor relations shape the ways in which firm-level actors abstain from or utilize early exit under the given constraints and opportunities. Informed by three complementary perspectives of protection-related pull, production-related push, and partnership-related mediation, I adopt here an encompassing and multidisciplinary approach (see Figure 1.2).

Seen from the protection-oriented *pull* perspective, social transfer programs provide incentives and opportunities to retire from employment before statutory pension age (around age 65). There are often multiple exit *pathways* or institutionalized social transfer programs that allow older workers to retire early: 'A pathway is an institutional arrangement or—in most cases—a combination of different institutional arrangements that are sequentially linked to manage the transition process, that is, the period between exit from work and entry into the normal old-age pension system' (Kohli and Rein 1991: 6). Different social policy programs

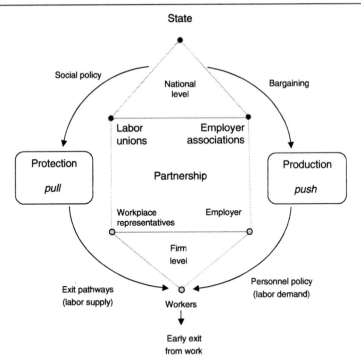

Figure 1.2 Pull and push in multilevel and multiple actor constellation model

provide alternatives that facilitate early withdrawal from work: flexible old-age pensions, disability pensions, special preretirement schemes, long-term unemployment as well as partial pension benefits (Kohli et al. 1991).

Concentrating on only one social security program is insufficient to fully grasp pull factors because there are several alternative pathways, even when they are not necessarily complete functional equivalents. While in one country early exit from work may be facilitated by drawing on seniority pensions early, in another country long-term unemployment benefits provide a 'bridging pension' (Guillemard and van Gunsteren 1991). Although one pathway may serve as an alternative for another, the eligibility conditions, the generosity of benefits, and control over access often vary considerably. Given the various pathways, we need to go beyond a policy study of one particular social insurance program. Early retirement presents a prime case of the *regime* approach's utility (Esping-Andersen 1990), as it emphasizes the systemically interwoven web of institutions and their interaction within particular environments. In comparative perspective, we can expect that different welfare regimes provide varying opportunities of income support for early exit from work.

The welfare regime analysis cannot confine itself to the public programs of the welfare *state*, but must acknowledge the importance of the *public–private mix* (Esping-Andersen 1999; Rein and Rainwater 1986a). Not only public policy but also private occupational benefits—provided by employers or negotiated by the collective bargaining partners—may offer additional opportunities or supplement insufficient public benefits for preretirement. In recent years, several comparative studies have highlighted the need to examine the involvement of firms or the social partners in the provision of occupational welfare, often previously overlooked (Rein and Wadensjö 1997a; Shalev 1996). In addition, recent studies point to employers' roles in the social policy arena and their influence on public policy (Mares 2001a; Martin 2000; Swenson 2002). These complement previous research on the role of labor movements in welfare-state expansion (Esping-Andersen 1985; Korpi 1983; Stephens 1979). The public–private mix is particularly relevant to the study of early exit from work (Casey 1992). What seem to be—in the protection-oriented *pull* perspective—income transfers to individuals that provide strong incentives to withdraw from work are economically-motivated labor-shedding measures when seen from the firm-oriented *push* perspective. In this case, public or private welfare policies are not politics *against* markets (Esping-Andersen 1985), enforcing redistributive social rights on free market economies, but politics *for* markets, enhancing the adaptability for social market economies (Ebbinghaus and Manow 2001a).

To fully understand early retirement, we should take into account the reasons firms shed older workers—the production-related *push* factors. In addition to institutionalized exit pathways and their incentive structures that affect labor supply, there are economic forces at work that influence the labor demand side (Lazear 1979, 1986). Most importantly, labor shedding or retaining of older workers will depend on firms' age-related hiring, training, and firing policies. The economic environment in which the firm operates will in turn influence the management's human resource strategy (Sørensen 1994). Since the 1970s, firms have been under increased pressure to downsize or restructure due to advancing deindustrialization, new production methods, pervasive shareholder demands, and intensified international competition (Sengenberger 1992; Streeck 1987a). The firm's organizational development interacts with the life courses of its workers (Kohli 1986): The firm's production method, demographic composition, wage structure, and skill profile can put additional pressure on management to shed older workers. Finally, management may be further constrained by legal employment protections for older workers, statutory state approval of dismissals, collective agreements with seniority rules, or workplace representatives' codetermination rights (Buechtemann 1993a). Early retirement is one major socially acceptable response to these pressures and constraints (Naschold and de Vroom 1994). As *institutional complementarities* (Milgrom and Roberts 1994), preretirement benefits help socially buffer firms' labor shedding strategies.

However, neither protection-oriented nor production-oriented accounts sufficiently explain early exit. The labor supply perspective assumes that incentives determine the decision of older workers to retire, while the labor demand perspective perceives early exit as the outcome of firms' human resource strategies. In this study, I maintain that the social partners play a crucial mediating role between such push and pull factors. Protection systems provide the pathways and the incentives for early retirement; the production systems induce pressure to shed older workers. Yet the partnership institutions are crucial in shaping the ways in which the social actors react to push and pull factors. At workplace level, the main actors—management, worker representatives, and the older workers—interact to find adequate responses, given constraints and opportunities provided by the protection and production systems. The worker's decision to retire early as well as management's policy to shed older workers is thoroughly embedded in workplace labor relations, and in the relationships between management and workplace representatives (statutory works council, shop stewards, or local unions) in particular.

The opportunities offered by protection systems and the constraints of production systems did not develop without continuous action by the social partners in the national policy and bargaining arenas. Organized labor and capital, together with the government, influence and implement policies affecting early exit from work. The social partners not only regulate wages, employment conditions, and workplace relations through collective bargaining, they also influence social policymaking and implementation through their political channels and involvement in social insurance or occupational welfare programs. We should thus expect that the national traditions of *partnership*, that is, the institutionalized relations between the state, organized labor, and employer associations as well as the workplace relations between management, workers, and their representatives would have a major influence on national exit policies and on the everyday social practice of early retirement.

In this study, I claim that an explanation of the cross-national variations in early exit from work must take into account the varying institutional configurations of welfare regimes, production systems, and labor relations (see Figure 1.2). The explanatory model assumes a multiple actor constellation on at least two levels (see Heinelt 1991; Naschold and de Vroom 1994): (*a*) that of the national policymaking and collective bargaining arena and (*b*) the firm level at which management, workers, and workplace representatives make decisions. While, due to data limitations, I will not be able to empirically analyze micro-level data in this comparative macro-institutional study, I do theoretically separate firm-level and macro-level explanatory factors (see Chapter 2). It would be erroneous to assume that the policies pursued by the national-level corporate actors, employer associations, and trade unions merely reflect the aggregated interests of their members at firm level. Similarly, the actors at the firm level may diverge considerably in the practice of early retirement from the intentions of policies enacted or bargained at national level.

1.4 Comparing Regimes

This study adopts the comparative-historical method (Skocpol 1984; Tilly 1984) to answer two main research questions: (*a*) Why are there differences in early exit from work over time and across countries? (*b*) Under which conditions is reversal in early retirement possible? In order to approach the first question, I undertake a comparative study of long-term developments in early exit from work, combining both quantitative indicators and qualitative institutional analysis. I systematically analyze not only both push and pull factors but also the social partners' mediating role by comparing cross-national variations in protection, production, and partnership regimes. The second, more policy-oriented question requires qualitative analysis of policy and institutional change, following case study design (Ragin and Becker 1992).

Adopting a *variation-finding* comparative design (Tilly 1984), I seek to explain cross-national variations in early exit patterns with particular regime constellations. Under which production, protection, and partnership regimes do we find early exit from work to be most common? The *interregime comparison*, using the most-dissimilar-country design (Przeworski and Teune 1970), helps to single out the impact of specific institutional configurations on the development of particular early exit trajectories. While the regime comparison helps to account for the path-dependent trajectories of early exit from work, it cannot unravel path departures through policy and institutional change. Embracing an additional most-similar-country design (Dogan and Pelassy 1990), the *intra-regime comparison* enables analysis of the opportunities for policy reform and institutional change within similar regime configurations. However, since there are fewer cases than possible regime combinations, I complement the macro-regime comparison with more detailed historical institutional analysis of the pull and push factors and the role of social partners in fostering, maintaining, and reforming early exit from work.

In order to allow systematic inter- and intra-regime comparison, I chose a selected group of ten OECD countries that share not only enough commonalities but also sufficient differences in both dependent and independent variables. The chosen countries represent cases from different configurations along the main conceptually defined dimensions of protection, production, and partnership regimes (see Chapter 3). For pragmatic reasons, the study is limited to a manageable number of countries for which crucial quantitative indicators were available (Eurostat, OECD, and ILO) and additional qualitative case studies already existed.[2] Instead of using cross-national pooled time-series analysis that exhibits serious limitations for the purposes of this study (Ebbinghaus 2005*b*; Kittel 1999), I opt for a smaller-N design that allows the combination of intensive case studies with enough cross-national variations to systematically explore differences in institutional configurations (Ragin 1987). My comparative method thus follows Ragin (1987) in analyzing countries as theory-relevant *cases* that allow us to explore context-dependent, process-oriented analyses, and to check for alternative hypotheses (Mahoney 2003; Savolainen 1994). They are not observations of a larger country sample to gain statistical leverage (Lieberson 1991, 1994).

This study applies an *institutionalist* approach (for overviews, see Hall and Taylor 1996; Thelen 1999). The decisions of actors at the workplace level or in the social policy and bargaining arenas are embedded in institutional environments that shape actors' orientations and interests as well as the opportunity structures for the actor constellations. Following Esping-Andersen (1990), I use 'regime' to refer to the ways in which institutions hang together and interact systemically, using the term as an

---

[2] The most important secondary case study sources consulted were the country-by-country readers on early retirement policies in general (Jespen, Foden, and Hutsebaut 2002*a*; Kohli et al. 1991; OECD 1995*a*), old-age pensions (Hughes and Stewart 1999, 2000; Reynaud 2000; Reynaud et al. 1996), disability pensions (Aarts, Burkhauser, and de Jong 1996*a*; Reinhard et al. 1998), gradual pensions (Delsen and Reday-Mulvey 1996*a*), unemployment (Compston 1997; Esping-Andersen and Regini 2000), and welfare policies by firms (Naschold and de Vroom 1994; Rein and Wadensjö 1997*b*; Shalev 1996). The operationalization of the quantitative indicators (absolute and relative exit rates) is provided in the Appendix Note.

analytical construct of the interrelations between institutions and their interaction with their environment. It is a heuristic tool to conceptualize complex institutional arrangements as a holistic system. A regime approach can help us understand how social protection is institutionalized, production systems are organized, and labor relations are governed. The regime approach is particularly useful in comparative analyses in order to conceptualize distinct regime typologies in which to classify empirical similarities and differences (Lange and Meadwell 1991; Sartori 1994). While regimes should be theoretically grounded, representing ideal-types, much comparative work nevertheless seeks to use typologies to classify empirical cases or real-types (Rieger 1998).

In this study, I use regime typologies from three different fields to map the main differences across countries with respect to protection, production, and partnership institutions (see Chapter 3). Although these regime typologies were developed largely independently and dealt primarily with different social systems, they share a similar systemic view of institutions (Ebbinghaus and Manow 2001a).

First, for a regime typology of *protection* systems that provide the pull towards early exit, I rely on Esping-Andersen's well-known welfare regime typology (1990, 1999). Three regime clusters are distinguished: (*a*) social-democratic *universalist* welfare states in Nordic countries, (*b*) Christian-democratic *conservative* social insurance states in Continental Europe, and (*c*) *liberal-residual* basic social security systems with substantial private pensions in the United Kingdom, Ireland, the United States, and Japan.

Second, for a classification of *production* systems and their economic governance, I borrow from similar typologies (Albert 1991; Amable 2005; Hall and Soskice 2001a; Streeck and Yamamura 2001) that juxtapose two political economy models: (*a*) Anglophone *liberal* (uncoordinated) market economies and (*b*) *coordinated* (nonliberal) market economies (Germany and its Rhenish neighbors, Scandinavia, and Japan).

Finally, for the analysis of *partnership* traditions, I draw on comparative studies of labor relations and organized interests (Crouch 1993; Ebbinghaus and Visser 1997). These delineate three different management–labor modes: (*a*) *voluntarist* (or 'give-and-take') bargaining traditions in Anglophone labor relations, (*b*) contentious labor relations in Latin Europe, and (*c*) cooperative labor relations in the remaining countries.

There is no clear one-on-one relationship between these institutional configurations; nevertheless, there are some intriguing *Wahlverwandtschaften* (Weber {1922}) or institutional affinities between welfare regimes, production systems, and labor relations. The liberal market economies (LMEs)

(United Kingdom, United States, and Ireland) all combine residual welfare and voluntarist labor relations. Among the coordinated market economies (CMEs), there are several combinations between welfare regimes and labor relations. In fact, we may need more subtle distinctions for these coordinated market economies: central coordination in Nordic countries, sectoral coordination for Germany and the Netherlands, and state coordination for Latin Europe (Ebbinghaus 1999; Kitschelt et al. 1999).

The purpose of locating countries in these analytical typologies is to provide a *conceptual map* (Rokkan 1999), which explains particular outcomes based on the institutional configurations. Thus, not one 'master-variable' alone is sufficient to explain the divergent early exit trajectories, but rather the particular interaction of protection (pull), production (push), and partnership (mediation). The comparative regime typologies also help in delineating the institutional obstacles and opportunities for policy reversal as they provide the basis for evaluating the degree of path departure from regime-specific trajectories. Thus, the purpose of this Rokkanian *encompassing comparison* (Tilly 1984) is to generate hypotheses about institutional macro-configurations and confront these with more process-oriented historical case studies (Rokkan 1999).

For this study, I selected eight member states of the European Union, representing four regime configurations, and added two major non-European OECD countries, the United States and Japan (see Table 1.1).

Table 1.1. Conceptual map of protection, production, and partnership regimes

Cluster countries	Protection (pull)	Production (push)	Partnership (mediation)
Center 　Germany 　Netherlands	Conservative	Coordinated	Cooperative
Latin 　France 　Italy	Conservative	Coordinated	Contentious
Nordic 　Sweden 　Denmark	Universalist	Coordinated	Cooperative
Anglophone 　United Kingdom 　Ireland 　United States	Liberal-residual	Liberal	Voluntarist
Asian 　Japan	Liberal-residual	Coordinated	Cooperative

Notes: See Chapter 3 for details on these three typologies.

These two global players are not only major economic competitors with these European economies, but also prime examples of opposing political economy models: The United States is a case of an (uncoordinated) LME, Japan of a (nonliberal) CME (Hall and Soskice 2001a; Soskice 1999; Streeck 2001). Explaining early exit from a production-oriented view, these two juxtaposed political economy models pose a puzzle. Because these countries with opposing production systems both have low exit rates, the differences in production regime (i.e. the push factor) alone cannot explain such a similar outcome. Conversely, taking into account the pull factor, the liberal-residual welfare regimes cannot be sufficient cause for low early exit since Sweden has also had relatively low early exit from work, despite sharing a relatively generous social security system with high exit Continental European welfare states.

In addition to this variation-finding comparative strategy, the *intra-regime* comparison allows us to test claims of path dependence, while exploring the nation-specific potentials for path departure (Ebbinghaus 2005a). A major criticism of regime approaches is their tendency to assume path-dependent change, if not institutional inertia (Crouch 2001). This study's second part, in analyzing the obstacles and opportunities for policy reversal, can compare and contrast parallel or divergent paths within a particular regime constellation. Although analogous regime constellations may provide similar problem loads and actor constellations, there may well be intra-regime differences in policy and institutional change. Adapting a most-similar-country design (Dogan and Pelassy 1990), *binary* comparisons—France versus Italy, Germany versus Netherlands, Britain versus Ireland, and Sweden versus Denmark—offer new insights on the path dependence or path departure debate. Rather small, often hidden intra-regime differences can be crucial in differing opportunities for change (see Chapter 7). Indeed, an important precondition for policy reversal is the reformability of social governance, that is, changes in the involvement of social partners in policymaking and implementation in the areas of social policy and labor market regulation.

1.5 An Overview of the Study

The first part introduces the analytical and theoretical foundation of this study's approach. Chapter 2 develops a general analytical framework for the analysis of interest organization and intermediation. From a micro-level perspective, one may ask: What are workers' interests in retiring early, and what are those of employers and worker representatives at the workplace? I then turn to the national corporate actors (the state, employers, and unions) and discuss their interests in early exit policies. This analysis remains abstract, discussing the potential interests of the social partners and the state in using early exit. To explain cross-national differences, however, we need to place this analysis within the institutional contexts. Therefore, Chapter 3 reviews the established typologies of welfare regimes, production systems, and labor relations, synthesizing these into a combined heuristic tool to discuss the *institutional affinities* between the spheres of protection, production, and partnership that provide unique institutional configurations for the social actors' interests. The particular institutional configurations help to explain divergent early exit trajectories as well as the current reform process examined in the subsequent two empirical parts.

The second part focuses on the emergence of early exit from work and the institutional configurations for its development. Chapter 4 establishes the observed phenomena, analyzing the trend toward early exit from work across the ten selected countries since the mid-1960s. Cross-national variations are studied using several indicators on changes in employment patterns for older workers, including cohort-adjusted measures of exit rates. The following two chapters analyze the merits of the pull and push theses in explaining the observed early exit trajectories. Chapter 5 looks at the *pull* factors, the incentives provided by the multiple pathways of (semi-) public welfare programs, as well as the roles of the social partners in promoting early retirement policies and even administering their own collective schemes. Chapter 6 takes a different angle, looking at the *push* factors in early exit from work: firm-sponsored occupational welfare, organizational capacity of unions, labor relations at workplace level, employment regulation, production-related human resource policies, and corporate and financial governance. It focuses on the following question: How far have capital and labor colluded in externalizing adaptation costs onto public programs or internalized the costs through firm-sponsored occupational plans or continued (re)employment of older workers?

The third part reviews opportunities for and problems of *policy and institutional change*. Chapter 7 discusses reform efforts to reverse the trend of early retirement through narrowing or closing early exit pathways. Reform-minded governments have attempted to raise the statutory retirement age, tighten eligibility for disability pensions, close special preretirement schemes, shift from passive to active labor market policies, and foster gradual partial pension schemes—all in order to reduce public expenditure and to increase activity rates among older workers. However, they encounter considerable obstacles owing to substitution effects, mere cost-shifting, and counteraction by the social partners. In order to overcome externalization strategies, some governments have moved from retrenchment policies to a reform of social governance, aimed at instilling more social responsibility. Finally, Chapter 8 reviews the study's findings and arguments and reconsiders its implications for the theories of institutional change. It stresses the study's contribution to a better understanding of the complex influences of protection, production, and partnership institutions on early exit from work. It also unravels the obstacles to and opportunities for policy changes and institutional reforms that are prerequisite to a reversal of the early exit trend.

Chapter 2

Actor Constellations and Interest Coalitions: Labor, Employers, and the State

Early retirement as a policy and as a social practice has been analyzed from very different theoretical backgrounds (rational choice, institutional) and disciplines (economics, sociology, and political science, among others). Major perspectives can be distinguished as (*a*) those that focus on labor supply and (*b*) those that emphasize labor demand. The 'pull' protection-oriented perspective centers on the incentives provided by existing early retirement benefits to individuals to withdraw from the workforce (lowering labor supply) and the availability of public or private exit pathways in a given welfare society. The 'push' production-oriented perspective focuses on the economic and social factors that lead employers, workers, and their representatives to utilize early exit from work to restructure the workforce, thus adjusting labor demand.

Two main levels are important: (*a*) the workplace that shapes the social practice of early exit from work (the micro level) and (*b*) the national policy and collective bargaining arenas in which early retirement policy decisions are made (the macro level). In this chapter, I first focus on the micro-level workplace perspective. At this level, economic models seek to explain the individual workers' rational decisions, based on pull incentives to retire early, while sociological analyses point to other individual or contextual factors (e.g. health impairments and retirement of partner). Workers hardly decide on early retirement in a social vacuum. Employer and worker representatives, in particular, shape early exit patterns at workplace level. These two social actors are important to the push perspective because their strategies affect labor demand. Moreover, partly as a result of exchange with workplace representatives, employers provide additional incentives for early retirement through private occupational benefits or severance pay, thus supplementing the pull from public benefits.

Next, I turn to the macro-level perspective. The state and the 'social partners', employers and labor, are the main corporate actors shaping the policies that affect early exit in both the political system and the collective bargaining arenas. Even though all three actors (the state, the employers, and unions) have interests in early retirement, they are quite varied. These actors not only aggregate and represent the interests of their constituencies or membership but they also enter strategic alliances with other actors in pursuing these interests. This leads to different interest coalitions: between state and unions, between state and employers, and between the social partners. I discuss six different concerns that are shared by at least two main actors. Yet the analysis remains largely abstract in this chapter, disregarding the impact of varying national contexts (see Chapter 3).

2.1 Actor Interests at Workplace Level

Different perspectives in economic and sociological studies seek to explain early retirement as decisions made at the micro level: the retirement decision of an older worker, the labor-shedding strategy of firms, and the influence of workplace representatives. An individual's decision to retire at a particular point in time is at the center of economic theories seeking to explain the determinants of labor supply: to work or not to work (Lazear 1986). According to this perspective, incentives provided by available public income programs or private retirement plans 'pull' individuals into retirement. The decision to retire is a voluntary rational decision undertaken by the older worker, given the available incentive structure. On the other hand, labor demand theories in economics along with many sociological studies point to the 'push' factors that induce labor shedding (Lazear 1979). That is, personal circumstances that force workers to retire despite potential financial losses, economic rationales for employers to shed older workers, and reasons why workplace representatives support early exit.

These perspectives also help to explain why employers and worker organizations, at the workplace level and beyond, have been lobbying for public early retirement policies, and were instrumental in setting up private occupational plans. Governments and unions will not be able to ignore the fact that many workers value a gain in leisure time and are thus in favor of early retirement options. More importantly, governments, unions, and employers advance early exit from work as a primary solution to economic and social circumstances that compel firms to shed labor. Before I discuss the national politics of early exit, I explore the pull and push factors leading to early exit from work seen from a micro-level perspective. First, the section analyzes the major reasons why older workers choose to retire, taking into account economic and sociological theories. Second, it focuses on the perspective of labor demand and investigates the reasons why firms have an interest in early retirement and why workplace representatives readily support it.

2.1.1 *Why Would Older Workers Retire Early?*

Focusing on the pull factors, economic theories of labor supply explain an individual's decision to retire early based on the (financial) incentives provided by preretirement programs (Lazear 1986; Lumsdaine and Mitchell 1999). In this view, an individual chooses to stop working when the future income loss due to early exit will be less than the expected gain from leisure (Gruber and Wise 1999*a*; Stock and Wise 1990). Thus, the decision entails the individual comparison of the asset value of the two different income streams: the net earnings from continued work plus the normal pension with full contribution records versus the posttax preretirement benefits plus the expected pension minus any deductions for the shortened contribution period (Quinn and Burkhauser 1990; Stock and Wise 1990). Even if the overall asset value from early exit might be less than from continued work, an individual may still prefer to withdraw early given the 'welfare gain' of extra leisure time (not to mention illicit work as additional preretirement income). Thus, generous preretirement incentives would account for an individual's decision to withdraw from the labor force prematurely; this corresponds to a reduction in labor supply on the aggregate level (Lazear 1986).

Central to the policy recommendations of the economic incentive model is the concept of an 'implicit tax' on continuing to work (Gruber and Wise 1999*b*). In this view, two parameters of preretirement programs could provide a 'subsidy' to early exit: (*a*) a high *net replacement value* of preretirement benefits and (*b*) low or no *actuarial adjustment* of old-age pension after statutory pension age. Therefore, we would expect that basic tax-financed pensions paid before statutory age (e.g. due to disability) and contributory old-age pensions (with low or no actuarial adjustment to early drawing) provide a disincentive to continue working, while actuarially fair flexible pensions with strict equivalence of contribution-benefits or *defined contribution* (DC) systems would not subsidize early retirement.[1] There are indeed social security systems that provide such incentives, functioning as a major pull factor in influencing the timing and scope of early withdrawal from work (see Chapter 5). Econometric studies have shown some support for the protection-related pull thesis: there is a considerable correlation between preretirement incentives and participation rates (Blöndal and Scarpetta 1998). Also the timing of exits from work by and large follows retirement benefits' availability and generosity (Gruber and Wise 1999a). Proponents of the pull-incentive view, including the OECD and IMF, recommend flexible pensions with actuarial fair deduction (i.e. reducing benefits by the shorter contributions and therefore lower interests) and a change to funded DC schemes, which would no longer provide a disincentive to work. However, preretirement incentives are not the only factor inducing early exit from work.

Age-related health impairments are a major (individual) push factor in early exit and, depending on the disability insurance rules, the 'generosity' of public benefits might be an additional pull factor (Bound and Burkhauser 1999). Because the risk of health impairment increases over the life course, a larger share of older workers may be unable to continue working or to find suitable work, being pushed out of employment as a result (Delsen 1996a). Disability insurance schemes commonly grant income support based on full inactivity; although some systems also award partial benefits for reduced inactivity that can be combined with part-time work (Aarts, Burkhauser, and de Jong 1996b). Disabled individuals or people with impairments may value the trade-off between work and nonwork differently than those who do not yet have an impairment or disability. Until mature pension systems were built up, health- and functioning-related reasons were the main causes of retirement, particularly in order to draw pension benefits early.

In all countries, long-term disability benefits exist prior to statutory retirement age, but the requirements and benefits for these programs vary considerably, as do the award rates (Aarts, Burkhauser, and de Jong 1996a; Kuptsch and Zeitzer 2001). In some countries, disability pensions have become a major pathway to early retirement, particularly where eligibility criteria are not only strictly linked to medical criteria but also include an evaluation of available employment chances (Aarts,

---

[1] Nevertheless, actuarially flexible public pensions and private DC pensions could be used to retire early. If an individual has enough private savings to fill in for the actuarial reduction of flexible pensions, or if a pension fund provides above average returns on capital, an individual may still be able to afford an early retirement.

Burkhauser, and de Jong 1996*b*). The reasons for receiving disability benefits in older age are varied; they are also contingent on the welfare program's eligibility and 'generosity'. Depending on national rules, partial
disability pensions may be allowed and thus provide options for part-time
work that in some cases prolong labor market participation (Delsen and
Reday-Mulvey 1996*b*). Moreover, stringently regulated disability programs
(e.g. in the United States) that require full withdrawal make a return to
employment unlikely (O'Day and Berkowitz 2001). Where eligibility rules
are less strict and nonmedical considerations are also taken into account,
and where the net replacement rate of such programs is relatively high, the
value of benefits compared with either work or the risk of unemployment
can be considered a further pull factor. However, early exit due to impairment or disability may also be due to push factors when employers discriminate against disabled people in hiring, firing, and training or by not
reducing barriers at the workplace level and alleviating work conditions
accordingly.

Unemployment is a major factor contributing to both pull and push into
early retirement among older workers. In many countries, favorable long-
term unemployment benefits for older workers provide a 'bridging pension' until an individual can draw on an anticipated or statutory pension,
thus often combining unemployment and other preretirement benefits
(Guillemard and van Gunsteren 1991). In this case, unemployment is
largely voluntary and results from an agreement between employer and
employee, often requiring the consent of workplace representatives. Yet
involuntary unemployment also results when employers push workers out
of employment through individual dismissal or large-scale redundancy. In
some cases, individual dismissal and particularly mass layoffs are subject
to approval by public authorities or consultation of workplace representatives. Unemployed workers, whether voluntary or involuntary, may also
choose not to seek reemployment due to unavailability of job opportunities, and in some countries, older workers are not required to actively seek
a job (they may also not be entitled to participate in retraining programs).
Due to age discrimination in hiring, unemployed older workers have a
much lower chance of finding employment than prime-aged (age 35–50)
colleagues (Lumsdaine and Mitchell 1999: 3292). Given the social stigma
of going 'on the dole', an older worker may therefore prefer the alternative
role of early retiree when facing the prospect of unemployment. For older
workers with low (re)employment chances, involuntary unemployment
(or the threat of unemployment) provides a push toward early exit, while
long-term unemployment benefits and waived job-seeking rules can be

seen as a pull factor. In both cases, the older unemployed have in fact already retired early, like their colleagues on other preretirement benefits.

In addition to any economic incentive effects, *social and personal context factors* are, of course, critical in shaping an individual's decision to retire early. Personal circumstances, such as coordination with a spouse's retirement or the need to provide personal care for a family member, can also lead to early retirement, even when it entails financial losses. Thus, in addition to the individual's own health conditions, the family situation as well as gender roles have to be taken into account if we want to explain the observable differences in old-age employment and retirement behavior between men and women or between singles and couples (Allmendinger and Hinz 1998; Oswald 2001: 46–9). For instance, the unavailability of public (long-term) care services may force women into earlier retirement or 'inactivity' in order to take care of family members in need (Daly 2000). Moreover, even if economic incentives were the only factor, the decision to retire early is dependent on the prospective combined household income, not merely the individual's income; this could either be high enough to facilitate or too low and thus hamper early retirement of one or both partners.[2]

Seen from a *life course perspective* (Sackmann 2001; Settersten and Mayer 1997), there are cohort, age, and status-specific personal, social, and labor market factors that not only shape the available alternatives but also lead to specific retirement decisions. There are often large differences in eligibility and sufficiency of preretirement benefits depending on cohort-specific work histories, gender, health, and family status. Thus, women with lower rates of labor market participation will have fewer contribution years and may, therefore, face a different benefit-work trade-off than their male colleagues (Allmendinger 1994). We also find different life course profiles of special social or occupational groups. White-collar employees or public servants, for instance, who have final salary pension schemes, will have different concerns than blue-collar workers who have their retirement benefits calculated over their entire working life. This perspective also points out the fact that different cohorts can differ considerably in their employment and retirement patterns over the life course. Each subsequent cohort of women tends to have been employed at a higher rate during and after the childrearing years, leading to rising employment levels for older women aged 55–64 over the last half century, though

---

[2] For instance, married women who are helping family members on a family farm or in a family-owned shop tend to work as long as their spouses, especially when their household needs the income from self-employment due to lack of sufficient public or private pensions.

women have the same or higher likelihood of retiring early as do men (see Chapter 4).

In addition, *norms and social pressure*, especially by the peer group at work, may influence older workers to retire early. Works councils and colleagues may exert social pressure on older workers to retire early as part of a social plan, especially in order to prevent dismissal of middle-aged workers who have no preretirement opportunities. Moral pressure on older workers to retire early was exercised by appeals such as 'Make room for the young!' in interwar Germany or 'Incomes for the old, jobs for the young!' in the United States during the Great Depression (Kohli and Rein 1991: 11). In general, social norms influence perceptions of 'earned' retirement rights after long working lives—retirement is not merely a solution to unemployment risks but a 'just' social right in a 'moral economy' (Kohli 1987). Since the 1960s, a 'normal' (statutory) retirement age has been established as a social institution (Atchley 1982) and early retirement subsequently became an additional right in many welfare states. Thus, the rising trend toward early exit, especially in particular industries and larger firms, has shortened the 'socially expected duration' (Merton {1984}) of working life among older workers (and, as we will see, also among employers).

Complex eligibility and benefit rules of the various exit pathways, paired with difficult predictions of personal life expectancy, future health status, job security, and future income from work (Lumsdaine and Mitchell 1999: 3299–301), result in individuals making 'bounded' decisions under high levels of *uncertainty*. Therefore, older workers especially face difficulty in rationally estimating cost and benefits of early exit from work. They may seek advice from others (friends, colleagues, workplace representatives, and personnel departments), or they may just follow perceived common practice, rules-of-thumb, or social norms. Thus, social norms may guide individual rational decisions on early retirement.

The increased proliferation, variability, and unpredictability of early exit from work have in fact led to a *deinstitutionalization* of state-sanctioned 'normal' retirement at a specific age (Guillemard and van Gunsteren 1991). Hence, the state has increasingly lost its capacity to steer the timing of transitions from work to retirement, while early retirement has become a rather unregulated, diverse phenomenon influenced by multiple push and pull factors and by many actors in a multilevel social field. Accounts that focus on individualistic pull effect in a rational choice framework have, therefore, been criticized as 'utterly incomplete' (Guillemard and Rein 1993: 479–81). For instance, early retirees may be 'discouraged' workers, involuntarily shed by employers and without much chance of becoming reemployed due to age discrimination. Although available pathways may play a role, the impetus to withdraw from work can come from the employer and thus reflects mainly *push*—not pull—factors. We thus need to look at the complex, interrelated push and pull factors at the workplace level as well as the interests of employers and workplace representatives in fostering early exit from work before we can turn to national corporate actors that influence policies affecting early exit.

2.1.2 Why Would Employers Induce Early Exit from Work?

The employer (or management) plays an important role in early exit from work (Naschold and de Vroom 1994), a fact stressed by the push view that focuses on factors affecting labor demand instead of labor supply.[3] Most obviously, employers may enforce 'mandatory retirement' rules in employment contracts (Lazear 1979), thereby requiring workers to exit the firm at a particular age. As an alternative, especially when mandatory retirement is not legal, employers may also induce retirement through firm-sponsored occupational pensions, topping up public benefits, or providing 'golden handshakes' (lump sum severance pay) to induce older workers to retire (early). Hence, what seems to be a pull factor seen from the perspective of the individual—the availability of a private pension—is also a push factor when seen from the firm's perspective. Why do firms have an interest in supporting (early) retirement?

According to the *diminished productivity* view shared by many employers, older workers have declining marginal productivity; therefore, 'buying them out' of the workforce enhances efficiency. The basic assumption is that productivity levels off or even declines toward the end of the working lifespan (Casey 1997). Age-related cognitive and physical wear as well as increased incidence of impairment are often held by employers to be responsible for productivity declines. In this view, labor shedding of older workers and replacement by younger workers enhance overall productivity and reduce labor costs. However, gerontological research has not confirmed such broad claims. Variations in job performance across age

---

[3] Interestingly, the economic literature on labor demand (or push) factors is less developed than on individual incentive (or pull) factors (see Oswald 2001: 40). Lazear (1986: 320) notes about incentive models: 'None of the models considered makes any serious attempt to ask whether constraints on worker retirement behavior are important, why such constraints exist, what the relation of pensions to earnings is, and indeed, why there are pensions in the first place.' An exception is his own work on the practice of mandatory retirement (Lazear 1979) and on pensions as deferred wages (Lazear 1990).

groups are as large as within age groups (Warr 1994). Moreover, diminished cognitive capacities due to senescence are often compensated by selection of tasks and optimized use of relevant skills as well as job- and task-related experience (Baltes 1997). Although empirical evidence tends to disconfirm the age-related 'diminished productivity' thesis, it remains a powerful belief among employers (or at least among personnel managers). Information campaigns and public mandates to require age-adapted workplaces could counteract such age discrimination practices (Jespen, Foden, and Hutsebaut 2002b).

Insufficient or outdated skills are a further rationale for many employers to replace older with younger workers. Cross-sectional data on skill levels by age groups seem to confirm the view that older workers are, on average, less skilled and have more outdated skills than younger people (OECD 1998d). However, the cross-sectional differences are largely due to cohort-specific differences in opportunities for attaining skills. The cohorts that entered the labor market later have more formal education on average and up-to-date vocational training than earlier cohorts. Similarly, an organization's age and recruitment policy will impact the demographic age profile of its workforce (Kohli 1986). More recently founded firms tend to be located in 'newer', growing sectors and have a younger workforce with up-to-date skills than 'older' firms located in more traditional, declining sectors with an aged workforce with less skilled workers (Stinchcombe 1965). Thus, on average, older workforces tend to be less skilled and less in accord with the modernization of production and technological innovations. However, older workers with the same initial skill level as their younger colleagues will have acquired more job-related and task-specific experience. Therefore, we would expect that the less a firm needs experienced and skilled workers, the more its managers would be interested in (and capable of) replacing older workers with inexperienced, unskilled younger workers who are paid lower wages.

Employers' *low investments in training* are closely related to the 'outdated'-skill problem of older workers. Yet whether the skills are up-to-date or not remains a function of the opportunities for postapprenticeship retraining, which in turn depends on employer strategies and public policy relating to education and training systems (Crouch, Finegold, and Sako 1999; Culpepper and Finegold 1999). Secular changes, such as more complex and frequently changing production processes, have required a shift from former practices that emphasized front-load vocational training and instead foster lifelong learning and continuing training (Gauron 2000). Although training investments are more likely to be lost among younger workers who tend to switch employers more often than older workers with higher tenure rates, employers are still reluctant to provide training for older workers (Casey 1997). For employers, the time span for returns on training investment, that is the remaining years in service, is too short for older workers (Naschold, de Vroom, and Casey 1994). The resulting catch-22 is that firms foster early retirement due to the 'outdated skill' argument and then, with the expectation of even shorter remaining durations, stop investing in skill updating even earlier. For their part, public policies often deny older workers retraining measures due to similar considerations. Only recently have calls for lifelong learning and 'active aging' attempted to alter these prevalent attitudes and incentive structures (Jespen, Foden, and Hutsebaut 2002b; Tuijnman and Schömann 1996; Walker 2000).

Employment contracts with seniority wage and tenure also add pressure on employers to shed older workers in an effort to reduce labor costs. According to the efficiency wage theory (Sørensen 1994), firms that rely heavily on high-quality production pay skilled workers seniority wages: they pay higher wages to older workers than to younger ones in order to retain and motivate them over their tenure with the firm. Cross-sectional studies show that wages rise, on average, until around age 50 and then level off or decline somewhat, showing an asymmetric hump-shaped relationship between age and wage (OECD 1998d).[4]

Given union policies enforced by collective agreements at industry or firm level, seniority wages are not adapted to the productivity level, and employers thus have an interest in mandatory or early retirement (Lazear 1979). Yet as was argued earlier, lower marginal productivity is not as much a problem as a consequence of employers' premature termination of training investments for older workers. As Sørensen (1992) argues, there are three different employment contracts (for tasks, jobs, and careers), each with specific consequences for the retirement process. Tenure employment rights that are part of the closed employment contract (under the 'jobs' or 'career' contract model) may also make continued employment of older workers less attractive due to reduced numerical flexibility given employment protection. In fact, in order to uphold tenure claims, firms may even be interested in maintaining mandatory retirement or inducing early retirement to ensure that tenure time is limited (Lazear 1979).

Occupational welfare schemes and particular firm-level retirement arrangements thus become a means to and further rationale for early

---

[4] However, such cross-sectional data on age-related wages masks cohort and selection biases since newer cohorts tend to have on average higher skills, and early retirement may affect the wage level for older age groups.

retirement. Many larger firms have set up deferred compensation schemes, such as occupational pension funds, to bind their core workforce to the company and to facilitate timely retirement (Rein and Wadensjö 1997*b*; Shalev 1996). Employer-sponsored occupational pensions can provide an incentive for retirement; most defined benefit (DB) plans and employer-sponsored pension funds actually allow early retirement (see Chapter 6). In addition, employers may 'top up' public preretirement benefits, using severance pay and other transfers to 'buy out' older workers. Special 'window plans' may also be devised to provide additional one-time incentives for older workers to voluntarily retire.

Yet nonwage labor costs also tend to rise with age, especially due to occupational welfare schemes such as employer-provided sickness insurance plans or pension plans (Casey 1997). Firms completely exclude or limit recruitment of older workers due to occupational welfare cost considerations, especially those due to DB and final salary pension schemes. Since occupational pensions entail a risk for workers who seek to change employers or in cases of insufficient funding or bankruptcy, statutory or collective regulation enforces some degree of vesting rights and prudent investment practices, which can however limit the incentive of firms to bind workers or reinvest funds into the firm (Davis 1995).

Peaceful workforce restructuring remains a major strategic reason for firms to use and sponsor early retirement. The causes and patterns of restructuring vary over time, cross-nationally, across sectors, and by type of firm (Sengenberger 1992). Short-term business cycles and long-term structural changes commonly induce pressure on firms with falling demand or on particular industries with structural problems to downsize or restructure their workforces. We might expect older workers to be somewhat exempt from layoffs, given (implicit) employment tenure, union enforced seniority rules ('last in, first out'), and age-related statutory employment protection. However, favorable public early retirement options and private topping up of pension arrangements provide a means and additional reasons to circumvent older workers' typical employment protections. In cases of mass dismissal, the workplace representatives (works councils or union shop stewards) may, through statutory rights or through provisions in collective agreements, play a central role in negotiating social plans (Morin and Vicens 2001). Some special preretirement schemes stipulate reemployment of younger or unemployed people as a condition for public benefits or state subsidies to employers. In these cases, public authorities will check eligibility conditions, and employers are constrained in their employment policies. When a firm can use early exit to avoid mass dismissal of prime-aged workers, it can uphold its tenure commitment and maintain social peace at the workplace level.

Employers have preferences for both exit *control* and risk *externalization* in preretirement polices. In her studies of employer preference for social policy, Isabella Mares (2001*a*, 2003) argues that employers prefer to maximize control and risk redistribution instead of mandated social policies, particularly in the case of early retirement (Mares 2001*b*). Since employers like to use early retirement as an element of their particular human resource strategy, they prefer to exercise control over the exit process, steering who leaves and who does not. Mandatory retirement clauses in employment contracts are the most obvious employer-imposed control; however, legislators have increased the age limit or banned such rules in countries with such employer practices (the United States and Japan). Firms can exercise control over exit by voluntarily topping up public benefits, providing customized 'window' plans, offering part-time jobs in line with gradual pensions, cofinancing bridging pensions until public pensions take over, or making a job replacement pledge under a public scheme. Of course, dismissal is the most obvious employer-controlled exit, though this step may be agreed upon with the older worker (and workplace representatives) in order to use unemployment benefits as a 'bridging pension' until statutory retirement.

There are also *constraints on employer control* when decisions are contingent on individual, social, or political actors at workplace level and beyond. With the exception of involuntary discharge (which is often legally restricted, costly, or requires works council consent), employers need to obtain the consent of older workers to implement voluntary early retirement. In addition, when preretirement is a social right, as with many flexible pension schemes and most disability pensions, employers have no direct control over their employees' exit decisions. That employers prefer to 'externalize' costs onto public schemes while limiting their own costs is relatively easy to understand, yet there is often also a trade-off between the externalization of costs and control possibilities (Mares 2001*a*, 2003). National actors, especially governments or the collective bargaining partners, are more reluctant to grant control options to individual firms if there is a danger of externalization. In particular, national unions will seek to negotiate conditions of early exit through collective bargaining, thus limiting employers' control capacity and enforcing early retirement as a social right, while workplace representatives may go along with employers in externalizing restructuring costs to the public.

33

2.1.3 *Why Would Workplace Representatives Support Early Retirement?*

Depending on statutory or bargained rights of *workplace representatives*, employers may have to consult worker representatives (works councilors or local union officials) about early exit policies. In some countries, workplace representatives are works council members, that is, elected representatives of all employees at the workplace (or company level) whether union member or not (Rogers and Streeck 1995). Additionally, union representatives at the workplace may be either voluntarily recognized by the employer or empowered by collective agreements (Tolliday and Zeitlin 1985). Consultation rights (in Germany: codetermination rights) may involve individual dismissal (of older workers or those with long tenure), mass redundancy plans, 'window' plans offering one-time early exit opportunities, and occupational welfare arrangements (such as private pensions). Collective agreements may also stipulate restrictions on personnel policy in general or with respect to older workers, thus employers would need the consent of the workplace representative or union to diverge from these collective rules. Even if no formal rights are granted or recognized, there is still the potential threat of collective action (strike action or public protests) against 'unfair' individual discharge and particularly against mass dismissal (Batstone, Borston, and Frenkel 1977; Golden 1997). Under these circumstances, worker representatives may influence employer decisions on personnel policy and even negotiate social plans to accommodate mass restructuring (Morin and Vicens 2001). But why would workplace representatives 'collude' with employers in shedding older workers?

Workplace representatives and local union officials represent the *'insider' interests of the core workforce*. Prime-aged and older workers are the core workforce groups; in larger companies with internal labor markets, they represent the majority of the works council's electorate, of union members, and of elected union officials (see Figure 2.1). Union membership rises with age among employed workers; the unemployed tend to be less organized (except where union-run unemployment insurance exists); and in most union movements, retired workers remain organized, paying reduced dues (Ebbinghaus 2002; Ebbinghaus and Visser 2000). Union-enforced seniority employment and wage rules thus serve the interest of the majority of the long-term employees—the 'insiders'—at the expense of the new entrants, temporary workers and particularly the job-seekers—the 'outsiders'. Note that seniority wage and employment rules also protect the prime-aged workers (aged 35–50) with medium tenure (five to ten years) since they will expect to remain employed and enjoy the rights of

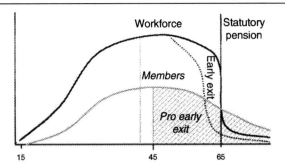

Figure 2.1 Age distribution model of workforce and union membership

senior workers (aged 50–65) with long tenure (above ten years). On the other hand, the more encompassing unions are, the more workers they tend to organize, the less likely they are to represent the 'insider' interests (Anderson and Meyer 2003).

Workplace representatives might play a crucial role in *selecting the groups affected by adjustment policies*. When employers plan workforce reduction or restructuring, workplace representatives may first seek to block such moves and propose a hiring freeze, thus making (early) retirement the only adjustment strategy. If they can only influence the distribution of the layoffs, however, they will face a selection problem: Which groups should be targeted? The large group of prime-aged workers with long-term tenure expectations will be in the strongest position to defend their seniority rights, while the employees with new or temporary contracts (and apprentices) will be in the weakest position. Yet employers may be unwilling to limit job cuts only to employees with already relatively flexible contracts; instead, they may seek to reduce the more costly and yet better-protected core workforce. In order to maintain the seniority employment system, workplace representatives might then be willing to negotiate an early exit deal for older workers on favorable conditions. Such a plan would be the preferred option for the prime-aged workforce since they will be exempted from layoffs, while they expect to profit from similar early retirement options in the future. Such an interest coalition between senior and prime-aged workers will hold not only for the case of exceptional redundancy plans but also for long-term gradual restructuring in internal labor markets. Hence, early retirement policies are often a consequence of seniority wage and employment policies advanced by unions and worker representatives as well as a way to maintain them.

Early retirement may also be offered as part of *political exchange* with workplace representatives or unions for political support vis-à-vis the state or public. When larger firms or whole industries are under economic distress and are forced to eliminate mass redundancies, the two sides may form a coalition to press public authorities to help restructure via direct subsidies or via early retirement provisions. Particular state-owned or large companies with national champion status are able to mobilize public opinion and convince public authorities to assist a firm in avoiding or smoothing mass layoffs. The 'political exchange' (Pizzorno 1978) is based on the militancy of the workers affected by potential restructuring and the political authorities' willingness to provide assistance in return for restoring social peace. Indeed, public authorities have frequently intervened in the restructuring process of coal mines, steel factories, and shipyards (Bovens, 't Hart, and Peters 2001). This is one example in which we see the interaction between workplace and corporate actors in the national political or bargaining arenas. I now turn to these social actors and their interests in fostering early exit from work.

2.2 Why Do Unions, Employers, and the State 'Collude'?

With few exceptions, the main policy decisions shaping early exit from work are taken at the national level in the social policy and collective bargaining arenas by the three main corporate actors: 'the *state*' (government, lawmakers, and courts), the *employer associations*, and the *trade unions*. While in this theoretical exposition I refer to these corporate actors as the state, employers, and unions, these actors are in fact often composed of various organizations—some hierarchically ordered by a peak organization (central government or confederation), others by rival organizations competing in a fragmented organizational space (e.g. politically split union movements). Furthermore, these corporate 'collective' actors are not autonomous from their members.[5] Employer associations and trade unions are membership organizations set up to represent the interests of their members (firms and workers, respectively). The selection of leaders and aggregation of interests are done via democratic processes. A large share of their resources, legitimacy, and representativity are gained through the mobilization of their membership (Schmitter and Streeck {1981} 1999; Streeck 1987b). In the case of the state (we focus here mainly

[5] In this case, Scharpf (1997: 54) uses the term 'collective' actors to denote 'that they are dependent on and guided by the interests of their members'. We will nevertheless follow common usage and use the term 'corporate' actors here, while acknowledging the limited autonomy of these membership organizations or of democratically elected governments.

on the government), public policymaking is also bound to the interests of the electorate by democratic means. Although these corporate actors have strategic capacities, I assume that—to a large degree—they are bound in their 'actor orientations' (Scharpf 1997) to the interests of their constituencies or membership.

I presume that all three corporate actors take an interest in shaping early exit policy for various reasons that are discussed in more detail later. Here, I assume that the interests advanced by these corporate actors derive largely from electoral considerations or membership logics. Governments will support early retirement policies when policymakers believe that such policies are popular with their constituencies just as membership organizations will foster early exit from work when their leaders deem that policies are in the interests of their members (or affiliated organizations). However, the process of aggregating and weighing the various and diverse interests of their constituencies or membership bases is not an easy one. I expect that differences in the constituency or membership base may well lead to differing aggregated interests. For instance, employer associations that are dominated by large-scale firms would tend to represent the interests of these firms, or a union that represents largely unskilled workers would advance the interests of this group. However, in this general theoretical discussion, I must abstract from such empirical questions, which are examined in more detail in later chapters.

In addition, strategic considerations will enter the 'games' these actors play (Scharpf 1997). I will assume that one actor alone is not able to shape early exit policy successfully unless there is one other main actor that shares similar interests. For instance, employers have an interest in enforcing employment contracts with mandatory retirement clauses (Lazear 1979); however, this practice cannot be maintained if the state intervenes and limits or abolishes such practice—as occurred in Japan and the United States. For analytical purposes, I distinguish different interest coalitions as I discuss the potential for 'collusion' between at least two main actors in supporting early exit from work.[6] There are different pairs of actors that form coalitions (see Figure 2.2): organized labor and the state; organized capital and the state; and the employers and the unions. In the empirical chapters that follow, I will see that several interest coalitions have evolved parallel to each other and thus a multitude of factors share responsibility for the empirically demonstrated rise in early exit from work trends.

[6] Although I refer to it as 'collusion', this is not meant to signify that these interest coalitions are based on illegal complicity; instead, I only denote that the two actors, at least implicitly, share the same kind of interests in advancing early exit.

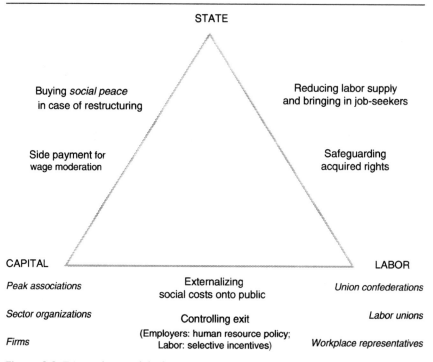

Figure 2.2 Triangular model of interest 'collusion' in early retirement policy area

A total of six main interest coalitions explain how the three pairs of actor constellations, with two separate rationales each, support early exit from work. Organized labor and the state could join for two reasons: they share an interest in extending social rights, thereby facilitating early retirement, and they have an explicit interest in using early exit from work as means to reduce labor supply. Employers and the state have two concerns in common: In early exit policies they see a means to buy social peace during needed economic restructuring, and they offer early retirement options as a side payment for wage moderation by trade unions. Organized labor and employers build coalitions seeking to control and regulate early exit from work independently, and they have an interest in externalizing the costs thereof to the state or the public (i.e. the tax and social insurance payers).

Speaking of 'collusion', I do not claim that these actors have come together and explicitly agreed on all these matters. In many cases, the confluence of underlying common interests of relatively independent actions seems the more likely origin. Moreover, early exit from work was not always planned or even intended. In fact, it has often been an 'unanticipated consequence of purposive social action' (Merton 1936) and tacitly accepted side effect of policies chosen for different reasons. As I argue later, the extension of social rights (or the use of early retirement as a side payment) was not necessarily chosen because it would facilitate labor shedding; nevertheless, once it had been decided upon, it had considerable consequences for early exit. However, we assume that the main actors would not immediately intervene if the policy outcome did not follow their initial aims. In fact, there were considerable time lapses before governments began to intervene due to negative consequences for public finances and labor costs of early exit from work (see Chapter 7).

2.2.1 *Organized Labor and the State: Extending Social Rights*

Early retirement must be seen in the wider context of the long-term expansion of social rights in the twentieth century (Marshall 1950). Three important theoretical arguments provide partial explanations for the rise of social rights in modern welfare states (Quadagno 1987): (*a*) the economic functionalist school, (*b*) the state-centered theories, and (*c*) the power resource approach. *Functionalist* accounts, which apply the logic of industrialization thesis, claim that, with increased economic growth, the need for supporting social policies will increase, while economic resources also become available (Wilensky and Lebeaux 1958). *State-centered* theories focus on the importance of bureaucratic elites, which used the extension of social rights as a strategy to promote nation-state building and support regime stabilization in face of demands for democratization and the increased problem load of industrialization (Alber 1982; Flora and Heidenheimer 1981; Heclo 1974; Weir, Orloff, and Skocpol 1988). The *power resource* approach points to the mobilization of organized labor and differences in opportunity structures for the advancement of social rights (Esping-Andersen and Korpi 1984; Korpi 1983, 2001). In this view, welfare policies are 'politics against markets' (Esping-Andersen 1985) imposed by social-democratic governments in coalition with strong labor movements against the will of employers and bourgeois parties. Welfare reforms were pushed from below instead of being granted from above by the state elites or merely emerging by functional necessity as a consequence of industrialization (Pampel and Williamson 1989; Wilensky and Lebeaux 1958).

Seen from the *state-centered* perspective, reform-oriented governments sought to extend pension rights to larger sections of the population as a response to problems and demands caused by industrialization. Lowering the normal retirement age in general and granting more favorable rules for women were reforms motivated by social concerns (sometimes paternalistic reasons), not as explicit early retirement policies, although de facto they did foster earlier exit from work. Initially, disability benefits (then usually called 'invalidity' pensions) were an insurance against age-related incapacity to work, and were meant to cover a social risk. Part of the extension of social rights was also due to judge-made law in the postwar period. Even before the rise of mass unemployment, older workers had difficulties regaining employment once lost. Social reforms aimed at exempting workers from de facto job-search and provided early retirement options as a matter of social—not employment—policy. However, these measures had the (unintended) consequence of allowing early exit when labor market conditions deteriorated in the mid-1970s.

In the *power resource* interpretation, the postwar welfare reforms were based on the political support of grand coalitions of left and center parties (Esping-Andersen and van Kersbergen 1992; Huber, Ragin, and Stephens 1993; van Kersbergen 1995). Governing parties could solidify their electoral base by granting favorable benefits without increasing payroll or income taxes through shifting to pay-as-you-go (PAYG) schemes, which had great 'front-end' political benefits (Myles and Pierson 2001: 310): 'Since there was no preceding generation of entitled pensioners, politicians could immediately offer a potent combination of modest payroll taxes, generous promises of future pensions, and "unearned" benefits for those near retirement age'. Special pension rules for women and benefits for widows also helped to extend public support among the female electorate. As long as the systems were not yet mature and contributors far exceeded pension recipients, the retirement age and necessary contribution period could be lowered as well as special early retirement options introduced for particularly unhealthy professions or other social concerns—all without immediate financial repercussions.

The power resource approach also provides an explanation for the expansion of social rights for which *union* movements have traditionally advocated (Katznelson and Hanagan 1991; Korpi 1983). Initially, pensions were defended as redistributions of societal resources to those unable to work and earn their living after the 'wear and tear' of a long working life. According to this political economy approach, organized labor advanced the call for a 'social wage': All citizens ought to have the right to a basic pension to retire on in old age and thus share in the economic wealth created during their working life (Myles 1989; Whiteside 1995). Pensions were seen as *deferred wages*: both employers' and employees' contributions to pension schemes were part of withheld social wages. Given the long-term struggle for the expansion of social rights, workers commonly see retirement as an 'earned social right', which the unions subsequently defend. The generational contract enshrined in pension systems with payroll contributions and PAYG financing further strengthens this tendency (Myles and Pierson 2001).

In addition, the more older workers fell victim to Fordist and Taylorist rationalization of production methods, and were discharged by formal or informal mandatory retirement rules, the more trade unions sought to protect their members by pushing for sufficient pension arrangements (Myles 1983, 1989). Early retirement was seen as a necessary state intervention in capitalist markets that would mend one of the consequences of intensified production processes, but lead to a fairer redistribution of the benefits gained from increased efficiency. Moreover, in those industries where workplace safety and health issues were particularly salient, such as mining and steel production, unions were well organized and successfully pressed for earlier retirement not only as a workplace safety measure but also as fair compensation for the additional risks over the working life. Thus, the more employers insisted on shedding older workers for reasons of efficiency, the more unions identified their role in protecting their members by compensating them with (early) retirement packages. However, this strategy could only be successful when unions could press the state and receive government support to expand social policies as 'politics against markets'. Regardless of whether the expansion of early retirement rights followed the interest of state bureaucracies or was rather a consequence of union mobilization, both the progressive government and unions saw early retirement as a social right, independent of labor market considerations.

2.2.2 Organized Labor and the State: Reducing Labor Supply

To a significant degree, early retirement was a deliberate policy to reduce labor supply (Esping-Andersen 1996c) following the rise in mass unemployment since the mid-1970s. Nevertheless, the 'management of unemployment' through the institutionalization of retirement (Atchley 1982: 271) has a longer history.[7] In all welfare states, public pensions were

---

[7] For instance, the US Social Security Act of 1935 made old-age pensions conditional on labor force withdrawal through an earnings limit. Following the Great Depression, retirement under the New Deal was partly 'a method of alleviating unemployment' (Graebner 1980: 266).

a means to reduce poverty in old age but could also serve to reduce labor supply—and it remains difficult to empirically separate social reform from labor market policy aims. When pension benefits were insufficient to maintain a certain living standard, full early retirement was not a viable choice for workers who were still capable or work and were fully employed. However, older workers faced involuntary unemployment at a higher rate, and the problems were amplified at times of high cyclical unemployment. Therefore, unions were already pushing for employment protection and earlier pensions in the bargaining and political arenas before the onset of mass unemployment in the mid-1970s.

With the rise of mass unemployment following the first oil shock in 1973, unemployment among older people (age 55–64) increased rapidly. Under these conditions, governments and trade unions supported the use of early retirement as a labor reduction strategy, especially in those countries where Keynesian employment stimulation had no longer been successful or where it was no longer pursued (Esping-Andersen 1990, 1996c). However, the 'labor reduction' thesis presumed a macro- and a micro-economic logic: (a) aggregate unemployment could be significantly lowered by 'buying out' older workers through early retirement and (b) positions freed by retiring workers would be replaced with younger workers or job-seekers. Yet many factors affected labor supply and the creation of new job opportunities, such as long-term increase in female labor force participation and the rationalization of jobs that were made redundant through early retirement. Nevertheless, for a long period, governments and unions put hopes in the labor reduction effect, even risking potentially higher social expenditures due to massive drawing of early pensions, which could be higher than savings from unemployment benefits.

National unions tended to support early retirement as a labor reduction measure for similar reasons to workplace representatives: The core union membership were prime-aged and senior workers who would hope to profit or who immediately enjoyed such early retirement (see Figure 2.1). At the workplace level, however, early retirement may have been supported at first not only as a labor reduction policy but also as a means to secure employment of the prime-aged workers, that is, the insider interests of those already in employment. Opening up jobs for 'outsiders', young workers or job-seekers, was not necessarily in the self-interest of the core workforce. Nevertheless, the rhetoric of replacing older workers with young job-seekers advanced by national unions served here as a legitimating device to argue for early retirement as a redistribution of employment opportunities at a time when youth unemployment and lack of apprenticeship positions had also risen precipitously.[8]

At least in the past, left or center *government* coalitions (social-democratic or Christian-democratic parties with ties to trade unions or workers' wings) on the Continent promoted early retirement as a means to reduce unemployment, an important measure of their success by the electorate. Labor reduction via early retirement seemed a possible solution to the particular problems of unemployment among older workers and a way to bring younger people into work. Governments set up special preretirement programs, which were conceived as short-term and tailored measures with often-stringent reemployment rules, to fight mass unemployment. Indeed, these special programs tended not to last due to high costs and mixed success (see Chapter 5). Yet in the case of other exit pathways that were not designed for this particular purpose, a more *implicit* consensus between governments and unions allowed their extended use, despite the rising costs. Employers were largely against such passive labor market policies for two main reasons: (*a*) lack of control and (*b*) increases in labor costs.[9]

2.2.3 *Employers and the State: Buying Social Peace*

Early retirement can serve as a socially acceptable form of 'buffering' employment reductions caused by industrial restructuring. For local unions and workplace representatives facing plant closures or mass redundancies, early retirement was an immediate means to protect older workers in a socially acceptable way (Casey 1992; Morin and Vicens 2001; Russig 1986). Nevertheless, it was the employers and the state that had an interest in 'buying social peace', not the unions or workplace representatives. The crisis of overcapacities in heavy industry sectors, especially mining, steel production, and shipyards brought first experiences with

---

[8] Not all unions were in favor of shortening the work life; some saw their primary goal in a reduction of weekly working time without earning losses, e.g. the German metal workers union during the 1980s (Jacobs, Kohli, and Rein 1991*b*: 208–12). A shortening of the work week would follow a similar reduction of labor supply logic, though it would bring a more equal distribution of the gain in leisure time, but it would also require a wider reorganization of work to open up new jobs.

[9] While employers supported early retirement for other reasons, they did not subscribe to the labor reduction thesis. Employers were reluctant to accept state regulations, demanding the most possible leeway in choosing new workers to replace retired workers. For employer associations, a reduction in unemployment would have the side effect of increasing the bargaining power of labor. The increased social security costs of this passive labor market policy would also increase nonwage labor costs.

social plans aimed at easing the downsizing process (Dudley and Richardson 2001). It was largely accepted as fair to allow workers with long working lives of physical work and in dangerous working environments to retire early. Moreover, political considerations about industrial policies and manpower management played a role in those sectors that were nationalized or at least dependent on state regulation or, within the European Coal and Steel Community, on supranational regulation (Ferner, Keep, and Waddington 1997). With increased limits on direct state subsidies to industries under European Union law, early retirement schemes often provided indirect assistance to industries under restructuring pressure.

Governments, as (quasi-)employers, would then use special retirement programs to dampen political resistance to industrial restructuring policy.[10] Special 'soft landing' plans devised by governments for ailing industries could then spread across other sectors where the driving concern of employers was not so much downsizing for capacity reasons but rather the enhancing of efficiency. Unions and workplace representatives would have to be lured by favorable early retirement deals to accept an increase in productivity through a downsized or rejuvenated workforce.

Early retirement as 'appeasement' may not only be eminent in individual cases of firm restructuring but also may emerge in the political context of more contentious labor relations. The late 1960s witnessed the *'resurgence of class conflict'* (Crouch and Pizzorno 1978): strike mobilization and political radicalization of worker movements, and also an economic downturn and new technologies that made further redundancies necessary. Increased social rights, including improvement in early retirement options, were not only a demand made by the strikers but also a means to help restore social peace, particularly for the state. As labor market problems aggravated economies, governments expanded the policies of 'soft landings', initially devised for ailing industries, to the whole economy. With the growth to limits of welfare states in the late 1970s (Flora 1986a) and increased calls for privatization of the public sector since the 1980s (Wright 1994), early retirement policies also became an attractive 'appeasement' to bring unions to accept public employment cuts (Clayton and Pontusson 1998).

Private sector employers found in early retirement a preferred route to 'soften' the impact of industrial restructuring and offer acceptable deals to

---

[10] For example, the French government set up a fund for preretirement allocations to older workers in firms that signed a modernizing agreement as early as 1963 (Guillemard 1991: 134).

workplace representatives who had gained in power through rank-and-file mobilization and extended participatory rights during the 1970s. Early retirement could be a bargaining chip in the hands of governments or employers as part of the 'political exchange' with union and workplace representatives (Pizzorno 1978). Even later, when strike mobilizations and the strength of workplace representatives were waning (Shalev 1992), the increasing need to enhance flexible production in the 1980s and 1990s made the previously institutionalized social practice a socially acceptable adaptation strategy. Such a strategy is particularly attractive to firms when there is a possibility of externalizing the costs of restructuring onto the public social insurance system (Naschold, de Vroom, and Casey 1994). Even when public benefits are insufficient, employers are willing to cofinance early retirement because of the benefit of peaceful labor relations. For governments, facilitating industrial modernization, and thus enhancement of productivity, is a positive side effect in addition to the expected labor reduction effect on overall unemployment. The costs of socially acceptable early retirement are seen to be lower than the unknown negative effects of increased industrial strife and social costs of high unemployment due to mass dismissal.

2.2.4 Employers and the State: Negotiating Wage Moderation

As part of the *political exchange* in corporatist income policies in the 1970s, the expansion of social rights was one possible side payment (Lange 1984). Governments and employers had an interest in keeping rising wages in check to combat inflation and enhance international competitiveness. Pay-as-you-go financing of extended social rights allowed provision of immediate benefits and postponement of liabilities of mature rights into the future. Depending on the financing of such side payments, employers may also have had the advantage of externalizing their adaptation costs and thus enhancing productivity. Even if there were no cross-subsidization, employers would probably prefer the financing of deferred social wages that allow for early exit policies to paying higher consumptive wages. The advantage of cofinancing for employer-sponsored plans was that firms could then control the exit process better than through social rights of public programs or state-regulated public subsidies (Mares 2001*b*). Yet governments may have been reluctant to allow externalization of cost and leave control over exit entirely to employers. Thus, the actual trade-off depends on the employers' bargaining vis-à-vis the government and unions. Over the long run, the side payments could be rather costly for governments as demographic shifts increase the expense of PAYG (pre)retirement programs (Myles and Pierson 2001). Thus, a major intervening variable here is the degree to which politicians can discount long-term financial liabilities for the sake of short-term electoral gains.

For *unions*, the exchange of wage moderation in return for social rights is more difficult to accept. Union leaders would have to discount the short-term interests of their members to insist on wage increases in times of high inflation and emphasize instead the long-term positive effects of moderate wage policies (Lange 1984). Here, a side payment of extended social rights could provide an additional incentive to accept such an exchange (Hassel and Ebbinghaus 2000). Early retirement could be such a compensation for wage moderation, yet the benefits of such a deferred wage are unequally distributed across age groups. While some senior workers (above age 50) may profit immediately or within a few years and prime-aged workers (aged 35–50) may expect to profit from such rules in the foreseeable future, younger workers (under age 35) and many women with insufficient contribution periods or part-time employment may not profit at all from this side payment. Therefore, the idea of 'old out, young in' replacement effects is important to maintain broad support across all age groups of workers and particularly union members. Here moral, altruistic appeals help to legitimize policies that are only indirectly beneficial to younger workers or job-seekers.

2.2.5 Organized Labor and Employers: Controlling Exit

A major issue between organized labor and employers is the control of early exit policies; this involves both the administration of programs and the decisions about individual exits. The state also has an interest in governing early exit policies, especially when it makes benefits dependent on replacement conditions or in the case of disability pension awards. Interesting issues arise when preretirement programs are self-administered by the social partners, or when they self-regulate private occupational benefits. In these cases of delegated self-administration or subsidiaristic self-regulation, the social partners have an interest in and the capacity to shape the conditions of early exit from work.

For *unions*, participation in self-administration of social insurance programs has several advantages: (*a*) unions can gain legitimacy through their representative role; (*b*) they can enhance their political role beyond traditional collective bargaining issues; (*c*) they have influence on delegated decision-making and implementation; (*d*) they have access to additional resources and positions; and (*e*) they may also be able to provide services to their members. In the case of the union-led voluntary unemployment insurance, the so-called Ghent system, unions profit from the 'selective incentives' (Olson 1965) via high membership levels (Ebbinghaus and Visser 1999; Rothstein 1992). When union-run unemployment funds also provide preretirement allocations (as in Denmark), early exit policies can provide additional 'selective incentives' to join a union. However, when unions are involved in the self-administration of mandatory social insurance or social partnership funds under collective agreements, discrimination against nonmembers will not be possible. Nevertheless, unions may receive credit for their involvement, and be able to provide special information services to their members.

Issues of early exit policies and the supporting social benefits can also become subject to collective bargaining between unions and employers. Unions or workplace representatives could thus assume a role in addition to wage bargaining at industry or workplace levels (Ebbinghaus 2003). On the one hand, at the workplace level, works council and union representatives can also play an important role in negotiating the conditions for firm-specific early exit plans. Workplace representatives, however, will be more likely to seek a particular solution for the firm and advance the particularistic interests of workers in the firm. On the other hand, national unions will tend to call upon the government to institutionalize early exit as a general social right to all employees or, in collective negotiations with employers for a given sector, seek to limit employer digression and institutionalize general rules. Thus, there is potential for some tension between national union policies, which uphold general rights, and local workplace representatives' strategies, which seek to exercise some joint control on early exit policies with employers.

For the *employer*, control of the exit process remains crucial for human resource management purposes (Mares 2001*b*). Firms would like to control the 'who, when and how' of early exit, retaining those with needed skills and high productivity, while shedding those with redundant skills and low productivity. Employers have substantial control over early exit decisions when early retirement requires some cofinancing (topping up of public benefits by the firm, sponsoring of employer-financed pension funds, special 'window plans') or employment decisions by the firm (mandatory retirement contract clauses, reemployment pledge, part-time employment contract, and discharge of employee to meet 'bridge' unemployment rules). Where early exit is a social right (and only conditional on approval by public authority), employers have much less control over the process.

As long as such public programs provide an attractive alternative in terms of eligibility and benefit generosity, employers will not be in a strong position to steer the early exit process.

Employer associations seek to represent their members' preferences for sufficient control of early exit at the firm level. However, insisting on more firm control will not come without costs: A larger share of these will be borne by employers, since governments and unions will be less willing to cofinance programs that are largely employer-controlled. As a result, the trade-off between control and financial responsibility entails a potential conflict of interests within a peak or sectoral employer association, as some member firms or sectors will expect to use early exit more extensively than others. Moreover, in systems in which risks are pooled beyond the firm—be it through a sector fund or through national social insurance—smaller firms that can rely less on early exit but still pay into these funds will be against the 'free riding' of larger firms that extensively use the early exit route and thus externalize the costs onto others (Mares 2001*b*).

2.2.6 *Organized Labor and Employers: Externalizing Social Costs*

While organized labor and capital may have opposing views as to the control over early exit processes and therefore need to find compromises, they both tend to 'collude' in externalizing the costs of early exit onto third parties (Naschold, de Vroom, and Casey 1994), especially the state, the community of social insurance payers, or other firms within an industry. Externalization of restructuring costs can easily occur within an economy when the financial burden on employers is not matching the actual costs incurred by the state or the public at large.

Unions seek to insure that restructuring policies and age-related labor market risks are not placed unduly on the shoulders of individual workers, but borne by society or by firms responsible for shedding workers. Depending on the welfare regime (Palier and Bonoli 1995), the risks may be shared among all employees (in Bismarck-type social insurance schemes) or among the citizens (in Beveridge-type basic pension schemes): the costs are collectivized through payroll taxes or state financing, respectively. Early retirement policies would not be subject to externalization problems if they were a collective insurance against age-related unemployment or disability, and everyone would be similarly at risk. However, to the degree that the availability of early exit options creates moral hazard problems and allows employers' opportunistic strategies, these policies are externalizing strategies: Not everyone will benefit from them, and some will use them for other reasons than the covered risk. When early exit policies serve other aims than covering the risk of unemployment or incapacity due to old age, such as labor reduction and industrial restructuring, the rationale of a social insurance—pooling social risks—is no longer given.

In addition, early retirement may lead to intergenerational cost externalization: Later cohorts may have paid for current recipients but may not profit from the scheme themselves when such a scheme is closed down or phased out. Therefore, the first generation that received benefits from a PAYG scheme but did not contribute to it, or earlier cohorts of recipients that were smaller than later ones, will have profited from such an arrangement at the expense of later cohorts. Thus, in the case of early exit arrangements financed by PAYG systems, a political problem arises: Those who have paid into the system in the past consider it an acquired right (Myles and Pierson 2001) and want to receive the same benefits as those that have already taken early retirement. As will be discussed in Chapter 7, it has been more difficult to undo preretirement options that are tied to mature general pension programs than those that were set up for the purpose of early retirement without being based on long-term contributions.

For firms, early exit schemes offer possibilities to externalize the costs of restructuring at least partly onto public or collective social insurance (Naschold, de Vroom, and Casey 1994). An internalization of these costs would require employers to seek working conditions adapted to older workers, and to be willing to hire, retain, and continue training older workers. Instead of internalizing these adaptation costs, firms often either use a *market-oriented* strategy of dismissing older workers without providing sufficient preretirement and severance pay, or use an *externalization* strategy by relying on public welfare systems (Naschold, de Vroom, and Casey 1994). The available choices depend in large measure on state policies and the state of labor relations: To what degree do these actors go along with the externalization strategy or seek to foster or even mandate an internalization course? Given all these vested interests of the myriad actors involved in early exit practice, reversing the course of early retirement proves quite difficult, despite its increasing costs for the public (see Chapter 7).

2.3 Bringing in Institutions

The discussion thus far has been rather theoretical, ignoring empirical variations and institutional contexts. Indeed, micro-level economic theories take these incentive structures as given; they do not seek to explain the institutional variations across countries. Labor demand theories may be able to explain why employers enforce early retirement in the case of an internal labor market, but they do not explain why production systems differ across countries, some relying more on internal labor markets than others. However, individual decisions to retire as well as firms' labor-shedding policies—shaped by employers and workplace representatives—occur in the context of existing welfare states, production systems, and labor relations.

The discussion of workplace representatives also pointed out their potential roles in shaping early retirement policies, but we need to know more about institutionalized labor relations to be able to explain substantial cross-national differences. Similarly, the discussion of interest coalitions remains largely abstract, stressing potential reasons for the three main actors to support early retirement policies. Here, the analysis must also be contextualized to be able to explain real world cross-national differences.

As the previous discussion makes abundantly clear, it remains impossible to discuss the development of early retirement policies without taking into account the larger welfare regimes in which they are embedded. Decisions taken by employers at national and workplace levels must also be placed within the context of different systems of production and economic governance. Finally, we need to examine the different labor relations in the collective bargaining arenas and the forms of social partnership in the administration of social insurance to understand the crucial roles the social partners play in mediating myriad pull and push factors. I turn to these significant institutional differences in the following chapter.

Chapter 3

Protection, Production, and Partnership Institutions: From Institutional Affinities to Complementarities

Institutions shape interests; they not only structure interest formation but also mold political opportunities. In this chapter, I map the institutional affinities and complementarities between protection, production, and partnership regimes. While in the previous chapter I discussed the latent interest collusion of social actors at national and workplace levels by deliberately disregarding the institutional settings, this chapter focuses on the ways in which historically evolved institutional arrangements structure the alternatives and opportunities for the social partners and the state. We thus expect cross-national variations in welfare regimes, production systems, and labor relations to impact interest politics differentially in the case of early retirement. To understand the interests at stake and the role played by the social partners, it is necessary to analyze the institutional configurations within which the social actors act.

Drawing on comparative studies in a variety of sub-fields, this chapter sketches the main cross-national differences in welfare-state regimes, social systems of production, and labor relations across Europe and in comparison to the United States and Japan. Three typologies are points of reference: Gøsta Esping-Andersen's *Three Worlds of Welfare Capitalism* (1990), Peter Hall and David Soskice's *Varieties of Capitalism* (2001b), and Colin Crouch's *Industrial Relations and European State Traditions* (1993). By bridging the gaps between these well-developed but thus far largely unconnected research traditions, I seek to overcome an apparent gap in theory building and empirical research.[1] While in the past disciplinary

---

[1] A number of programmatic statements called for a study of these linkages: the interaction between welfare states and labor relations (Bonoli 2003; Crouch 1999; Esping-Andersen 1992;

divides permitted further specialization of research, there remains also a need to reflect on the linkages between the spheres of protection, production, and partnership. Early exit from work is a case where such a comprehensive perspective is not only warranted but also necessary. Welfare regimes vary in their pull toward early exit from work, as they provide more or less generous preretirement benefits. On the other hand, specific production systems more or less push firms to shed older workers. Moreover, depending on the country's social partnership tradition, organized capital and labor are more—or less—inclined to mediate between these pull and push factors, cooperating in the development of early exit policies. All three institutional arrangements—protection, production, and partnership—influence early exit from work.

In this chapter, I contend that there is a need to overcome the disciplinary divides in studying welfare regimes, production systems, and labor relations. Max Weber's search for *elective affinities* constitutes a major part of the macro-comparative project: Recent attempts to map institutional variations and explore possible institutional complementarities between the spheres of protection, production, and partnership have given this classic conceptualization new life. Drawing on established comparative typologies, this chapter reviews the main differences across welfare regimes, two opposing varieties of capitalism, and diverse state traditions in industrial relations. For each of these comparative approaches, I discuss the theory-based typology and the empirical variations for the countries considered in this study. In the final section, I explore institutional affinities between particular regimes of production, protection, and partnership by asking two questions: How would these different institutional complementarities affect early retirement? What reform problems would result from particular regime constellations?

3.1 Comparative Typologies as Heuristic Tools

Comparative institutional analysis commonly employs typologies to map institutional variations (Lange and Meadwell 1991). Typologies can be used to construct theoretical models of causal relations between variables; they may also serve as categories for comparing empirical variations. Following Max Weber's concept of *ideal-types*, typologies can be

Jefferys 1995) and between the sphere of production and protection (Ebbinghaus and Manow 2001*b*; Hall 1997; Huber and Stephens 2001*a*).

constructed as theoretical models of causal relations between institutions that represent a model of reality, not reality as such. However, typologies may also classify different empirically observable patterns of social phenomena or *real-types*. For instance, while economists use the market model as a pure ideal-type model of exchange, economic historians would use classifications to describe different historically emerged types of national economic systems. Typologies can be developed inductively by classifying a posteriori social patterns of a set of cases or deductively by defining a priori theoretical dimensions that serve as conceptual lenses or as a 'yardstick' for empirical analysis. The heuristic value can thus move in two directions: ideal-types serve as a theoretical tool to produce hypotheses for empirical testing, while in inductive analyses—for instance, 'cluster analysis' of real welfare regime worlds (Obinger and Wagschal 1998; Shalev 2006)—classifications reduce empirical complexity to a few typical patterns (Kohl 2000: 116).

Despite their significant usefulness in systematizing myriad dimensions of social worlds, ideal-types must be constructed carefully. Several considerations require attention before proceeding with the building of a parsimonious typology, including boundaries between cases, clearly articulated analytical dimensions, and the crucial distinction between ideal-types and 'real' cases. For example, the fact that some cases are not clearly definable into only one category is not by itself a refutation of the theoretically constructed ideal-type but may reflect the existence of a *hybrid case*, which shares features of more than one ideal-type. However, there is the danger of mistaking 'real' cases for ideal-types. This happens when we confuse an empirically observable clustering of countries with conceptually derived typologies (Rieger 1998: 78). This pitfall can also arise when we look at single cases as prototypes of an ideal-type and disregard intra-regime variations. In order to explain cross-national variations, ideal-type typologies can only sufficiently guide the mapping of empirical cases by providing the *main* analytical dimensions. When classifying empirical cases, either we need realistic classifications to sort individual cases into analytical categories (Ragin 1987) or we have to allow partial membership in 'fuzzy sets' (Ragin 2000).[2] When we accept that categories of a typology need not necessarily be mutually exclusive, there is consequently no

---

[2] For instance, when classifying welfare states, we may look at income security across the four main social risks (old age, accident or impairment, sickness, and unemployment) by their degree of universalism and then code a welfare state as 'universalist' when it achieves universal coverage for at least three out of four risks. For an application of Ragin's *fuzzy sets* (2000) to welfare regime analysis, see Kvist (1999).

reason to assume that real cases have to fall fully within only one of the analytically derived conceptual boxes. Hybrid cases are then a mix of partial overlaps in several analytical types.

Comparative institutional analyses on welfare regimes, industrial relations, or production systems go beyond the classification of particular institutions; more ambitiously, they aim to capture cross-national variations in 'regimes' (or systems).[3] Most prominently, Esping-Andersen uses his welfare (state) *regime* approach 'to denote the fact that in the relation between state and economy a complex of legal and organizational features are systematically interwoven' (Esping-Andersen 1990: 2). More recently, he speaks of 'welfare regime', not welfare *state* regime, to indicate that private actors and families or households play important roles in providing welfare functions or supports (Esping-Andersen 1999; see also Wincott 2001). Similarly, the Varieties of Capitalism approach (Hall and Soskice 2001*b*) or similar political economy studies (Dore 2000; Hollingsworth and Boyer 1997*a*) stress the 'systemness' of institutional arrangements leading to different types of market economies. For a regime analysis, typologies have 'an obvious attraction in being able to characterize whole systems with the related implication that different systemic features hang together' (Lange and Meadwell 1991: 84). However, as Esping-Andersen concedes, the welfare regime approach implies a trade-off: 'Since our intention is to understand the "big picture", we shall not be able to dwell on the detailed characteristics of the various social programs' (Esping-Andersen 1990: 2).

Regime typologies are heuristic tools to understand the systemic interaction between a particular system and its environment. They describe the particular functioning of a set of given institutions on a general level. However, different institutions can provide the same function, while similar institutions may have very different functions. Therefore, we may find more variation in particular institutions within the same regime type, yet their functioning may nevertheless be very similar. As we discuss in Chapter 5, there are several *pathways* (Kohli and Rein 1991) to early exit from work; that is, multiple social transfer programs allow early retirement, many of which may be functional equivalents and are often substituted (Casey 1989). For instance, Continental European welfare states may differ

---

[3] Some authors use *system*, for instance 'social systems of production' (Hollingsworth and Boyer 1997*a*), while others use 'production regime' (Soskice 1999) to describe the configuration of institutions. Most prominently, Esping-Andersen (1987, 1990) introduced 'regime' in comparative welfare state analysis, a term which had previously been largely limited to the political sphere (e.g. Rose and Urwin 1969).

in the social policy programs that are available to sponsor early exit, but they share similar extensive use of public programs to shed older workers, externalizing the costs of restructuring to the public (Esping-Andersen 1996c).

Linkages between institutions from different social systems play a prominent role in these macro-regime analyses (Ebbinghaus and Manow 2001a). Esping-Andersen stresses the importance of public–private mix in welfare regimes, that is, the way in which these welfare functions are divided among state, market, and family (Esping-Andersen 1999). Colin Crouch's analysis (1993) of industrial relations uses the concept of 'sharing public space' (Crouch 1986) to describe cross-national differences in state–society relations that provide the collective bargaining partners with more or less influence in public policymaking. Peter A. Hall and David Soskice speak of 'institutional complementarities' when analyzing interactions between particular production methods and nation-specific socioeconomic institutions such as vocational training or corporate governance (Hall and Soskice 2001b; Soskice 1999). Following Hall and Soskice (2001b: 17), we can refer to *complementarity* between two institutions 'if the presence (or efficiency) of one increases the returns from (or efficiency of) the other'. An example of institutional complementarities between protection and production is the case of generous long-term unemployment benefits that help skilled workers to maintain their skills during unemployment spells. Consequently, well-developed unemployment benefits would be an institutional complementarity to skill-intensive production systems (Estevez-Abe, Iversen, and Soskice 2001).

Already Max Weber ({1922}: 202) had stressed the importance of studying *Wahlverwandtschaften* (elective affinities) to understand these linkages: '[We] can generalize about the degree of elective affinity between concrete structures of social action and concrete forms of economic organization; in other words, we can state in general terms whether they further, impede or exclude one another—whether they are "adequate" or "inadequate" in relation to one another' (Weber 1978: I/341). In Weber's view, the linkage between economy and society is not unidirectionally determined—as Marxism presumes—but rather the result of historical processes of mutual reinforcement (or friction). Nevertheless, even this affinity is constrained by external crosscurrents as well as *Eigendynamik,* i.e. institution-specific momentum (Mayntz and Nedelmann 1987; Rieger 1991). Weber's concept goes beyond mere functionalist accounts by analyzing these systems' historical coevolution. Indeed, we should not commit the functionalist fallacy of assuming that institutions that perform a particular function were created for that purpose (Stinchcombe 1968). The institutional complementarities may have been the *unintended consequences* of past decisions (Merton 1936) and the result of long-term mutually reinforcing but open feedback processes (Pierson 1993). In many cases, the actors that later profit from *beneficial constraints* (Streeck 1997*a*) of an institutional arrangement were often initially opposed to it. Only after its establishment did the actors adapt their behavior accordingly and the institution become 'institutionalized'. Early retirement, as I show in later chapters, arose partly as the unintended consequence of policies devised for an altogether different purpose, but once established, they assumed important complementarities to the exigencies of the particular production systems.

3.1.1 *Three Worlds of Welfare-State Regimes Revisited*

In his influential study, Esping-Andersen (1990) distinguishes three 'worlds' of welfare-state regimes: (*a*) the liberal, (*b*) the conservative, and (*c*) the social-democratic. Titmuss (1958, 1968) had already developed a similar triad of social policy principles, distinguishing residual, merit-oriented, and institutional welfare states. In contrast to many empirical studies, the welfare regime approach advocated by Esping-Andersen goes beyond a one-dimensional analysis of social spending levels; instead, it focuses on the locus of welfare provision, the scope of social rights, and the stratification of outcomes (Esping-Andersen 1990). Following Marshall (1950), Esping-Andersen (1990) stresses the redistributive function of social policy; in particular, whether universal citizenship rights correct market inequalities. Drawing on Polanyi's thesis of increasing commodification of labor within the self-regulated market economy (Polanyi 1944), Esping-Andersen measures the scope of social protection by its degree of *decommodification* (Esping-Andersen 1990), that is, whether social rights are independent of market outcomes (such as previous employment and earnings).

As the labels of the welfare-state regimes indicate, Esping-Andersen conceives three political traditions as important sources of welfare-state development that also shape the dominant principles of social protection (see Table 3.1):

- *Liberal* conceptions of a residual welfare state that should not intervene in 'free' markets by limiting work incentives and individual choice. Welfare policies should therefore only provide relatively low (or flat-rate) benefits to deserving citizens. They should not interfere

Table 3.1. Three worlds of welfare regimes

Regimes: (prime examples): Dimensions	Universalist (Sweden, Denmark)	Conservative (Germany, Italy)	Liberal (United States, United Kingdom)
Decommodification	High	Medium	Low
Social rights	Universal rights	Employment-related	Basic citizenship
Welfare provision	Public services	Transfer payments	Public–private mix
Benefits	Decommodified	Contribution-related	Flat benefits

Sources: Esping-Andersen (1990, 1999); see also Ebbinghaus and Manow (2001*b*); Kohl (1993).

with individual self-help and market mechanisms such as private occupational welfare benefits (Esping-Andersen 1996*a*).

- *Conservative* authoritarian-state traditions and Christian-social conceptions of 'subsidiarity' that rely on the solidarity of family as well as occupational and community ties. This conception has been particularly propagated by Christian-democratic parties (see van Kersbergen 1995). This type of welfare state is largely based on social transfers to maintain social status, particularly through using employment-related social insurance with contribution-related benefits.

- According to the social-democratic conceptions of a *universalist* and redistributive welfare state, advanced by strong labor movement and allied parties (Korpi 1983), a largely tax-financed welfare state should provide universal social benefits, guarantee full employment, and extend public services to all citizens.

At the analytical level, we can distinguish three welfare principles and main providers of solidarity (see Esping-Andersen 1999): (*a*) liberal-residual welfare regimes that rely on *market* forces; (*b*) conservative-familiaristic welfare regimes that rely on social *intermediary institutions* (family, occupational groups, and community); and (*c*) social-democratic universalist welfare regimes that rely on the *state* as provider of income security and social services. These distinct conceptions about the responsibility of welfare entail important differences in the *public–private mix* (Rein and Rainwater 1986*b*) of welfare provisions that are consequential for early exit policies. The more market-competitive welfare regimes are, the more we would expect production-related *push* forces to have an impact on early exit from work. In the two other cases, we would assume public welfare policies to produce a larger *pull* force, given the more generous benefits. We would expect conservative welfare regimes to be more favorable to early retirement due to the strong employment-related orientation and differences between status groups (Esping-Andersen 1996c), whereas universalist welfare states with a full employment goal would be less inclined to provide special retirement options to some but not all citizens (Stephens 1996).

Esping-Andersen's usage of these welfare regimes as both ideal-types and real-types leads to some debate about the addition of further distinctions to better fit welfare state realities (Esping-Andersen 1993). No 'real' welfare state comes close to the ideal model, Esping-Andersen concurs: 'Since they are, in a sense, ideal-types there are bound to be ambiguous cases' (Esping-Andersen 1999: 86). Following some of Esping-Andersen's critics (Ferrera 1996; Rhodes 1996), I distinguish five real world clusters of welfare states, taking into account the Southern European conservative welfare regimes (Ferrera 1996; Rhodes 1996) and the 'hybrid' case of Japan (Esping-Andersen 1997; Guillemard 2003).[4] The Latin European countries (France and Italy) are not only welfare laggards, but also rely more on traditional intermediary institutions: Church and family—ensuing from the importance of 'subsidiarity' in these societies (Ebbinghaus and Kraus 1997). In contrast to Germany, the Latin welfare states did not introduce compulsory social insurance until after World War I; in some cases even later.[5] Thus, in this revised scheme, a typology of five welfare-regime clusters helps to analyze the real world institutional affinities between protection, production, and partnership.

(1) *Liberal universalism* is the welfare-state model that combines free market principles and basic social security, and is dominant in the United Kingdom, Ireland, and the United States. The Beveridge welfare reform extended basic *social citizenship* rights (Marshall 1950) in Britain in the 1940s, though without abandoning liberal welfare principles. Its main aim is to eradicate 'want' and poverty, but not to interfere with individual self-help and free market principles (Cochrane and Clarke 1993; Marshall 1950). The Irish Republic inherited the early British welfare policies but did not develop a full Beveridge-type postwar welfare state and only in 1993 reformed and consolidated the fragmented social policy legislation (Quin et al. 1999). In response to the Great Depression, the United States introduced social security as part of the New Deal in the 1930s, overcoming

---

[4] Another model, which lies outside the scope of this study, has also been suggested: the 'radical' welfare states of Australia and New Zealand (Castles and Mitchell 1993).

[5] A borderline case is France, which shares many features of both the Latin and the Germanic tradition (Ashford 1991; Korpi 1995). Nevertheless, it is classified here together with Italy as a Latin regime because of the importance of old-age pensions, special public sector schemes, and strong familist tendencies (high youth unemployment combined with extensive protection of older workers) (MIRE 1997).

the troubling experiences with veterans' pensions following the Civil War (Graebner 1980; Skocpol 1992). American tax-financed 'welfare' policies are even more strictly divided from contributory social security and are limited to families with dependent children and disabled people with full work incapacity. While US social security or the British and Irish basic pension systems provide basic income security in old age, the liberal welfare states leave ample space for voluntary or private insurance such as occupational (company) pensions (Davis 1997; Rein 1996). The reluctance to intervene in the market is also eminent in meager unemployment insurance benefits of brief duration and limited active labor market policies. While Britain and Ireland depart from American extreme residualism (postwar Britain introduced a national health system universalizing basic health care), all three liberal welfare states are much less redistributive than Continental or Nordic welfare states; they come relatively close to the liberal ideal-type (Korpi and Palme 1998).

(2) *Social-democratic universalism* has been the success story of Scandinavian welfare states for a very long time, particularly in Sweden and to a lesser degree in Denmark. Thanks to the relatively homogeneous societies and the dominance of social democracy (partly in coalition with agrarian interests), these welfare states expanded rapidly (Esping-Andersen 1985; Esping-Andersen and Korpi 1984). The traditional flat-rate benefits and means-tested schemes were transformed into universal citizenship rights with considerable income redistribution and decommodification (Esping-Andersen 1990; Korpi 2001). In addition to social transfers, the Scandinavian welfare states also relied extensively on the provision of social services, expanding the public sector (and providing employment opportunities to women) in the process (Kolberg and Esping-Andersen 1991). Although earnings-related occupational pensions are supplementary to basic public pensions, only Sweden added a mandatory second pillar to its pension system in 1960 (Baldwin 1990) and in 1999 integrated both tiers in one new pension (Wadensjö 2000a). In the past several decades, Keynesian macro-economic management and active labor market policies have prevented mass unemployment in these export-oriented economies (Scharpf 1991). While the dominance of the Social Democratic party and the feasibility of Keynesianism have been increasingly undermined since the 1980s (Benner and Vad 2000), both Scandinavian welfare states come closest to the ideal-type social-democratic *universalist* regime.

(3) *Continental corporativism* relies largely on a social insurance model, first introduced in Bismarckian Germany, followed later by its neighbor

the Netherlands. In these socially and culturally segmented societies, the Christian-social doctrine and subsidiarity principles became a major political force (van Kersbergen 1995). In addition to a weaker social-democratic labor movement, this conservative socio-political legacy influenced the development of these corporativist welfare states, which delegated some regulatory functions to occupational and societal groups. Contributory social insurance that provided solidarity within—but not necessarily between—social groups was gradually extended to more and more sections of the population. In return for their contributions, employees and employers were granted self-administration in social insurance (as in Germany) or the social partners assumed self-regulative functions (as in the Netherlands). In the postwar Netherlands, basic old-age and disability pensions were introduced in addition to earnings-related occupational insurance.[6] Different occupational schemes as well as increased benefits (and, in tandem, contributions) served to maintain previous living standards in cases of social risk. Given employment-related contributions and benefits, social insurance is less decommodifying than the universal Scandinavian systems, but more redistributive than residual systems (Esping-Andersen 1990). The social insurance state relies, however, largely on social transfer payments, and less on state-provided social services. Both conservative welfare states faced a problem of increased social wage costs and high inactivity, leading to a 'welfare without work' syndrome (Esping-Andersen 1996c). Thus, Germany and the Netherlands (to a lesser degree) come close to the conservative (or Christian-democratic) ideal-type (van Kersbergen 1995).

(4) *Latin subsidiarism* is a variant of the conservative welfare state, represented by France and Italy. The Latin welfare states first copied Bismarckian earnings-related insurance that provides status maintenance for different social groups (Ashford 1991; Ferrera 1984). The differences from the other Continental welfare states result from a multitude of factors: the stronger impact of subsidiarity and 'familist' principles, a historical conflict of modernizing state elites and the conservative Catholic church (Rokkan 1999), more contentious left–right politics, larger regional disparity in industrial development, and a tendency, at least in Italy, toward clientelist

---

[6] Esping-Andersen (Esping-Andersen 1990: 53) subsumes the Netherlands under the conservative heading, attributing its high level of decommodification to the influence of a strong social-democratic labor movement after 1950. Some have followed suit in classifying the Netherlands as universalist (Goodin et al. 1999), while Esping-Andersen's later work (1996c; Esping-Andersen 1999) followed van Kersbergen (1995) in placing the Netherlands in the group of Christian-democratic welfare regimes (see also Huber, Ragin, and Stephens 1993; Huber and Stephens 2001b).

politics (Ferrera 1996; Rokkan 1980). Given the French state elite's role in modernization and Italian clientelism, the public sectors have been used as employment and regional policy instruments with public employees granted favorable benefits. Due to its familist tradition, social policy relies on subsidiaristic self-help functions of the family and local community (Paci 1989). While providing social protection for the male breadwinner, the welfare state was less supportive of young people and women. In both France and Italy, youth unemployment remains particularly high, while the rights of older workers are particularly well protected (Samek Lodovici 2000*a*). This leads to an even stronger insider–outsider cleavage than in the Northern Continental European countries (Esping-Andersen 1996*c*), thus France and Italy represent a special Latin variant of the conservative welfare regime.

(5) The *Japanese familist-residual welfare regime* is a particular combination of public–private 'welfare mix' and societal arrangements (Maruo 1986). The Japanese 'welfare state' emerged belatedly, with the main social policy legislation implemented only since the 1940s (Gould 1993). Japan is a hybrid case that relies on all three social institutions—the market, the state and family—in a unique way (Esping-Andersen 1997; Leibfried 1994; Seeleib-Kaiser and Thränhardt 2000). The firm assumes a particularly important role in providing occupational welfare benefits; indeed, firms can partially opt out of the state scheme (Kimura 1997). Over time, the state has extended its social policy scope, particularly for those who are not employed in the primary labor market made up of large firms. The state bureaucracy assumes a powerful role in society and enjoys particular privileges. The family remains an important societal institution, with strong traditional gender roles that are also reinforced by a highly segmented labor market (Brinton 1993). Based on its residual welfare state and firm-sponsored benefits (with an opt-out option as in Britain), Japan could be seen as partly following the liberal-residual model (Kimura 1997). Nevertheless, Esping-Andersen sees this hybrid case as a conservative welfare society with strong familist tradition (Esping-Andersen 1997).

Although a first glance at some general indicators on welfare-state regimes (see Table 3.2) of the period prior to recent reforms indicates some clustering, there are also significant deviations. Esping-Andersen's (1990) measure of decommodification summarizes the generosity and comprehensiveness of social security for three social risks (old age, sickness, and unemployment) at the height of welfare-state expansion around the early 1980s; it serves as the basis for his clustering of countries. As expected, the

Table 3.2. Welfare states in Europe, Japan, and the United States

Country	Decommodification index	SE % GDP	Social contributions and state subsidy (%)				Pension % SE	LMP % SE
			SC % SE	Employees	Employers	State		
	1980s	1980–95	1980–95	1980–89	1980–89	1980–89	1980–95	1980–95
	(1)	(2)	(3)	(4)	(5)	(6)	(7)	(8)
Conservative								
Germany	28	26.8	53.4	39.8	36.2	19.9	48.7	7.9
Netherlands	32	29.4	63.7	40.9	31.8	45.2	43.8	14.1
Latin								
France	28	27.0	71.1	26.0	56.4	14.4	48.5	7.5
Italy	24	22.4	56.9	19.7	50.9	28.3	62.4	4.7
Universalist								
Sweden	39	32.5	42.5	9.3	42.8	45.2	33.8	10.0
Denmark	38	28.6	5.3	17.6	4.4	80.1	27.4	19.3
Liberal								
United Kingdom	23	20.9	30.2	27.0	26.4	46.3	45.5	8.7
Ireland	23	19.9	25.3	21.5	19.7	61.5	17.4	15.0
United States	14	14.5	45.2	33.8	50.0	11.5	51.2	5.3
Familist								
Japan	27	11.7	74.3	22.4	29.0	30.0	47.7	3.7

Notes: (1) Decommodification index (1980): combined additive measure of benefit quality, coverage, and conditions for pension, sickness, and unemployment benefits; (2) SE: social expenditure (OECD definition); (3) SC%SE: social contributions as percentage of social expenditure; (7) Pension: old-age and disability pensions as percentage of social expenditure; (8) LMP: Labor market policy (active and unemployment) as percentage of social expenditure.

Sources: (1) Esping-Andersen (1990: 52); (2–3) OECD (1999); (4–6) ILO (1980–89); (7–8) OECD (2001c).

two Nordic universalist welfare states show the highest scores, followed by the conservative social insurance systems of the Netherlands, Germany, France and Italy, and finally by the Anglophone liberal welfare states (the United Kingdom, Ireland, the United States). The Japanese residual welfare state ranks higher than Italy. Comparing social expenditure (in percentage of GDP) over the long run (1980–95), we find a similar pattern: the Swedish welfare state spends most, followed by the Netherlands, Denmark, and the other Continental social insurance states, and tailed by the Anglophone countries, but Japan also lags considerably behind.

More pronounced cross-national variations can be found with respect to the form of financing and the type of expenditures. The Nordic welfare states, particularly Denmark, are largely financed by general taxation (in Sweden payroll taxes are also paid by employers). The more moderate liberal welfare states also have a relatively small share of social expenditure financed by mandatory employment-related contributions. In contrast, the Continental social insurance states do follow the Bismarckian model more closely, with more than half of current expenditures financed by payroll taxes. Yet not in all Bismarckian welfare states do the two sides of industry shoulder the burden equally: in France and Italy, the employers contribute a considerably larger share than workers.

In terms of overall expenditure patterns, measured here by labor market exit (old-age and disability pensions) and labor market policies (active and passive), cross-national variations are less clearly clustered within these regimes. Conservative welfare states and also the United Kingdom, the United States, and Japan have spent a larger share on benefits allowing labor market exit than Scandinavian welfare states or Ireland. The pattern is more varied with respect to active and passive labor market policies. Nordic countries spend more on active policies, while the Continental European and Irish economies spend relatively more on unemployment insurance due to higher unemployment. While this brief overview of indicators only provides illustrative evidence of the different clusters, it does reveal underlying qualitative differences that cannot be captured with aggregate data.

3.1.2 *Varieties of Capitalism Juxtaposed*

Michel Albert, most prominently, has juxtaposed 'Anglo-Saxon' with 'Rhenian' capitalism (Albert 1991). Several academic studies have more systematically compared the different economic governance modes and production strategies across industrial economies (see Table 3.3), using

Table 3.3. Two varieties of capitalism

Prime examples	Liberal market economy (United States, United Kingdom)	Coordinated market economy (Germany, Japan)
Financial and economic govern-ance	Short-term financial markets equity financing (shareholder value); limited business coordin-ation, antitrust laws	Long-term patient capital debt financing (stakeholder value); strong business associations, intercompany networks
Production system	Low-skill production; mass products; numeric flexibilization	High-skill production; high-quality products; flexible specialization
Management–labor relations	Decentralized bargaining; contentious workplace relations	Coordinated bargaining; statutory worker representation
Training and employment	General education; short tenure, high turnover, and interfirm mobility	Vocational training; long tenure, low turnover, and intrafirm mobility

Sources: Hollingsworth and Boyer (1997*a*); Soskice (1991, 1999); see also Ebbinghaus (1999).

polarized models of liberal market economy (LME) versus coordinated market economy (CME) (Hall and Soskice 2001*b*; Soskice 1991; Streeck and Yamamura 2001).

Firms in LMEs draw on short-term investment capital, thus seeking high profits for shareholders. They also rely on competition by low-wage mass production, which in turn requires a flexible labor market and wage structure. Given a fragmented and decentralized system of industrial rela-tions, 'free riding' on the institutional benefits without contributing to them is common, while the production of collective goods such as non-firm-specific vocational training is rare due to a lack of state support and weak associational capacity. Following voluntarist and pluralist traditions, the union movement is weak and fragmented. Moreover, it pays off for a company to be a 'non-union' workplace, or to weaken union rights, as happened under the Reagan and Thatcher governments (Freeman 1993).

In contrast, CMEs profit from far more patient long-term investment capital, 'good' employment relations and stable producer–supplier ties (Hall and Soskice 2001*b*; Soskice 1999). These institutions have not emerged by themselves; they result from historical legacies and past de-cisions taken by collective actors (Streeck and Yamamura 2001). Nonlib-eral capitalism, instead of relying merely on market mechanisms, enforces collectively imposed 'beneficial constraints' (Streeck 1997*a*), such as high wages that compel employers to seek cost-saving technological changes. In order to keep wages out of the competition between firms and allow above market-rate wages, a high degree of organization and compliance is needed among employers and unions. For the success of a high-value growth strategy, encompassing interest organizations (Olson 1982) are also important in providing other public goods—for instance, long-term investment into vocational training and up-skilling of the workforce (Streeck 1992). Firms made up of small-scale handicraft employers and workers have to be convinced by their associations to invest in production of collective goods such as vocational training. Institutions, such as life-long employment, high wages, skill transferability, and further training in case of technical change, are all important to motivate investment in the upgrading of skills.

Although the Varieties of Capitalism approach (Hall and Soskice 2001b) juxtaposes two ideal-typical models, we should also acknowledge considerable intra-regime variation and hybrid forms (see Table 3.7); these real world clusters assume importance in explaining divergent trajectories (see also Amable 2005; Kitschelt et al. 1999).

(1) *Sector-coordinated market economies*. In Germany and the Netherlands, the governance structure is traditionally different from the Anglophone free market model (Soskice 1991). Here, long-term patient capital provided by *Hausbanken* (banks with traditional links to a firm) has played a much larger role, as has the state, in providing the needed infrastructure and social protection. These 'social market' economies are all export-oriented (Katzenstein 1985). Given relatively high wages, companies can only compete in today's world markets with high-quality products and flexible specialization, requiring high-skilled labor and technological innovation (Streeck 1997b). However, these wage levels, tailored to the skilled, industrial, and male breadwinner, have also led to structural mass and long-term unemployment since the mid-1970s. Female, part-time and service employment have been traditionally low. In recent years, the Netherlands has exceptional employment growth through increased part-time and female employment (Visser 2002). At the workplace level, statutory works councils have institutionalized forms of worker participation (on German management boards, even codetermination). Worker representatives can secure employment rights, mediate in case of grievances, and codetermine restructuring due to technological change. Moreover, because of the consensual style and strike-ban until the end of a collective agreement, firms profit from the absence of industrial unrest, which would be particularly harmful to a just-in-time quality production strategy.

(2) *State-coordinated market economies*. Even though the Latin model shares many features with the German coordinated market model, it also

has some distinct features due to the importance of state intervention. Southern Europe evidences many small- to medium-sized firms, and the significant role of the state in modernizing the economy via nationalized banks, state-controlled conglomerates, or public subsidies due to the lack of private capital (Lane 1995; Schmidt 1996). Recent privatization efforts have increased market pressure, but the dualism between relatively monopolistic national industrial champions and a more or less flexible small-scale sector remains. State intervention is also necessary in the realm of labor relations, collective bargaining, and employment regulation, given the politically fragmented union movement, traditions of worker mobilization, and intransigence of employers in the private sector (Shorter and Tilly 1974). Both France and Italy face a severe employment problem: high unemployment, in particular for the young and foreign-born populations, widespread early retirement, and low female participation rates. While part of the labor market is relatively well protected by seniority rights and employment law, those with atypical work contracts, younger job-seekers, or those in the informal sector do not enjoy the social protection their fellow workers do.

(3) *Nordic centrally-coordinated market economies.* The Scandinavian economies come close to the nonliberal market models, with similar production systems to those in Germany. However, these welfare states channel a higher proportion of economic resources, provide more public services, and shelter a larger share of employment from market competition. In the private sector, the export-dependent high-quality, high-skill industrial sector has long been sustained by a financial system with neo-Keynesian macro-economic steering and long-term, patient capital through state-financed co-operative loans, at least until entry into the European currency system and recent liberalization of capital controls (Huber and Stephens 1998; Stephens 1996). Moreover, a system of centralized bargaining between encompassing and well-organized unions and employer associations provided relatively high and equalizing 'solidaristic' wage structures that forced restructuring, particularly in Sweden (Pontusson 1997). Denmark's economic structure is more marked by smaller and specialized export-oriented companies (Schwartz 1994). In the past, the social partners have been involved in nationwide corporatist interest intermediation that went beyond income policies and included active employment policies. However, following the employment growth in and wage push by the public sector, as well as state intervention into management prerogatives, private employers have sought to decentralize wage bargaining and have called for

labor market deregulation since the 1980s, undermining the postwar neo-corporatist system (Kjellberg 1992; Lash and Urry 1987; Swenson and Pontusson 2000). Sweden's exceptional record in maintaining full employment ended in the late 1980s; while Denmark suffered earlier from high unemployment, the labor market situation has improved since the late 1990s (Benner and Vad 2000; Jochem 2000).

(4) *Anglophone liberal market economies.* The British–American model, particularly since the Thatcher government or Reagan administration, followed the 'free market' model in applying supply-side macro-economic policies. The financial markets had always played a larger role in the United Kingdom and the United States than on the European Continent or in Japan (Dore 2000). The privatization of Britain's postwar nationalized industry and public service sector on the 1980s added to the dominance of short-term shareholder values, searching for immediate returns on invested capital. Ever since the late nineteenth century, a debate on the 'industrial decline' of Britain has pointed to some of this strategy's shortcomings: the lack of long-term investement in infrastructure, research and development, a skill-deficit in the labor force, and relatively low levels of productivity. While the British Conservative government was able to attract some foreign capital and help industry through deregulation, it bet on a low-wage mass production strategy (Soskice 1991). Even though 'Fordist' mass production for large consumer markets was a hallmark of American postwar success, it entered into crisis in the 1970s. Deregulation, flexible labor markets, wage concessions by unions, increased anti-union policies, and a wave of innovation in new technologies helped US economic growth to rebound in the 1990s (King and Wood 1999). In these countries, the low-wage mass production strategy finds institutional support through decentralized voluntarist labor relations and unregulated employment that allows 'hiring and firing', and a liberal welfare state with low reservation wages. Compared with the European Continent, LMEs' employment levels are relatively high, especially for women, given larger service economies and more stringent eligibility for nonwork income transfers.

(5) *Japanese firm-coordinated model.* Japan is also seen as a proponent of the Rhenian model (Dore 1997). However, in contrast to Germany, Japanese labor relations at the national level and state social policy are less developed. Patient capital and lifelong employment have provided the backbone of the Japanese model of diversified production (Dore 2000). Special features of the Japanese business system include the special

relations between producers and suppliers and the interlocking financial interdependencies within business groups. Unlike European economies, the Japanese export-oriented economy remained relatively closed to international competition, protecting its own home market. The recent crisis in its financial system, rising cost pressure on its aging society, and the need for reform of its relatively rigid institutions call the future of the traditional Japanese system into question.

A brief comparison of economic indicators shows some systematic differences between LMEs and CMEs (see Table 3.4). Europe's CME countries are more open to trade than the United States and Japan, which both have large domestic markets. Stock market capitalization is particularly high not only in liberal countries but also in Japan, the Netherlands, and Sweden, partly due to pension funds' investments. Wage inequality is more pronounced in LMEs than in CMEs.

Employment levels and unemployment performance are not clearly divided into the two market models, however. Employment regulation and skill profiles show the expected empirical variations: employment

Table 3.4. Market economies in Europe, Japan, and the United States

Regime Country	Trade (% GDP) 1990–96 (1)	Stock market 1990–95 (2)	Wage spread 1994–2003 (3)	Employment rate 1995 (4)	Unemployment rate 1990–6 (5)	Median tenure 1995 (6)	Vocational training 1990s (7)
Sector-coordinated							
Germany	42.8	22	1.37	64.9	7.4	10.7	34
Netherlands	76.3	55	1.56	65.2	6.8	5.5	43
State-coordinated							
France	39.6	31	1.60	59.0	10.9	7.7	28
Italy	39.1	15	1.65	51.2	11.4	9.9	35
Centrally coordinated							
Sweden	54.3	52	1.36	77.9	6.0	7.8	36
Denmark	55.7	31	1.38	72.9	8.4	4.4	31
Liberal							
United Kingdom	45.9	105	1.74	68.3	8.5	5.0	11
Ireland	87.0	40	—	55.3	14.2	5.3	6
United States	20.9	76	2.13	73.3	6.2	4.2	3
Firm-coordinated							
Japan	17.4	78	1.60	74.1	2.6	8.3	16

Notes: (1) Trade (export and imports in % GDP); (2) market capitalization (in % GDP); (3) wage spread (men): D1/D9; (6) median tenure: median length of job tenure with current employer; (7) share of young people in (post)secondary vocational training.

Sources: (1), (3)–(5) OECD (1999); (2) OECD (1998*b*); (6)–(7) Estevez-Abe, Iversen, and Soskice (2001).

tenure tends to be lower in LME countries and higher in CME countries, particularly in Germany, Italy, France as well as Japan. Vocational training is more common in the CME countries, with the exception of Japan where firms provide extensive on-the-job training (Marsden 1999). Empirical studies on the varieties of capitalism indicate a clustering of institutional variables and economic indicators along the two poles (Hall and Gingerich 2004). Country case studies (Crouch and Streeck 1997; Streeck and Yamamura 2001) also indicate that CME countries not only differ from the United States model, but that there are also relatively important variations within this large cluster of CMEs (see also Ebbinghaus 1999; Ebbinghaus and Kittel 2005). One of the institutional variations that has often been subsumed in the broader political economy models of the Varieties of Capitalism approach is the differences in labor relations that also have bearing on production systems' coordination capacity. As the later analysis shows labor relations and production systems do not overlap, particularly in the case of CMEs. This also corroborates my assumption that production-related differences may explain the push factors to early exit from work but that the social partners assume an important role in mediating between pull and push. Therefore, I separate here the overall economic governance and production system from labor relations.

3.1.3 Labor Relations Compared

In terms of industrial relations systems, Colin Crouch distinguishes three modes of interest intermediation (Crouch 1993): contentious relations, pluralist bargaining, and neo-corporatism (see Table 3.5). Informed by early analyses of neo-corporatism (Lehmbruch and Schmitter 1982; Schmitter 1974; Schmitter and Lehmbruch 1981), Crouch develops a formal model of the exchange relations between organized labor and capital, that is, between the organizations of workers and employers.

Table 3.5. Three ideal-typical modes of labor relations

Modes (Prime examples)	Contentious (France, Italy)	Pluralist (United Kingdom, Ireland)	Corporatist (Sweden, Germany)
Interest organization Perspective	Fragmented Antagonistic class conflict	Particularistic Short-term group interests	Encompassing Long-term common interests
Role of the state Mode of change	State intervention Waves of protests	Noninterventionist Economic stop-and-go	Enabling/cooperative Consensual

Sources: Crouch (1993); Ebbinghaus and Visser (1997).

Contentious relations are characterized by an antagonistic conflict of interests between both sides, the unlikelihood of cooperation given a zero-sum bargaining situation, deficits in self-organization, and underdeveloped mutual recognition. When waves of social mobilization during a conflict arise, state intervention frequently attempts to mediate and restore order. Historically, *pluralistic* bargaining arose when employers supported by political and legal changes altered their strategy from outright antagonistic conflict to 'the development of procedures for conducting conflicts with labor in such a way that mutually damaging action is avoided' (Crouch 1993: 36). However, such voluntary bargaining still suffers from short-termism and particularistic interest representation, while the state remains reluctant to intervene in material bargaining issues. Finally, the third mode of interest intermediation (*corporatist*) is based on long-term 'positive sum' conceptions of the common interests among all organized actors. This presumes relatively centralized and encompassing organization of interests (Schmitter 1974) as well as institutionalized support by the state (Traxler 1999). After a crisis of neo-corporatist arrangements in the 1980s, tripartite concertation reappeared in many European countries (Berger and Compston 2002; Fajertag and Pochet 2000) as they coped with the challenges of a European single market and the European Economic and Monetary Union (EMU). The new 'competitive corporatism' (Rhodes 2001) covered not only income policies, negotiating wage moderation to boost competitivity, but also welfare-state reforms in order to reduce public deficit and lower labor costs (see Ebbinghaus and Hassel 2000). However, given their need for bargained consensus, such corporatist relations have also been criticized for their institutional inertia and slow adaptations (Berthold and Hank 1999).

Building on Crouch's three modes (1993) of interest intermediation, I make further distinctions in analyzing varieties in corporatism (see also Ebbinghaus and Visser 1997): Nordic neo-corporatism and Continental social partnership. The need for this differentiation becomes particularly clear when we consider the interaction of welfare states and labor relations. When we look at the welfare state–labor relations nexus, we observe that Nordic corporatism was developed under a more favorable social-democratic welfare state, while Continental social partnership depended on and reproduced the Conservative welfare state. Crouch does plot two possible variants of neo-corporatism that largely coincide with this dichotomy—the distinction between neo-corporatism with 'strong' and 'weak' organized labor (Crouch 1993: 43)—and this is the difference between Nordic neo-corporatism and Continental social partnership applied in the labor relations typology here. While the Nordic unions are relatively centralized and are strong in union membership, the Continental European unions have much lower membership and have been at least historically more politically divided (Ebbinghaus and Visser 2000). Finally, Japan easily fits into neither corporatist category, given the importance of firm-level labor relations (Shirai 1983). Nor can it be subsumed under pluralist voluntary bargaining since Japanese management–union relations are cooperative.

Let us briefly review the five empirically observable patterns of interest intermediation in Europe, Japan, and the United States:

(1) *Anglophone pluralism* has been dominant in the United Kingdom, Ireland, and the United States (Edwards et al. 1998; Kochan, Katz, and McKersie 1994; von Prondynski 1998). According to a voluntarist conception, employers and labor should promote their particularistic interests via 'free' collective bargaining without state intervention. Labor–capital conflicts are regulated by common law traditions and legal regulations (Fox 1985). The interest organizations are rather fragmented and weak, on both sides: labor and capital. The main power resource of trade unions relies on membership and strike mobilization, in particular at the firm or plant level. It provides the means to force the other side to collective negotiations and finally to an agreement. Only partially or occasionally can organized labor—via lobbyism or affiliation with the Labor Party as in Britain or the Democratic Party as in the United States—influence government politics in its favor (Taylor 1989). Antiunion policies in the 1980s under the Reagan administration in the United States and the Thatcher government in the United Kingdom represented a break with noninterventionist traditions (Card and Freeman 1993; Freeman and Pelletier 1990). On the other hand, in Ireland since the late 1980s, tripartite national social pacts on income policies and other social issues have been agreed, a development that has brought Ireland closer to corporatist policymaking (O'Donnell and O'Reardon 2000). Even though the voluntarist legacy is strong in all three countries, developments have diverged: toward more intervention in the United Kingdom and the United States, but more corporatist consensus-seeking in Ireland.

(2) *Nordic corporatism* is the dominant form of concertation in the Scandinavian welfare states of Sweden and Denmark (Kjellberg 1998; Scheuer 1998). These welfare states have traditionally maintained Keynesian economic policies of full employment and assumed a mediating role in labor relations. Thanks to union-led unemployment insurance and strong local

workplace unionism, the Swedish and Danish union movements have exceptionally high levels of union density (Rothstein 1992; Western 1998). Traditionally, Swedish and Danish organized interests are relatively centralized and the organizations enjoy a high degree of membership compliance. However, there is a trend toward decentralization of collective bargaining in both countries since the 1980s (Kjellberg 1998; Scheuer 1998). The main cleavage in the union movement is between blue-collar and white-collar unions, the first movement historically linked to social democracy. The Danish union movement tends to be more fragmented and dominated by general versus craft unionism, while Sweden has a more centralized industrial union movement. The labor market partners recognize each other and are also consulted by the state in political decision-making. With the support of the state, the collective bargaining system is highly institutionalized. It fulfills self-regulatory functions mainly via bipartite central agreements or through political exchange with the state in return for social policy legislation. However, since the 1980s, the Swedish employers have grown more critical of centralized bargaining and corporatist institutions, while in Denmark the system has always been less centralized (Kjellberg 1998).

(3) *Continental social partnership* is a further variant of corporative labor relations through both sectoral bargaining and statutory works councils present in Germany and the Netherlands (Jacobi, Keller, and Müller-Jentsch 1998; Visser 1998). Both societies are traditionally more segmented than the largely homogenous Nordic societies. Unlike the North, the labor–capital conflict has been crosscut by religious and/or linguistic cleavages (Rokkan 1999), leading to fragmentation and even *verzuiling* (pillarization) of associational life, though unitary movements gained in importance after 1945 in Germany and after several mergers from the 1970s in the Netherlands (Visser 1990). Associations have acquired an important role in socio-political consensus-building. Even though the state partially intervenes in labor relations and defines the general collective bargaining rights, it also leaves crucial self-regulatory functions to the 'social partners'. Statutory workplace codecision rights have extended social partnership institutions into the firm: the works councils represent the stakeholder interests of the employees vis-à-vis management (Streeck 1995). Nevertheless, German and Dutch unions organize a much smaller share of the workforce and are more indirectly present at the workplace level than Scandinavian unions (Ebbinghaus and Visser 1999).

(4) *Roman polarization* is the dominant pattern in France and Italy (Goetschy 1998; Regalia and Regini 1998). These countries have strong 'Etatist' traditions (van Waarden 1995), crosscutting and politicized labor cleavages, and weak institutionalization of peaceful state–society relations (Ebbinghaus 1995). Employer associations and unions do not always recognize each other's rights as legitimate collective bargaining partners; their bipartite relations as well as those with the state are rather contentious, which in turn provokes further state intervention. Given the fragmented and polarized systems, the employers and labor organizations strive for representational rights and recognition by the state. Due to their weak membership ties, labor unions rely on social and political mobilization to demand state intervention: only this can force employers to recognize and negotiate with the political union movements and/or to settle labor conflicts with state support (Shorter and Tilly 1974). However, in the 1990s, concertation on major reforms of bargaining system has been possible in Italy (Regini and Regalia 1997), while the state-imposed workplace bargaining right has not helped the divided and weak unions in France (Howell 1992).

(5) *Japanese firm-level cooperation* emerged during the postwar period, though Japanese labor relations were initially rather contentious, with a politicized and divided labor movement and relatively exclusionary government policies. While employers have good corporatist relations with the government, national unions tend to be excluded from national policymaking (Knoke et al. 1996). Union density is higher than the United States, but lower on average than in Europe and gradually declining, as in most countries. However, within the larger firms, decentralized 'enterprise unionism' (Shirai 1983) emerged in more cooperative and consensual relations between management and unions. Although they are loosely federated beyond the firm, there is some coordination of firm-level bargaining through *shuntō* (the Spring offensive). Thus, Japanese labor relations are relatively centralized and less codified than in the Anglophone voluntarist tradition. Nevertheless, in practice, management–labor relations are cooperative and enterprise unions play a crucial role in maintaining the occupational welfare and employment tenure system.

A comparison of Western industrial relations systems according to qualitative and quantitative indicators reveals some clustering in the five regimes (see Table 3.6). First, in terms of the organization of labor, we find systematic differences with respect to cleavage structures and mobilization patterns. When we look at the number of main confederations and the nature of splits within the labor movement, we find important differences.

Table 3.6. Labor relations in Europe, Japan, and the United States

Country	Organized labor		Employers		Conflict	Collective bargaining		
	Cleavage	Density	Peak	Coverage	Days lost	Level	Coverage	Extension
	(1)/(2)	(3)	(4)	(5)	(6)	(7)	(8)	(9)
Cooperative								
Germany	Unitary	32.9	EA	80–90	29	Sector	W. 90	Mandatory
Netherlands	Unitary	25.5	BA	70–80	1	Sector	81	Mandatory
Contentious								
France	Political	10.8	BA ind.	30–40	91	Firm	82	Mandatory
Italy	Political	38.8	BA	70–80	1352	Sector	70	None
Corporatist								
Sweden	Collarline	82.5	EA ind.	90–100	112	Nation/sector	83	Voluntary
Denmark	Collarline	71.4	EA	90–100	114	Nation/sector	>80	Voluntary
Voluntarist								
United Kingdom	Craft–ind.	39.1	BA	20–30	344	Firm	47	None
Ireland	Craft–ind.	50.8	BA	30–40	374	Nation/firm	>70	Mandatory
United States	Craft–ind.	14.9	None	—	245	Firm	15	None
Firm-cooperative								
Japan	Firm	23.8	BA		50	Firm	20	None

Notes: (1) Functional cleavage: collarline (white vs. blue-collar), craft vs. industry; (2) cleavages: religious, political vs. unitary; (3) density: union members as percentage of dependent labor force; (4) major peak employer association: ind. = industry only; EA = employer association proper, BA = business association (employer and trade association); (5) employers covered: percentage of employees in organized firms; (6) conflicts: working days lost by strike (or lockout) per 1,000 employed 1974–89; (7) level: main level of collective bargaining; (8) coverage: share of employees covered by collective agreements; Germany (West), East: 63 (1992); (9) extension: *erga omnes* extension of collective agreements: mandatory for all firms.

Sources: Ebbinghaus and Visser (1997, 2000).

The Nordic countries all have a social-democratic labor confederation that organizes the blue-collar workers (largely in industrial unions) in particular, while some white-collar workers have founded separate peak organizations. The British and Irish union confederations, on the other hand, are the only peak associations, though they are a relatively weak umbrella for a variety of craft, general and industrial unions, some of which are affiliated with the Labor party. Political and religious splits are particularly pronounced in the Latin labor movements, while these cleavages have some residual importance in the Netherlands, and in Germany they have been overcome through nonpartisan unitary confederations after 1945.

With respect to the level of unionization, measured by union density, Scandinavian countries lead the ranks in steady, high unionization levels, while the Roman labor movement has relied more on cycles of political mobilization (Ebbinghaus and Visser 2000). The Continental labor movements have a medium level in membership mobilization—membership decline occurred earlier in the Netherlands than in Germany. Although Britain and Ireland had somewhat higher levels in the past, British unions, in particular, have witnessed a dramatic decline in unionization since the Thatcher government introduced new labor legislation (Freeman and Pelletier 1990). Partly as a consequence of the concentration or fragmentation and strength or weakness of unions, important differences exist with respect to strike propensity and volume of industrial conflicts (Korpi and Shalev 1980; Shalev 1992): polarized Latin and Anglophone labor relations, but also more recently in Scandinavian countries, show a higher level of strikes and lockouts compared with the more 'peaceful' Continental social partnership countries or Japan.

On the capital side, we also find considerable differences in organization, although for less political reasons. Some countries, in particular Germany and Sweden, have specialized employer peak associations that are relatively centralized and well organized, whereas in other countries general business associations combine labor market and producer interests within their ranks. A low level of membership, weak centralization, and often paternalistic union opposition is especially problematic in Anglophone and Latin labor relations. Consequently, collective bargaining covers fewer workers, which is the case in Britain and Ireland. In the Scandinavian countries, employers and unions are well organized and they can enforce collective agreements by themselves, which is not the case elsewhere. Particularly in Latin labor relations, such state intervention can be crucial in extending collective agreements that have been negotiated by relatively less-organized and unrepresentative bargaining partners to larger sections of the economy (Traxler 1999). Britain, however, has no legal extension mechanisms at its disposal, which is quite harmful given the increased decentralization of collective bargaining and the lessening recognition of unions at the workplace level.

3.2 From Institutional Affinities to Complementarities

3.2.1 Institutional Affinities and Complementarities under Pressure

The different real world regime clusters show intriguing institutional affinities between particular regimes of protection, production, and partnership institutions (see Table 3.7). The comparative analysis indicates that there is only one complete overlap between welfare regimes, production systems, and labor relations. The uncoordinated LMEs go together with liberal welfare states and voluntarist labor relations; the liberal principle of non-intervention into the market has put its mark on social policy and labor relations. The CMEs, however, show a larger variety of welfare regimes and labor relations combinations. If we classify the Japanese welfare state as liberal-residual due to its reliance on occupational (company-level)

Table 3.7. Institutional affinities between protection, production, and partnership

Countries	Protection (welfare regime)	Production (market economy)	Partnership (labor relations)
Center			
Germany	Conservative	(Sector-)	Cooperative
Netherlands	(corporativist)	Coordinated	(social partnership)
Latin			
France	Conservative	(State-)	Contentious
Italy	(subsidiaristic)	Coordinated	
Nordic			
Sweden	Universalist	(Centrally)	Cooperative
Denmark		Coordinated	(neo-corporatist)
Anglophone			
United Kingdom	Liberal-residual	(Uncoordinated)	Voluntarist
Ireland		Liberal	
United States			
Asian			
Japan	Liberal-residual	(Firm-)	Cooperative
	(familist)	Coordinated	(firm-level)

Notes: Sub-types in brackets.

welfare, we would find all three welfare regimes among nonliberal CME countries. Similarly, in the past, labor relations were centrally coordinated in neo-corporatist Nordic countries, sectorally coordinated under social partnership in Germany and the Netherlands, state-coordinated due to contentious employer–labor relations in France and Italy, and firm-level coordinated under management–enterprise union relations in Japan. Therefore, it makes sense to make finer distinctions when analyzing CMEs than to use only a polar typology (un/coordinated). Only when we juxtapose them with Anglophone liberal capitalism do these different subsystems seem to fall in the same conceptual box.

These postwar institutional affinities evolved in tandem, often facilitated by the evolving postwar social compromise that reaffirmed some of the historical legacies but modernized them nonetheless. The main institutional framework of labor relations, welfare-state expansion, and production regimes was set during the Golden Age of postwar growth. With the economic success following the Marshall Plan, expansive welfare policies, mass production, and collective bargaining became the major pillars of these postwar political economies.

The 'loose coupling' (Pfeffer and Salancik 1978) of relatively autonomous but interdependent spheres of protection, production, and partnership for the first time came under considerable strains during the political and social mobilization of the late 1960s (Crouch and Pizzorno 1978), leading to some reforms in workplace labor relations and industrial participation (Rogers and Streeck 1995; Sorge 1976). The real problem of the loosely coupled regimes arose after the oil shocks of the 1970s, when the postwar compromise and social institutions were seen as 'social rigidities' and as the cause of the economic problems (Olson 1982). Mass unemployment and low economic growth rates strained the traditional linkages between protection, production, and partnership institutions. Calls for welfare retrenchment, deregulation of mixed economies, decentralization of collective bargaining, and flexibilization of employment relations now dominate the political debate.[7]

Yet the debate on the global pressure which national economies face failed to take into account the distinct national diversity and the crucial institutional complementarities that could offer institutional advantages (Hall and Soskice 2001*b*). If we assume institutional affinities to be well entrenched, three general problems of institutional adaptation arise. First,

---

[7] For recent comparative analysis of welfare reform efforts, see Pierson (2001*c*), and Scharpf and Schmidt (2000).

each national configuration that comes under global challenges produces a specific problem constellation. For instance, we would expect different welfare regimes to face different challenges. Moreover, given very different power and opportunity structures these national political systems may be more or less able to cope with globalization and societal changes. Second, given these different institutional logics, the national responses to the challenges require nationally specific adaptation. There is hardly a 'best solution' for all systems. Even if there were, each nation state will have to pursue a particular path given its different starting position. Third, while loosely coupled systems allow a considerable degree of systemic adaptation, these may be uncoordinated and contradictory, leading to incompatibilities and strains between them. In fact, changes are occurring at different levels, at varying speed, and in relatively unconnected ways. For instance, decentralization of collective bargaining occurs on the one hand, and centralized intervention in social security systems on the other. Therefore, we need to understand the institutional affinities and complementarities before we can evaluate current problem configurations and reform capacities.

3.2.2 *Institutional Affinities and their Consequences for Employment Regimes*

For the ten countries considered here, we could detect five institutional affinities between protection, production, and partnership (see Table 3.8). We should now inquire: What are the consequences of the interaction of protection, production, and partnership institutions for the employment regime, particularly with respect to early exit from work? What are the particular reform problems that arise from the specific constellation of the protection–production–partnership nexus? For the moment, my arguments will be speculative and general, whereas in the later empirical part of this study I confront the hypotheses derived from the regime analysis with the evidence from the cross-national comparison of early exit policies.

(1) *Conservative 'welfare without work' problem:* Historically, the linkage between the social insurance state, CME, and social partnership was tightly coupled in the postwar period (Hemerijck and Manow 2001). The social insurance schemes have been linked to the employment relationships and both employers and workers play an important role in their administration (Manow 1997). Moreover, following the corporative orientation, social security schemes are tailored to particular social groups, and organizationally fragmented into many occupational schemes. Unions have tended to opt for employment security, for higher family wages, and for full-time work for the

Table 3.8. Mapping the socioeconomic models

	Center	Latin	Nordic	Anglophone	Japan
Protection: Financing	Medium expenditure, largely wage tax	Medium expenditure, public debt, wage tax	High public expenditure, largely tax-financed	Medium expenditure, tax- and private-funded	Medium expenditure, public- and firm-funded
Regime	Social insurance state, transfer-oriented	Subsidiaristic, 'familist', transfer-oriented	Universalist, social service-oriented	Liberal welfare state, increased privatization	Residual welfare state, company welfare
Production: Governance	Long-term, patient capital from banks	Nationalized banks, state intervention	Long-term, patient capital from banks	Short-term, financial markets (shareholders)	Long-term, patient capital from banks
Production regime	Export-dependent, high-quality, high-skill flexible specialization	Nationalized mass production, flexible small firms	Export-dependent high-quality, high-skill flexible specialization	Low-skill mass production, privatization	Export, dependent, high-quality, high-skill flexible specialization
Partnership: Organized interests	Sectoral unions, membership declining, works councils	Weak, fragmented labor, intransigent employers, strike propensity	Centralized organizations, high density, local union	Fragmented unions, membership crisis, no-union strategy	Enterprise unionism, weak political unionism
Bargaining system	'Social partnership' coordinated bargaining but exit threat	Decentralized bargaining, ad hoc state intervention, state–union crisis pacts	Corporatist intermediation coordinated bargaining but decentralization	Decentralized bargaining, voluntarism, lobbyism	Firm-level bargaining but interfirm coordination (Spring offensive)
Employment: Trend	Medium employment rate, mass unemployment	Low employment rate, large public sector, mass unemployment	High employment rate (also female, part-time), recent unemployment	High employment rate (also female, part-time), cyclical unemployment	High employment rate, low unemployment, mandatory retirement
Labor market	Regulated labor market, lifelong employment, skilled workforce	Regulated labor market but flexible work, informal sector	Regulated labor market, lifelong employment, skilled workforce	Flexible deregulated labor market	Tenured employment of skilled; segmentation (old, women)

Sources: Adapted from Ebbinghaus (1999: Table 2).

skilled core workforce at the expense of female labor force participation, the expansion of part-time and service work, and the inclusion of outsider interests (Esping-Andersen 1996c). Given the involvement of social partners, in particular unions, in social insurance systems and the 'earned' rights due to contributory PAYG schemes, we would expect that the interests of the older workers are well defended. With rising unemployment and restructuring problems, we would expect the social partners to seek consensual solutions. Here, early retirement could serve as a socially acceptable means for labor shedding (Manow and Seils 2000; Trampusch 2005).

In the Continental European cases, we would expect the scope for collusion between labor and capital on externalizing adaptation costs to be most prominent. Yet this practice will add to the reform problems of Continental welfare regimes; high unemployment, high social expenditure, and future liabilities of PAYG systems. Thus, the Continental European welfare states face a severe 'welfare without work' problem (Esping-Andersen 1996c), as even more people are inactive and need to be supported by growing welfare states which in turn, through rising nonwage labor costs, prices even more people out of work (Scharpf 2001). While these employment and labor cost problems are particularly pressing for these export-oriented economies, a reform of the welfare state and the labor market is only possible when governments and the social partners assume responsibility and coordinate their actions, as was the case in the Dutch 'miracle' (Visser and Hemerijck 1997). Hence, we would expect that a reform can hardly be pressed through unilaterally, instead requiring a concertation strategy that brings the social partners into a reform coalition at national and workplace levels.

(2) *Latin clientelist pensioner states*: While the Latin welfare states share some of the institutional features and thus problems of the Continental conservative social-insurance states (Esping-Andersen 1996c), they are also distinctive, given the greater importance of the public sector, familialism, and clientelism (Ferrera 1996; Rhodes 1996). We would expect the same favorable welfare policies as in the other Continental European countries, but with an even stronger bias toward the rights of senior workers and public sector workers (Lynch 2001). Given the rather contentious labor relations, we would expect early retirement to be one of the few consensual solutions to economic adaptation problems (Ferrera and Gualmini 2000; Levy 2000). Any attempt to change these rights would also meet more contentious union response, since labor movements are competing politically and social mobilization remains stronger. In fact, welfare cuts proposed by governments provoked waves of social mobiliza-

tion in the 1990s, leading to negotiations between governments and the social partners in Italy (Regini and Regalia 1997). The young, women, and workers with atypical jobs still mainly shoulder the costs of the failure to adjust. These welfare states face the problem of reducing the insider or seniority bias and help the outsiders against the strong mobilization of insider interests.

(3) *Scandinavian full-employment goal*: In the Nordic countries, the interdependence of the universalist welfare state and neo-corporatist labor relations have been increasingly evident and well understood (Esping-Andersen 1985; Kolberg 1992; Stephens 1996). As long as full employment and public employment growth could be maintained, a large part of the economy was sheltered from market pressure and adaptation in the exposed sectors was aided by active labor market policies in which the social partners played an important role (Benner and Vad 2000; Scharpf 2000). Hence, we would expect that universalist welfare states would be more reluctant to provide early retirement options to some groups, since they would uphold full employment aims and universal rights for all citizens. As long as the Scandinavian welfare states achieve the goal of full employment, active labor market policy, and public employment growth, we would not expect much pull or push for early exit from work. However, these more tightly coupled Keynesian corporatist welfare states came under strain from the global economic changes, increased decentralization of bargaining, and the crisis of public finance. This should undermine the full employment promise and intensify the economic push toward early exit from work through dismissal, while the public sector can no longer provide an employment buffer. Thus, the reform problem of Scandinavian welfare states is how to meet the fiscal limits of public sector growth and still maintain its high employment level necessary to provide universal welfare benefits and services. Reforms could thus entail some cuts in welfare benefits and a strengthening of work incentives but also foster integrative active labor market policies. However, this would not be politically feasible without broad political and societal consensus, including large sections of the powerful labor movement.

(4) *Anglophone flexible labor market*: The Anglophone societies show a neat institutional affinity between liberal-residual welfare state, uncoordinated market economy, and voluntarist labor relations. The relatively modest involvement of the state in welfare provision relies more on, and shuns interference with, the self-regulatory market mechanism. According to the liberal credo, early retirement should rarely be financed by public programs,

except in the case of incapacity to work; individuals who could continue working, but seek to retire early of their own will, would have to rely on their own savings or means from a firm-sponsored plan. Given the unregulated labor market, LME companies will seek to use numerical flexibility to respond to downturns, thus also shedding older workers. While in unionized workplaces, seniority rights may lead to some protection for older workers (employers may have to provide golden handshakes), in unorganized plants we would expect older workers to be particularly affected by downsizing without sufficient financial support; they would either have to seek new employment or face poverty. We would expect the push toward early exit to be largely market-driven, while the pull of public programs would be rather limited. For many dismissed older workers, the costs will be largely borne on their shoulders, especially those without sufficient private insurance and no chances to find postcareer reemployment. Social assistance (or US 'welfare' benefits) will be insufficient since—according to the liberal market principles—the reservation wage should be held at a low level. The particular welfare predicament of the liberal model is the inequality and poverty problem in old age, especially for laid-off older workers without sufficient occupational pensions, and for older impaired or disabled people without sufficent public benefits.

(5) *The Japanese tenure employment model*: Although Japan shares a rather residual welfare state which relies on occupational welfare like the United States, Japanese corporate welfare policies lead to a substantially different outcome. In this CME, large companies assume welfare functions that are performed by nonliberal welfare states. Tenured career employment systems attract and bind blue- and white-collar workers to the firm (Watanabe 2000). Following the stakeholder model, large Japanese firms assume social responsibility for their employees, including severance pay, and reemployment opportunities for permanent workers after their mandatory retirement from their career job (Kimura et al. 1994). However, this employment tenure system is only enjoyed by one-third of the working population, while most women, older workers, and many less-skilled men work under far less secure employment conditions, largely in the small-sized firm, small shop, and agricultural sectors (Brinton 1998). Declining birth rates and a rapidly aging population challenge both the traditional permanent employment system and the pension system (Endo and Katayama 1998). Since more and more career-job workers are approaching retirement and given the current economic and financial problems, the reemployment system of older workers comes to its limit. While the government wishes to

postpone if not eliminate mandatory retirement by firms, the larger firms are increasingly reluctant to maintain the reemployment pledge. Moreover, a labor shortage among young entrants could in the future help revise the gender-segmented labor market, and bring about a change toward more equalized opportunities for Japanese women.

3.2.3 *Regime Configurations and Early Exit from Work*

The cross-national comparison of the macro-configurations of welfare regimes, production systems, and labor relations has revealed significant variations across Europe, Japan, and the United States. Certainly, there are many exceptions and inconsistencies, but we can nevertheless detect some clustering into five (in Europe: four) institutional affinities. Moreover, the specific form of the protection–production–partnership nexus has an impact on the political economy at large as it structures the institutional environment for the labor market, and early exit from work in particular. Surveying the different regimes with the help of some general macro-indicators, this chapter mapped some of the general variations across the five clusters of institutional affinities between the spheres of protection, production, and partnership. We encountered a number of inconsistent and deviating patterns; thus individual countries share not only features of their regime-group but also some traits of different models. Therefore, as pointed out in the introductory chapter, the analysis of *intra*-regime differences will be an important test in addition to the analysis of cross-regime variations. The macro-analysis sketched here provides the general hypotheses and theoretical puzzles that will be the focus of the empirical research on early exit from work in the subsequent chapters.

Given these institutional variations, we should not consider ideal-typical classification as an exclusive category; instead we find in each country mixtures of principles, often borrowed from different regimes. How much we make of the intra-regime variations and whether we highlight more subtle differences depends on the analytical lens. While some patterns of *institutional affinities* could be highlighted in this chapter, a more detailed analysis of the *institutional complementarities* is needed to show how these different institutional configurations interact with and impact on early exit patterns. For the empirical analysis of 'pull' (protection) and 'push' (production) factors toward early exit from work in the subsequent chapters, we need a more concrete empirical analysis of what institutional arrangements contribute to the phenomenon of early retirement. The typologies developed thus far are heuristic devices to sort institutional variations across countries and look for regime-specific similarities and intra-regime differences. For instance, one can ask: What makes relatively generous Nordic universal welfare states less prone to the pull toward early retirement than the Continental European welfare regimes? Why does labor shedding by Japanese enterprises not lead to massive exit from work as in Germany, although in both countries larger firms rely on internal labor markets and face the problem of seniority wages and employment tenure? The institutional variations sketched thus far have provided sufficient evidence to expect regime-specific institutional complementarities to be at work in fostering or limiting early exit from work.

Finally, the analysis of labor relations thus far has provided some clues to the possible regime-specific potential for collusion of interests between the social partners (see Chapter 2). In the case of contentious labor relations, governments and employers may be tempted to buy social peace through 'social shock absorbers' when economic restructuring is needed. Also when management–labor relations are cooperative, early retirement can be a socially acceptable adaptation strategy to maintain the internal labor market system and high-skill wage system. Adaptation will depend on the support by public programs, endorsement by the social partners, or employer recognition of corporate social responsibility. In voluntarist systems, employer-sponsored early retirement may only occur in unionized workplaces where seniority rights can be negotiated, while most dismissed older workers will be without sufficient social protection due to lacking employment regulations.

Moreover, we would expect the different institutional configurations of protection and production to lead to specific reform problems and capacities. We have discussed some of the regime-specific problem constellations: (a) the working poor problem of Anglophone liberal welfare states; (b) the growth to limits of Nordic universalist public services; (c) the labor cost problem of the 'welfare without work' strategy of Continental conservative welfare states; (d) the particular problems to overcome reform opposition in Latin countries with contentious labor relations; and (e) the future problem of the career-job and reemployment pledge of Japanese companies. In the following parts of this study, I discuss the particular reform process in early retirement and more generally with respect to pension and employment policies in these nation states. Further, the different opportunity structure entailed in the various forms of partnership traditions should have an important impact on the reform process.

Part II

Comparing Early Exit Regimes

Chapter 4

Ever Earlier Retirement: Comparing Employment Trajectories

Early retirement has become an increasingly widespread phenomenon in modern industrial societies. Although retirement can mean receiving pension or similar benefits that allow continued income during old age, it also entails the notion of exit from work. In this study, I focus on the latter concept: early retirement is seen as the early withdrawal from employment—early exit from work—before age 65 (the most common retirement age across the OECD countries). In this chapter, I describe the dependent variable: early exit from work. Although early retirement does not necessarily entail complete exit from work, and the statutory retirement age varies across countries, for the purpose of this study, we look at indicators that measure a decline in employment rates in the age groups prior to age 65. The chapter analyzes the trend toward early exit from work over time, by examining time-series data covering more than three decades, and studies cross-national differences in the scope of early exit across eight European countries, Japan, and the United States.

In the first section, I analyze the long-term institutionalization of a statutory pension age around age 65 and the decline in activity above that age. This trend alone accounts for some of the decline in the mean year of exit from work, but most of this phenomenon can be attributed to premature exit by those under age 65. Therefore, I compare over time and cross-nationally participation level, unemployment, and employment rates as well as part-time employment for men and women in the age groups prior to age 65. This allows us to observe the effect of early exit on declining activity rates among older men. However, the employment patterns among older women are more difficult to observe due to countervailing trends of increasing female participation over time and also ongoing early exit among older women. For this reason, in the main section, I complement my analysis with cohort-adjusted early exit rates (see Appendix Note), which provide a superior indicator to study both cross-national differences and long-term developments in early retirement trends. The analysis will show that there are at least two main trajectories of high versus low exit countries, Continental Europe vis-à-vis the other (Anglophone and Nordic) countries, with few significant exceptions.

4.1 The Rise in Inactivity among Older Workers

4.1.1 *The Institutionalization of a 'Normal' Pension Age*

With the expansion in coverage of public pensions and the improvement of benefits, the statutory retirement age became a major juncture in the transition from work to retirement. 'As pension systems developed, a norm emerged whereby the life course was divided into three major phases: youth as the time for education; adulthood, for work; and old age, for inactivity' (Guillemard and Rein 1993: 470). The first public pensions, however, only supplemented income loss due to reduced working capacity from age 70 (or later age 65) onwards, such as Germany's 'invalidity' pension of 1889 (reformed in 1913). All European countries introduced public pension systems in the interwar period with the United States and Japan following in 1935 and 1944 respectively (Alber 1982; Inkeles and Usui 1989). Although old-age participation declined in the 1930s and 1940s as a consequence of the Great Depression and World War II, the main advancement in 'exit from work' after age 65 occurred only with the expansion of postwar welfare states (Jacobs, Kohli, and Rein 1991*a*: 38–41, Table 2.1). By the 1960s, nearly all ten countries granted public pensions to a majority of their citizens at least at age 65 with the exception of Denmark (age 67 until 2003), Sweden (age 67 until 1976), and Ireland (age 70 until 1973).

Nevertheless, a considerable share of elderly men (age 65+) was still working in the mid-1960s (see Figure 4.1): particularly in Japan (56 percent), Ireland (48 percent), Sweden (35 percent), and Denmark (32 percent), partly due to farming and insufficient or late pensions. These participation rates were somewhat lower in France (27 percent), the United States (26 percent), Britain (23 percent), Germany (23 percent), and Italy (17 percent). Since women had a much lower participation rate before age 65, less than 8 percent of elderly women (age 65+) were working during the age of industrialism and male-breadwinner households (see Figure 4.1), except for Japanese (1966: 22 percent), Irish (13 percent), French (11 percent), and

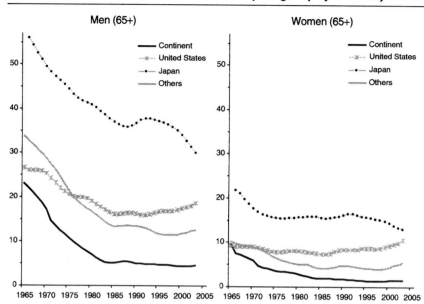

Figure 4.1 Participation rates, men and women aged 65+, 1965–2003

Notes: Five-year moving average of labor force participation rates (%); multiple country averages—Continent: Germany, the Netherlands, France, Italy; Others: Denmark, Sweden, Ireland, United Kingdom.

Sources: OECD, *Labour Force Statistics 1965–2004*; and own calculations.

Swedish women (10 percent) due to a large share of family farming with wives helping. Moreover, during the first postwar decade, welfare states in Germany, Italy, the United Kingdom, Japan, and Denmark (until 1970) granted some groups or all women an earlier pension than men, though in many cases women without longer work histories remained dependent either on their husbands' income or on survivor pensions.

The final decline in elderly employment occurred during the 1970s, leveling off thereafter (see Figure 4.1). Japan stands out as the society with the longest working life (and also the longest life expectancy): Nearly 40 percent of Japanese elderly men (age 65+) still work, mostly to supplement insufficient pensions through self-employment in agriculture, small crafts, or commercial family shops.[1] Besides Japan, a still significant—though gradually declining—activity rate for elderly men (age 65+) can be observed in the United States, Ireland, and Sweden, followed by Denmark and the

---

[1] Even in 2001, every second Japanese man aged 65–69 had not yet left the labor force; more than 40 percent of those were self-employed (nearly every fifth man aged 65–69) and nearly 30 percent were employees in small firms with under thirty employees (JAP-LFS 2001).

United Kingdom, largely due to widespread self-employment and/or family farming (see Table 4.1). Most of those working as elderly wage and salary earners (age 65+) work reduced hours (e.g. two-thirds of German and British men aged 65–69 work part-time), often because of pension rules that restrict combinations of earnings and pensions.

A similar long-term decline (see Figure 4.1), albeit at a level two to three times lower, occurred among women age 65 and over, with American and Japanese women again the exception with activity rates of 10 and 15 percent respectively, mostly self-employed or family members helping out in agriculture and commercial shops (see Table 4.1).[2] In contrast,

Table 4.1. Men and women aged 65+ by employment status, 1999

	Employed (% population)			Self-employed (% employed)			Helping family members (% employed)		
	65–69	70–74	75+	65–69	70–74	75+	65–69	70–74	75+
Men									
Germany	7.1	3.8	1.5	50.4	56.9	55.6	8.1	13.8	—
(West)	7.9	4.3	1.7	52.9	58.2	60.0	8.3	14.5	—
Netherlands	8.4	3.2	2.7	70.8	75.0	87.5	—	—	—
France	3.1	1.6	0.6	56.8	50.0	50.0	18.9	25.0	—
Italy	10.4	4.3	2.4	73.8	81.6	62.9	4.1	12.2	14.3
Sweden	17.6	7.7	—	60.6	61.5	—	12.1	—	—
Denmark	8.3	—	—	40.0	—	—	—	—	—
United Kingdom	15.6	7.0	2.4	44.8	43.7	45.7	2.8	—	—
Ireland	24.2	—	7.1	66.7	—	80.0	—	—	—
United States	30.1	17.9	8.0	—	—	—	—	—	—
Japan	50.7	23.4 *		38.7	55.6 *		1.7	4.9*	
Women									
Germany	3.3	1.6	0.6	21.1	25.7	33.3	16.9	20.0	19.0
(West)	3.8	1.8	0.7	23.4	28.1	35.0	17.2	21.9	15.0
Netherlands	2.4	—	—	62.5	—	—	—	—	—
France	1.3	0.7	0.2	52.6	50.0	—	21.1	—	—
Italy	2.8	1.6	1.2	50.0	54.5	34.5	15.2	31.8	24.1
Sweden	4.8	—	—	30.0	—	—	—	—	—
Denmark	4.5	—	—	—	—	—	—	—	—
United Kingdom	8.9	2.9	0.8	18.6	27.8	38.1	3.4	—	—
Ireland	6.1	—	—	—	—	—	—	—	—
United States	18.8	9.9	3.5	—	—	—	—	—	—
Japan	25.4	10.1*		21.6	32.6*		35.1	41.1*	

Notes: 1999 except for the United States: 2000 and Japan: 2001; *Japan: 70+.

Sources: Eurostat (2005), US-CPS (2000), JAP-LFS (2001); and own calculations

---

[2] In 2001, every fourth Japanese woman aged 65–69 was still working, with the large majority either helping family members (35 percent) or self-employed (22 percent) (JAP-LFS 2001). In the same age group, nearly every fifth American woman was still employed or seeking work, with 5 percent of black women 65–69 unemployed (US-CPS 2000).

participation rates for women aged 65 and over declined to under 5 percent in the European countries, except in Sweden during the high unemployment years of the 1990s. Except in Japan, statutory pension age at age 65 or earlier has become the threshold by which most people leave work and enter retirement. Thus, all welfare societies with the exception of Japan have seen a dramatic decline in post-65 employment; only those self-employed and helping family members tend to be somewhat more likely to continue working after age 65.

4.1.2 *The Decline in Participation Levels*

Whereas during the late 1960s, the workless period after age 65 became institutionalized as the transition to the Third Age, we can observe a *destandardization* (Guillemard and van Gunsteren 1991) of the timing of the transition from work to retirement since the 1970s due to the rise of early retirement. The actual age of withdrawal from work has become earlier, but less predictable. The trend toward early exit from work is partly observable in the declining labor force participation rates for older people under age 65, at least among men. In all countries, older men (age 55–64) have experienced a decline in participation rates, that is the rate of all employed and unemployed in the age group, with Japan least affected by this trend (see Figure 4.2). Participation rates dropped very dramatically from around 75 percent for men aged 55–64 in the early 1970s to less than 55 percent in Germany and less than 45 percent in France, Italy, and the Netherlands in the late 1990s. In these Continental European welfare states, massive labor shedding occurred during the last three decades of mass unemployment: Today only every second older man aged 55–64 is working or seeking employment.

We can detect a second group, the Anglophone and Scandinavian societies with medium levels of decline. The United Kingdom and Ireland went through a significant reduction from the highest rates to medium levels above 60 percent in the 1990s. The United States experienced a more gradual decline, with the level stagnating since the 1980s above 65 percent. The level also fell in Scandinavian countries, but the decline began earlier and the participation level was lower in Denmark (65 percent) than in Sweden (70 percent). Japan once again demonstrates an exceptional maintenance of high-level labor supply: Since the 1960s, four out of five older Japanese men (age 55–64) remain in the workforce. Finally, for very recent years a slight rebounding of participation levels can be observed for most countries, particularly for the Netherlands.

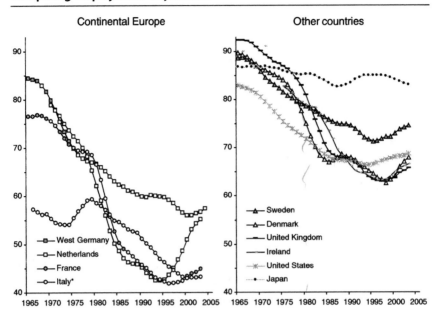

Figure 4.2 Participation rates, men aged 55–64, 1965–2003

Notes: Five-year moving average of labor force participation rate (%); *Italy 1965–72: trend estimated with rates for 50–59 and 60–64.

Sources: OECD *Labour Force Statistics 1965–2004*; West Germany, 1991–: Eurostat, *Labour Force Surveys 1991–2004* (2005); Italy 1973–: Eurostat, (2005) *Labour Force Surveys 1973–2004*; and own calculations.

Early retirement among female workers is more difficult to trace due to changes in participation rates (see Figure 4.3) because two processes tend to cancel each other out. Each cohort of older women tends to have a higher participation rate because women increasingly stay in employment during or return to work after raising children. But each subsequent cohort of women also tends to retire earlier, at the same—or at an even earlier—age than men. The time series of participation rates for women only shows the net effect of both trends. Sweden is exceptional in experiencing a substantial net increase in participation among older women (age 55–64) despite ongoing early retirement thanks to early and massive increases in female (prime-age) participation. The American rate has slightly increased the second highest level, while Japan's rate has stagnated, and the British rate has oscillated around a medium level. In contrast, Germany and France at times show real declines, and the Netherlands, Italy, and Ireland traditionally have a very low employment level among older women, although all these countries with low female participation levels have experienced net increases since the 1990s.

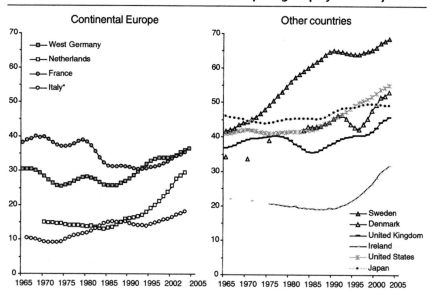

Figure 4.3 Participation rates, women aged 55–64, 1965–2003

Notes: Five-year moving average of labor force participation rate; *Italy 1965–72: trend estimated with rates for 50–59 and 60–64; and own calculations.

Sources: OECD, *Labour Force Statistics 1965–2004*; West Germany only, 1991–: Eurostat, *Labour Force Surveys 1991–2004* (2005); Italy 1973–: Eurostat, *Labour Force Surveys 1973–2004* (2005).

4.1.3 *Unemployment as a Bridging Pension*

The risk of both job loss and long-term unemployment is relatively high among older workers not only for reasons related to low labor demand for this age group but also as a consequence of social policies. Unemployment has become a de facto 'bridging pension' until preretirement or statutory pensions are available. Moreover, older workers are often exempted from actively searching for jobs or are not eligible to participate in active labor market measures. When such an unemployment pathway does exist, companies in need of restructuring may particularly single out older workers for (voluntary) dismissal. On the other hand, dismissed workers may seek other preretirement benefits that offer the socially acceptable role of 'retiree' instead of 'being on the dole'. Unemployment rates, therefore, may not reveal the actual degree of involuntary unemployment among older workers, as many are discouraged workers who have left de facto the labor market because they do not expect to find a job because of their age.

Before the first oil shock in 1973, unemployment among older men aged 55–64 was relatively low (less than 4 percent unemployment rate) with the exception of Britain (1972: 6.6 percent) and Ireland (1971: 9.4 percent). However, the rising of mass unemployment during the late 1970s resulted in notable increases in joblessness among older men, particularly in Germany and France (around 5 percent in 1980). The unemployment pathway became an early labor-shedding strategy in the two countries (Guillemard 1991; Jacobs, Kohli, and Rein 1991*b*). Yet only after the second oil shock, during the early 1980s, did unemployment among older workers become a major problem in nearly all countries (see Table 4.2): Britain and Ireland again led with average unemployment rates around 10 percent, followed by the German, French, and Dutch welfare states (in the exceptionally difficult year 1983–84, nearly 25 percent of Dutch men aged 60–64 were unemployed). At first, it was the older age group (age 60–64) that was most affected by unemployment. However, with more alternative preretirement pathways becoming available from age 60 onwards, unemployment decreased in this age group and spread to the earlier age group (age 55–59) as people combined long-term unemployment benefits before 60 with

Table 4.2. Unemployment rates, men and women aged 55–59 and 60–64, 1965–2003

	55–59				60–64			
	1965–74	1975–84	1985–94	1995–2003	1965–74	1975–84	1985–94	1995–2003
Men								
Germany	1.1	4.9	8.4	13.1	1.7	5.5	7.8	11.8
Netherlands	1.9	4.4	4.8	2.6	2.4	5.9	3.7	2.4
France	1.8	4.5	8.1	8.3	1.6	4.5	7.0	7.5
Italy	—	1.4	2.7	4.3	—	1.5	2.5	4.2
Sweden	1.6	1.4	2.8	6.6	2.0	2.3	3.4	7.4
Denmark	—	6.2	7.5	5.1	—	6.5	6.2	4.6
United Kingdom	3.3	6.5	10.0	6.6	3.2	10.3	10.2	6.6
Ireland	—	9.4	10.9	5.0	8.4	9.1	9.1	4.5
United States	2.5	4.1	4.4	3.3	2.6	4.1	4.3	3.3
Japan	1.8	3.5	2.8	3.9	1.6	4.2	4.2	6.2
Women								
Germany	1.1	6.3	10.2	15.7	1.3	4.6	5.0	6.3
Netherlands	1.6	3.2	5.8	3.5	2.5	5.2	5.1	3.5
France	2.4	5.7	9.0	8.7	3.3	5.1	4.8	4.0
Italy	0.7	3.3	4.4	4.8	0.1	4.9	2.2	3.4
Sweden	1.4	1.7	2.0	4.9	2.2	3.6	4.3	7.3
Denmark	—	8.2	8.8	6.3	—	2.7	5.3	3.3
United Kingdom	—	3.9	6.0	3.4	—	0.9	4.9	1.8
Ireland	—	6.3	14.1	10.0	—	8.7	9.9	8.1
United States	2.9	4.3	3.6	3.0	2.5	4.1	3.4	3.0
Japan	0.7	1.7	1.8	2.7	0.3	1.2	1.7	3.6

Notes: Average unemployment rate by period; Italy: age 50–59; Ireland (women): partly missing data.

Sources: OECD, *Labour Force Statistics 1965–2004*, except Ireland (1983–) and Sweden (1995–): Eurostat, *Labour Force Surveys 1983–2004* (2005); and own calculations.

preretirement benefits after 60.[3] During the 1990s, older German and Japanese men (age 55–64) had unemployment rates 50 percent higher than the overall rates and the French, Swedish, Danish, and British older age groups came close (70–100 percent) to the overall rates (see Table 4.2). In the other countries, the risk of unemployment was lower in this age group, partly due to the availability of other more generous exit routes (the Netherlands and Italy) or the limited duration of unemployment benefits (the United States and Ireland).

Older women have been exposed to unemployment risks to a similar degree to men, with a few significant exceptions (see Table 4.2). Until the onset of mass unemployment in the late 1970s, unemployment rates of older women (age 55–64) remained below the level of their male colleagues in most countries, except in France and the United States. Since then, however, women have been affected as much as their male colleagues, except in Japan (the female rate was lower by two-thirds), the United Kingdom (lower by half) and Italy (lower by a fifth, until recently) due to lower statutory pension ages for women in these three countries. By contrast, women were exposed to a higher risk of unemployment in France (traditionally higher by 20 percent), the Netherlands (higher by 50 percent in the 1990s), and Denmark (higher by 30 percent). Again, in postunification Germany, unemployment was particularly high among women aged 55–59 and exceeded the rate for men (by 20 percent in 1990s) as a consequence of a major influx of women to the labor market.

Only in a few cases were unemployment rates higher than the overall level, indicating the availability of other preretirement pathways rather than a lower real risk of unemployment. For most unemployed older men and women, receiving long-term unemployment benefits was a bridge to retirement, largely forced upon them by employers through dismissal and limited chances to find employment above age 50. The unemployment pathway is, therefore, the most cyclical exit route and follows waves in overall unemployment and mass dismissal. However, some special early retirement programs (e.g. in Britain and Germany during the 1980s) served as functional equivalents, by allowing governments to lower unemployment figures through provision of preretirement benefits on a temporary basis.

---

[3] In France, the incoming Socialist government lowered the 'normal' pension age from 65 to 60 as of 1983 in order to relieve the unemployment funds (Guillemard 1991). As a consequence, the unemployment bridging pension shifted to the earlier age group: The unemployment rate for men aged 55–59 increased from 5.3 percent in 1981 to 9.1 percent in 1986, ranging below 5 percent for men aged 60–64.

4.1.4 *The Decline of Employment Rates in Preretirement Age*

Since unemployment benefits for older workers allow de facto early retirement, the subsequent analysis of early exit from work is based on the *employment rate* (see Appendix Note). A drop in the employment rate indicates that fewer older people remain in gainful employment, while the others—nonworking people—are most likely to be dependent on pension, unemployment, other welfare benefits, or—especially in the case of housewives—their spouse. For more detailed analysis, we also need to disaggregate the early exit trends into at least two age groups: (*a*) early exit (age 60–64), for which many preretirement options exist and (*b*) *very* early exit (age 55–59), for which few preretirement opportunities, other than unemployment benefits, exist.

The most significant decline in employment rates occurred among men in the age group 60–64 (see Table 4.3). With the exception of Italy, which already had low employment rates (around 50 percent), all other countries experienced a long-term decline from the employment level of the 1960s (above 70 percent). The drop was most pronounced for Germany, France, and the Netherlands during the 1970s; more gradual thereafter, but plunging in the 1980s even below Italy's traditionally low level. All four Continental welfare states stand out as having the lowest levels of active employment among men aged 60–64: less than every third West German and Italian, less than every fourth Dutchman, and every sixth Frenchman and East German.

Early retirement among men aged 60–64 is less common in the Nordic and Anglophone countries (see Table 4.3). Nevertheless, the United Kingdom, the United States, and Ireland have seen a drop to medium employment levels: Only every second man aged 60–64 works, despite a later statutory retirement age of 65. Sweden maintained a higher level until the surge in unemployment during the early 1990s that led to a drop from 60 to 50 percent in employment rates. Neighboring Denmark saw an even more severe drop—to an employment rate of less than 40 percent in 2000, coming close to Germany around the turn of the century (30 percent). In terms of the timing of labor shedding, Sweden and Ireland experienced their major declines in the 1990s; Denmark and Britain in the 1980s; and the United States even earlier. Finally, Japan stands out with a more gradual decline during the mid-1980s and again since the mid-1990s. In 2003, about 65 percent of Japanese men still worked after the age of 60 when they could draw the second-tier contributory pension. While most of the larger Japanese companies enforce mandatory retirement by the age

Table 4.3. Employment rates, men aged 55–59 and 60–64, 1965–2003

	1965	1970	1975	1980	1985	1990	1995	2000	2003	Δ1970–85	Δ1985–2003
Men 55–59											
Germany	—	—			—	73.0c	64.1	66.0	68.9	—	−0.48c
(West)	90.5	89.0	82.1	78.4	76.2	74.8c	67.5	67.8	70.2	−1.02	−0.46
(East)	—	—	—	—	—	65.4c	50.0	58.7	62.1	—	−0.43c
Netherlands	82.9	87.0b	78.4	72.9	60.3	63.5	60.4	68.7	74.4	−2.58b	+1.17
France	76.2a	81.5	81.3	77.4	62.6	63.0	60.4	60.5	60.1	−1.74	−0.22
Italy	92.8	74.5	76.0	69.6	68.1	66.0	57.9	51.5	55.2	−0.60	−1.16
Sweden	~92.0	89.7	88.8	86.8	85.6	86.3	79.0	80.4	79.9	−0.31	−0.38
Denmark	95.7	~88.0	82.6	83.0	77.7	81.6	77.2	79.7	80.7	−0.83	+0.22
United Kingdom	~88.0	92.4	89.7	84.7	74.8	75.0	66.1	70.8	73.8	−1.40	−0.07
Ireland	88.0	~86.0	82.5	80.4	73.9	69.1	66.7	71.6	73.1	−0.73	−0.06
United States	85.7	85.7	79.8	79.0	76.1	76.8	74.6	75.2	74.2	−0.79	−0.14
Japan	90.4a	89.3	89.2	88.4	86.8	90.0	91.6	90.0	88.8	−0.19	+0.13
Men 60–64											
Germany					—	31.1c	26.2	27.8	31.1	—	−0.01c
(West)	78.1	74.0	53.3	41.5	33.0	32.9c	29.6	30.1	33.1	−5.23	+0.01
(East)	—	—	—	—	—	23.0c	12.6	18.1	23.0	—	−0.01c
Netherlands	—	73.8b	62.5	46.3	26.7	22.4	20.5	27.1	31.1	−7.01b	−0.86
France	68.8	66.6	55.1	45.1	29.4	22.1	16.4	14.7	14.5	−5.30	−3.85
Italy	52.8a	47.8	42.1	39.0	38.2	35.4	30.3	30.1	30.5	−1.48	−1.24
Sweden	83.0	78.1	72.3	67.4	61.8	62.4	50.8	51.2	59.1	−1.55	−0.25
Denmark	~85.0	~77.0	71.4	55.5	45.5	48.8	47.4	37.7	50.0	−3.45	+0.52
United Kingdom	89.2	80.5	74.6	60.6	49.7	49.4	45.1	47.4	53.3	−3.15	−0.38
Ireland	~85.5	~78.0	73.5	69.4	58.2	50.8	53.7	52.0	54.3	−1.93	−0.38
United States	79.2	69.9	61.6	58.7	53.2	53.6	51.3	53.6	54.5	−1.80	+0.13
Japan	82.5a	79.8	76.9	74.2	67.4	69.2	69.3	65.0	64.6	−1.12	−0.23

Notes: a1966, b1971, c1991, ~=estimated value; Δ1970–85, Δ1985–2003: annual natural growth rate (%): $\Delta X_{t_0} - t_{0,n}\% = ((X_{t_0,n}/X_{t_0})^{1/n} - 1) \times 100$ (where n = 1970–85 = 15, 1990–2003 = 18, b1971–85 = 14, c1991–2003 = 12).

Sources: OECD, *Labour Force Statistics 1965–2004*, except: Germany: 1991–2003 German Statistical Office internal data; Italy 55–59 (1966–72 estimated based on 50–59, 1973–); Sweden 1997–2003, Denmark 1975–83, and Ireland: Eurostat, *Labour Force Surveys 1973–2004* (2005); and own calculations.

of 60 (Kimura et al. 1994), these workers seek reemployment in order to supplement their pension and severance pay income.

During the 1960s, all societies had high levels of employment among men aged 55–59 (around 90 percent), except the United States (85 percent), France (80 percent), and, most notably, Italy (only around 75 percent). All countries experienced a decline in employment rates in this age group during the 1970s, but the Nordic, Anglophone countries, and Japan went through the decline more slowly than Continental Europe. After relatively slow decline throughout the 1970s and 1980s, with high unemployment in the 1990s, Swedish employment among men 55–59 also dropped rapidly from 86 percent in 1990 to 76 percent in 1995. The downward trend in Denmark already started in the 1980s and continued until the mid-1990s. Britain and Ireland have had a more rapid decline since the late 1970s, due to high and fluctuating unemployment in this age group: every third man aged 55–59 was inactive by the mid-1990s. In comparison, the United States performed somewhat better, starting from a lower level and experiencing a slower decline: every fourth American man aged 55–59 was not (or no longer) employed in the 1990s.

The Continental European welfare states are distinct in their significant drops in employment rates in this early age group. Italy always had a low employment level: Until the mid-1970s only three out of four Italian men aged 55–59 were working and by the 1990s it was only every second man. France and the Netherlands had higher employment rates in the early 1970s, but thereafter witnessed a major drop to only 60 percent by the mid-1990s. West Germany's decline was somewhat less dramatic than in the Netherlands but by the late 1990s both countries had reached the same level of inactivity: Every third man aged 55–59 was not working (in East Germany, it was 40 percent).

Analyzing early retirement among women with the help of employment rates produces the same shortcoming as previously discussed for participation rates. Nonetheless, the disaggregation into two age groups provides some additional information (see Table 4.4). In 1970, nearly the majority (around 40–50 percent) of women aged 55–59 were working in all countries, except Germany (37 percent), Ireland (below 20 percent), the Netherlands (18 percent), and Italy (14 percent). The most dramatic increase in employment occurred in Sweden, reaching a level beyond 70 percent in the mid-1980s, followed by gradual increases in Denmark, the United Kingdom, the United States, and Japan; all these countries had reached levels between 50 and 60 percent by the 1990s. The Continental European

Table 4.4. Employment rates, women aged 55–59 and 60–64, 1965–2003

	1965	1970	1975	1980	1985	1990	1995	2000	2003	Δ1970–85	Δ1985–2003
Women 55–59											
Germany	—	—	—	—	—	37.4[c]	40.2	46.8	51.0	—	+2.61[c]
(West)	36.3	37.0	36.2	37.5	36.1	39.6[c]	41.6	46.6	50.6	−0.16	+1.89
(East)	—	—	—	—	—	29.3[c]	34.5	47.8	53.0	—	+5.07[c]
Netherlands	—	17.8[b]	17.4	18.1	17.4	23.9	27.0	38.2	42.7	−0.18[b]	+5.13
France	41.2	44.8	41.9	44.8	39.2	41.4	44.9	47.2	48.3	−0.88	+1.16
Italy	8.8	8.5	16.2	17.5	19.1	19.2	18.8	22.9	27.4	+2.64	+2.03
Sweden	46.6	52.3	60.0	67.8	72.7	78.0	71.6	76.4	76.9	+2.22	+0.31
Denmark	—	—	46.0	45.6	54.3	57.6	51.4	64.3	70.8	+1.67[d]	+1.48
United Kingdom	44.5	49.6	51.8	51.9	48.6	51.9	53.1	55.8	61.2	−0.13	+1.29
Ireland	—	—	21.1	20.4	27.0	29.1	32.1	34.1	40.6	−0.13[d]	+3.78
United States	44.9	47.4	45.1	46.9	47.9	53.7	57.4	59.9	63.0	+0.08	+1.53
Japan	50.2[a]	48.7	48.0	49.8	49.9	53.1	56.0	56.9	56.8	+0.16	+0.72
Women 60–64											
Germany	—	—	—	—	—	9.9[c]	10.1	12.2	15.9	—	+3.99[c]
(West)	23.3	22.4	14.9	11.8	10.8	11.4[c]	12.0	13.9	17.2	−4.73	+2.61
(East)	—	—	—	—	—	4.4[c]	2.8	5.6	10.9	—	+7.92[c]
Netherlands	—	11.8[b]	10.5	9.2	6.1	7.4	8.2	11.2	14.9	−4.56[b]	+5.05
France	31.7	33.3	28.9	25.9	17.6	16.1	14.0	12.8	12.0	−4.16	−2.10
Italy	13.4	10.5	8.5	10.4	10.0	9.9	7.5	7.8	9.9	−0.32	−0.05
Sweden	30.9	35.2	37.5	40.1	43.0	52.0	43.3	43.2	52.6	+1.33	+1.13
Denmark	—	—	29.2	26.4	25.3	26.9	20.0	23.4	27.5	−1.43[d]	−0.46
United Kingdom	25.8	27.9	28.6	22.4	17.6	21.7	24.6	25.4	27.3	−3.03	+2.47
Ireland	—	—	18.4	16.1	14.1	14.5	14.7	18.9	24.1	−2.64[d]	+3.02
United States	34.5	34.0	31.3	32.2	32.2	34.6	36.6	39.2	43.7	−0.36	+1.71
Japan	40.4[a]	39.1	37.6	38.4	37.8	38.9	38.7	37.7	37.6	−0.22	−0.04

Notes: [a]1966, [b]1971, [c]1991; Δ1970–85, Δ1985–2003: annual natural growth rate (%): $\Delta X_{t_0}-t_{0+n}\% = ((X_{t_{0+n}}/X_{t_0})^{1/n} - 1) \times 100$ (where $n = 1970$–85 = 15, 1990–2003 = 18, [b]1971–85 = 14, [c]1991–2003 = 12, [d]1975–85 = 10).

Sources: OECD, *Labour Force Statistics 1965–2004*, except: Germany: 1991–2003 German Statistical Office internal data; Italy 55–59 (1966–72 estimated based on 50–59, 1973–); Sweden 1997–2003, Denmark 1975–83, and Ireland: Eurostat, *Labour Force Surveys 1973–2004* (2005); and own calculations.

countries and Catholic Ireland showed stagnating levels until the 1990s. During this time, female employment rates particularly improved in the Netherlands, Ireland, and Italy.

A comparison with the employment rates for the later age group (age 60–64) shows considerably lower levels and often falling employment rates; this indicates that early retirement supersedes the trend of increasing female participation in this age group. In particular, where women can draw on pensions earlier, employment rates are particularly low: British women receive the basic pension at age 60, while German, Danish, Italian, and Japanese women can, under some conditions, draw pensions earlier than men, though often receiving lower benefits than if they worked their remaining years until statutory retirement. In Sweden, employment levels still increase from cohort to cohort; at least they did before the unemployment crisis of the 1990s. In Japan, with the second highest employment rates (just under 40 percent), there is no visible change over time. The United States and at a lower level the United Kingdom and Ireland have experienced some increase in recent years, while Denmark has a much lower (and unstable) employment level among women aged 60–64 due to the use of unemployment insurance as a bridging pension. In all Continental European countries, the level of employment has been falling as in Germany and France or remains very low as in the Netherlands and Italy. However, falling employment rates are an incomplete means to detect the scope of early retirement, particularly among women since each female cohort tends to have a higher likelihood to be working at age 55. In order to take cohort-specific effects into account, we need to adopt a perspective that studies employment patterns over the life course and across cohorts.

4.1.5 *Partial Exit and Temporary Employment*

Early retirement, measured in declining employment rates, implies 'full' exit from work, not reductions in working hours through part-time work or the transition from a permanent job to temporary employment. Yet part-time employment and to a lesser degree atypical employment contracts have also increased over time and are more frequent among older workers than among prime-aged workers, a trend that holds not only for women but also for men. Part-time employment allows a more gradual transition from work to retirement; a less demanding workload often postpones final exit. Part-time work has been fostered by partial pension arrangements that at least partially provide income support for the loss in earnings due to reduced working time (see Chapter 5). Sweden was the leader in gradual pensions during the 1980s, with other countries following with less favorable arrangements (Wadensjö 1991). Not all gradual retirement schemes lead to real part-time employment; thus the German part-time pension (*Altersteilzeit*) is often used to finance two 'time blocks': one of full-time work and a subsequent one of full retirement (Barkholdt 2001). The practice of mandatory retirement in larger Japanese firms forces workers around age 60 to leave, but they commonly receive a temporary or part-time job thereafter (Kimura et al. 1994). Similarly, American or British workers who have been 'downsized' find themselves forced to work part-time to supplement their insufficient public or private occupational pensions (Chen 1996; Taylor and Walker 1996). In these cases, part-time work is an indicator of insufficient opportunity to find full (re)employment in older age or the consequence of insufficient retirement benefits. If sufficient, gradual-pension arrangements foster higher employment levels and prolong employment (Delsen and Reday-Mulvey 1996*b*); they allow a smoother transition for the individuals affected; the 'human capital' or expertise of older workers remains available for a longer period for the firm; and part-time workers still continue to pay income and payroll taxes.

Although part-time work remains rather unusual among male industrial workers and the self-employed, there is an increasing tendency toward part-time employment among older male workers. The Netherlands has the highest level of overall part-time employment among women and among older men (Delsen 1996*b*): Already in the early 1980s, around 12 percent of employed Dutch men aged 60–64 and 7 percent of those aged 55–59 held a part-time job, increasing to nearly 40 and 20 percent respectively in 1999 (see Table 4.5). Part-time work has also increased among older men in other Continental European countries, particularly in France in the 1990s and Germany in the late 1990s, but their levels remain below those of the other countries. Thanks to the gradual pension, over 40 percent of Swedish employed men aged 60–64 were in part-time work in the 1980s (Wadensjö 1991) but cuts in the favorable gradual pension led to a drop below 20 percent in the late 1990s (Wadensjö 2002). In the United Kingdom and the United States, part-time employment has grown in importance among older men (8–9 percent for men aged 55–59 and 15–18 percent for men aged 60–64 in the late 1990s), partly as workers have had to combine pensions and earnings. In Japan, nearly every fourth male employee aged 60–64 works part-time, often after mandatory career retirement at age 60, and every tenth aged 55–59 (OECD 2001*a*, Table 5.4, p. 92).

Table 4.5. Male and female part-time employment, age groups 15–64, 1999

	Male part-time employment (%)				Female part-time employment (%)			
	15–64	50–54	55–59	60–64	15–64	50–54	55–59	60–64
Germany	4.3	2.4	4.0	12.8	37.2	43.0	46.1	69.8
(West)	4.5	2.4	3.6	11.3	41.1	48.2	51.4	71.1
Netherlands	17.6	9.6	19.3	38.9	69.2	75.3	81.0	—
France	5.7	3.5	11.3	13.0	32.2	28.3	37.6	47.9
Italy	3.2	2.7	2.9	6.0	15.8	12.2	14.5	8.2
Sweden	8.8	3.5	9.2	17.1	40.8	32.9	40.0	50.6
Denmark	9.9	5.4	4.2	18.6	34.4	32.8	34.5	54.2
United Kingdom	7.6	4.8	8.8	17.4	43.0	45.0	51.4	66.7
Ireland	7.6	7.3	8.6	—	29.8	42.1	45.0	45.5
United States	7.9	—	7.3	15.1	18.2	—	22.0	33.2
Japan	11.8	—	11.3	23.9	39.4	—	39.5	46.0

Note: EU countries: part-time employment in percentage (no response excluded); United States and Japan: part-time employees in percentage.

Sources: Own calculations based on Eurostat, *Labour Force Surveys 1999* (2005); United States and Japan: OECD *full-time/part-time database*, cit. in OECD (2001a): Table 5.4, p. 92.

Part-time employment has been much more common among women across all age groups, ranging from 30 to 70 percent, with the exception of Italy (16 percent in 1999). Nevertheless, part-time employment increases as female workers age (see Table 4.5): More than half of employed older women 55–64 work part-time in the Netherlands, Germany, and the United Kingdom, followed by Sweden, Denmark, Ireland, France, and Japan, while it remains less common in the United States and particularly Italy. Just as partial pensions—as a pull factor—may either foster early exit or prolong exit, part-time employment—as a push factor—is ambiguous since it can be either involuntary (no full-time work available) or voluntary (a deliberate choice to prolong work). A notable exception is the Netherlands, where part-time work is quite frequent for both older men and women, although employment rates are also low in old age. For the other countries, we find a significant positive correlation between the prevalence of part-time employment among older people and overall employment rates.

Since higher employment rates and part-time employment go together in the Nordic countries, Britain, and Japan, we need to reevaluate the relatively high employment rates in these countries. When we measure full-time equivalents (counting two part-time jobs as one full-time job), male employment rates at age 60–64 drop by less than 5 percent points (Japan: 7 percent points) for the high (partial) exit countries (including the Netherlands) and only slightly for the remaining Continental European countries with insignificant part-time rates among older workers. Even though higher part-time rates go together with higher employment rates, as the full-time equivalents indicate, partial pension alone cannot explain the significant cross-national differences between high and low early exit trajectories.

4.2 The Trend Toward Early Exit from Work

4.2.1 *Measuring Early Exit from Work*

Seen from a life course perspective, we should measure exit from work by cohort-adjusted employment rates, particularly in the case of women with rising participation levels and in countries where early retirement has lowered participation levels for several age groups. While some studies have used average retirement age (based on labor force participation rates by age groups) to analyze early retirement processes,[4] the analysis here will be based on the rates of withdrawal from work (based on employment rates) that provide a more clear indication of the incidence and timing of early exit. Following a life course perspective (Settersten and Mayer 1997), we study the impact of cohort and historical changes on early retirement patterns with the help of cohort-adjusted *exit rates* or 'net withdrawal rate' (Blöndal and Scarpetta 1998; OECD 1995*b*).[5]

Two measures are calculated for this study (see also Appendix Note):

- *Absolute* exit rate (change in percentage points), i.e. the cohort-adjusted withdrawal—the difference between the five-year age group's (e.g. age 60–64 in 1995) employment rate and the same birth-cohort's employment rate five years earlier (e.g. age 55–59 in 1990)—as a proportion of the age group's population (e.g. age 60–64).

- *Relative* exit rate (percentage change), i.e. cohort-adjusted withdrawal rate (e.g. absolute exit rate) as a proportion of the population 'at risk' of exiting work, those in the same birth-cohort who were employed five years earlier (e.g. age 55–59 in 1990).

[4] The 'average age of retirement' (Latulippe 1996) is a summary estimate based on labor force participation rates across older age groups (five-year age groups from 45 to 80). In addition to the common cross-sectional *static* indicator, Scherer (2002) also provides a *dynamic* indicator, adjusted for cohort effects (see also Johnson 2001).

[5] The publicly available labor force statistics of OECD, Eurostat, ILO, and national sources provide aggregate data by age group that can be transformed into cohort-adjusted *exit rates* (see Appendix Note). Exit rates for men or women aged 60–64 (1970–2000) were calculated from OECD data. Employment and exit rates (1988–99) for age 55–59 were calculated from Eurostat (limited to European Union countries) and Swedish labor force sources.

We may find a larger difference between the two rates when the population at risk is small. For instance, absolute withdrawal and relative exit at age 60–64 diverge when early retirement (or low overall participation) has already reduced the population at risk, that is, if the initial employment rate for the age group 55–59 five years earlier is already low. While absolute exit rates give an indication of the *incidence* of early retirement within an age group's population (whatever their previous employment status), relative exit rates show the *likelihood* of early exit among those that were previously employed. The subsequent analysis mainly analyzes *relative* exit rates since they are the best indicator of the likelihood of early exit from work, while the absolute rates provide additional information on the labor reduction effect in particular age groups. Absolute exit is a measure of the net labor reduction effect in the age group (i.e. the share of the age group that left work), relative exit the actual incidence of early exit from work (i.e. the percentage of those in the age group who were previously employed and left their job over the last five years).

4.2.2 *Early Exit from Work Before Age 65*

Early exit among men aged 60–64 follows similar cross-national differences to those discussed for the decline in employment rates, with some minor differences. The Continental European countries show the same pronounced trend of rapidly increasing early exit and high levels of early retirement, while the trajectories in the other countries are more gradual and remain at a lower exit level (see Figure 4.4). Given declining or low employment levels for the previous age group, the two withdrawal measures diverge over time: absolute exit rates, the share of the age group 60–64 leaving work, fall behind the relative exit measure, which shows the propensity of those previously (age 55–59) employed to leave work upon reaching ages 60–64.

During the first growth period (from 1970 to the first peak in 1985), the Continental European countries witnessed acceleration (with annual growth rates of 8–9 percent) in *relative* early exit from work (see Table 4.6). An exception is Italy, which had a more gradual annual increase (2.6 percent) due to an already high level of early retirement in 1970 (30 percent). By the 1980s, more than 40 percent of the age group 60–64 retired early and more than half of those initially employed before 60 stopped working within the next five years. During the second period, beginning in the mid-1980s, we also see some stagnation and short-term fluctuations, with the exception of France, where early retirement

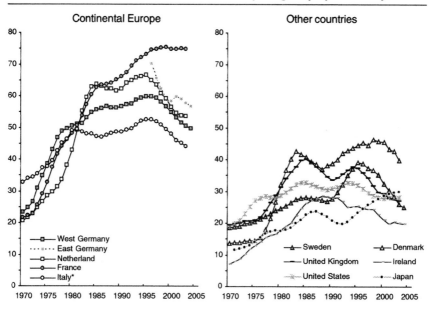

Figure 4.4 Relative exit rates for men aged 60–64, 1970–2003

Note: Five-year moving average of relative exit rates (see Appendix Note); Italy* 1965–72: 55–59 partly estimated.

Sources: OECD, *Labour Force Statistics 1966–2004*, except Ireland 1983–, Sweden 1997–: Eurostat, *Labour Force Surveys* (2005); and own calculations.

continues to increase. Given the considerable labor shedding among older male workers occurring throughout Continental Europe, one can refer to these countries as 'welfare states without work' (Esping-Andersen 1996c). They all show a long-term growth trajectory that follows an S-curve for both men (see Figure 4.4) and women (see Figure 4.5), suggesting a *diffusion process* (Pemperton 1936) that first acceleates during the 1970s and since the 1980s has reached saturation at a very high level of 'penetration': Early retirement some time between 60 and 64 has become the dominant social norm in Continental Europe.

In contrast, the other countries on average show less dramatic increases and reach lower levels of early exit among men aged 60–64 (see Table 4.6), though they also go through more pronounced cyclical ups-and-downs (see Figure 4.4). During the first period (1970–85), growth in early exit was slower (4–5 percent) and reached a much lower level (below 33 percent in 1985) than on the Continent (above 45 percent) with two exceptions. Denmark and Britain show fast growth rates (7–8 percent), albeit starting from a somewhat lower level (about 15 percent in 1970) but (nearly)

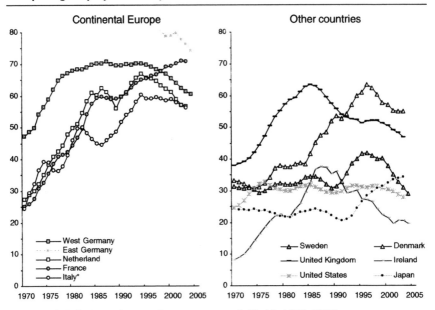

Figure 4.5 Relative exit rates for women aged 60–64, 1970–2003

Note: Five-year moving average of relative exit rates (see Appendix Note); Italy* 1965–72: 55–59 estimated.

Sources: OECD, *Labour Force Statistics 1966–2004*, except Ireland 1983–, Sweden 1997–: Eurostat, *Labour Force Surveys* (2005); and own calculations.

reaching the Italian level in net withdrawal (45 percent in 1985). Sweden, the United States, Ireland, and Japan had relatively low early exit rates; nevertheless, every fifth to fourth man aged 60–64 left work early. While early retirement declined somewhat during the late 1980s, the early 1990s brought another cyclical upturn, most dramatically in Sweden and Denmark. Interestingly, despite high levels of old-age employment, more than every fourth Japanese older man aged 60–64 had left employment in the 1990s. Differences between the two measures are relatively minimal, given the high employment rates among men aged 55–59. As a result, there is less divergence between absolute and relative exit (see Table 4.4).

We draw a much clearer picture of early retirement when we analyze early exit rates and adjust for cohort effects than if we look only at employment changes in aggregate. We find three distinct groups of countries for early retirement among men aged 60–64: the Continental European high early exit countries, the in-between cases of the United Kingdom and Denmark with medium-level early retirement, and the remaining countries (Sweden, Ireland, the United States, Japan) with

Table 4.6. Absolute and relative exit rates, men aged 60–64, 1970–2003

	1970	1975	1980	1985	1990	1995	2000	2003	Δ1970–85	Δ1985–2003
*Absolute exit**										
Germany	—	—	—	—	41.8[c]	46.6[d]	36.4	33.0	—	−1.96[c]
(West)	16.5	35.6	40.7	45.3	44.3[c]	45.4[d]	37.4	33.0	+6.97	−1.74
(East)	—	—	—	—	42.4[c]	50.9[d]	31.9	32.6	—	−2.17[c]
Netherlands	18.5[a]	25.8	32.1	46.2	38.0	43.0	33.4	33.8	+6.30	−1.71
France	16.3	26.4	36.2	48.0	40.5	46.5	45.7	46.6	+7.46	−0.17
Italy	29.6[b]	32.4	37.0	31.4	32.7	35.7	27.8	21.1	+0.41[b]	−2.19
Sweden	14.7	17.4	21.4	25.0	23.2	23.5	25.1	18.1	+3.64	−1.57
Denmark	12.5[a]	13.5[a]	27.1	37.5	28.9	34.2	39.5	25.6	+7.60	−2.10
United Kingdom	15.2	17.9	29.1	34.9	25.4	29.8	18.7	16.2	+5.69	−4.17
Ireland	6.3[a]	12.9[a]	13.1	22.1	23.1	15.4	13.1	12.8	+3.67	−3.02
United States	15.8	24.1	21.1	25.8	22.5	25.4	20.3	21.8	+3.32	−0.94
Japan	10.6	12.4	15.0	20.9	17.6	20.7	25.1	26.4	+4.64	+1.30
*Relative exit***										
Germany	—	—	—	—	57.3[c]	63.8[d]	56.7	51.5	—	−0.90[c]
(West)	18.2	40.0	49.5	57.9	57.4[c]	60.7[d]	55.5	49.9	+8.00	−0.81
(East)	—	—	—	—	64.8[c]	77.7[d]	63.7	58.6	—	−0.83[c]
Netherlands	19.8[a]	29.0	41.0	63.4	62.9	67.7	58.3	52.1	+8.67	−0.47
France	19.7	32.4	44.6	62.0	64.7	73.9	75.6	76.3	+7.95	+1.11
Italy	31.0	36.2	48.7	45.2	48.0	54.1	48.1	40.8	+2.74	−0.35
Sweden	15.8	19.4	24.1	28.8	27.1	41.1	32.9	24.2	+4.10	+0.74
Denmark	13.3[a]	14.8[a]	32.8	45.2	37.2	41.9	51.1	33.9	+8.49	−0.69
United Kingdom	15.9	19.3	32.4	41.3	34.0	39.8	28.3	23.4	+6.55	−2.07
Ireland	6.8[a]	13.7[a]	15.9	27.6	31.3	22.3	19.8	19.0	+5.10	−1.81
United States	18.4	28.2	26.5	32.6	29.6	33.1	28.2	28.5	+3.89	−0.81
Japan	11.8	13.9	16.8	23.7	20.3	23.0	29.0	29.0	+5.14	+1.13

Notes: * Absolute exit rate (decline in cohort-specific employment rate, see Appendix Note); **relative exit rate (decline in cohort-specific employment rate as percentage of previous employment rate, see Appendix Note); [a] 1970/75 estimated based on participation rates (ILO); [b] 1971, [c] 1991 (estimated), [d] 1996; Δ1970–85, Δ1985–2003: annual natural growth rate (%): $\Delta X_{t_0} - t_{0+n}\% = (((X_{t_{0+n}}/X_{t_0})^{1/n} - 1) \times 100$ (where $n = 1970–1985 = 15$, 1985–2003 = 18, [b] 1971–2003 = 14, [c] 1991–2003 = 12).

Sources: OECD, *Labour Force Statistics 1965–2004*, except: Germany: 1991–2003 German Statistical Office internal data; Italy 55–59 (1966–72 estimated based on 50–59, 1973–), Sweden 1997–2003, Denmark 1975–83, and Ireland: Eurostat *Labour Force Surveys 1973–2004* (2005); and own calculations.

oscillating, but overall lower levels (see Figure 4.4). In contrast to employment rates, the analysis of cohort-adjusted exit rates indicates a very similar increase in early retirement for older women aged 60–64 in Continental Europe, with the exception of Italy, which maintained a medium level until the early 1990s (see Figure 4.5). In general, all four countries show parallel trends for women and men with only a few exceptions: Germany's exit rates among women exceed those for men; Italy's gender gap has increased since the 1980s; there is no large difference in the Netherlands; and in France, women are less prone to retire early in the age group 60–64. Moreover, the *absolute* exit rates diverge more significantly than the relative rates, as female employment rates are overall lower and vary between these countries (see Table 4.7). Thus, Germany and France have medium-level absolute exit rates, with nearly every fourth woman aged 60–64 withdrawing from work. The high relative exit rates in the Netherlands and Italy are less important in absolute numbers because fewer women were employed at all before age 60. The other countries show lower early exit rates for women too, again with the partial exception of Denmark and Britain.

Such different societies as Sweden, the United States, and Japan show very similar early retirement patterns for women aged 60–64, with cyclical ups-and-downs around a low level of early retirement (between 20 and 35 percent) in the 1980s. Yet in the early 1990s, female exit rates increased in

Table 4.7. Absolute and relative exit rates, women aged 60–64, 1970–2003

	1970	1975	1980	1985	1990	1995	2000	2003	Δ1970–85	Δ1985–2003
Absolute exit*										
Germany	—	—	—	—	27.5[c]	26.9[d]	27.9	27.7	—	+0.05[c]
(West)	13.9	22.1	24.4	26.7	25.2[c]	27.1[d]	27.7	26.5	+4.44	−0.05
(East)	—	—	—	—	24.9[c]	25.9[d]	28.9	32.2	—	+2.18[c]
Netherlands	4.2[a]	7.3	8.3	12.0	9.9	15.7	18.1	16.7	+7.17	+1.86
France	7.9	15.9	16.0	27.2	23.2	27.5	32.0	32.2	+8.58	+0.93
Italy	2.8	4.4	5.7	7.5	9.2	11.8	11.4	11.8	+6.70	+2.56
Sweden	11.4	14.7	19.9	24.9	20.7	34.7	30.0	20.4	+5.36	−1.10
Denmark	13.7[a]	11.8[a]	19.7	20.3	27.4	37.6	28.0	32.1	+2.66	+2.57
United Kingdom	16.6	21.0	29.4	34.3	26.9	27.3	27.7	25.4	+4.96	−1.66
Ireland	1.6[a]	3.5[a]	5.0	6.4	6.3	7.2	4.3	5.1	+4.03	−1.26
United States	10.9	16.1	12.9	14.7	13.3	17.1	18.2	16.2	+1.97	+0.57
Japan	11.7[b]	11.1	9.6	12.0	10.9	14.5	18.3	19.9	+0.18[b]	+2.85
Relative exit**										
Germany	—	—	—	—	73.4[c]	71.8[d]	69.6	63.5	—	−1.20[c]
(West)	38.4	59.8	67.5	71.2	69.0[c]	68.4[d]	66.6	60.6	+4.20	−0.89
(East)	—	—	—	—	85.1[c]	88.6[d]	83.9	74.7	—	−1.07[c]
Netherlands	27.0[a]	41.2	47.4	66.1	57.2	65.7	65.8	52.8	+6.15	−1.24
France	19.2	35.4	38.2	60.8	59.0	66.3	71.4	72.8	+7.97	+1.01
Italy	22.4	42.3	49.4	40.6	47.6	61.0	59.6	54.2	+4.04	+1.62
Sweden	24.4	28.2	33.1	36.7	28.5	44.4	40.2	27.9	+2.75	−1.50
Denmark	34.4[a]	28.8[a]	42.7	44.6	50.4	65.3	54.5	53.9	+1.74	+1.06
United Kingdom	37.3	42.4	56.8	66.1	55.3	52.5	52.2	48.2	+3.89	−1.74
Ireland	7.1[a]	16.1[a]	23.7	31.1	30.4	32.8	18.4	17.4	+10.31	−3.18
United States	24.4	34.0	28.6	31.3	27.8	31.9	31.7	27.1	+1.68	−0.80
Japan	23.3[b]	22.8	20.0	24.1	21.9	27.2	32.7	34.6	+0.23[b]	+2.04

Notes: *Absolute exit rate (decline in cohort-specific employment rate, see Appendix Note); **relative exit rate (decline in cohort-specific employment rate in percentage of previous employment rate, see Appendix Note); [a] 1970/75 estimated based on participation rates (ILO); [b] 1971, [c] 1991 (estimated), [d] 1996; Δ1970–85, Δ1985–2003: annual natural growth rate (%): $\Delta X_{t_0} - t_{0+n}\% = (((X_{t_{0+n}}/X_{t_0})^{1/n} - 1) \times 100$ (where n = 1970–85 = 15, 1985–2003 = 18, [b] 1971–85 = 14, [c] 1991–2003 = 12).

Sources: OECD, *Labour Force Statistics 1965–2004*, except: Germany: 1991–2003 German Statistical Office internal data; Italy 55–59 (1966–72 estimated based on 50–59, 1973–), Sweden 1997–2003, Denmark 1975–83, and Ireland: Eurostat, *Labour Force Surveys 1973–2004* (2005); and own calculations.

Sweden and Japan as a result of more severe labor market conditions. Another exception is Catholic Ireland, where despite low overall female participation a substantial share of older women withdrew from work during the unemployment crisis of the 1980s, a trend that was reversed with improved labor market conditions in the 1990s. The two major outliers are Denmark and the United Kingdom. Given the statutory female pension age of 60, British women tend to withdraw at rates comparable to Continental Europe (66 percent in 1985, declining to 52 percent in 2000). Since the late 1970s, Danish women aged 60–64 withdrew from work at an increasing rate, such that by 1995 two-thirds had left employment; this has been largely possible through disability pensions that allowed retirement long before the normal pension age of 67.

4.2.3 *Even Earlier Exit Before Age 60*

Early retirement has not been limited to the age from 60 to 64, as the longitudinal analysis of employment rates for men aged 55–59 showed. Based on Eurostat data, we also calculated cohort-adjusted exit rates for the two age groups before 60 from the late 1970s onwards, though we lack comparable data for the United States and Japan. While early exit in the age group 55–59 is significant in several countries, it is very rare before age 55 and largely due to cyclical unemployment in all countries.[6] Continental Europe is again leading in early exit among men aged 55–59 (see Figure 4.6). Every third French or Italian and every fifth German or Dutch working man is today no longer employed by the age of 60. While the decline in employment was still relatively small in the mid-1970s, ever earlier retirement led to a doubling of the *relative* exit rate by the late 1990s. French men led the pre-60 retirement trend in the 1980s, followed by Italian men in the 1990s. A particular situation existed in Germany after unification: Initially two out of three East German men were without work before age 60, but the relative exit rate declined over the 1990s to the French and Italian level. The other European countries show considerably lower tendency to early retirement before age 60 (exit rates age 55–59

---

[6] An exception is Italy, where nearly every fifth person left work before age 55 in the 1990s. Only during major downturns have other European countries achieved levels of around 7–8 percent, e.g. the United Kingdom in the early 1980s and France and Germany in the 1990s. Thus, the Italian pre-55 early retirement pattern seems to be the main exception that accounts for the low employment rate among men aged 55–59, a fact to keep in mind when analyzing Italian post-55 early exit rates that seem to be lower than those of other Continental European countries.

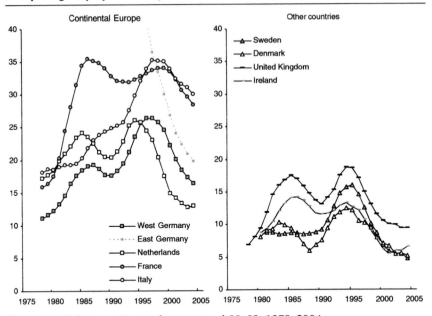

Figure 4.6 Relative exit rates for men aged 55–59, 1978–2004

Note: Five-year moving average of relative exit rate in percentage (see Appendix Note).

Sources: Eurostat, *Labour Force Surveys 1973–2004* (2005); Sweden (1976–95): Swedish Labour Force Surveys (2005); and own calculations.

range below 20 percent) and follow a more cyclical trend. Nevertheless, the impact on labor reduction is around 8–13 percent; that is, about every tenth man has lost work in the age group 55–59. National data suggest that the American pre-60 retirement rates rank with those of the United Kingdom and Ireland, while hardly any Japanese men quit working before age 60.

Exit from work before age 60 is even more important among women, partially due to early statutory retirement age (see Figure 4.7). In Continental Europe, exit before 60 is as common among women as men, with the exception of Italy. Italian women are even more prone to leave before 60 (every third woman instead of every fourth man) thanks to a statutory pension age five years earlier than for men. In France, exit before 60 was somewhat less common among employed women than men, but the gap has begun to close in recent years: Every third French woman aged 55–59 who had been in employment left work—the same rate as among men. After lower rates in the 1980s, Dutch women in recent years have surpassed their male colleagues in very early exit. In the 1980s, West German women had lower rates than men, but have now surpassed their

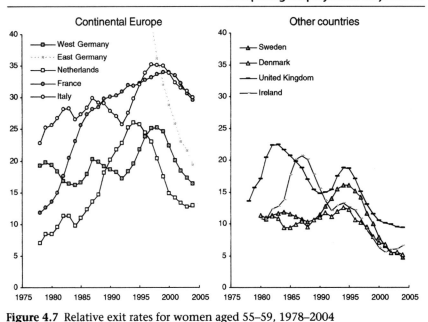

Continental Europe

Other countries

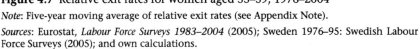

Figure 4.7 Relative exit rates for women aged 55–59, 1978–2004

Note: Five-year moving average of relative exit rates (see Appendix Note).

Sources: Eurostat, *Labour Force Surveys 1983–2004* (2005); Sweden 1976–95: Swedish Labour Force Surveys (2005); and own calculations.

male colleagues. In contrast, East German women were even more likely than men to be pushed out of the labor market before age 60, which had been the German Democratic Republic's statutory retirement age for women (Ernst 1995). In the other countries, pre-60 retirement seems to be more common among working women, especially during an economic slowdown. Over the last two decades (1981–99), relative exit in the age group 55–59 on average has been more likely for women than men in the United Kingdom (19.7 percent vs. 15.5 percent), Denmark (14.8 percent vs. 9.6 percent), Sweden (12.6 percent vs. 10.8 percent), and in Japan (13 percent vs. 5 percent), while relatively similar in Ireland (11.2 percent vs. 12.1 percent) and the United States (10 percent for both). Given the traditionally lower participation rate of women in Continental Europe, similar pre-60 exit rates have a more moderate impact on labor reduction than for men, whereas moderate exit and high participation in the United Kingdom, Denmark, and Sweden add up to the same labor reduction effect (around 10 percent of the female population aged 55–59) as in France or Italy.

4.3   How Many Early Exit Trajectories Are There?

The analysis of long-term trends in early exit from work for the age group 60–64 revealed two different early exit *trajectories* within the overall trend: (*a*) Continental European countries showed an S-curve-like *diffusion* process from low to high early retirement over the past three decades (with the partial exception of Italian men, who maintained an already high level of early exit); whereas (*b*) in the other countries early exit from work grew less rapidly and continued *fluctuating* during the 1980s and 1990s with the exception of early exit among British and Danish women that came close to Continental levels during the 1980s and 1990s, respectively. By the mid-1990s, we can distinguish three different worlds of early exit: (*a*) the Continental European *high* early exit countries (Germany, the Netherlands, France, and Italy), (*b*) the British and Danish *medium* exit levels (particularly among women), and (*c*) the other countries (Sweden, Ireland, the United States, and Japan) with *lower* levels of early exit.

Would the inclusion of early exit before age 60 alter these findings? Not significantly. Indeed, the difference between the Continent and the other countries might even be enhanced. All four Continental European countries have high exit rates that are rising, while the other countries show more cyclical patterns due to unemployment waves that remain below the Continental European level. Very early exit (age 55–59) follows similar patterns to exit after age 60, though the groups of very early exit clearly stand out: Italians, French, and Eastern Germans. Moreover, earlier exit before age 55 occurs occasionally (with the exception of Italy) but remains limited to some occupational groups (e.g. miners) and to cyclical unemployment due to lacking other institutionalized public exit pathways for this age group. The three worlds of exit regimes—high exit Continental Europe, medium-level outliers Denmark and Britain, and low exit countries—are still observable in the 1990s.

Cohort-adjusted early exit rates provide a better tool to study early withdrawal from work, particularly for women. Continental Europe's main trend in early exit for the age group 60–64 shows an S-shaped diffusion curve with fast growth in the 1970s and early 1980s and a leveling off thereafter. In the other countries, however, early exit from work increased more gradually and cyclically, with the exception of relatively significant trends in early exit among women in the United Kingdom and Denmark. Although the level of very early exit before age 60 remains considerably lower, it increased rapidly during the 1980s and remained substantial in the 1990s in Continental Europe, while the other countries show a lower but cyclical trend. Premature early exit before age 55 remains rare, with Italy a major exception.

Based on the results for early exit trajectories in the age groups 55–64, there are clear country clusters that partly overlap with the regime typologies discussed in the previous chapter (see Table 4.8). The four Continental European welfare states show highest levels of early exit from work for both men and women. While Italy traditionally has had very early exit (age 50–59) and France showed increasing exit from work in the age group 55–59, very early exit before age 60 by and large remains limited to unemployment in Germany and the Netherlands. With the exception of France, the rise in early exit has leveled off in recent years, and there has even been some improvement, particularly in the Netherlands. The remaining countries—universalist and residual-liberal welfare states— have moderate or lower levels of early exit. Denmark and the United Kingdom are outliers among the non-Conservative welfare states with relatively high levels of early exit among older women (age 60–64). They also stand out due to relatively high levels of male early exit during the 1980s, continuing in Denmark into the 1990s. Sweden and the United States have moderate levels of early exit for men and women, while Japan and Ireland have comparatively low levels of early retirement. The trend among the non-Continental countries is less marked by a general diffusion curve, following a cyclical pattern instead, indicating that early retirement results more from changing labor market situations than solely

Table 4.8. Cross-national variations in early exit from work for men and women

Men/Women (relative exit rates by age group)	High and early (60–64: ≥40%) (55–59: ≥25%)	High (60–64: ≥40%) (55–59: ≤25%)	Moderate (60–64: ≤40%) (55–59: ≤15%)	Low (60–64: ≤35%) (55–59: ≤15%)
High and early (60–64: ≥45%) (55–59: ≥30%)	France Italy			
High (60–64: ≥45%) (55–59: ≤30%)		Germany Netherlands		
Moderate (60–64: ≤45%) (55–59: ≤15%)		Denmark United Kingdom	Sweden United States	
Low (60–64: ≤35%) (55–59: ≤15%)				Japan Ireland

Notes: Relative exit rates for age groups 60–64 and 55–59 in brackets; based on period averages 1980s–90s (see Tables 4.6 and 4.7; and Figures 4.6 and 4.7).

because it has become a socially accepted role. This holds also for Denmark and Sweden where exit increased during periods of high unemployment in the 1990s but then receded. While British and Irish early exit trends declined with labor market improvements during the 1990s, Japan, after long periods of low early exit, experienced an unusual increase with the economic downturn in the late 1990s.

In subsequent chapters, I analyze more closely not only the impact of the main protection and production institutions but also the role of the social partners in order to unravel the causes for the cross-national variations. In Chapter 5, I first discuss the pull factor: the public pathways to early exit provided by specific welfare regimes. Further, I consider the following question: Why do Continental European welfare states foster early exit from work to a much larger degree than Scandinavian universalist, Anglophone liberal, and the Japanese residual welfare states? In Chapter 6, I turn to the push factors, looking more closely at the structural changes in the economy and the varieties of production regimes and partnership institutions in shaping labor-shedding strategies across these economies. Here, I focus on the question: Do LMEs always lead to lower employment rates, while CMEs rely more heavily on early exit? Why have both Sweden and Japan, which share more features with the German system than the liberal model, been able to achieve higher employment levels for older workers? Thus, the exit regimes clusters delineated here will be analyzed from these 'pull' and 'push' perspectives, considering first the impact of welfare regimes, and then of production systems and labor relations.

Chapter 5

The Protection-Pull Factors:
Multiple Pathways to Early Exit

According to the *pull* perspective, welfare states provide incentives for workers to retire early by granting public income transfers prior to age 65. In fact, there are multiple institutional arrangements or *pathways* (Kohli and Rein 1991: 6) leading to early retirement, often combining multiple income programs that can (and sometimes must) be linked sequentially. For instance, a worker who has been dismissed may first receive long-term unemployment insurance, followed by a preretirement pension, before finally becoming eligible for a public pension—and each step may be conditional on the earlier one. Moreover, we find considerable cross-national variations in these pathways' availability, eligibility conditions, and generosity of benefits. Thus, the main question addressed in this chapter is: Do differences in exit pathways of the welfare regimes analyzed here explain the rise in early exit from work and the considerable cross-national variations?

We need not assume that all of these institutional arrangements were initially tailored toward advancing early exit from work; I argue that many opportunities to retire from work are the *unintended consequences* of policies designed for quite different purposes. For instance, long-term unemployment benefits for older workers were originally conceived as a social policy for the hard-to-reemploy, but, with rising mass unemployment since the mid-1970s, these rights became the first step on an increasingly popular pathway leading to early exit. Thus, it would be misleading to look only at the formal designation, institutional locus, or initial intention of these policies: Different pathways can serve similar preretirement functions, though they may have quite different implications in terms of eligibility, generosity, and control. I thus consider not only schemes explicitly set up for early retirement but also major (semi-)*public* exit pathways that provide income support for withdrawal from work before age 65. Although this chapter discusses collective schemes financed by the social partners, it excludes firm-sponsored income support for early retirement (ranging from severance pay to occupational pension funds) because such policies are attributable to push (production) more than pull (protection) factors (see Chapter 6).

In this chapter, I thus focus on the institutionalized (public or collective) pathways to early exit, whether they were explicitly intended for this purpose or have assumed such a function over time. I first review the main pathways for early exit from work, highlighting the multiple arrangements that have emerged across and within different social security programs. Given very different social protection arrangements, focusing only on one program, for instance pension insurance, would be insufficient to map the entire opportunity structure for early exit from work. This review of the multiple pathways also reveals that there are cross-national variations in the importance of the various programs and that there are salient differences between countries as to the 'openness' (eligibility, generosity, and control) of these pathways. In this chapter, I focus on the expansion of early exit pathways, discussing the politics of *reversing* early retirement (see Chapter 7).

In Section 5.2, I analyze the evolution of exit pathways and reveal the underlying social and political forces that gave rise to the multiplication—even explosion—of early exit opportunities since the 1960s. Was early retirement a planned labor reduction policy or was early exit rather the *unintended* consequence of policies created for other purposes? Which political and social interests propagated early retirement policies and facilitated the expansion of early exit from work? In a comparative regime analysis, I explain cross-national variations in early exit patterns by differences in both multitude and openness of institutionalized pathways inherent in the different welfare regimes. I evaluate the degree to which the pull thesis explains early exit: Do the observed cross-national differences in early exit from work match the number and openness of institutionalized pathways?

5.1 Institutionalized Pathways to Early Exit

A multitude of exit pathways have emerged in advanced welfare states (Jespen, Foden, and Hutsebaut 2002*a*; Kohli et al. 1991). In the following, I distinguish six pathways (see Figure 5.1): (1) early statutory (old age) pensions providing benefits before age 65, (2) flexible pensions and partial pensions that allow part-time work, (3) special preretirement schemes,

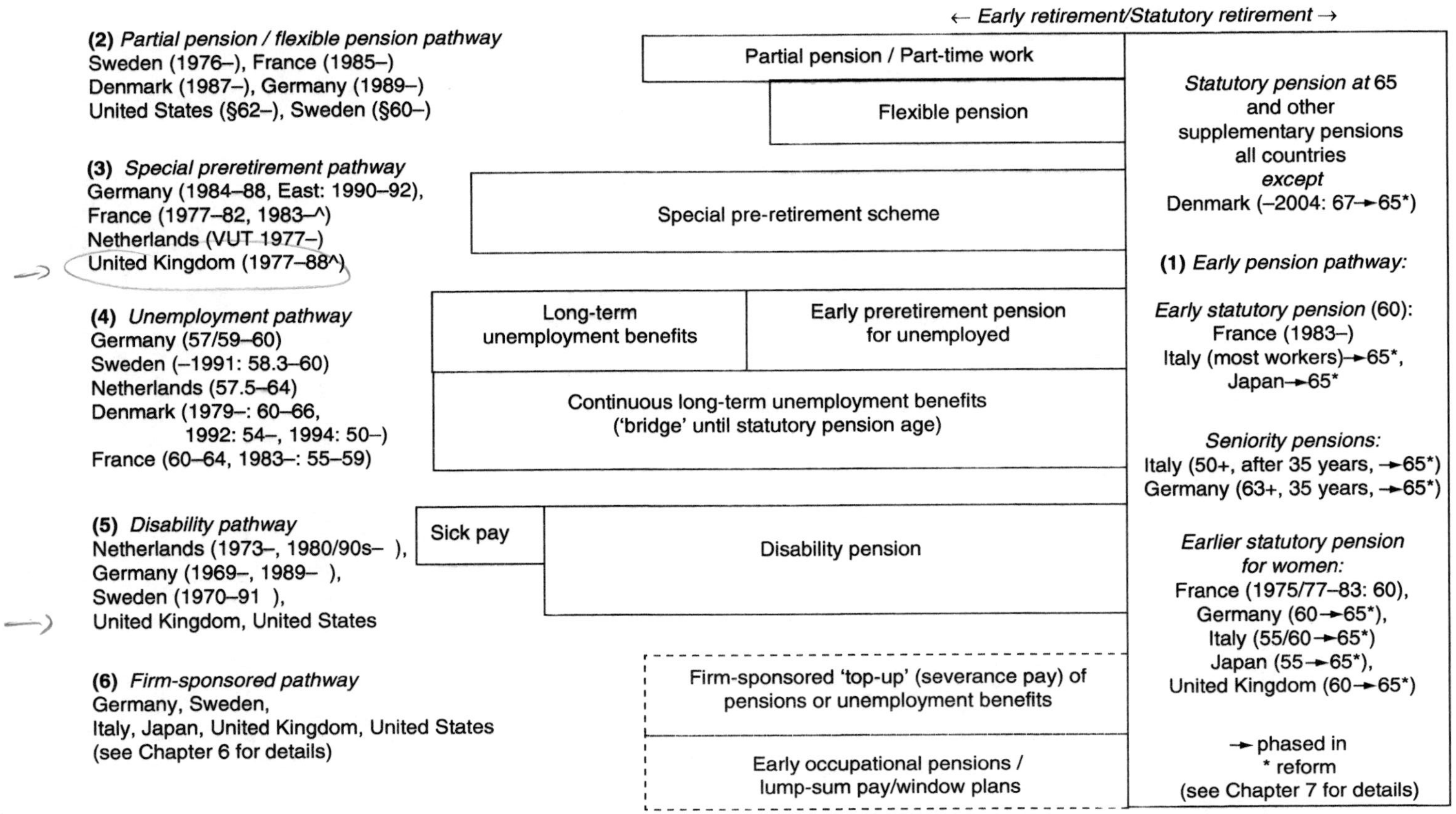

← Early retirement/Statutory retirement →

Partial pension / Part-time work

Flexible pension

Special pre-retirement scheme

Early preretirement pension for unemployed

Long-term unemployment benefits

Continuous long-term unemployment benefits ('bridge' until statutory pension age)

Disability pension

Sick pay

Firm-sponsored 'top-up' (severance pay) of pensions or unemployment benefits

Early occupational pensions / lump-sum pay/window plans

Statutory pension at 65 and other supplementary pensions all countries except
Denmark (–2004: 67→65*)

(1) *Early pension pathway:*

Early statutory pension (60):
France (1983–)
Italy (most workers)→65*,
Japan→65*

Seniority pensions:
Italy (50+, after 35 years, →65*)
Germany (63+, 35 years, →65*)

Earlier statutory pension for women:
France (1975/77–83: 60),
Germany (60→65*),
Italy (55/60→65*)
Japan (55→65*),
United Kingdom (60→65*)

→ phased in
* reform
(see Chapter 7 for details)

(2) *Partial pension / flexible pension pathway*
Sweden (1976→), France (1985–)
Denmark (1987–), Germany (1989–)
United States (§62–), Sweden (§60–)

(3) *Special preretirement pathway*
Germany (1984–88, East: 1990–92),
France (1977–82, 1983–^)
Netherlands (VUT 1977–)
United Kingdom (1977–88^)

(4) *Unemployment pathway*
Germany (57/59–60)
Sweden (–1991: 58.3–60)
Netherlands (57.5–64)
Denmark (1979–: 60–66,
    1992: 54–, 1994: 50–)
France (60–64, 1983–: 55–59)

(5) *Disability pathway*
Netherlands (1973–, 1980/90s–),
Germany (1969–, 1989–),
Sweden (1970–91),
United Kingdom, United States

(6) *Firm-sponsored pathway*
Germany, Sweden,
Italy, Japan, United Kingdom, United States
(see Chapter 6 for details)

Figure 5.1 Multiple pathways to early exit from work
Notes: * reforms (see Chapter 7 for details); § with actuarial reduction; ^ with reemployment duty;→ phased in; # with labor market criteria.

(4) long-term unemployment benefits for older workers, (5) disability pathways with or without labor market considerations, and (6) firm-sponsored policies ranging from severance pay to occupational pensions.

Each pathway has its own particular 'logic' of *eligibility* (conditionality of benefits), *generosity* (net income replacement rate of benefits), and *control* (individual, firm, or administrative codecisions), but each also implies different financing rules and cost-sharing implications. In general, old-age pension policies, whether early statutory pensions (early pension age for some groups) or flexible/partial pensions (allowing early drawing or part-time pensions with or without reduction in benefits) are granted as individual rights, require some minimum contributions, and are financed by the public through taxes or social contributions. Special preretirement programs and age-related unemployment pensions, however, have been set up as part of labor market policies and are often tied to conditions for job replacement, thus also involve employer decisions (dismissal of older workers, hiring of younger workers as 'replacements', topping up of insufficient benefits). Quite in contrast, disability pension eligibility is largely dependent on an individual's health status, the programs' medical, social and labor market criteria, and administrative procedures. Finally, firm-sponsored early exit policies (such as occupational pensions, severance pay, or 'social plans') depend on firm-specific human resource strategies, the workers' interests and influence at firm level, and interactions with existing public or negotiated programs (these are discussed in Chapter 6).

The review of these multiple pathways also reveals a multitude of actors involved—with consequences for both the growth of early exit and the difficulties of its regulation or reversal (as discussed in Chapter 7). Although public policy plays a large role in the social security systems of most welfare states, we find that exit pathways exhibit a broad *public–private* mix (Casey 1992; Rein and Rainwater 1986a; Russig 1986). Early exit pathways include tax-financed public policy, mandatory but self-administered social insurance, collectively negotiated funds administered by the social partners, union-led (so-called 'Ghent') unemployment funds, and firm-sponsored voluntary welfare policies.

5.1.1 *The Early Pension Pathway*

The *institutionalization* of 'retirement' (Atchley 1982) as the right to income maintenance in old age that enables full withdrawal from work was a crucial precondition for the trend toward 'preretirement'. Although old-age pension insurance was introduced in all ten countries before 1945 (see Table 5.1), only the major *postwar* reforms made old-age insurance encompassing and pension benefits sufficient to induce the full transition from work to retirement. In countries with Bismarckian pension systems (not only Germany, France, and Italy but also the United States), the coverage of mandatory old-age insurance extended to include nearly all the dependent employed and partially also the self-employed. Following the Beveridge postwar reforms in Britain, basic pensions for all citizens were also improved in Denmark, Sweden, and Ireland or newly introduced in the Netherlands and Japan (Alber 1982; Korpi 2001). Pension benefits were subsequently improved by enlarging the earnings-related element in one-tier systems (the United States, Germany, and Italy). A second earnings-related tier was added to the basic pension systems (Baldwin 1990) in Sweden, Denmark, and the United Kingdom. In the United States, the United Kingdom, and Japan private occupational funds with taxation or opt-out advantages complement public pensions, while supplementary pensions based on collective agreements top up the first-tier public pensions in France and the Netherlands (Rein and Wadensjö 1997*a*; Reynaud et al. 1996).

Indeed, after World War II, all countries eventually lowered their age limit to 65 or below. Sweden lowered its age limit to 65 in 1976, granting all citizens the same rights that had previously been enjoyed only by some employees through collective agreements.[1] While Sweden lowered the pension age (Øverbye 1997), Denmark first raised the age limit from 60 to 67 over the immediate postwar decades and maintained its high statutory retirement age, despite growing early exit, while the *1999 Reform* has finally granted pensions at age 65, starting in 2004 (Hansen 2002), though this is, paradoxically, part of an effort to *delay* exit from work and reinstate old-age pension as the main exit pathway through a more 'realistic' retirement norm.

On the other hand, Japan, Italy, and France introduced relatively early pensions for industrial workers, whereas agrarian workers and the self-employed tended to retire later. Japanese workers can draw on public earnings-related pensions at age 60 (and basic pension, though *actuarially reduced*, i.e. lowered by benefits for shorter contribution periods), at a time when larger companies enforce mandatory retirement. However, as shown in Chapter 4, most Japanese men and women remain in employment

---

[1] Even before the 1976 reform, public sector and white-collar employees were customarily granted exit at age 65. The 1971 SAF agreement financed pensions at age 65 for blue-collar workers from 1973 onwards (Wadensjö 1991).

Table 5.1. The expansion of public pension pathways

Country	First law	−1945 age♂	Reform year	1945+ age ♂/♀*	Flexible pension	Public pension	Replacement	
							1975	1995
Germany	1889	70	1949/1957	65/65(60: 15 y)*	1973–: 63 (35 y)	Contributory	59.6	55.0
Netherlands	1913	70	1957	65		Basic (+)	48.0	45.8
France	1910	65	1975/1982	60		Contributory	62.5	64.8
Italy	1919	65	1958/1965	60/55*	50+ (35 y)	Contributory	62.0	80.0
Sweden	1913	67	1976	65		Mixed	77.1	74.7
Denmark	1922	65	1956/1970	67	60+ (−0.5% p.a.)	Basic +	42.3	56.2
United Kingdom	1908	70	1948	65/60*		Basic (+)	33.8	49.8
Ireland	1908	70	1973/1977	66(65)†		Basic	28.9	39.7
United States	1935	65			62+ (−0.5% p.a.)	Contrib	49.1	56.0
Japan	1941	60	(1962)	EP: 60/55*	PP: 60–64 (−90%)	Basic PP + Contrib EP	54.1	52.1

Notes: *Gender difference for (♂) men / (♀) women in retirement age; PP: public pension; EP: employee/occupational pension; Germany: 60 optional pension for women with 15 contribution years; Italy: age for employees, for self-employed (m/f): 65/60; Denmark: lower age for (single) women before 1970; basic PP (+): basic public pension with state supplement or (opt-out) occupational pension; gross replacement rate (average benefit replacement ratio as percent of former in come); † with means test.

Sources: For reforms until early 1990s: Alber (1982); Delsen and Reday-Mulvey (1996); Flora (1986b); Inkeles and Usui (1989); Kohli et al. (1991), for replacement rate: Blöndal and Scarpetta (1998).

beyond age 60 (or are self-employed long beyond age 65), often combining income from work and pensions.

Until the reforms of the 1990s, most male wage earners in Italy could retire at age 60 (women at age 55), while self-employed men had to wait until age 65 (women until age 60) (Klammer 1997). Italian politicians used the expansion of a generous (but underfunded) old-age system to compensate their electoral clientele, making up for the lack of effective unemployment insurance and accommodating the major need for industrial restructuring (Ferrera and Gualmini 2000). Additionally, older Italian workers in the private sector could retire on 'seniority pensions' once they had contributed for 35 years (i.e. already at age 50 if they had entered the labor force at age 15), though they were then officially forbidden to work. Introduced in 1965, seniority pensions only became important from the late 1980s onwards, when cohorts that had entered the labor market in the immediate postwar period were seeking early retirement.[2] In the public sector, civil servants had even more favorable retirement options: They could receive benefits after only 20 years (sometimes even after 15 years due to credited noncontributory social years), without being forced to retire from the workforce. As a consequence of the 1990s reforms, which were negotiated with the unions, conditions were tightened, though only gradually since the seniority scheme was very popular with unionized workers (Baccaro 2002; Regini and Regalia 1997).

In France, allowing special groups a lower retirement age on public pensions, postwar social reforms also predated explicit early retirement policies.[3] While this opened the door for a lowering of the retirement age on social grounds, increasing usage of the unemployment pathway augmented the pressure on the government to respond. The newly elected Socialist government lowered the pension age from 65 to 60 starting in April 1983 (Guillemard 1991). Although some employers would have liked to retain control of early exit by continuing the previous dismissal scheme, the French unions were in favor of a state-guaranteed individual right to retire at age 60 (conditional on 37.5 years of contributions). Since the new public pension rule would relieve the unemployment insurance of the social partners, they followed suit and also introduced a lower

[2] In 1990, 289,000 people were benefiting from the 'seniority pension' arrangement in Italy. Only five years later, the number had swelled to 865,000 people and it had become the most important early exit pathway besides early pensions (SZW 1997: 92–9).
[3] The French government granted early pensions to veterans and prisoners of war from 1974 onwards (over 300,000 beneficiaries) and some groups of women before the general lowering of the pension age to 60 in 1983 (Guillemard 1991).

pension age for their supplementary pensions by agreement in February 1983. With the lowered age limit, the government sought to resume the (public) pension fund's 'power to regulate definitive exit, at least of 60- to 64-year-olds' (Guillemard 1991: 143) and reduce early exit costs by shifting from expensive unemployment to less generous pension benefits.

The institutionalization of a 'normal', that is, *statutory retirement age* had significant impact on the timing of exit from work. As discussed in Chapter 4, employment rates among very old working people (age 65+) dropped in all ten countries over the postwar period thanks to the expansion of public pension and have reached very low levels (particularly among dependent employed workers), except in Japan. However, the statutory pension age for men does not explain the large cross-national differences found in early exit patterns. Certainly, Denmark, Sweden, Ireland, the United Kingdom, and the United States stipulate a statutory pension age of 65 (or even later) and have relative low early exit rates for men. Japan has a lower pension age limit, by five years, for dependent employed men and women, but it also has the lowest early exit rates of all ten countries; this can only be explained by the combination of pension and work income. Among the Continental European countries, France and Italy have an early statutory retirement age, which partly explains the high early exit before age 65, though in the case of France the early exit trend preceded the lowering of pension age to 60 in 1983. The Netherlands maintains a statutory pension age of 65 but has a high level of early exit. Of importance for early exit, particularly among men, is thus not only the statutory retirement age but also the various other institutionalized pathways to early exit prior to the usual pension drawing age.

In the case of women, there is more evidence for a reduction in labor supply through a lower statutory pension age. In Italy, the United Kingdom, Japan and for some insured women with few contribution years in Germany and France, women were given the right to draw pensions five years earlier than men (see Table 5.1) on the 'paternalist' reasoning that married women (who tended to be younger than their husbands) could retire at the same time as their spouses and would not have to continue working longer than their husbands. In Italy, until recent changes, women who were dependent employed (at age 55) or self-employed (at age 60) could enjoy pensions five years earlier than their male colleagues. In the 1940s, British women were granted their own basic pension at age 60, five years earlier than men. With the German 1957 reform, women with interrupted employment careers could choose an early pension at age 60 (instead of 65), although these pension benefits were considerably lower due to shorter contribution periods.[4] And selected groups of French women had been granted a similar right some years prior to the 1983 pension reform.[5]

Granting an earlier 'normal' pension age to women was largely motivated by social (if not paternalist) considerations; however, it became a de facto labor-shedding strategy, particularly as female labor force participation increased from cohort to cohort. Among the 60–64-year-olds, the relative exit rate of British women was significantly higher than for men due to earlier public pensions, though not all women withdrew at age 60. Markedly higher early exit rates during the 1970s and later somewhat higher rates for women in Germany and Japan can also be attributed to the favorable age limits. In Italy, the earlier pension age has only played a role in recent years, as more women participate in the labor market, thus fulfilling the early exit criteria. Nevertheless, somewhat higher relative exit rates for women can also be found in some countries that have no gender gap in pension rules. Thus, earlier statutory pension ages than 65 have had an impact in countries with gender-specific rules. Due to future increases in female labor market participation rates this earlier pension age would contribute even further to early exit—if the gender gap in pension rules were not to be gradually phased out in all countries considered here, following European Union and national equal opportunity legislation but also financial concerns about pension sustainability (see Chapter 7).

5.1.2 *The Flexible and Partial Pension Pathways*

In addition to drawing full benefits at statutory pension age, *flexible* pensions allow anticipated or deferred drawing within a predefined timeframe. Depending on the eligibility rules and actuarial treatment, the flexibility pathway can provide an important though often hidden pull on early exit. If actuarial treatment is quite favorable or deferment does not lead to benefit increase, pensioners will tend to retire earlier than later (Casey 1997; Gruber and Wise 1999*b*). In France, workers in the private

---

[4] To draw benefits early, women in Germany needed 15 contribution years, ten of them after age 40. With the increasing return of women to the labor market after childrearing years, the share of women entering the public pension system at age 60 grew from an initial 10 percent in 1958 to around one-third in the early 1980s. Following legal restrictions in 1984, the share dropped to 25 percent, but in the late 1990s, it rebounded (VDR 2002).

[5] Before the general reform of 1982, the French Conservative government granted pensions at age 60 to working mothers (with 30 years of contributions and three children) in 1975 and to all female wage earners (with 37.5 years of contributions) in 1977, resulting in about 60,000 beneficiaries from 1978 until the general change in pension age in 1983 (Guillemard 1991: 144, Table 5.8).

sectors have no incentive to continue employment once they have reached 37.5 (since 1993: 40) contribution years because benefits will not be raised by additional contribution years and drawing a state pension is incompatible with continued employment.

As of 1973, the German left-liberal coalition introduced a 'flexible' seniority pension (*flexibles Altersruhegeld*) for workers with 35 contribution years from age 63 onwards. Although the German system had an actuarial appreciation for postponement of pension until age 67, the legislators did not depreciate the anticipated flexible retirement pay.[6] Following reforms in the 1990s, the flexible seniority pension was phased out at age 62 by 2004 and replaced by an actuarially reduced flexible pension.

Since 1961, the United States public pension system does allow benefits to be drawn prematurely at age 62, but with relatively 'fair' actuarial reductions (−0.5 percent p.a.). This voluntary preretirement option is relatively unattractive unless employers top up such benefits or individuals have sufficient private income. Nevertheless, after increased labor market problems since the 1980s, more Americans left the workforce at the flexible pension age of 62 than at the statutory pension age of 65 (Gruber and Wise 1999b: 18, Fig. 12). Flexible pensions can thus have effects in both directions, leading either to delays in retirement or to early withdrawal—depending on actuarial treatment and availability of additional resources. A similar Swedish flexible pension with actuarial reduction from age 60 onwards has not been very popular due to more attractive alternatives (Wadensjö 1996).

In addition, *partial* pensions are designed to smooth the transition from work to retirement by combining a gradual pension and part-time work (Delsen and Reday-Mulvey 1996b). Such a program may help some workers to stay in the labor force longer, while it may induce others to withdraw earlier particularly when it allows a full exit at mid-term. The first such partial pension program for working people aged 60–65 who reduced their working hours by at least five hours per week was introduced in Sweden as early as 1976 (Delsen 1996c; Wadensjö 1991, 1996). The original tax-financed program soon became more widely used than expected because it had attractive conditions: It replaced up to 65 percent of the reduced gross earnings and it had no negative repercussions for old-age pensions after age 65. Later stop-and-go changes in benefit generosity have caused

[6] Indeed, the flexible seniority pension was initially very popular among older men (few women achieved 35 contribution years): 30 percent of new male pensioners retired at 63 in the mid-1970s, but since the 1980s, it has fluctuated between 12 percent and 20 percent (VDR 2002).

the numbers to drop or increase accordingly, but the scheme was phased out by 2000 and replaced by the actuarially reduced flexible pension (Wadensjö 2002).

A decade after Sweden started offering gradual pensions, Denmark (1987–), France (1988–), and Germany (1989–) followed, but these programs had limited success due to less favorable terms, more attractive alternatives, and little employer support for part-time jobs (Delsen and Reday-Mulvey 1996a; Laczko 1988; Latulippe and Turner 2000). Since 1987, Danish workers (age 60–66) with ten years (today 20 years) of contributions to the flat-rate supplementary labor market pension and part-time work (12–30 hours) are entitled to a partial pension (*delpension*), though benefits are means-tested with other private occupational benefits. Given other options for full withdrawal with good net replacement for lower income groups, Danish partial pensions remained unattractive.

The French part-time schemes have similar disadvantages compared with more generous alternatives for full exit (Jolivet 2002; Reday-Mulvey 1996). The French *préretraite progressive* (PRP) is part of the French state redundancy program (introduced in 1982, extended in 1993, and reformed in 1997). The Ministry of Labor signs an agreement with a firm that is willing to meet stringent job replacement conditions for using partial preretirement of its workers (age 55–60) in return for receiving payroll tax reductions and state subsidies. A similar gradual retirement scheme also exists since 1982 in the public sector for workers aged 55–60 with 25 years of service (EIRO: TN0109184S). The French gradual preretirement pensions have become a means to retire even earlier than the relatively low statutory retirement age of 60, whereas the French partial pension (*retraite progressive*), which since 1988 has allowed the combination of part-time work and partial pension at age 60, has not been able to prolong full exit from work.

The German part-time pension (*Altersteilzeit*) for older workers (58+) paid by the Federal Employment Office was short-lived (1989–92), mostly due to employer resistance (Schmähl, George, and Oswald 1996). Following a tripartite consensus and new legislation in 1996 (Bispinck 1997), unions and employer associations have implemented the new part-time pension rules through sectoral collective bargaining (Barkholdt 2001). Nearly all employers apply a 'block' model (not possible under the old law): During the first segment, the 'part-time' employee works full time and during the later segment the 'part-time' pensioner retires fully from the firm, but the firm continues to pay the employee a part-time wage on top of the partial pension paid by the social insurance program for the entire period.

The social partners in the Netherlands and Denmark also negotiated partial retirement options in several collective agreements within the context of their special preretirement schemes (EIRO: TN0109184S). These are discussed in Chapter 6 later. No partial pension schemes exist in the liberal-residual welfare states (United Kingdom, Ireland, and the United States). The Irish means-test pensions at 65, and the US old-age social security is granted conditional on full withdrawal from work or with earnings-tests (e.g. flexible US old-age pensions for those aged 62–64), and reduction of benefits in cases of continued employment. Following Anglo-American free market and liberal welfare principles, public benefits should be paid as income replacement to those unable to work, not as wage subsidies. Nevertheless, we find increased part-time work (up to the income ceiling of public benefits) among older British and American workers. Japan, however, allows a combination of earnings-related pension and income from work (Kimura and Oka 2001; Takayama 1996), which explains the high share of working pensioners among older male workers aged 60–64 and 65–69.

Only in Sweden have gradual pensions been a major success, though this result depends on the financial incentives in place. At its peak, one-third of all older employed people worked part-time, thus partial pensions have contributed to Sweden's high employment record. Combining public benefits and part-time work still plays an important role in the mid-1990s, with half of working men aged 60–64 combining benefits with partial employment. The recent termination of the gradual pension will, therefore, have major implications for Swedish older workers (Wadensjö 2002). All other countries, including Denmark, delayed introduction of programs to facilitate gradual transitions from work to retirement. The intended positive effect—to retain older people in the labor force—awaits fulfillment, partly due to the availability of more favorable full exit options and partly due to the unwillingness of employers to accommodate older workers' part-time employment. The German 'block' model shows the complicity of employers, workers, and their representatives in using partial pensions for full early withdrawal from work instead of as the intended measure to retain older workers.

5.1.3 *The Special Preretirement Pathway*

Traditionally, particular occupational groups with particular age-related health risks or work safety concerns were granted special preretirement pensions. Some manual industrial occupations (in particular, miners and steel workers) and some public sector groups (military and police officers) as well as transport workers (seamen, pilots, and train conductors) enjoyed these benefits. Germany, France, Italy, and Japan have such special pension funds that grant earlier retirement for selected occupational groups. In other countries, occupational pension schemes offered by private or public employers provide DB pensions that in some cases also allow early exit (see Chapter 6). Although these favorable conditions were set up to resolve specific concerns, they may also provide opportunities for managing ailing industries and for downsizing public employment.

Special preretirement programs that went beyond single occupational groups have been set up since the mid-1970s in order to relieve the labor market by reducing labor supply and replacing older with younger workers (Mirkin 1987). Although labor reduction was the main aim, they could be justified on social grounds when they assisted older workers who would otherwise become unemployed or were unlikely to find work. Some of these early retirement measures were initially limited to particular industries that were under restructuring pressure.

In 1963, the French state set up a national employment fund (*Fond National pour l'Emploi*, FNE) to distribute special allocations to dismissed workers (aged 60–64) in particular industrially depressed areas, facilitating industrial restructuring, especially in heavy industry. Even though the French state used its first state-sponsored preretirement scheme as part of industrial policy, steering the modernization of French large-scale industry through state–firm agreements, the scheme fell out of use during the 1970s.[7] Only in the early 1980s, after increased redundancy among older workers and escalating use of unemployment benefits, did the French state seek to reintroduce more control (Guillemard 1991). The new special allocation (FNE *allocation spéciale*, FNE–AS) made benefits conditional on agreements between firms and public authorities, requiring a replacement of old workers by younger workers. It provided for the preretirement of redundant workers across all sectors (aged 55/56+), following the example of the FNE's cofinancing of the iron and steel collective restructuring agreement of 1979.[8] During the late 1980s, the FNE–AS scheme granted new benefits to about 50,000 workers per year (Guillemard 1991: 148,

[7] This fund reached its peak around 1969–72 with 14,000 beneficiaries per year (Guillemard 1991: 138, Table 5.4).

[8] As an additional temporary measure older workers (age 55–59) would be able to retire under the new pension age of 60 (beginning in April 1983); a 'solidarity contract' (ACS) scheme was set up in 1982 but closed after 200,000 workers signed up by the end of 1983. The temporary ACS scheme required the replacement of workers with younger unemployed persons (for at least one year), but it covered those that had resigned voluntarily instead of dismissed workers (Guillemard 1991).

Table 5.9). Yet sign-up rates have declined since 1995 as a consequence of state restrictions on the FNE–AS scheme (Jolivet 2002) and the availability of new pathways under the unemployment scheme.

The Italian government introduced preretirement pensions of three years before statutory pension age as early as 1968, but benefits remained insufficient and take-up rates were low. After it was initially closed in 1979, a new *prepensionamento* scheme for redundant industrial workers was reinstituted in 1981 (OECD 1995*a*). Financed by the special unemployment fund, it provided five years of preretirement benefits (men from age 55 and women from age 50; with 15 years of pension contributions) and included contributions to the normal pension scheme. The preretirement scheme was initially planned as a temporary measure but became a structural means to limit the impact of mass dismissal, without having any impact on bringing younger people into work (Gualmini 1998: 137). Over the 1980s, it was extended to steel workers (men at age 50), port workers (at age 52), and employees of the publishing and building sectors, leading to a 'boom' of more than 40,000 new cases per year (1984–8). After firm copayments were introduced in 1989 and further retrenchment measures were implemented, this pathway became less attractive for firms than seniority pensions.

Special state-financed preretirement programs were rather short-lived in the other countries where they were created (the United Kingdom and Germany). Initially no more than a regional experiment under the British Labour government in 1977, the Job Release Scheme (JRS) became an important early retirement pathway, running for twelve years until the Conservative government closed it down after numerous changes (Casey and Laczko 1989; Laczko and Phillipson 1991*b*). While women could draw on public pensions at age 60, older men had to wait until age 65. Within two years, the JRS was extended beyond its limited scope—to areas with high unemployment. Until it was ended in 1989, several stop-and-go measures changed the age limits, conditions and eligible groups; thus only 250,000 workers, mainly lower skilled male industrial workers, received JRS benefits for one or more years during its existence (1977–88).[9]

In Germany, the newly elected conservative-liberal Kohl government introduced a similarly short-lived scheme for preretirement (*Vorruhestand*),

[9] The age limit (64 for men and 59 for women) and duration (one year) were relaxed for disabled male workers (since 1979: 60). It was subsequently lowered for all men to age 63 (1979–80, 1981–4) or age 62 (1979–80, 1982–4), and part-time JRS was also available, but only for a short time (1983–6) (Laczko and Phillipson 1991*b*: 229). It was most popular among un- or semi-skilled manual workers since the allowance was a flat-rate benefit. JRS was concentrated among metal manufacturing and transport workers and employees in public administration (Laczko and Phillipson 1991*b*: 231, Table 7.5).

1984–8. This occurred at a time when the metal workers' union (*IG Metall*) was fighting for the 35-hour week and the government wanted to side with the more moderate unions in favor of reducing lifelong working time (Jacobs, Kohli, and Rein 1991*b*: 208–9). While the two largest unions (metal workers and public sector) were uninterested in pursuing a collective agreement for its implementation, other sectors (such as chemicals and construction) were more willing to negotiate preretirement. The scheme was relatively favorable, paying out about 65 percent of former earnings (plus social insurance contributions) to 200,000 workers, mostly men over 58 years of age. Despite a job replacement rate of about every second redundant job, the scheme was seen as too costly, especially given the knock-on effect on the public preretirement schemes. The program was replaced by the unsuccessful part-time scheme in 1989, which was reformed in 1996 again.

In the Netherlands, the social partners developed a collective scheme for early retirement (*Vervroegde Uittreding*, VUT) in the late 1970s that first financed only one year of the 'bridge' until pension age, but later was extended to five years of preretirement. 'VUT is an example of a scheme that was intended to be temporary but has become semipermanent' (OECD 1995*a*: 185). The trade unions pushed for this more socially acceptable alternative to disability or unemployment benefits, believing that it would open up new opportunities for younger job-seekers. 'Once launched, the growing number of preretirement schemes attracted not only "troubled" blue-collar workers but also more highly educated and better paid employees' (de Vroom and Blomsma 1991: 109). Negotiated and administered at the branch level (including the public sector), VUT benefits were initially financed on a PAYG basis with contributions based on the firm's wage bill.[10] As 'the main instrument to phase out personnel in company reorganizations' (Delsen 2002: 304), one in five older persons (age 60–64) or about 120,000 persons received VUT during the 1990s. Since then, the government and, increasingly, the social partners have sought to transform VUT into a flexible retirement scheme, although this change has to be implemented through a large number of collective agreements (Rein and Turner 2001: 133).

---

[10] A few years after its start in 1976, 80 percent of employees in larger firms were covered by such collective agreements at the branch level (OECD 1995*a*: 182). Although conditions varied from one branch agreement to another (each VUT fund is an independent private foundation), 80 percent of gross pay and joint payment of social insurance contributions was a common practice in the 1990s. Since 1983, VUT schemes (under public law) have also existed in the public sector for full- (at age 60) and part-time exit (at age 59). In the late 1980s, 45 percent of all VUT beneficiaries worked in the public sector.

In 1978, when overall *Danish* unemployment had reached high levels, a voluntary 'preretirement pay' (*efterløn*) was set up on the initiative of trade unions, most importantly the general workers' union (Petersen 1989). Older workers, whether employed or unemployed, with ten years of contribution to the voluntary union-run but state-subsidized unemployment insurance fund could receive preretirement pay from age 60 until public pension at age 67. In line with the relatively generous unemployment benefits in Denmark, during the first half of the period the preretirement benefits were based on 90 percent of gross wages and thereafter on 82 percent gross replacement, while the later basic public pension was unaffected. In the 1980s, the program reached 100,000 recipients or 60 percent of the insured (including the self-employed) in this age group (Petersen 1989: 74). With rising unemployment in the 1990s, a transitional preretirement benefit (*overgangsydelse*) was introduced in 1992 for long-term unemployed persons aged 55–59 and in 1994 for those aged 50–59. By 1999, 180,000 older people were on preretirement pay, of which 30,000 were already receiving preretirement before age 60 (Hansen 2002). Facing a massive early exit wave during the 1990s, the government intervened: Since 1996, the early preretirement program has been phased out and reforms of the *efterløn* scheme in 1999 will limit future early exit via this scheme (Hansen 2002).

In response to an aggravated labor market situation and increased old-age redundancy, special preretirement schemes were largely set up during the late 1970s or early 1980s by the state unilaterally (France, Britain, and Italy) or the state in cooperation with the social partners (Germany, the Netherlands, and Denmark). The schemes were often temporary and were closed down or substantially altered due to changing labor market conditions and cost concerns. The British and German schemes were closed down altogether in 1988, while the French and Italian schemes have become less attractive since the early 1990s. The Danish and Dutch systems' financing was substantially reformed in the late 1990s, when they were transformed into funded schemes. Neither Sweden nor the liberal-residual welfare states (with the exception of Britain) set up special preretirement schemes. When no other pathways were available cyclical redundancies would still lead to unemployment among older workers.

5.1.4 *The Unemployment Pathway*

Unemployment insurance is another major pathway to early exit (Casey and Laczko 1989; Knuth and Kalina 2001). Initially, special policies for older unemployed persons were legitimized as social policy for those with age-related difficulty in finding reemployment in tight labor market situations. Granting special long-term unemployment provisions to older workers would make it a quasi-preretirement scheme and bridging pension until other early retirement or 'normal' pension benefits could be drawn (Guillemard and van Gunsteren 1991). In some cases, older unemployed persons who received preretirement benefits were excluded from unemployment statistics since they were no longer considered to be seeking work. More importantly, governments and social partners saw a means to reduce labor supply in unemployment bridging pensions. Furthermore, when preretirement was made conditional on replacement by young job-seekers or the long-term unemployed, it could be defended as an 'active' employment measure—bringing the younger unemployed into work. In all European countries except the United Kingdom, benefits from unemployment insurance (or, in Italy, restructuring funds) were paid to older workers for at least one year (see Table 5.2). These long-term unemployment benefits for older workers made it possible to bridge the time from dismissal to the normal pension at statutory retirement age.

Unemployment benefits became a major pathway for early exit of private sector workers in France (Guillemard 1991). The unemployment fund (*Union Nationale pour l'Emploi dans l'Industrie et le Commerce*, UNEDIC) was set up by a collective agreement in 1958 and remains under the control of the social partners outside the public social security system (Palier 1997). In 1972, before the onset of mass unemployment, the French social partners agreed to set up a guaranteed-income scheme (*Garantie de ressources licenciement*, GRL) for dismissed workers (above age 60) in the private sector that would not require approval by public authority as the FNE scheme would. The GRL benefits (70 percent of last gross wage) were higher than later pension benefits and old-age pensions after 65 were unaffected. Additionally in 1977, the social partners negotiated a similar scheme (*Garantie de ressources démission*, GRD) for workers who resigned from their jobs voluntarily; GRD was renewed every two years and by 1981 grew to surpass GRL in new enrollments.[11] In order to regain control over early exit, the Socialist government lowered retirement age for all workers (with 37.5 contribution years) from 65 to 60 in 1983 and launched new preretirement state–firm contracts for workers aged below 60 (Guillemard 1991).

---

[11] By 1982, each of the two schemes had a stock of about 200,000 workers aged 60–64 (Guillemard 1991: 138, 148, Tables 5.4 and 5.9).

Table 5.2. The expansion of unemployment pathways

Country	First law	Insurance principle	Major reforms	Benefits duration	No search requirement	Extended benefit duration	Preretirement pension	Replacement rate 1961	Replacement rate 1975	Replacement rate 1995
Germany	1927	State	1969/97	−2 y.	1986: 58+	57+: 3 y.	1959: 60+	0.41	0.40	0.39
Netherlands	1949	State	1986	−2.5 y.		57.5+: 3.5y.; 1975−: 60−64	(1977−: 50+ VUT)	0.03	0.39	0.52
France	1940/67	Collective	1958	−5 y.	56+	1972/77−83: 60+; 1996−: 55+	1962−82: 60+ state 1982−: 55+ state	0.17	0.43	>0.23
Italy	1919/47	State	1988/91	−0.5 y.	(on list)	1969−: CIGS	1969−79: 57/52+; 1983−: 55/50+	>0.14	>0.29	>0.74
Sweden	1934	Voluntary	1997	−1.1 y.		57+: 1.7 y.	1972/76−91: # disability 62/60+	0.03	0.14 #0.77	0.14
Denmark	1907	Voluntary	1970	−2(−5) y.	50+	1992−96: 50−59	1978−: 60−66	0.18	0.35	0.72
United Kingdom	1911	State	1992/95	−0.5 y.	1983: ♂60 / ♀55+			0.22	0.18	0.17
Ireland	1911	State	1993	−1.25y.		65+: 3 y.	1995: 55−66	0.01	0.16	0.24
United States	1935	State		− 0.5 y.				0.02	0.08	0.06
Japan	1947	State	1975/98	− 0.5 y.		45+: 1 y.		>0.04	>0.04	>0.03

Notes: y.: years; # disability pension (Sweden); > retirement age lower than 65, will affect calculations; gross replacement rate (average benefit replacement ratio as percent of former in come).

Sources: For reforms until early 1990s: Mirkin (1987), MISSOC (1998–2003); SSA (1999). For replacement rate: Blöndal and Scarpetta (1998).

Moreover, French workers who are not yet eligible for preretirement can draw on 'normal' long-term unemployment benefits and they do not have to register as job-seekers when they reach age 57 and six months. Since 1987, employers are no longer required to gain public permission for individual or collective dismissals (instead there is a fine for dismissing workers aged 50 and over). Since the mid-1990s, when the state tightened the public FNE schemes, the social partners set up a new 'job substitution allowance' (*Allocation de replacement pour l'emploi*, ARPE) for workers aged 55–60 and further special measures (Jolivet 2002). Policies to induce progressive retirement as an alternative to full exit (most important since 1993: PRP) have not had the hoped-for success. Thus, twice in recent French history, the social partners have taken the lead in early exit when they believed the public program to be insufficient, while the state was incapable of containing early exit from work. Indeed, France is the only country in which early exit has continued to grow until today.

The Dutch unemployment rate, particularly long-term, remains very high among older Dutch workers, and despite improvement in the general labor market situation, it continued to increase in the mid-1990s. Since 1982, the older unemployed have been exempted from job-seeking ('57.5 rule') and thus old-age unemployment also serves to bridge the time before VUT benefits (around age 60) or old-age pensions (age 65) can be drawn (de Vroom and Blomsma 1991).

In addition to the special Danish preretirement scheme financed by unemployment insurance, long-term unemployment benefits (for seven years; since 2000: for four years) are available for workers before age 60. Special rules allowed older workers to extend this period until they could receive preretirement pensions at age 60, thus also functioning as a *pre*-preretirement bridge. In the mid-1990s, before the pre-60 scheme was closed (in 1994), a jobless Danish worker could—at least in theory—combine unemployment benefits and preretirement pay for up to 25 years until public pension began at age 67 (Hansen 2002).

In Germany and Sweden, long-term unemployment insurance was the first of several steps in the preretirement bridge, becoming a common practice in workplace agreements on voluntary dismissal. German preretirement pensions (*Altersruhegeld*) for unemployed persons have provided an alternative exit pathway for jobless older workers (age 60–64) since 1957. Against the government's intentions, this unemployment provision became 'a vehicle for firms to shed their unwanted workers and to externalize the costs of this operation' (Jacobs, Kohli, and Rein 1991*b*: 202). With mass unemployment growing since the late 1970s, firms negotiated workplace agreements to dismiss older workers at age 59 (the so-called '59er' rule). These workers received a year of unemployment benefits, followed by a five-year jobless pension (age 60–64) and topped up by severance pay. Long-term unemployment benefits were extended in several steps during 1985–7 to 32 months; thus the unemployment pathway could begin as early as age 57 and four months. Indeed, Germany is the country with highest level of unemployment among older workers: around 8 percent for male workers aged 55–59 in the late 1980s and above 14 percent in the late 1990s.

Similarly, Sweden's long-term unemployed older workers could, from 1973 till 1991, receive a disability pension (age 60–64) and since 1974 can draw on unemployment benefits for one year and nine months (Øverbye 1997). Using the '58.3' rule, companies and unions agreed on shedding older workers (at age 58 and three months) who could receive first unemployment pay and from age 60 onwards the disability pension for older unemployed (Wadensjö 1991). Until the closing of the age-related disability pension in 1991, this combination of pathways largely helped firms to externalize restructuring costs (Olofsson and Petersson 1994), even though firms usually 'topped up' the lower unemployment benefits to bring them up to the previously received net wage.

Italy's compulsory unemployment insurance for private sector employees is rather meager (30 percent of gross wage) and short in duration (only half a year). This has been counteracted by relatively severe regulation of dismissal first via collective agreement and since 1970 by the 'Labor Statute' (Gualmini 1998). In order to respond to short-term demand crises, a special allowance (*Cassa Integrazione Guadagni Straordinaria*—CIGS) for temporarily underemployed industrial workers was introduced.[12] It became a widespread means to facilitate industrial restructuring without mass dismissal and help industrial unions control seniority rights. Since CIGS benefits were much higher (80 percent of wages) and could last up to five years, 'CIGS became a *de facto* unemployment benefit for workers who had been definitively laid off even if they were still formally employed' (Samek Lodovici 2000*b*: 281). During the economic recession of the early 1990s, coverage was extended beyond industry and construction to the private service sector. Until the 1990s reform, older workers on the 'mobility lists' could receive CIGS benefits until they were entitled to early retirement pensions. These *ammortizatori sociali* ('social shock absorbers')

---

[12] The *Cassa Integrazione Guadagni Straordinaria* (CIGS) or special wage guarantee fund was first introduced as an 'exceptional' measure in 1969, following the example of a similar scheme in construction as early as 1963—it has remained in force ever since (Gualmini 1998).

thus functioned as a bridging pension not unlike the Dutch, German, or Swedish age-related unemployment bridges.

Quite in contrast to the Continental European and Scandinavian welfare states, the Anglo-American liberal and Japanese residual welfare states foreclosed the long-term pathway by providing only low, short-term unemployment benefits (Schömann et al. 2000). In the United Kingdom, the 'job-seeker's allowance' is a flat-rate benefit paid to the unemployed for only half a year before being reviewed (prior to 1995: one year) (Tonge 1997). Thereafter, means-tested social assistance is the only 'fall back' for older jobless workers. The Irish unemployment insurance provides somewhat higher benefits and for a longer duration (15 months or three years from age 65). There is also a (means-tested) preretirement allowance for Irish workers aged 55–64 after unemployment benefits have run out. In the United States, most, but not all, dependent employed have been insured under unemployment insurance since 1935. The relatively meager benefits (about half of gross wages) are unavailable to those resigning voluntarily and in most states they do not last much longer than half a year (in depressed areas: one year) (Hutchens 1999). Japanese unemployment insurance is also only available to dismissed workers; the maximum length for unemployment benefits (60–80 percent of gross wages) paid to workers aged 45–65 is 300 days (210 days for 'short-term' workers) and an extra three months under particular circumstances. In these residual welfare states (with the partial exception of Ireland and Japan), unemployment insurance remains relatively less accommodating to older unemployed workers, requiring employer dismissal and active job search, and providing meager resources for limited durations of time. Nevertheless, unemployment for older workers (age 55–64) was very high in Britain and Ireland from the late 1970s until the mid-1990s, while unemployment among older workers in the United States and Japan was slightly higher but followed the overall business cycle.

Unemployment has increased dramatically for some, but not all, Continental and Scandinavian countries—depending on the particular unemployment pathways used. While the French, Dutch, and Danish social partners (or unions) used special preretirement schemes to manage early exit and reduce employment, the German, Italian, and Swedish social partners relied on public pathways of unemployment (or CIGS) to externalize adaptation costs. Italy and the Netherlands are exceptions, as they have low unemployment rates but high early exit. Italy's low unemployment figures are due to the particularities of CIGS-dismissal-avoidance and the preretirement scheme (both do not count as unemployment), while the decline in the Netherlands is due to the rising importance of VUT as an alternative to the unemployment pathway since the 1980s. While Denmark had higher unemployment rates among older workers than Sweden and increasingly used preretirement pay as an alternative pathway, unemployment among older workers was considerable during the labor market crisis of the 1990s (the unemployment rate among men aged 60–64 was 10 percent in 1995), partly a consequence of the closing of other preretirement options.

Firms and workers have thus often used the unemployment pathway as a bridge to other preretirement programs. When unemployment-bridging pensions that provided good replacement values were available, workers (and workplace representatives) agreed to dismissal or voluntary resignation. Yet in other cases where alternative pathways were lacking, job protection was weak, and employment possibilities were low, dismissal by employers would force workers into unemployment, even if no sufficient long-term benefits were available. The use of the unemployment pathway justifies the decision to count long-term unemployment among older workers as quasi-exit from work due to the use of unemployment as an intended bridging pension or de facto inactivity until pension age.

5.1.5 *The Disability Pathway*

Disability pensions are another pathway (see Table 5.3) that may lead to early exit from work, especially for those older people who, after long working lives, have acquired age-related health problems or impairments and cannot find 'commensurate' employment (Kohli et al. 1991; Wadensjö and Palmer 1996). However, access to the disability pathway is highly contingent on restrictive eligibility criteria and award procedures, regardless of whether solely medical or a combination of social and functioning factors—especially the likelihood of finding employment—are taken into consideration (Aarts, Burkhauser, and de Jong 1996b; Bound and Burkhauser 1999; Reinhard, Kruse, and von Maydell 1998; Prinz 2003). Although the risk of impairment increases with age, disability pension arrangements are commonly not age-related with the exception of labor market considerations for older workers. The decision to apply for disability pensions is voluntary, and individuals are not dependent on employer support as in the case of the dismissal-unemployment or preretirement-replacement pathways.

Take-up rates of disability pensions vary considerably across OECD countries and are highly fluctuating across time (see Table 5.4), suggesting

Table 5.3. The expansion of disability pathways

Country	First law	Major reforms	Labor market criteria	Age	Full or partial disability pension	Replacement rate 1961	1975	1995
Germany	1889	1972, 1984	1969, 1976	–65	Full, 1/2, 1982: 60+	0.48	0.49	0.44
Netherlands	1913	1966, 1997	1967/73/82–87	–65	Full, 2/5–1/4	0.66	0.88	0.70
France	1930	1945	1971–	(see pension)	Assisted, full, 2/3	0.50	0.50	>0.25
Italy	1919	1984	1970–	(see pension)	Full, 2/3	>0.22	0.56	0.06
Sweden	(1913)	1970, 1972	1972–91	–65	Full, 3/4, 1/2, 1/4	0.63	0.77	0.74
Denmark	1921	1984	1977: 50+	1984–: –59, 60+	Full, 2/3, 1/2, 60+	0.24	0.33	0.39
United Kingdom	1911	1994	No	–65/60	Full only	0.31	0.33	0.28
Ireland	1911	1993	No	–66	Full only	0.28	0.25	0.32
United States	1934		No	–65	Full only	0.31	0.39	0.45
Japan	1944		No	–65	Full, partial	>0.06	>0.19	>0.25

Notes: > Retirement age lower than 65, will affect calculations; gross replacement rate (average benefit replacement ratio as percent of former income).

Sources: For reforms: Aarts, Burkhauser, and de Jong (1996a); Kohli et al. (1991); Jespen, Foden, and Hutsebaut (2002); MISSOC (1998–2003); SSA (1999); for replacement rate: Blöndal and Scarpetta (1998).

Table 5.4. Recipients of disability, preretirement, and unemployment benefits

Country		Disability 55–65	Special 55–65	Unemployed 55–65	All 55–65	55–59	60–65
Netherlands	1985	23.3	9.7	5.6	38.5	28.9	48.6
	1990	24.0	12.2	3.1	39.2	30.5	48.7
	1995	23.5	13.3	5.7	42.5	34.1	51.7
France	1985	—	—	—	—	—	—
	1990	—	3.3	6.4	9.7	14.7	4.4
	1995	—	3.5	6.7	10.1	15.6	4.7
Italy	1985	8.1	2.5	—	10.9	17.5	3.9
	1990	5.5	4.8	—	10.3	15.6	4.6
	1995	4.0	11.2	—	15.2	19.9	10.3
Denmark	1985	23.5	15.5	4.2	43.2	23.3	57.5
	1990	24.8	17.6	5.2	47.6	26.4	63.3
	1995	23.5	24.1	7.7	55.3	37.2	70.6
Sweden	1985	22.3	6.0	2.7	31.0	16.9	44.2
	1990	25.7	6.0	1.1	32.8	18.7	46.5
	1995	25.6	6.5	5.0	37.0	24.3	51.5
Britain	1985	9.9	—	5.7	16.9	13.2	24.0
	1990	12.4	—	2.7	15.1	12.0	21.7
	1995	18.6	—	2.6	21.2	18.2	28.0

Notes: Recipients in percentage of age group; excluding normal retirement pensions.

Sources: Own calculations based on SZW (1997).

that differences in institutional contexts are extremely important since such wide variations in health status and impairment are not reasonable (Aarts, Burkhauser, and de Jong 1996*b*). Of particular importance for this exit pathway are: whether disability benefit rules recognize varying degrees of disability or only 'severe' disabilities, whether they provide partial pensions and allow part-time work or require full exit from work, and whether the insurance seeks rehabilitation and reintegration or grants permanent pensions without periodical reconsideration. The disability pathway must be seen in the context of the other alternatives, especially as there may be other more easily accessible exit options, which entail fewer stigmas and provide better benefits. Nevertheless, in some cases, disability will be the only available publicly financed long-term benefit for those workers who cannot find work. Finally, we note that the pull-incentive perspective remains insufficient: High 'disability' pension take-up rates may also be a consequence of push factors such as lacking employment opportunities due to discrimination and insufficient adaptation of workplaces to provide access for and adapt working conditions to people with impairments or disabled persons (Delsen 1996*a*).

In the liberal-residual welfare states, which lack long-term unemployment insurance, disability pensions constitute (with few exceptions) the only public program allowing older workers to receive long-term income support for diminished working capacity in old age (Aarts, Burkhauser, and de Jong 1996a). Applying primarily medical considerations, the British, the Irish, the US, and Japanese disability schemes have traditionally required 'full disability' or set stringent criteria for partial pensions. Since 'the first task of liberal social welfare policy, as such, is to separate out those who are genuinely *unable* to make any productive contribution from those who are merely *unwilling* to do so' (Goodin et al. 1999: 42, italics in original), disability pension benefits are highly targeted by applying strict medical and earnings tests. These countries implemented two schemes: a mandatory disability insurance for the dependent employed, with contribution requirements, and a means-tested disability allowance for those who do not have sufficient insurance coverage. Although these schemes do not consider the impaired or disabled person's chances to find 'commensurate' employment, the number of claims and the acceptance rates for disability awards—based on medical indications—tend to increase in a more aggravated labor market situation (Berkowitz and Burkhauser 1996; Lonsdale and Aylward 1996).

Moreover, the all-or-nothing character of the severe earnings test has made it difficult for those on disability benefits to return to work, especially if their benefits, including health care, are immediately terminated (O'Day and Berkowitz 2001). Disabled people have particular problems finding jobs and remaining employed (Delsen 1996a). Especially during economic downturns and when there is a large pool of job-seekers, employers may discriminate in hiring and firing against people with disabilities, although antidiscrimination laws have been enacted in the United States and the United Kingdom which outlaw such action. Since 1994, the Americans with Disabilities Act guarantees disabled people civil rights and requires firms (with 15 or more employees) to make 'reasonable accommodations' for disabled workers (Berkowitz and Burkhauser 1996). Similarly, the United Kingdom Disability Discrimination Act (1995) strengthens the Disabled Persons (Employment) Act, initially enacted in 1944, which relies on a strategy of integrating disabled people into work using quotas, though these penalties are rarely enforced (Lonsdale and Aylward 1996). Nevertheless, the question remains whether the right-based strategy will be sufficient to foster retention of older disabled workers and to help jobless older workers to overcome both age and disability discrimination.

In contrast, the Scandinavian and Continental European welfare states have been more 'generous' and 'flexible' in their disability pensions (Aarts,

Burkhauser, and de Jong 1996*a*; NOSOSKO 1998). Following a less medical, more social conception of disability, these welfare programs attempt to take into account labor market prospects as they consider whether older workers will be able to obtain 'commensurate' employment with a given 'degree of disability'. These employment considerations were introduced as administrative practices (sometimes advanced by courts) as early as 1967 (and 1973) in the Netherlands, 1969 in Germany, 1970 in Italy and Sweden, and 1971 in France (see Table 5.3).

Sweden has implemented not only a full pension but also partial disability (half and two-thirds) pensions since 1963 (reformed in 1970). They provide higher wage replacement than the flexible old-age pension (with actuarial reduction) and the partial pension, particularly from 1981 to 1987 when the latter was reduced from 65 to 50 percent of gross replacement (Wadensjö 1991). In addition, in 1972, disability preretirement pensions of five years were granted to older long-term unemployed people at age 62. After the change of statutory pension age from 67 to 65 in 1976, the age limit of the disability preretirement pension was lowered to 60 (Wadensjö 1991).[13] The regular disability pension and the pension for unemployed workers became major exit pathways in the 1980s, while partial pensions were cut back.[14] Although the numbers in the unemployment-disability pathway declined to below 4,000 in 1991, the government closed this route to prevent its use in the new labor market crisis, but this led to a further increase in general disability rolls during the early 1990s (Wadensjö and Palmer 1996).

In Denmark, disability insurance (enacted in 1921) also remains a major pathway to early exit from work, especially since social and labor market considerations were introduced for workers above age 55 in 1977, while statutory retirement age remained at 67. Danish disability pensions allow for three degrees of reduced working capacity (full, two-thirds and half) for people aged 18 to 60 and extended by the medium preretirement pension from age 60 until old-age pension (Petersen 1989). With the introduction of social criteria and labor market considerations, two special age-related schemes were enacted.[15] Danish women, in particular, have profited from

---

[13] Throughout the 1970s, new awards for the unemployment disability pension fluctuated around 2,500 or 6 percent of all new disability pension awards. These early exit pensions increased considerably until 1985 when more than 10,000 (or nearly 10 percent) such awards were granted (see Carlsson 1995: 205, Table 3).

[14] Fifteen percent of all Swedes aged 55–59 and 29 percent of those aged 60–64 were on disability pension benefits in 1985, while only a small minority (10 percent) of the 200,000 beneficiaries in the two age groups were on partial (two-thirds, or half) pensions (SZW 1997).

[15] Two age-related disability pensions (*førtidspension*) exist: the general 'anticipatory' pension (age 60–67) and the increased general 'anticipatory' pension (age 50–59). Since 1984 all

anticipatory disability pensions: In 1998, twice as many women as men received the very early (age 50–59) pension and more than three times as many the later (age 60–66) pension (NOSOSKO 2000: 120, Table 7.9). This particularly gendered disability pathway, including not only labor market but also social criteria for older working people, to a large degree explains the relatively high exit rate among women in Denmark, despite the equal age rules in statutory pensions.

Disability insurance in the Netherlands grew to become one of the most noted social expressions of the 1980s: the 'Dutch disease' (Aarts and de Jong 1996a). In 1976, in addition to earnings-related disability insurance for employees in the private sector (civil servants have had a special scheme, the *Algemene Burgelijke Pensionenwet*, ABPW scheme, since 1966), the Dutch left-center government introduced general (flat-rate) disability insurance (*Algemene Arbeidsongeschiktheidswet*, AAW) as a social right to every citizen. Moreover, since 1973 the insurance boards, administered by the social partners, assumed that 'poor employment opportunities result from discriminatory behavior unless the contrary could be proven. The ensuing administrative practice was to treat partially disabled applicants as if they were fully disabled' (Aarts and de Jong 1996a: 26). The improved benefits and relaxed eligibility criteria led to the massive use of the disability pathway for older workers (aged 52 and over) during the late 1970s and early 1980s (Aarts and de Jong 1993). Every third Dutch older man aged 55–64 received a disability pension in the mid-1980s (de Vroom and Blomsma 1991: 103, Table 4.2). Increasingly, the collectively negotiated VUT replaced the disability pathway for redundant male workers, whereas for women who had (re-)entered the labor market, the disability pension became a more important pathway to early retirement—one-third of disability pensioners in the early 1990s were women, compared to one-quarter in the 1980s (Aarts and de Jong 1996a: 43, Table 2.7).

The disability pathway played a much less important role in neighboring Germany because disability pension awards are less favorable and more advantageous alternative routes exist (Frick and Sadowski 1996: 118; Jacobs, Kohli, and Rein 1991b). With the exception of civil servant schemes (Rothenbacher 2004), all disability benefits are part of the employment-related old-age pension system, which initially started as an 'invalidity pension' under Bismarck in 1889 (Eghigian 2000). Two disability pensions were granted to people with at least five contribution

disability schemes are integrated with the old-age and survivor pensions, and payments are based on the same rules. In 1985, 17 percent of Danes aged 55–59 and 29 percent of those aged 60–64 were on disability benefits, quite similar to the Swedish rates (SZW 1997).

years (no general disability pension exists): *Berufsunfähigkeit* (incapacity to pursue one's occupation) and *Erwerbsunfähigkeit* (incapacity to work). While initially both disability pensions were awarded strictly on medical grounds, court decisions in 1969 and 1976 granted those who were 'partially disabled' a full pension if there was no part-time work available, thereby introducing labor market considerations into eligibility criteria (Jacobs, Kohli, and Rein 1991*b*: 188). This change led to an increase in disability pensions, especially for older workers who could not receive any other pension benefits. A 1972 reform introduced a new pension for 'severely handicapped' people aged 62 and over, which remained relatively unimportant until the age limit was lowered to 60, in 1981.[16] Another change in 1985, excluding those without a recent work history, led to a major shift from disability to 'normal' pensions, but due to the fact that most of the affected persons were housewives, this change had only a minor impact on early exit from work. Disability pensions remained an important pathway in the 1990s, particularly for German men (more than every fourth man claimed a disability pension); nevertheless, since the year 2000 occupational incapacity pensions are being phased out and replaced by a less generous disability pension.

Disability pensions assumed some importance in Italy, particularly before the 1984 retrenchment (Ascoli 1988). Compared to low unemployment benefits, Italian disability pensions are higher and either renewable (twice for three-year terms) or last until retirement age (given twelve years of prior contributions). Particularly in the South, these pensions became a quasi-unemployment benefit as part of clientelistic practices, especially after local labor market considerations were introduced in 1970. A less stringent criterion of white-collar disability (one-half), introduced in 1939, was extended to blue-collar workers in 1971, but after rapid increase of awards the more stringent criteria (two-thirds) was applied to all groups in 1984 (Ascoli 1988). After another boost in disability pensions in the 1990s, retrenchment reforms in 1995 led to reductions in take-up (Hohnerlein 1998).

The labor market criterion, initially introduced as a social right, has provided for an important (sometimes unintended) pathway to early exit. With the exception of British women who have early state pensions (age 60+), disability rates were higher for older workers than for younger

[16] In the early 1980s, every third German male pensioner received one of the three types of disability pensions (only 15 percent waited until age 65 to receive the statutory pension), while nearly every second woman received a disability pension (less than 20 percent received a 'normal' pension) in 1985 (VDR 2002).

ones, in countries with more generous eligibility criteria, especially in Sweden, less so in Denmark, Italy, and Germany (Aarts, Burkhauser, and de Jong 1996b). There are also marked gender differences across countries in how disability benefits are drawn reflecting differences in roles and attitudes: Older men and women in Sweden exhibit the same take-up rates, German women were more likely to receive such pensions before 1985 but this has changed, British and American men are more likely to draw benefits than women, and the practice has been more widespread among Dutch and Danish women than men since the 1980s. In contrast to the pull-incentive thesis, increasing or high take-up rates are not necessarily indicative of a disincentive to work effect, as is often implied by looking solely at generosity of benefits (Gruber and Wise 1999b). Indeed, push factors, such as individual health impairment, discrimination in hiring and firing, and insufficient adaptation of workplaces, have also contributed significantly to this trend toward full (or partial) early exit from work (Kuptsch and Zeitzer 2001).

5.2 The Institutionalization of Early Exit Regimes

Thus far, I have analyzed cross-national variations for each of the multiple (semi-)public pathways of early exit from work; now, I will switch perspectives to analyze the evolution of early exit *regimes*. Myriad claims have been made in analyses of early retirement. One macro-level pull thesis emphasizes the 'collusion' of unions and governments to reduce labor supply in Continental European welfare states facing mass unemployment (Esping-Andersen 1996c; Esping-Andersen and Sonnberger 1991). Other micro-level push theses focus on early retirement as serving individual firms' interests to restructure in a socially acceptable way and to externalize the ensuing costs onto the public (Naschold and de Vroom 1994; Rosenow and Naschold 1994). Quite in contrast are pull interpretations of early retirement as a consequence of social rights extensions, the spread of the social norms of early retirement as part of the generational contract in a 'moral economy' (Kohli 1987).

In the remainder of this chapter, I thus ask whether these exit pathways were *explicitly* set up for the purpose of labor shedding: Did they serve primarily the interests of firms or were they actually unintended consequences of social policies for older workers? The comparison of available pathways has already shown that not all programs were tailored to early exit from work. Indeed, while some were explicit 'early retirement' programs, other followed non-age-related rules and emanated from more general policies. We need to look more closely at the timing and rationale for this increasing diversity of early exit opportunities as well as their—sometimes vastly—increased use. Finally, I review the major cross-national differences to sort out which welfare regimes are particularly prone to provide certain early exit pathways. This step enables us to reevaluate the pull-protection thesis: Do welfare states with more open exit pathways foster early exit from work?

5.2.1 *The Unintended Consequences of Past Reforms*

Even before the onset of mass unemployment, several reforms of social policy had provided opportunities to retire at an age earlier than 65. Lowering the statutory retirement age was not initially a policy to promote labor shedding, but rather one motivated by social or paternalist welfare concerns, such as the special treatment of occupational groups with particular health risks or for women generally. Often, women were granted earlier pensions in order that they could retire at about the same time as their, presumably, older husbands. Germany, Italy, the United Kingdom, and Japan as well as Denmark before the 1970s and France before 1982 had such policies. With rising labor force participation of older women beginning in the late 1960s, the (unanticipated) effect of such policies was a massive increase in early exit from work among women.

With the welfare-state expansion in the late 1960s, new social reforms were initiated, responding to labor movement demands and following large electoral support (Korpi 1983; Stephens 1979). Until the mid-1970s, most government policies grew out of extending social rights. They were intended neither to appease labor during ongoing restructuring nor as labor-shedding policies to alleviate labor market difficulties. Largely due to social concerns, the French, German, and Italian governments granted earlier exit to (manual) workers who had long working histories, benefiting those cohorts that had lived as adults during the Second World War. Even when governments did respond to union demands, such as in the German 1972 pension reform, these were largely seen as *social rights*—not as labor-shedding strategies.

In particular, the opening up of the *disability* pathway through introduction of labor market or social eligibility criteria resulted from administrative decisions or court-made changes and was motivated by social concerns about the plight of older unemployed persons with limited working 'capacity' (Guillemard and van Gunsteren 1991). When labor market criteria were introduced in disability insurance, this had happened largely before the onset of mass unemployment in the late 1970s (see Table 5.4). The extension of disabled people's social rights led to the *unintended* consequence of increasing early exit from work during labor market turmoil and rationalization of production following the first oil shock (1973). Resulting rises in unemployment reduced the probability that older workers with chronic illnesses or impairments would find employment—due to *double* discrimination, against age *and* disability. In countries where other early exit pathways are limited or disability pensions are the only public long-term program, we see cyclical trends of increased disability applications, even when decisions exclude a labor market consideration. In countries that do have a labor market consideration and suffer high unemployment rates, disability pensions for older workers have become more widespread, particularly among those persons with 'partial disability' who have been less likely to find part-time work. The interaction of the expansion of social rights and labor market criteria thus led to the unexpected rise.

We might expect the *unemployment* pathway to be the most likely area for explicit labor reduction strategies pursued by governments and unions. Nevertheless, its beginnings are found in smoothing the processes of restructuring due to ongoing deindustrialization. The Italian redundancy scheme (1969) and the French preretirement benefits for dismissed workers (1972) were set up to help firms restructure and appease labor at times of 'resurgence of class conflict' (Crouch and Pizzorno 1978). Early retirement options for dismissed or unemployed older workers were also a part of the *political exchange* (Pizzorno 1978) of neo-corporatist income policies. Preretirement benefits were part of deferred 'social wages' in return for wage moderation under conditions of rising inflation (Lange 1984). Thus, long before the onset of mass unemployment in the mid-1970s, preretirement options were already being granted—the first step toward early exit from work had already been taken.

Although reforms of seniority pensions, disability benefits, and unemployment compensation predated the oil shock of 1973 in some countries, the opening up of such pathways enabled later massive exit from work when competition and labor market disequilibria increased pressure on firms to shed labor. In contrast to functionalist accounts, the origins of many exit pathways were not necessarily driven by the rationales that their later use during mass unemployment suggests. In fact, they were often the *unintended consequences* of policies devised for very different purposes. Nevertheless, social actors fostered their subsequent development and use, while government interventions failed to effectively reverse early exit during the ensuing mass unemployment period. The 'collusion' thesis cannot account for developments before 1973, and it would need to prove that in the subsequent evolution of pension policies, the social partners and government deliberately added further steps to foster early exit or were unwilling to reverse its course since it unexpectedly now served their interests.

5.2.2 Muddling through Rising Mass Unemployment

The oil price shocks of 1973 and 1979 led to major economic downturns and high unemployment waves in the late 1970s and early 1980s (Scharpf 2000). Adverse labor market conditions not only brought the end of full employment but they also led to high unemployment and dismissal rates among older workers. According to the labor reduction thesis, governments and social partners 'colluded' in utilizing early retirement options as a foil to make mass dismissals more socially acceptable and simultaneously reducing labor supply and creating job opportunities for younger job-seekers (Esping-Andersen 1996c; von Rhein-Kress 1993). But even during the turbulent late 1970s, governments and social partners pursued ad hoc policymaking. They used 'bricolage' (or tinkering) with available 'repertoires' of action (Guillemard and van Gunsteren 1991). Importantly, their expectations that the crisis was cyclical and not structural led them to see special preretirement options as merely temporary measures.

Unintentionally opened and hastily widened, the available pathways led to surging early exit from work during the late 1970s. Between 1970 and 1985, early exit from work among older men aged 60–64 increased on average by around 8 percent annually in Germany, France, and the Netherlands. By 1985, more than 60 percent of male and female workers aged 60–64 had left the workforce in these three Continental European countries, while in Italy participation rates had been relatively low even before the 1970s. Despite relatively similar exit rates in the early 1970s, these ten countries weathered the economic problems of the 1970s and 1980s very differently. While the Continental European countries showed rapidly increasing early exit, the other countries experienced more gradual and cyclical increases. Two exceptions were Denmark and the United Kingdom, which both witnessed medium to high levels of early exit for men in the 1980s and especially for women ever since. Partly these exit patterns resulted from unintended consequences of the different welfare regimes, which were institutionalized prior to the mid-1970s. Certainly tacit collusion between governments and social partners also promoted increasing use of existing pathways, added new exit options or simply produced leniency toward their diverse negative effects.

During the first five to ten years of the mass unemployment crisis, various past and new pathways were increasingly trodden, but all directions facilitated growth in earlier exit from work. Particularly the Continental European welfare states expanded their exit options, in terms of individual life courses and in retirement policies. In Germany, the seniority pension at age 63, the unemployment pathway (age 59+), and the 'severe disability' pension (since 1981 at age 60) became the main new pathways for older men in addition to the preexisting general disability pension; for women, the general disability pension (age-independent) and the early pension at age 60 were used for early retirement (Jacobs, Kohli, and Rein 1991*b*). In the Netherlands, the welfare pathways—disability, unemployment benefits, and civil servants' preretirement—were the main avenues for early exit from work (de Vroom and Blomsma 1991). In France, the two preretirement benefits for the unemployed were the main pathways that had been opened by the social partners, not by the government (Guillemard 1991). In Italy, the disability pension and redundancy allowance schemes were the pathways to preretirement added to the already low retirement age for employees (OECD 1995*a*).

In all four Continental European countries, planned government action did not take the lead in developing this policy field. Already existing programs had built-in accelerators but no brakes, most prominently demonstrated in the labor market considerations institutionalized in disability pension rules before the mid-1970s. Unemployment compensation schemes—initially devised as social policies for the older unemployed workers (Germany since 1959 and Sweden since 1972) or as facilitators for redundant workers due to economic restructuring (France and Italy)—also became a major force in early exit. The social partners in both France and Italy pushed for these redundancy programs before mass unemployment became persistent during the 1980s. Similarly, the Swedish government's decision to lower the retirement age to 65 in 1976 only followed the precedent set by collective bargaining, while in Denmark the union-run unemployment schemes promoted early retirement beginning in the late 1970s.

5.2.3 *Putting on the Brakes without Slowing Down*

Following the second oil price shock in the late 1970s and periods of mass unemployment, increasing use was made of available pathways for early exit from work. By and large, governments abstained from intervening, at least initially. The social partners defended passive labor reduction policies, claiming that it was better to retire older workers early than dismiss young or prime-aged workers. By the early 1980s, governments in all countries, increasingly worried about the rising costs, began seeking means of shifting these considerable costs onto the firms (Casey 1989), and tried to regain control over the exit process (Guillemard and van Gunsteren 1991). In fact, some of the new, explicit 'preretirement' policies attempted to steer and fine-tune the labor reduction process by altering incentive structures and enforcing job replacement conditions. However, all these attempts at directing the tide of early exit ran into major problems.

Continental European welfare states, which had the highest level of early retirement already during the 1980s, faced the most acute pressure to react. In France, the new Socialist government sought to short-cut the social partners' costly unemployment pathway by granting less generous pensions at age 60 and by introducing state–firm 'solidarity' contracts that required the replacement of older workers with younger ones (Guillemard 1991). The German Conservative-Liberal government set up a preretirement scheme (1984–8) to shift costs onto employers and foster job replacement, though with limited success (Jacobs, Kohli, and Rein 1991b). The Dutch government attempted to restrict access to old-age unemployment benefits and particularly to disability pensions (1985–7), but this led the social partners to extend the scope of their sectorwide VUT preretirement schemes (de Vroom and Blomsma 1991). And in Italy, the disability scheme's exploding costs and widespread clientelist misuse led to its major reform (1984), though this led to other pathways (Ascoli 1988). Hence, state-induced early welfare retrenchment (or regulation at least) of early exit was largely unsuccessful and merely led to cost shifting and pathway substitution (Casey 1989), not to a decline in early exit from work.

The Continental European countries were indeed the most prone to labor shedding (Esping-Andersen 1996c). However, that two other countries—Britain and Denmark—followed closely behind them in the 1980s is often overlooked. Early exit from work among British and Danish women was remarkably high, which had repercussions for old-age activity rates, since women increasingly worked prior to retirement. While women could retire at age 60 in the United Kingdom, older British men were increasingly affected by unemployment during the 1980s. The Job Release Scheme, introduced by Labour in 1977, provided 5 percent of British men aged 60–64 with a preretirement pension in the mid-1980s. In the late 1980s, the British Conservatives closed down JRS and started to cut back welfare provisions, and indeed early exit from work declined for older men. In Denmark, it was union-administered preretirement pay that in 1978 provided an early exit pathway for older workers, particularly the less skilled. Disability pensions provided an additional pathway for older, especially female Danes, particularly after social criteria were introduced. Only after another major boost in early exit in the mid-1990s did the Danish government begin to reform early retirement policies and close down temporary programs that had provided preretirement even before age 60.

The other four countries had relatively lower levels of old-age unemployment and early exit from work, only gradually and cyclically increasing during economically rather difficult years. In the Swedish universalist welfare state, the combination of disability pension for unemployed older workers and the long-term unemployment benefit allowed early exit before age 59, but partial pension also helped keep older workers in (part-time) employment (Wadensjö 1991). The financial and employment crisis of the early 1990s forced the government to reduce unemployment disability pensions and phase out partial pensions; thus the Swedish model of work integration and partial pensions has come under increased pressure (Casey and Bruche 1983; Esping-Andersen and Sonnberger 1991).

In Europe, early retirement has been lowest in Ireland, given fewer preretirement options, the still largely agrarian workforce, and the relatively young population. Nevertheless, until the recent boom, mass unemployment and poverty among older workers were considerably higher than in other liberal countries (O'Loughlin 1999). Rather limited resources available from public programs provided no major pull for early exit from work, though those who were forced out of work faced high risk of poverty due to insufficient occupational pensions and employer window plans (Hughes and Nolan 1996).

Early exit from work increased during the 1970s and 1980s in the United States to a level even slightly above Sweden, though considerably lower than in Britain. Disability insurance with strict medical criteria and flexible pensions (aged 62–64) with actuarial reduction were the only public pathways, but even these led to an increase in early retirement. In particular, the flexible pensions grew even faster as many white-collar and blue-collar workers could complement the reduced public benefits with savings from their private pensions or employer-provided plans (Sheppard 1991: 267, Table 8.11).

Finally, Japan had the lowest rate of early exit from work, while larger Japanese companies were able to shed older workers using mandatory retirement rules (Kimura et al. 1994). Initially, the mandatory age at which firms could enforce retirement was 55. Later, the government pressed employers to raise the age to 60, while it promised to increase the public pension age in the future (Kimura and Oka 2001). The older workers in larger firms could draw on lump sum severance pay and occupational pensions (Kimura 1997). Many employees were also offered reemployment at lower pay by their former employer or were sent by 'secondment' to smaller suppliers (Kimura et al. 1994). When reemployment or unemployment benefits were not available, earnings-related and reduced basic pensions were the only social transfers available (Kii 1991). The situation was much more difficult for older women than for tenured blue-collar or white-collar men working in large companies, reflecting Japan's gender-segmented labor market (Brinton 1998).

5.2.4 Early Exit Regimes at Their Peak

By the mid-1980s, early exit trends had peaked in most countries. Different early exit regimes emerged that reflect considerable cross-national differences in the availability of early exit pathways (see Table 5.5). The combination of multiple pathways—whether explicitly intended for early exit or not—shapes the overall pull toward early exit from work. The Continental European welfare states provide the most generous and largest set of preretirement options, though there are intra-regime differences. Most importantly, the French and Italian public pension schemes provide relatively early pension benefits for older workers (at age 60 or even earlier) and except for disability pensions provide relatively open exit pathways. The German system granted some early 'normal' pensions (largely to women aged 60 with few working years), while the Dutch basic pensions are paid out only from age 65. Although all Continental European welfare states have had high levels of early exit from work since the late 1970s, the Latin welfare states show particularly high early exit rates (before age 60) in comparison with Germany and the Netherlands; this is also reflected in the index of pathway availability (see Table 5.7).

These regime-specific differences in the timing of early exit manifest themselves also in studies on *hazard rates* (Blöndal and Scarpetta 1998; Gruber and Wise 1999b), which measure the likelihood of exit from work at a given age. Such life course analyses indicate the variable impact of institutionalized public pathways on the timing of exit from work. For instance, French public pension rules induce two peaks in exit from work (Blanchet and Pelé 1999): for those with sufficient contributions at age 60 and for the others at 65. Italian public programs do not regulate the timing

Table 5.5. Overview of pathways to early exit from work

	Statutory pension	Flexible pension	Special schemes	Unemployment benefits	Disability pensions
Germany	1957–:65 (♀ 60)	1972–: 63 (35 y.)	1984–88: 58+ 1992: East, part-time	59/57–60, plus 60+ pension	1969 # 60+: severe disability
Netherlands	65		1976–: VUT 60+ (1983–: public sector)	1982–: 57.5+ (social plans)	1967/73 # contributory; 1976: AAW 52+
France	1983: 65–>60		1980/82–: 55+	1972–83: 60+, 1996–: 55+	1971 #: 60+
Italy	♂ 60 (s.e.: 65) ♀ 55 (s.e.: 60)	50+ (35 y.) (20 y. public sector)	1968–79: 3 y.; 1981–: 5y.	1969–: CIGS	1970 #
Denmark	1970–: 67	Partial 60+	1978: 60+; 1992/94–96: 55+/50+	7 y., 1996–: 4 y.	1977–: # (♀ social) 1984–: –59/60–
Sweden	1976: 67–>65	Partial 60+		58.3–60	1970– #; 1972–91: 60+ (unemployed)
Ireland	66	65 (means-tested)	(55–65)	–1¼ y.; 65+ 3 y.	(medical/means-tested)
United Kingdom	♂ 65 ♀ 60	(private OP: 60+)	1977–89: JRS	–½ y.	(medical/means-tested)
United States	65	Flex: 62–64 (private OP)		–½ y.	(medical/means-tested)
Japan	Basic PP: 65 (flex.: 60–64)	Earnings-related: ♂60, ♀55		45+: 1 y.	(medical/means-tested)

Notes: Opportunities for early exit: #: with labor market consideration; ♂ men; ♀ women; y.: years; PP: public pension; OP: occupational pension; flex.: flexible pension; s.e.: self-employed.

Sources: See Tables 5.1–5.3.

as much as in other countries (Brugiavini 1999). The largest spikes in early exit occur at age 65 for men and 60 for women, that is, the statutory retirement age for self-employed persons in Italy. However, the likelihood to retire is already high from age 50 onwards and increases over time until age 65. In particular, dependent employees enjoy a pension age five years earlier or they may be able to draw on a seniority rule that is not age-specific. The German pension rules induce several exit points which also show in peaks of yearly hazard rates (Börsch-Supan and Schnabel 1999): for men at age 65 (statutory pension), at age 63 (seniority pension), and to a lesser degree at age 60 (unemployment pension); for women it is at age 60 (early pension) and also at age 65 (statutory pension) with high exit in between. According to the yearly data, Dutch men and women tend to either leave at age 65 or retire early during the time window from age 55 to 65 with an increasing tendency toward ever earlier exit for both men and women (Kapteyn and de Vos 1999).

The two 'outlier' countries, Denmark and Britain, only partially follow the patterns of the Scandinavian universalist and Anglo-American liberal models, respectively (see Table 5.6). Denmark provides multiple pathways (5–6 index points for men and 6–7 for women depending on the period) unlike Sweden, which provided mainly the disability–unemployment pathway until the early 1990s (see Table 5.7). In the Danish case, preretirement pay, in particular, turned out to be a major exit route, as did disabil-

Table 5.6. Index of pathways ranked by exit opportunities

	Statutory pension	Flexible pension	Special scheme	Unemployment	Disability	Index of pathways	Exit trend
Italy	***	**	**	**	* {**}	10 {12}	Early, high
France	***		***	**	*	9	Early, high
Germany	* ♀ **	**	{**}	**	**	7 {9} ♀ 8	High
Netherlands			***	**	***	8	High
Denmark		*		** {***}	** ♀ ***	5 {6} ♀ 6 {7}	♂ Mod. ♀ High
United Kingdom	♀ ***	**	{♂**}		*	♂ 3{5} ♀ 6	♂ Mod. ♀ High
Sweden		*		*	* {**}	3 {5}	Moderate
United States	**				*	3	Moderate
Ireland		*		*	*	3	Low
Japan	**		*		*	3	Low

Notes: Opportunities for early exit (see Table 5.5 for details): Index of pathways: *** major pathway (3 points); ** conditional pathway (dismissal, unemployment, disability) (2 points); * limited pathway (means-tested, medical-test only, partial pension, actuarial reduction) (1 point); {} before policy reversal; exit trend for men (♂) and women (♀) (see Table 4.8).

Table 5.7 Three worlds of welfare regimes and early exit patterns

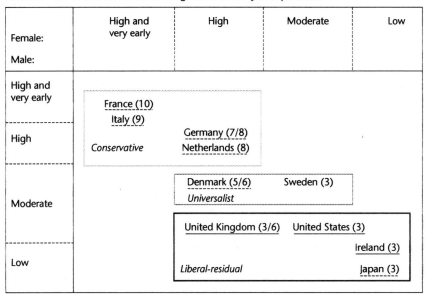

Female: Male:	High and very early	High	Moderate	Low
High and very early --- High	France (10) Italy (9) *Conservative*	Germany (7/8) Netherlands (8)		
Moderate		Denmark (5/6) *Universalist*	Sweden (3)	
--- Low		United Kingdom (3/6) *Liberal-residual*	United States (3) 	Ireland (3) Japan (3)

Notes: ( ): Index of pathways (see Table 5.6); see Table 4.8 for exit trends; welfare regimes in italics.

ity pensions, especially for women. The life course analyses confirm the intra-Scandinavian difference (Gruber and Wise 1999*b*): while Sweden shows relatively late exit and limited early exit for both men and women, Denmark's pattern resembles that of Continental Europe, despite the official retirement age of 67. Early exit for both men and women around age 60 became increasingly important during the 1990s. Sweden has, thus far, relied on part-time work and partial benefits (Palme and Svensson 1999), increasing the share of older working men who combine income from work with pension benefits.

In Britain during the 1980s, early retirement was common for men due to high unemployment, the JRS, and employer policies, but it is no longer common before age 65. Due to an earlier standard retirement age, British women do retire earlier than men (Blundell and Johnson 1999). However, insufficient means lead many to continue working, often part-time up to age 65. Indeed, an increasing share of older working men combine work and public or private pension benefits (OECD 2001*a*: 36). In respect to availability of pathways, British women have more opportunities to retire early than men (not least because of the earlier normal pension age), yet the available pathways have been larger for men during the 1980s (see

Table 5.6). In comparison, Ireland has fever institutionalized pathways than Britain (see Table 5.7). During the 1990s, old-age unemployment before 65 was common for Irish men, while for Irish women 65 was the 'norm' (Blöndal and Scarpetta 1998). Thus relatively similar welfare states, not only Denmark and Sweden but also the United Kingdom and Ireland, show significant intra-regime differences in early retirement pathways and actual exit from work patterns, at least with respect to particular time windows and gender variations. These differences are not merely the outcome of dissimilar government policies, but also the consequence of different strategies by the social partners and variations in the production regimes.

Finally, the United States and Japan are two welfare regimes with a liberal-residual orientation that allow companies significant scope in determining occupational welfare (Rein 1996; Rein and Wadensjö 1997b; Shinkawa and Pempel 1996). Both provide limited access to disability and unemployment benefits. In addition, pensions can be drawn earlier but these are insufficient, requiring additional occupational benefits. Moreover, in both countries, employers have used mandatory retirement rules in the past (Kimura et al. 1994; Lazear 1979). However, there are still marked differences in employment rates between both countries that reflect very different employer strategies and particular private–public mixes: American workers may be induced to retire early through employer-provided plans or may be let go through general downsizing, while Japanese employers provide reemployment opportunities for their 'retired' workers (see Chapter 6). The United States has less-developed public pathways and leaves a larger role for private pathways (see Table 5.6). Annual exit data show that for American men, the risk of retiring early increases with age until flexible retirement (age 62) and 'normal' retirement (age 65); for women, it increases similarly but with no particular spike at flexible retirement age due to lack of employer-induced plans (Diamond and Gruber 1999). In Japan, early retirement increases slowly up to age 60, when some Japanese men exit, but most continue working until after 65 (Yashiro and Oshio 1999). Early exit among Japanese women is even less clearly regulated. Japan and the United States are also the two countries in which older workers (aged 60–69) tend to combine work and some form of public or private pension benefits (Gruber and Wise 1999b; OECD 2001a: 36). Together with Ireland, the United States and Japan rank lowest on the index of pathway availability (see Table 5.7), and indeed range also among the countries with the lowest or medium level of early exit.

5.3 Is Early Retirement an (Un)intended Consequence?

We learn two main lessons from this comparative-historical analysis of the evolution of early retirement. First, to a large degree, early exit regimes derived from long-term *unintended consequences* of prior decisions that opened up several alternative pathways. Because many of the key decisions were taken before the mid-1970s and motivated by social concerns, early exit from work was initially less a deliberate strategy to reduce labor supply than a 'byproduct' of those other social concerns. Thus, functionalist explanations that account for the existence of multiple and generous pathways, particularly in Continental Europe, solely as an intended, passive labor market policy (Esping-Andersen 1996c), reverse the actual historical sequence. Nevertheless, deteriorating labor market situations due to technological changes and increased competition pressured firms to restructure and the available exit pathways did help to shed labor in a socially acceptable way (Naschold, de Vroom, and Casey 1994). In fact, as I argue in the next chapter, it is the 'collusion' between the social partners in response to the existing production regime and following the dynamic of the established labor relations that proves central to explaining the *use* by workplace actors of available early exit options.

Second, when governments finally intervened in early retirement policies, they aimed to regulate the process, though they initially failed to stem the tide. While explicit early exit measures, such as Germany's *Vorruhestand* or the British JRS, did not endure, problems associated with early exit from work continued. As I argue later (see Chapter 7), government efforts to reverse these trends toward early exit have proven very difficult given the multitude of alternative pathways and the need to bring the social partners into reform coalitions in both policymaking and implementation. Yet problem loads, reform capacities, and alternatives vary across welfare regimes.

Comparing the existing pathways, we find that some welfare states are much more prone to early exit than others (see Table 5.7). Continental European welfare regimes in particular provided a large set of early exit opportunities. These *conservative* welfare regimes have inbuilt amplifiers: Occupationally fragmented earnings-related social insurance schemes and the social partners' extensive involvement in their administration provide ample leverage for widening these exit pathways. Major examples include the French social partners' use of the unemployment bridge in the 1970s and again in the 1990s; the Dutch social partners' VUT retirement schemes responding to state cutbacks; the German employers' use of unemployment bridges and, more recently, collective bargaining on partial pensions; and the Italian unions' clientelist grip on both disability and redundancy schemes.

In the Scandinavian *universalist* welfare states, we observe that the social partners' influence also affects Danish early retirement pathways, but such initiatives were not common in Sweden with the exception of the 'occupational preretirement' pensions (age 65–66) that were replaced by the earlier state pension of age 65 in 1976. In comparison to Continental European high exit regimes, Sweden's (and partially Denmark's) utilization of partial pensions and more integrative policies stands out, though the success of these policies depended on the overall employment strategy (Jochem 1998). At a time when unemployment increased, Sweden was able to close down several pathways, while the Continental European welfare states and Denmark encountered much more resistance, though they have also begun to change course.

For the *liberal-residual* welfare states, I indicated the importance of the public–private pension mix and the role of employer policies; both issues are discussed in Chapter 6. Given the few publicly available pathways, the liberal-residual welfare states have much fewer incentives for early retirement. In fact, it is not so much the *pull* factors of public welfare programs but the *push* factors of employer-sponsored early retirement plans, financial market-driven downsizing pressure, and voluntarist labor relations that shape the timing and scope of early exit from work. The Japanese welfare regime, while sharing some similarities with the American liberal-residual and corporate welfare model, is very different in its production regime (Soskice 1999; Streeck 2001) and thus in public–private welfare interface (Estevez-Abe 2001; Jackson and Vitols 2001). The exceptionally low early exit rate for Japanese workers may be explained by the limited public pathways, but it remains a puzzle how such high activity levels for older workers could be maintained given that Japanese firms enforce mandatory retirement at age 60. The following chapter will look more closely at economic push factors, the strategies of companies and the role of the social partners in mediating pull and push toward early exit from work.

Chapter 6

The Production-Push Factors: The Political Economy of Labor Shedding

Explanations of early exit from work as solely induced by the incentive-pull of public social policies are insufficient. The production-related *push* factors must also be taken into account. Seen from the pull perspective, private preretirement pathways provided by the social partners or employers seem to be an incentive for older workers to retire early. However, viewed from the push perspective, employers have production-related interests in fostering early exit from work and are thus willing to (co)finance such benefits. In addition, production-related push factors can lead to early exit independent of the pull by generous pathways, for example when employers dismiss or simply do not hire older workers for efficiency concerns or due to age discrimination. As this chapter argues, early exit is no longer as aggregate of older workers' individual choices based on available public pathways; instead it is conditional on policies and interventions by the social partners at national level as well as by employers and workplace representatives at workplace level.

In this chapter, I first look at the employer-sponsored or collectively negotiated occupational pensions and their potential use as early exit pathways. Particularly in liberal-residual welfare states, where public pathways are limited, employers have set up voluntary occupational pensions and, at times, special early exit plans. However, not all workers are covered and firms have increasingly chosen to disengage from self-sponsored preretirement options. In Continental and Nordic welfare states with generous public pathways, employers have found fewer reasons to set up their own occupational pensions. However, in some cases, labor unions have pushed for collectively negotiated supplementary pensions or special preretirement schemes, especially when the state cut back on public preretirement options. Thus, the role of employer-sponsored or collectively negotiated preretirement pathways is highly contingent on employers or social partners' interests in complementing the public exit pathways with private ones.

This chapter thus adopts the *push* perspective in asking: Why has labor demand for older workers declined and why do employers and worker representatives 'collude' in shedding older workers? In a first step, we review some of the structural pull factors that affect labor demand: (*a*) the decline of the industrial sector and the growth to limits of the sheltered public sector; (*b*) the age-related skill profiles and sectoral early exit patterns; (*c*) the impact of cyclical and mass unemployment on early exit from work; and (*d*) the impact of labor shedding on overall, youth, and female employment growth. These sectoral push factors explain only part of the long-term trend toward early exit and largely fail to account for cross-national variations. Therefore, we need to go beyond a macro-economic push perspective and investigate more closely whether firms and social partners play a role in promoting early exit from work across Europe, Japan, and the United States.

Finally, I turn to the institutional push factors and adopt a comparative political economy perspective, drawing on the variations in labor relations and the varieties of capitalism. I first look at the variations between union movements in organizational structures and institutionalized power in the bargaining and workplace arenas. To what degree have union movements been strong enough to push for early exit policies and defend seniority rights? Moreover, the economic reasons to shed labor vary depending on the production system. I show that variations in production systems can also be linked to particular corporate governance and finance regimes. Although there are important intra-national variations, LMEs tend toward market-driven cyclical and individualized early exit, while CMEs induce more institutionalized early exit with a strong externalization tendency. However, the Japanese and Swedish firms differ from other CME firms in the ways in which they have been able to retain older workers in activity and partially internalize the resulting costs. The concluding section reviews the institutional affinities between protection, production, and partnership in explaining the specific push toward labor shedding of older workers.

6.1 Production-Related Pull Factors

6.1.1 *Private Occupational Pensions between Pull and Push*

Public early exit pathways are not the only pull factors providing incentives for older workers to stop working and retire early. Private occupational pensions provided by employers or the social partners also play an

important role in workers' retirement decisions and firms' personnel policies. Although they are protection-related *pull* factors for older workers,
these private or collective early exit pathways originate in production-
related *push* factors, i.e. the particular personnel strategies of firms.

Given the more limited first-tier public pensions typical of liberal-
residual welfare states, second-tier employer-provided occupational pensions have had more space to develop in Britain, Ireland, the United States,
and Japan (Goodin and Rein 2001; Rein 1996). To the degree that univer-
salistic or conservative European welfare states developed generous basic
pensions and/or earnings-related social insurance, occupational pensions
assumed a less important role after World War II (Esping-Andersen 1996*a*;
Kangas and Palme 1992). However, collective schemes negotiated by the
social partners provide (quasi) public second-tier pensions in France and
the Netherlands, negotiated supplementary pensions are also common in
Sweden and Denmark, and private pensions will gain in importance in
Germany and Italy as public pensions are cut back.

While comparative analyses of public policies have provided us with a
better understanding of the major differences in welfare-state regimes (most
notably Esping-Andersen 1990), the *public–private mix* has only recently
gained in attention (for an early study, see Rein and Rainwater 1986*a*). In
particular, the firm-provided or collectively negotiated occupational welfare
arrangements have been studied less, partly because they seem to be less
widespread, more fragmented, and in a state of flux.[1] The share of private
welfare provision of total social expenditure (including mandatory and
voluntary welfare benefits ranging from sick pay to occupational pensions)
is relatively high in the United States (34.7 percent in 1995) and probably in
Japan (firms can opt out of employee pensions), followed by the United
Kingdom (16.8 percent), the Netherlands (16 percent), and possibly France
(due to mandatory private second-tier pensions), while it is smaller in Germany (8.4 percent), Ireland (8.3 percent), Sweden (6.9 percent), and Denmark (4.1 percent) (Adema 1999: 15). I first review the use of occupational
pensions provided unilaterally by employers or negotiated by the social
partners, before considering their impact on early retirement.

According to the credo of *liberal* welfare states, public pensions should
only provide basic income support in old age and leave plenty of

---

[1] Recent comparative studies of occupational welfare have begun to fill the gap in research
(see Rein and Wadensjö 1997*b*; Reynaud et al. 1996; Shalev 1996; Turner and Watanabe 1995);
see also the recent OECD studies on private pensions (Davis 1997; Hughes 1994; OECD 1992;
Reynaud 1997*b*) as well as the activities of the European Commission (EU-Com. 1999*b*) and
ILO (ILO 2000).

opportunities for private initiative to secure earnings-related income maintenance (Esping-Andersen 1990). In Britain, most medium-sized to large private firms and the public sector provide occupational pensions as a supplement to the basic pension that has existed since 1908 (it was reformed in 1925 and again under Beveridge in 1946). Opt-in earnings-related pensions were only introduced in 1961 and the 1975 reform installed the state earnings-related pension scheme (SERPS) as of 1978, from which employer-sponsored pension funds could opt out (Davis 1997). Historically, occupational pensions were largely confined to male white-collar employees, but they have become more widespread: about every second employed person was covered by an occupational pension in the 1980s, that is, around 60 percent of working men and around one-third of working women—a lower rate due to the low coverage among female part-time employees (Lynes 1997).

Ireland inherited the same tradition of public basic pensions, which started under British rule in 1908, and to which a contributory pension was added in 1961. While there is no mandatory earnings-related scheme and coverage of occupational pensions is less widespread than in Britain (Hughes 1994), about 50 percent of all employees have been covered since the 1980s (Seitan 2001: 11). As a result of tripartite concertation, in recent years the need for pension reform and an expansion of occupational pension coverage has been put on the agenda in Ireland (Seitan 2001).

For lack of a sufficient public pension in the United States before the 1930s (Graebner 1980), larger firms provided occupational pensions as part of 'welfare capitalism' and some professions, such as education, established mutual funds (Sass 1997). Given the low social security benefits of the 'New Deal' of 1935, occupational pensions continued as voluntary supplementary pensions; these were especially common among white-collar employees with higher wages and in unionized firms (Sass 1997). In the 1940s, American unions pushed for negotiated ('integrated') company pensions that would guarantee income security for better-paid, skilled workers. Subsequently, employers lobbied Congress to increase social security benefits to lessen the financial burden of private pensions (apRoberts and Turner 1997: 361). During the 1990s, about 45 percent of employees in the private sector received employer pensions in addition to social security, while most public employees were entitled to participate in state pension schemes. Employers manage these pension funds individually or, in the case of collectively negotiated multiemployer plans, they administer them jointly with labor unions (Rein 1996).

Paternalistic welfare corporatism played an important role in Japan's residual welfare state (Kimura 1997; Maruo 1986). Acute skilled labor shortages in the early interwar period led to voluntary (since 1936 also to compulsory) small retirement lump sum allowances, while employer pensions expanded further with postwar tax incentives (since 1952). In addition, civil servants' retirement pay has a long tradition, with special mutual funds existing for specific groups—national authorities, local communities, and state firms, but also private school teachers. Since 1990, the Employees' Pension Funds (large company or group plans) have covered one-third of male private sector employees (and a somewhat smaller proportion of female employees), and nearly as many employees are insured under the tax-qualified pension plans, that is, mainly lump sum annuities in smaller firms (Kimura 1997). Under both schemes, employers can contract out of the earnings-related public pension since the 1960s (Shinkawa and Pempel 1996) and thus save a portion of the public pension contribution (3.2 percentage points of 14.5 percent payroll taxes in 1994) (Turner and Watanabe 1995: 34). In both private and public sectors, firm-provided occupational pensions (and severance pay arrangements) play an important role, reinforcing Japan's lifelong employment tenure system.

In contrast to liberal and residual welfare states, which left considerable room for private pensions to develop, occupational pensions assumed a less important role in Scandinavian *universalist* welfare states with well-developed basic pensions. Swedish unions have negotiated occupational pensions in both the private and public sectors (Kangas and Palme 1996). Even before the public second-tier pension (ATP) was introduced in 1960 as an earnings-related supplement to the basic pension, white-collar unions had negotiated occupational pensions (*Industrins och handelns tilläggspension*, ITP). The blue-collar unions affiliated to *Landsorganisation* (LO) also negotiated a private pension plan (*Särskild tilläggspension*, STP) in 1971, initially with the aim of providing 'earlier' retirement two years prior to the statutory public pension age of 67 (Wadensjö 1997). After statutory retirement age changed to 65 in 1977, STP became a supplementary pension financed with PAYG employer contributions, though it was turned into a funded scheme in 1996. In the public sector, there are two other major collective schemes, which have been negotiated for the central government (*Statens personalpensionsverk*, SPV) and local public sector (*Kommunernas pensionsanstalt*, KPA) (Wadensjö 1997). The 1999 Pension Reform, which integrates the basic and earnings-related pensions into a new scheme, is partly funded. The new integrated public pension has not led to a change in the supplementary function of negotiated occupational pensions, but it has put additional pressure on these schemes to become fully funded as well.

Quite in contrast to Sweden, Denmark's second-tier pension, initially introduced as a deferred wage in 1963 and later made mandatory by law, remained a flat-rate supplement administered by the social partners. Efforts prior to the late 1980s to expand the second-tier pension into a Swedish-type earnings-related and union-controlled investment fund failed due to political splits and opposition by the general worker unions (von Nordheim Nielsen 1991). While civil servants have a statutory pension scheme and other public employees are covered by a collective occupational pension, only one-third of employees in the private sector had an employer-provided occupational pension in the 1980s. However, from 1991, when the metal workers pushed for a collective agreement on occupational pensions, rapid improvements were made in expanding negotiated third-tier pensions, about two decades after the Swedish development (Green-Pedersen and Lindbom 2002). Before that, the Danish public–private mix, with tax-financed public basic pensions and pockets of private pensions, resembled Irish developments. In both countries, these could be attributed to the strong role of general unions, fragmented white-collar associations, and remnants of craft unions. Thus, neither mandatory earnings-related pensions nor collectively negotiated occupational pensions emerged in Denmark until the 1990s.

The scope for private occupational pensions was particularly limited in *Bismarckian* social insurance systems with earnings-related contributory pensions. In Germany, workers with low to medium income receive relatively high pensions under the earnings-related social insurance; therefore, occupational pensions are less important for them than for better-paid white-collar employees (Schmähl and Böhm 1996). Nevertheless, occupational pensions offered by private employers are widespread (about half of all private employees are covered), especially among larger firms, and benefits contribute to one-quarter of pension income for those receiving an occupational pension (Schmähl and Böhm 1996). Occupational pensions are also the rule in the public sector thank to a collective agreement.[2] The Riester Pension Reform of 2002 has introduced a new second-tier private pension that is voluntary but includes tax incentives for lower

[2] Civil servants (*Beamte*) are excluded from social insurance, receiving tax-financed retirement pay instead (Rothenbacher 2004), while the other non-tenured public employees have been covered (since 1967) under a collective agreement that guarantees a pay-as-you-go occupational supplementary pension to keep up with civil servants in old age (Schmähl and Böhm 1994).

income groups. This reform opened up new opportunities for unions to negotiate collective agreements on deferred wages; it also enables the reorganization of the exiting firm-provided occupational pensions as well as the supplementary pension scheme in the public sector (Bispinck 2002).

In Italy, the public old-age insurance was expanded after World War II to nearly all occupational groups, including the self-employed (Ferrera 1984). Italy's earnings-related public pension benefits have a high replacement rate and rank as one of the most expensive old-age income systems in the world (Brugiavini 1999; Regalia and Regini 1998). With the exception of employees in the public sector and banking, special occupational pensions were not common in Italy until government efforts sought to foster private pensions since the 1990s. However, a functional substitute to occupational pension is the 'end-of-service pay' (*trattamento di fine rapporto*), an accumulated portion of wages that is paid by the employer as a lump sum severance pay upon exit (Di Biase et al. 1997). First common as a deferred wage in collective bargaining, this measure was made mandatory for all employers in 1982. Since the pension reforms of the 1990s, the severance pay arrangements are gradually converted to occupational pensions. The new private pension funds have been collectively negotiated and are administered by the social partners in several sectors, though the development has been rather unequal across the economy.

Among the conservative welfare states, France and the Netherlands, however, divert from the Continental pattern: in addition to a first-tier public pension, important second-tier occupational pensions are administered by the social partners (Blomsma and Jansweijer 1997; Reynaud 1997a). While the high replacement rate of public pensions in Germany and Italy crowded out some of the developmental space for private pensions, collective occupational pensions have assumed a more important role in the Netherlands and France. In addition to the basic pension (reformed in 1957), most Dutch employees have been covered by private occupational pensions since the early 1950s. These supplementary pensions aim to close the replacement gap left by the basic pension—up to 70 percent of gross pay (Blomsma and Jansweijer 1997; Lutjens 1996). Larger firms commonly provide a pension fund, while smaller firms usually contribute to a sectorwide scheme under binding collective agreements; thus nearly 80 percent of all employees are covered. These sectorwide schemes were also the model for the PAYG early retirement (VUT) schemes of the social partners negotiated in the late 1970s.

Even more remarkable are the French supplementary pensions, initially negotiated by the social partners for higher grade white-collar workers in

1946 and then for all employees in the 1960s; these were made compulsory for all private employees in 1972 (Reynaud 1997a; 1997b).[3] In addition, civil servants are covered by a special scheme outside the general scheme of first-tier and second-tier pensions. The resulting fragmented public and mandatory private pension system reinforces the stratification of French society (Korpi 1995): privileged state pensions for civil servants, special higher earnings-related pensions for cadres, less generous general private and public pensions for the dependent employed, and occupationally fragmented schemes for the self-employed. The social partners, in particular the unions, assume an important role in the self-administration of public pensions and the self-regulation of second-tier pensions.

The administration of occupational pensions differs considerably cross-nationally (see Table 6.1). In the United Kingdom, Ireland, the United States, and Japan, occupational pensions are employer-sponsored plans by and large; only occasionally do workers contribute to them. In the German private sector, the occupational pension plans have thus far been mainly employer-sponsored, with workplace representatives playing a secondary role. On the other hand, because unions and employer associations have set up the French, Swedish, Danish, and Dutch schemes jointly, firms do not have much discretion. While the social partners initially set up the Italian severance pay scheme, the firms run the mandatory scheme except when negotiations have introduced sectorwide occupational pensions that are jointly administered by the social partners.

The private pensions' coverage rates (see Table 6.2) are lower where plan approval remained the voluntary decision of employers (Gern 1998; Turner and Watanabe 1995). Such is the case in the United Kingdom, Ireland, the United States, and Japan as well as in the German private sector and in Italy, compared to the collectively negotiated plans in Sweden, Denmark, and the Netherlands, not to mention the French mandatory plans. Although desirable from a public policy point of view, mandatory coverage and portability of pension rights from job to job under collective schemes undermine the micro-economic logic of selective benefits for employers who seek to attract and bind workers to their firm (Casey 1997; Steinmeyer 1996) and reward investments in firm-specific skills (Estevez-Abe, Iversen, and Soskice 2001). Competition for

---

[3] The first schemes were negotiated for cadres (managerial and technical personnel) in the private sector in 1946 (AGIRC) to close the replacement gap for those earning more than the contribution limit under the new general pension regime. Supplementary schemes for other, less-compensated groups emerged as a result of collective negotiations in the 1960s and were made compulsory by law in 1972. Of these schemes (over a hundered), most are organized in ARRCO. On average ARRCO pays benefits at one-third of what AGIRC pays for cadres.

Table 6.1. The public–private mix in pension schemes

	Germany	Netherlands	France	Italy	Sweden	Denmark	United Kingdom	Ireland	United States	Japan
First-tier: public basic pension	—	1947/57– AOW	(1905), 1930/45 general scheme	(1969 social pension)	1913/1948–	1891/1921/ 1960	1908/1946–	1908/1952–	—	1944, 1961 National pension
Second-tier: earnings-related state pension	—	—	—	—	1960–ATP fund	(1963 Flat-rate fund)	(1961–) 1978– SERPS or opt-out	—	—	1941 Employee pension or opt-out
Earnings-related social insurance	1889/1957– employees	—	—	1919/1939– employees; self-empl.	—	—	—	—	1935 Social security	—
Occupational pensions	Firm-OPs	Firm-OPs/ 1949: CAs	1947/1961: CA; 1972: mandatory	Law 1982: Trf; 1990s CA: OPs	CAs: white-/ blue-collar	Firm-OPs	Firm-OPs (opt-out)	Firm-OPs	Firm-OPs, (unionized firms)	Firm-OPs (opt-out)
Public sector	*Beamte*; 1969: CA	Special OPs (1990s: privatized)	1930–Special schemes	Special schemes	CAs: central/ local	Civil service pension; CA	Civil service; OPs	Civil service; OPs	Civil service; OPs	Special OPs
Private early exit pathway	Top-up benefits	Special ER (CAs: VUT)	1982: Top-up; Special ER (unemp.)	Top-up	–1976: exit at 65	Special ER scheme (*efterløn*)	Earlier exit –65/–60	(Top-up)	Top-up 63+; ERIPs –63	Top-up reduced earnings

Notes: OP: occupational pension; CA: collective agreement; ER: early retirement scheme; Trf: end of service pay; for other abbreviations see text.

Table 6.2. Occupational pensions and financial markets

	OP coverage (as %)	OP type	OP financing	Equities % fund	Fund assets (%GDP)	Stock market (%GDP)	Institutional assets (%GDP)
Germany	46 (1990)	OP	Books; funded	>35	6*	24	48
Netherlands	83 (1993)	CB/OP	Funded; books	>30	85	67	158
France	>90	Mand.CB	PAYG	None	3	34	75
Italy	>5	OP/CB	Funded		2		
Sweden	>90	CB	PAYG; funded		16	24	114
Denmark	80–90	CB/OP	Funded				
United Kingdom	48 (1991)	OP	Funded	>50	82	114	162
United States	46 (1992)	OP/CB	Funded	>35	72	75	171
Japan	61 (1990)	OP	Books; funded	>25	18*	50	77

Notes: CB: collective bargaining; OP: occupational pension fund (firm-level); * without book reserves; stock market capitalization (1994); institutional investors' assets (1995).

Sources: coverage and financing: Rein and Wadensjö (1997a); assets: Gern (1998): Table 1, pp. 3–7; OECD (1998b): 130–1.

better fringe benefits, between status groups and sectors, may emerge in more centralized bargaining systems or when employer benefits are voluntary. The increasingly decentralized labor relations and lack of state intervention in Britain, Ireland, the United States, and Japan have prevented an evolution toward sector- or nationwide schemes, as have developed in France and the Netherlands. Where voluntary employer-led occupational pensions exist, coverage is lower, benefit conditions vary, and inequality in pension income is more common, whereas collectively negotiated schemes have wider coverage (Sweden and Denmark) or *erga omnes* legal extension of collective agreements (France and the Netherlands) (Behrendt 2000; Turner and Watanabe 1995). However, in systems with nearly full coverage, firms no longer profit from the primary function of voluntary occupational pensions: to attract and retain (skilled) workers. Instead, supplementary pensions are deferred wages negotiated as part of wage bargaining. These variations in overall coverage and control opportunities for employers or social partners determine their opportunities to facilitate or hinder early retirement.

6.1.2 Occupational Welfare as a Private Early Exit Pathway

Occupational pensions in some cases provide an additional early exit pathway or help to supplement the incentives provided by public pathways. Most importantly, they affect whether firms can promote early retirement through occupational pension plans. Under DB plans, employers as sponsors may be able to offer early retirement pensions that are more favorable than normal actuarial deduction would dictate. This is not possible with DC plans, especially in individual savings plans. However, there is currently a shift from DB to DC plans that allows more portability, yet shifts the financial risks to individuals, thereby lowering the financial incentives to retire earlier.

In Britain, many of the larger occupational pension schemes allow earlier drawing than the state pensions (at age 65 for men and age 60 for women), providing a major private pathway to early retirement, especially for men (Blundell and Johnson 1999; Laczko and Phillipson 1991*b*). In addition, British employers have relied on 'voluntary redundancy' for downsizing, i.e. the payment of lump sum compensation based on years of service. Thus, older workers (alongside young workers with short tenures) are more likely to become redundant than prime-aged workers (Casey and Wood 1994: 367). Since 1988, the Conservative government made the SERPS less attractive and allowed not only firms but also individuals to opt out of it by signing up for a private pension.[4] Coverage among lower-income groups, however, remained relatively low due to the personal pension plans' high costs. For this reason, the New Labour government introduced a more affordable Stakeholder Pension Scheme in 2001. For the first time, the British Trades Union Congress offers its own DC scheme (Scarbrough 2002). Thus in the future, fewer people who exit early will be covered by DB schemes that would provide final salary pensions without limited actuarial reductions.

In the United States, occupational pensions provided a means to induce workers to retire, especially after Congress raised the mandatory retirement age in 1978 and abolished it in 1986. Some employers had already provided favorable early retirement options as part of their pension plans before flexible social security (at age 62 instead of 65) was introduced in 1961, and they later used the DB plans to top up any actuarial deductions under the flexible public pension (Hutchens 1994). Public policy did not abstain from regulating occupational pensions and introduced favorable tax rules to foster private pensions.[5] In addition, a firm can also devise an

---

[4] Nevertheless, there is a trend away from DB schemes: 14 percent of private sector employees already had a DC plan in 1991 (Lynes 1997: 339), especially smaller employer plans and all 'personal pension schemes'.

[5] The Employee Retirement Income Security Act (ERISA) of 1974 introduced important regulations on private sector pensions, requiring vesting of occupational pensions when an employee leaves a firm, forbidding benefit cuts after raises in social security benefits and introducing collective protection against bankruptcy. Favorable tax rules apply as long as a firm does not discriminate; a firm can design (or negotiate with its union) particular plans for subgroups, but it cannot restrict benefits only to higher management.

Early Retirement Incentive Plan (ERIP) to foster voluntary retirement. This occurs only at particular times (thus they are called 'window plans') when firms are forced to adjust their workforces, and is limited to older workers (Wise 1993). During the 1980s, when high interest rates and stock market profits increased pension fund assets, employers could use excess profits, which would otherwise be taxed, to finance early retirement options (Hutchens 1994). With falling unemployment during the 1990s, employers were increasingly worried about labor shortage, and cut back on these early retirement incentives. American firms finance and use early retirement provisions mainly as *downsizing* measures; early exit patterns thus follow a cyclical pattern. Since the 1970s, an important shift toward cash plans has occurred, reducing the early retirement incentives for an ever-larger section of the workforce.[6] This will increase even more the tendency of early exit to be driven by economic cycles.

Japanese occupational pensions are often DB plans that allow early drawing at age 60, i.e. at the age larger firms enforce mandatory retirement for their employees (Kimura et al. 1994). Further deregulations to boost contracting out and public pension reforms to increase the retirement age and lower benefits (Kimura 1997; Kimura and Oka 2001) have made occupational pensions more important for retirement since the 1990s. In addition, Japanese employers provide lump sum severance pay and use reemployment practices to enforce mandatory retirement from 'lifelong' career jobs (Kimura et al. 1994). Since the basic pension cannot be drawn earlier than age 65 without actuarial deduction, the occupational pension (including the lump sum severance pay) provides a subsidy during lower-paid follow-up work after mandatory retirement from the career job. Thus, a combination of partial pension and reduced earnings from work are common among older Japanese workers after age 60.

A variety of occupational schemes exist in Germany (Schmähl 1997; Schmähl and Böhm 1996): employers can choose between different financing methods with different tax and financial security regulations (Jackson and Vitols 2001).[7] Larger firms tend to have book reserves (or, less frequently, support or pension funds) during the 1990s, while more than half

---

[6] While two-thirds were entirely and one-fifth were partially DB plans in 1975, by 1992 only 19 percent of covered American workers had a DB plan, but already 44 percent had a DC plan and 37 percent had a mixed plan (apRoberts and Turner 1997: 366).

[7] Four models exist in Germany (Jackson and Vitols 2001; Schmähl and Böhm 1994): (*a*) support funds (employer-financed funds which can provide loans to the firm), (*b*) pension funds (independent trust funds consisting of employer and voluntary employee contributions), (*c*) direct insurance (life insurance financed by employers and voluntary employee contributions), and (*d*) book reserves (a commitment by employers to pay pensions out of reserves accumulated by the firm that are usually reinvested into the firm).

of smaller firms have direct insurance contracts. Book reserves and support funds function as deferred wages that are reinvested into the firm, though reinsurance against bankruptcy is mandatory. Since 1974, legal regulations only guarantee the right to an occupational pension after five years of service and former employees' pensions only have statutory accrual. Accrued occupational pensions are an important incentive to stay with a current employer, diminishing labor turnover. Most occupational pensions of larger private sector firms (above 1,000 workers) are earnings-related benefits and thus show the commitment of employers to safeguarding their employees' standard of living, especially for higher income groups (Schmähl 1997).[8] Nevertheless, German firms, and especially the larger firms, have mainly relied on public schemes to facilitate their older workers' early exit (Jacobs, Kohli, and Rein 1991*b*). Occupational pensions do play a role in topping up the benefits under the part-time scheme. In the late 1990s, collective negotiations on voluntary part-time pensions have gained in importance, making up for the phasing out of several public exit pathways (Barkholdt 2001). The new Riester pension as a DB scheme provides no particular support for early retirement.

Legal regulations require the second-tier Dutch private pensions to be funded (since 1956), and rights are already vested after one year of employment (after age 25). Moreover, portability across firms even outside sectoral schemes has become common since the 1980s and even legally required since 1994.[9] These occupational pension schemes thus provide no comparative advantage to any individual Dutch firm's personnel policies, and do not facilitate early retirement. However, since 1976, an increasing number of collective agreements have established early retirement plans (VUT) that, initially set up as PAYG schemes, are financed by employer and employee contributions and require at least ten years of contributions (Blomsma and Jansweijer 1997).[10] Especially for male workers in sectors with VUT agreements, employers could thus rely on these occupational schemes to shed labor (Trommel and de Vroom 1994). Yet increasingly these VUT schemes are being transformed from PAYG DB

---

[8] Occupational pensions are thus enjoyed more frequently by white-collar than blue-collar workers, among more qualified than lower-ranking employees, and among men than women (data from 1990, Table 4.4 in Schmähl 1997).

[9] Besides the civil servant scheme (covering more than 20 percent of all employees), which was recently privatized, there are around eighty sectoral plans (60 percent) and plans for companies with over 1,000 employees (less than 20 percent); (Blomsma and Jansweijer 1997: 240).

[10] In combination, private pensions and VUT plans can increase earnings replacement rates to 90 percent at age 59, compared to 60 percent at age 65 for those completely dependent on a public pension (Kapteyn and de Vos 1999: 284–5, Table 7.1).

preretirement pensions to funded flexible DC pensions, lowering the financial incentives to exit from work early (Rein and Turner 2001).

The mandatory French occupational pension scheme, like the general public scheme, provided no early retirement options before the government lowered the statutory retirement age from age 65 to 60 in 1983. The social partners then adapted their second-tier pensions to the new age limit, making them conditional on the government's willingness to subsidize a transitional fund (ASF) (Guillemard 1991).[11] In 1995, a job replacement scheme (ARPE) was introduced for workers aged 58 with 40 years of contributions (Jolivet 2002). The French social partners did not use the second-tier old-age fund, but rather the unemployment fund to facilitate early exit, since the unemployment benefit replacement would be much higher than the combined public and second-tier pensions. Moreover, the self-administered unemployment funds gave the social partners more control over the conditions of early exit. Thus, French firms have two outside sources for early exit policies: (*a*) the preretirement benefits of the unemployment funds and (*b*) the 'solidarity' state–firm contracts paid by the public labor market fund.

Like the French unions, the Danish unions used the unemployment funds (set up by the Social in Democratic government in 1979) to facilitate early retirement. Unemployment scheme benefits were, as in France, much higher than the public pensions' replacement rate after age 67; therefore, the preretirement benefits were paid in two periods to lower the benefits stepwise (after two and half years). Even though employers were critical of the preretirement scheme because they would not have much control over it, the unions, and in particular the general workers' unions (*Specialarbejdersforbundet i Danmark,* SiD), favored the preretirement pay scheme since it provides relatively high benefits for the lower-paid un- and semiskilled workers (Petersen 1989). In the 1990s, the preretirement scheme was first extended to exit before age 60 (Hansen 2002) and then thoroughly reformed as a consequence of a major turnaround in labor market policy.

All four Swedish collective supplementary pension schemes provide full retirement supplements after thirty contribution years, based on the last peak year's wage or salary, and allow earlier withdrawal, albeit with some actuarial reduction. The occupational schemes had granted 'earlier' benefits

[11] The ASF fund was initially set up by the social partners to finance 'bridging pensions' within unemployment insurance (UNEDIC), which is also run by the social partners following a collective agreement signed in 1958 (see Chapter 5). A joint agreement concerning UNEDIC in 1972 introduced the unemployment allowance for older dismissed workers (aged 60–64), guaranteeing 80 percent of net wages (and later full public pensions), and since 1977 for the voluntarily unemployed as well (Guillemard 1991: 136–7).

than did the public pensions (age 65 instead of 67), but this ended in 1976 when the statutory pension age was generally lowered to 65. Given the high organization rate of Swedish unions and employers, nearly all dependent employees are covered by the collective pension schemes, with the exception of employees working less than 16 hours per week. The occupational pensions not only supplement old age but also disability pensions; they also provide partial pensions for three out of four schemes (Wadensjö 1997). Recent moves away from PAYG and toward funded DC benefits will further reduce the already minor impact of Swedish occupational pensions on early retirement.[12] Unlike in other countries, the Swedish social partners have shown more constraint in using occupational pensions to support early retirement. When they wanted to shed old workers, Swedish firms have relied mainly on the public unemployment-disability pathways and the partial pension schemes until the retrenchment in the 1990s.

In contrast to the common view in public debate, this cross-national review of private exit pathways reveals that not only the public welfare state but also private pension funds and other occupational welfare arrangements—largely determined by employers or the social partners—pull older workers toward early exit. Indeed, occupational welfare policies provide supplements in closing the replacement gap of public benefits or maintain alternative private pathways when public schemes are less accessible or generous. The public–private mix and the governance of private pensions show interesting cross-national variations (see Table 6.3). In the residual welfare states with important private pension pillars (the United Kingdom,

Table 6.3. The public–private mix in exit pathways

Exit pathways	Occupational welfare	
	Private firm-provided occupational pensions	Negotiated supplementary pension
Public pathways only	Germany; Italy: Externalizing costs onto public exit pathways	Sweden: Partial internalization/public exit pathways only
Private additional pathways	Britain; Ireland; United States; Japan: Firm-sponsored private exit pathway	France (UI); Denmark (UI); Netherlands (VUT): Special preretirement schemes by social partners/union-run

Notes: UI: Unemployment insurance; VUT: Dutch preretirement scheme.

[12] After the public disability pension for the older unemployed was abolished in 1991, the blue-collar unions and private employers negotiated an occupational scheme to provide similar preretirement benefits (1993), but it lasted less than three years (Wadensjö 1997).

Ireland, the United States, and Japan), occupational pensions provided by employers played a more crucial role for early retirement, especially given the absence of generous or widely available public schemes. The British and American early exit pathways, in particular, were thus subject to economic rationales and cyclical trends, entailing more 'internalization' of labor-shedding costs by employers through cofinancing of occupational plans or increasingly by individuals through income losses.

In the Netherlands, France, and Denmark, special preretirement schemes negotiated by the social partners (or run by the unions as in Denmark) played an important role in the pervasiveness of early exit and externalization of costs at the sectoral or national level. Quite in contrast, German occupational pensions remained mainly supplementary; they do not contribute significantly to early retirement since employers and workplace representatives externalized early exit costs to public schemes. In Italy, severance pay has thus far been a supplement to workers leaving; however, the main incentive remained the pull of public benefits. Although the Swedish social partners had some experience with financing 'earlier' exit before 1976, the collective bargaining partners did not continue down that path, adopting instead an integrative strategy.

6.2 Structural Push Factors

6.2.1 *Deindustrialization and Public Sector Expansion*

We now turn from the perspective of pull factors—the private welfare policies—to the other side of the coin: *push* factors that induce a decline in labor demand for older workers. Before analyzing the institutional push factors, we need to ask whether structural changes in the economy are sufficient to explain early exit from work. Two possible structural shifts may have had an impact: (*a*) the decline of industrial employment (*deindustrialization*) and (*b*) the increase of the sheltered sector (*public employment*). These structural changes have not only been seen as major changes affecting welfare state spending (Iversen and Cusack 2000), but also as having repercussions for retirement patterns (Clark, York, and Anker 1999). While deindustrialization adds to the push toward early retirement, the growth of public employment provides a sheltered sector insulated from market push (Scharpf 2001).

Deindustrialization is considered a major push factor in labor shedding (Esping-Andersen and Sonnberger 1991). All industrial economies have experienced major reductions in industrial employment since the 1970s (see Table 6.4). More than one-third of all employed people (and an even larger share among men) worked in the secondary sector before the mid-1970s, but the industrial workforce shrank considerably to one-quarter by the late 1990s, although there are also considerable variations. Can the timing and speed of deindustrialization explain the timing and variations in early exit trajectories? The two countries with the largest industrial workforce (45 percent in the 1960s) showed very different trajectories: Britain's industrial workforce declined rapidly during the 1970s, while Germany's declined less rapidly and remains substantial at more than 30 percent in the 1990s. Japan, Italy, and Ireland expanded their industrial workforce throughout the 1960s, maintained their levels during the 1970s, and saw only a gradual decline thereafter. The other countries have a relatively similar drop in employment shares (between -1.0 and -2.3 percent). Thus deindustrialization explains solely the general trend toward early retirement, not the major cross-national variations in early exit from work. Only in the case of Japan, Ireland, and Italy, can one attribute the slow increase in early exit from work (albeit at different levels) to the more gradual decline in industrialization since the 1970s (see Table 6.4). Although deindustrialization in the heavy industry sectors led to initial efforts to downsize via early retirement during the 1960s, the rapid rise of early exit from the mid-1970s was not limited to declining industries, but spread across all sectors.

We would thus expect *public employment* to be sheltered from the economic push toward early exit, at least until fiscal austerity leads to budget cuts and privatization efforts (Clayton and Pontusson 1998). Countries with low public employment (see Table 6.4) would thus be less sheltered from market forces, while large welfare states would provide social buffers against market forces (Kolberg and Esping-Andersen 1991; Rose 1985). The Swedish and Danish welfare states were the only ones to continue to expand public employment during the 1970s and maintained high levels during the 1980s (Benner and Vad 2000). This may have taken some pressure off the economic push for early exit, partly explaining the higher levels of employment in the older age groups. Moreover, when Sweden cut down on public employment in the crisis of the 1990s (Benner and Vad 2000), early exit from work accelerated. From the 1980s, Britain privatized and cut back on public employment (Wollmann 2000), though only the early efforts of public sector retrenchment coincided with a major wave of early exit. For the other countries, public employment remains relatively stable and thus fails to explain either the level or the direction of change in

Table 6.4. Secondary sector, public employment, and early exit, 1960–2000

Sector	Labor force share (%)				Annual growth rates (%)			Exit growth (%)	
	1960	1970	1985	2000	Δ1960–1970	Δ1970–1985	Δ1985–2000	Δ1970–1985	Δ1985–2000
Secondary (%)									
Germany	47.0	48.5	41.5	33.4	+0.32	−1.03	−1.44	+8.00	−0.20*
Netherlands	40.5	38.9	28.1	22.2[a]	−0.39	−2.14	−1.96[a]	+8.57	−0.60
France	37.6	39.2	32.0	24.4	+0.41	−1.34	−1.79	+7.95	+1.33
Italy	33.9	39.5	33.6	32.4	+1.55	−1.07	−0.24	+2.55	+0.02
Sweden	40.3	38.4	30.3	24.6	−0.49	−1.57	−1.38	+4.10	+0.95*
Denmark	36.9	37.8	28.1	26.8[a]	+0.24	−1.96	−0.41[a]	+8.49	+0.83
United Kingdom	47.7	44.7	31.6	25.1	−0.64	−2.28	−1.53	+6.55	−2.46
Ireland	23.7	29.9	28.9	28.8	+2.33	−0.22	−0.02	+4.90*	−2.26*
United States	35.3	34.3	28.0	22.9	−0.28	−1.34	−1.33	+3.89	−0.91
Japan	28.5	35.7	34.9	31.2	+2.27	−0.15	−0.74	+5.14	+1.34
Public (%)									
Germany	8.1	11.2	15.5	11.4	+3.37	+2.20	−2.18	+8.00	−0.20*
Netherlands	–	11.1	14.3	10.6	–	+1.68	−2.10	+8.57	−0.60
France (1966–)	16.3	17.6	22.9	24.2	+1.90	+1.76	+0.39	+7.95	+1.33
Italy	9.0	12.2	16.7	16.6	+3.12	+2.10	−0.02	+2.55	+0.02
Sweden	12.8	20.9	33.3	32.0	+5.00	+3.15	−0.29	+4.10	+0.95*
Denmark	10.5	17.4	29.5	29.8	+5.20	+3.59	+0.07	+8.49	+0.83
United Kingdom (1961–)	21.0	26.0	26.7	17.9	+2.44	+0.17	−2.82	+6.55	−2.46
Ireland (1961–)	8.5	10.6	15.4	11.0	+2.50	+2.52	−2.40	+4.90*	−2.26*
United States	12.7	16.0	15.3	15.2	+2.34	−0.28	−0.05	+3.89	−0.91
Japan (1962–)	7.9	7.7	8.7	8.4	−0.23	+0.76	−0.19	+5.14	+1.34

Notes: [a] 1997; Δ annual natural growth rate (%): $\Delta x_t - t_{0-n}\% = (((X_{t_{0-n}}/X_{t_0})^{1/n} - 1) \times 100$ (where 1960–70 $n = 10$, 1970–85, 1985–2000 $n = 15$, [a]1988–2000 $n = 12$); exit growth rates: annual growth of relative exit rates for men 60–64 (*see Notes in Table 4.5).

Sources: own calculations based on OECD (1963); OECD, *Labour Force Statistics 1970–2000.*

early exit patterns. As a result, with the exception of the Scandinavian and British welfare-state growth and retrenchment, public employment has not changed early retirement patterns. Moreover, early retirement became as common in the public sector as in other sectors (Jacobs, Kohli, and Rein 1991c), and in Continental Europe it was facilitated even more by special pension arrangements for civil servants (Rothenbacher, 2004).

6.2.2 Age-Related Skill Profiles and Sectoral Exit Patterns

The sectoral shifts discussed thus far may be too broad to capture the structural push thesis; instead, labor shedding may take place only in particular industrial branches or even selected employment groups. Given 'social imprinting' (Stinchcombe 1965), the age profile of particular economic sectors varies considerably according to their 'age', thus older industries tend to have a more aged workforce than newer ones. The transformation from an industrial to a service society, and the transition from less-skilled to more-skilled workforces occurred largely by intergenerational mobility as young and better-trained workers took up employment in new sectors with more job opportunities, while less-educated older workers tended to stay in their industries, given seniority-protected jobs and fear of age discrimination in hiring (OECD 1998d). Therefore, older firms or sectors tend to have an older age structure and may be more likely to downsize than younger firms or sectors. When obsolete jobs in older firms or sectors are significantly affected by early retirement, such early exits hardly create job opportunities for young workers, as the 'old out, young in' replacement thesis claims.

Even though older workers on average have lower skill levels than their younger colleagues (see Table 6.5), this effect will decline from cohort to cohort with the increase in overall and occupational education.[13] We find much higher percentages of less-skilled men and women in the older workforce (age 55–64) than in the main medium-aged workforce (25–49): The age-related overrepresentation among less-skilled workers is particularly unfavorable in Japan (2.8 times for men, 3.8 for women) and the United Kingdom (2.8 and 3.7 respectively), followed by Sweden (2.1 and 2.4). The other countries still have a higher share of less-skilled older

---

[13] A comparison of educational levels of employed older men and women (aged 55–64) in comparison to the prime-age group (25–49) can, however, be deceptive since those remaining in the workforce may be a (self-) selected group (i.e. those with inadequate skills may have already retired). Therefore, we need to compare skill-related differences between active and non-active older workers (see Table 4.8).

Table 6.5. Age-related skill profile, men and women aged 55–64, 1999

Men	Employed 55–64			Inactive 55–64			Employed 55–64/ employed 25–49			Inactive/ employed 55–64		
	High	Med.	Low	High	Med.	Low	High	Med.	Low	High	Med.	Low
Germany	36.9	48.5	14.7	20.8	57.7	21.5	1.2	0.8	1.2	0.6	1.2	1.5
Netherlands	29.8	39.2	31.0	15.6	40.5	43.8	1.1	0.9	1.2	0.5	1.0	1.4
Italy	12.8	22.2	65.0	3.4	15.6	81.0	1.2	0.6	1.3	0.3	0.7	1.2
Sweden	23.3	41.7	34.9	14.6	37.8	47.6	0.8	0.8	2.1	0.6	0.9	1.4
United Kingdom	25.9	49.1	25.0	19.2	38.8	42.0	0.8	0.8	2.8	0.7	0.8	1.7
United States	37.3	48.3	14.4	21.6	50.8	27.6	1.0	1.0	1.4	0.6	1.1	1.9
Japan	20.6	43.9	35.5	13.8	40.9	45.3	0.5	0.9	2.8	0.7	0.9	1.3
Women												
Germany	18.4	52.4	29.1	7.9	49.3	42.8	0.8	0.9	1.9	0.4	0.9	1.5
Netherlands	21.8	30.0	48.2	8.4	26.1	65.5	0.8	0.6	2.0	0.4	0.9	1.4
Italy	12.0	24.6	63.4	3.2	12.4	84.4	0.7	0.5	1.8	0.3	0.5	1.3
Sweden	26.5	44.5	29.0	12.1	40.9	47.0	0.7	0.9	2.4	0.5	0.9	1.6
United Kingdom	22.0	37.6	40.4	12.6	31.2	56.2	0.7	0.6	3.7	0.6	0.8	1.4
United States	29.4	58.8	11.8	19.0	55.4	25.6	0.7	1.2	1.6	0.6	0.9	2.2
Japan	9.9	46.5	43.6	9.2	47.6	43.1	0.3	0.9	3.8	0.9	1.0	1.0

Notes: Educational level as percentage of age group; percentages do not necessarily add up to 100% due to nonresponses.

Sources: OECD (2001*b*): Table 5.4, p. 97; and own calculations.

workers in comparison to the main workforce, and the overrepresentation is higher among women than men. Due to Continental Europe's higher rates of early exit, the lower overrepresentation is the result of a selection process that sheds particularly the less-skilled older workers. The less skilled are also (although to a lesser extent) overrepresented among the inactive in comparison to active older workers, except among Japanese women. The medium and higher educational levels show more cross-national variations due to the larger differences in categorization, particularly in the middle category. Those with tertiary education tend to remain employed longer, probably due to the higher share of self-employed professionals. Hence, we find substantial evidence for the low-skill-labor-shedding thesis: Older cohorts tend to be less educated and are more likely to be inactive than those with more formal education. Thus, the fact of an overall lower skill profile in the older population and their concentration in 'old' (potentially declining) sectors represents a push factor for early exit from work.

Special programs for early retirement were introduced, largely in the late 1970s, to ease the industrial restructuring process, the decline of technologically outdated and uncompetitive industries with surplus capacity (Russig 1986; Tsoukalis and Ferreira 1980). In addition to specific preretirement programs that were at least initially confined to ailing industries, early exit soon became a more general trend. In fact, there is only limited evidence that early exit is specific to these declining industries. A *shift-share analysis*[14] of employment changes by industry during the 1970s for three countries (Germany, the Netherlands, and Sweden) concluded that a 'decrease in employment share of older men within all the industries, rather than changes in the distribution, is the main factor underlying the overall changes in the old-age share of male employment' (Jacobs, Kohli, and Rein 1991c: 83). Early exit, whatever its initial intention, became a quasi-social right claimed by anyone approaching retirement age: early exit has spread across nearly all sectors, including those that are not declining.

Nevertheless, there are some significant sectoral variations, and intra-sectoral patterns may well remain undiscovered in aggregate statistics. When analyzing Germany, the Netherlands, and Sweden over the 1970s, we find that in addition to the general trend of early exit in the three countries, there are some broader sectors that are affected more than others (Jacobs, Kohli, and Rein 1991c: 84–6, 90). Following the overall employment decline in agriculture and construction, a reduction in old-age employment is particularly dramatic in these sectors. The multiple manufacturing sectors, transport and communication, and mining and utilities, all have average levels of employment contraction for the older employed (above age 55). Differences with respect to the likelihood of very early retirement (before age 60) exist in particular sectors, with construction and agriculture again showing the strongest decline in the three countries. But the patterns of the age group 60–64 are very different with respect to the public and community service sector: Germany showed considerable relative decline, the Netherlands witnessed limited decline, and Sweden experienced an actual increase in employment. The authors of this shift-share analysis conclude that the 'pattern of exit across industries suggests that the troubled-industry hypothesis holds to some degree, but does not offer a sufficient explanation of the whole process of early exit from the labor market' (Jacobs, Kohli, and Rein 1991c: 94).

Employment data for 1995 (Blöndal and Scarpetta 1998) indicate that early retirement is not concentrated in declining industrial sectors; instead, it is relatively widespread, with the exception of the primary sector and private services (see Table 6.6). Certainly, workers in private industry

---

[14] Shift-share analysis holds one condition constant over time (*ceteris paribus*), for instance, the employment rate of older workers, and then applies this rate to a later point in time, comparing the actual value with the hypothetical result.

Table 6.6. Sectoral overrepresentation of retired men aged 55–64, 1995

Sector	Germany	Netherlands	France	Italy	Denmark	United Kingdom	Ireland
Primary sector	1.2*	0.2	0.9	0.7	0.3	0.5	0.4
Private industry	1.4*	1.2*	1.4*	1.7*	1.4*	1.2*	1.7*
Mining	6.2*	—	3.8*	2.3*	—	5.0*	2.9*
Manufacturing	1.5*	1.2*	1.5*	2.2*	1.4*	1.1*	1.6*
Construction	0.9	1.2*	1.1*	1.0*	1.3*	1.2*	1.7*
Public services	0.9	1.0*	1.4*	1.3*	1.1*	1.5*	1.7*
Utilities	1.1*	0.7	3.3*	1.5*	1.1*	3.9*	1.4*
Communication	1.1*	1.1*	1.8*	1.3*	1.1*	1.3*	1.9*
Administration	0.8	1.0*	1.0*	1.3*	1.1*	1.6*	1.5*
Private services	0.6	1.1*	0.6	0.5	1.0*	0.8	0.8
Commerce	0.7	1.1*	0.7	0.5	0.9	0.6	0.9
Catering	0.4	2.6*	0.5	0.6	8.3	1.0*	0.9
Finance	0.5	0.7	0.8	0.8	0.8	1.6*	2.1*
Business services	0.5	1.0*	0.4	0.4	0.2	0.5	0.8
Other services	0.5	1.0*	0.5	0.6	0.9	0.8	0.6

Notes: *Overrepresentation (≥1.0): sector share among retired men 55–64/sector share among employed men 55–64; 'no response' excluded.

Sources: Own calculations are based on Eurostat, *Labour Force Survey 1995* (2005), cit. in Blöndal and Scarpetta (1998: Table II.5, p. 58).

are more likely to be overrepresented among retired men (aged 55–64) than those in the private service sector or agriculture, but this also holds for the (semi-)public sectors. Even though the level of early exit varies across Europe, the lowest level of early exit is found in the private service sector (though not in the Netherlands) and agriculture (though not in Germany). With few exceptions, the industry-mix hypothesis cannot explain the cross-national variations in the overall level of early exit. Even though early exit from work often started as a deliberate labor-shedding strategy in declining sectors, it has become a general phenomenon across most industrial and public service sectors.

6.2.3 Cyclical and Mass Unemployment as Push Factors

In addition to economic restructuring, mass unemployment increased the push toward early exit from work (Esping-Andersen and Sonnberger 1991). High unemployment may induce politicians (and unions) to use labor shedding as a strategy to reduce labor supply, in the hope that it will create new employment opportunities for younger job-seekers and reduce the visibility of unemployment. Although early retirement of course already occurred before the mid-1970s, the major surge began during the rise in mass unemployment. The overall unemployment rate is negatively correlated with the employment rate, while losses in industrial employment are less significant but positively correlated.[15] While the first wave of mass unemployment was crucial in institutionalizing the social rights of early retirement, today it is relatively independent from business cycles and so entrenched that it is difficult to reverse. Especially in countries with high unemployment in the 1970s, particularly the Continental European countries, persistent early retirement 'increasingly took on institutional forms and became increasingly autonomous' (Naschold, de Vroom, and Casey 1994b), though the United Kingdom (and Ireland) reversed this trend in the 1990s. For the high early exit countries of Continental Europe, the trajectories follow a long-term *S-curve*, indicating a diffusion process (Pemperton 1936), while for the lower exit countries the trend oscillates in a more cyclical fashion, indicating more sensitivity to unemployment cycles (see Figures 4.5 and 4.6). Since these latter countries offer fewer preretirement opportunities, changes in older workers' unemployment rate affect early exit more than in countries that offer many preretirement options besides short-term unemployment benefits.

For some countries, we can detect particular periods when exit for male workers (age 60–64) rose in significant leaps that were connected to aggravated labor market conditions. This occurred in West Germany during the 1970s (and in East Germany in the 1990s), in France over the mid-1970s and again (due to a reduced statutory pension age) in the early 1980s. Both the United Kingdom and the Netherlands experienced dramatic increases in inactivity in the preretirement age groups in the late 1970s, leveling off in the late 1980s. For these four countries, the major post-oil-shock wave of high unemployment indeed triggered wider use of early exit (Casey and Bruche 1983; Esping-Andersen 1996c). These economic push-induced waves were also due to policy modifications, such as the opening and closing of special early retirement schemes and changes in eligibility rules, which take the labor market situation into account when granting long-term unemployment, disability or old-age pension benefits. Yet even in countries without such direct unemployment linkage, early retirement tends to go up with a downturn in the economy and labor market, since employers are more likely to dismiss older workers who in turn either remain unemployed or seek to retire via available preretirement programs.

---

[15] In a quantitative comparative study of German, Swedish, and American early exit patterns, combined models including unemployment and job loss in industry for the pre- and post-1973 period performed poorly, while 'the unemployment variable is significant, and the job loss variable, albeit insignificant, has become stronger' for a model dividing the two periods (Esping-Andersen and Sonnberger 1991: 244).

In Sweden and Japan, unemployment rate and early exit are relatively low during the 1970s–1980s, but both indicators increase together in the 1990s. For the Anglo-American market economies, both unemployment and early exit tend to follow the business cycle. However, while unemployment parallels early exit trends over time (with a few notable exceptions), the level of unemployment alone does not explain cross-national variations in early exit. Hence, it is only the timing and speed of early exit trajectories, not the overall level, that is influenced by aggravated labor market positions. The major differences between high-labor-shedding Continental Europe and the other countries with lower early exit trajectories cannot be explained by unemployment levels or growth, but instead by the interaction of institutional differences in pull and push factors.

6.3 Institutional Push Factors

6.3.1 Union Movements between Pull and Push

Before analyzing the different labor market regulations, particularly employment protection, this section compares the various traditions of labor relations, especially membership strength, organizational structure and bargaining power of unions, and their institutionalized role of worker representation at the workplace level. Particular partnership traditions and subsequent evolution of labor relations shape the opportunity structure for unions as they negotiate bargaining policy, codetermine workplace labor relations, and influence social policymaking. There are significant cross-national variations in labor relations at national and workplace levels (see Table 6.7). Moreover, over the last three decades, labor relations in general and union organizational capacities in particular have evolved, (re)shaping their opportunity structures to influence the course of early exit from work in the national political, collective bargaining, and workplace arenas. In most postindustrial societies, union power has decreased not only due to membership decline, but also because of increasing heterogeneity of interests, decentralization of collective bargaining, and weakened party–union ties (Ebbinghaus and Visser 2000). Thus, I ask two main questions here: (a) can cross-national variations in labor relations, particularly in union structure, explain these different early exit trajectories and (b) to what degree do union movements retain enough power to defend seniority employment and early retirement rights?

Table 6.7. Labor relations and early exit patterns

Early exit trend	Country	Labor relations	Union movement	Union density	Collective bargaining	Workplace relations
High/early	France, Italy	Contentious	Politically divided, political strike	Low (F)/medium (I) decline	State extension (central-local dualism)	Union local/works council (wildcat strikes)
High	Germany, Netherlands	Cooperative (sectoral)	Largely unified, strong industrial unions	Low/declining	Sectoral coverage (state extension)	Works council (strike/bargaining ban)
Moderate (♀ high)	United Kingdom	Voluntarist	Weak confederation, craft/general/collar unions	Low/declining	Decentralized	Shop stewards (wildcat strikes)
Moderate (♀ high)	Denmark	Cooperative (central)	Central confederations, craft/general/collar unions	High/stable	Central+decentral	Union representative (support by law/agreement)
Moderate	Sweden	Cooperative (central)	Central confederations, industrial unions (collar)	High/stable	Central+decentral	Union representative (support by agreement/law)
Moderate	United States	Voluntarist	Weak confederation, (industrial) company unions	Low/declining	Workplace (majority election)	Bargaining representative (majority election)
Low	Ireland	Voluntarist	(Central) confederations, craft/general/collar unions	Moderate/declining	Central+ (decentral)	Shop stewards (wildcat strikes)
Low	Japan	Cooperative (firm)	Weak confederations, company unions	Low–moderate/declining	Company	Union representative (cooperative relations)

Notes: See Tables 3.5 and 3.6.

Decentralized labor relations are dominant in those countries with voluntarist traditions (the United Kingdom, Ireland, and the United States) or cooperative enterprise unions (Japan). British, Irish, and American union movements, and also Japanese unions are fragmented and workplace-oriented. They also suffer from declining, low-union density: Every second Irish, third British, fourth Japanese, and merely every sixth American worker is unionized in the 1990s (Ebbinghaus and Visser 2000; Golden, Wallerstein, and Lange 1999: 200), and about as many are covered by collective bargaining (Traxler, Blasche, and Kittel 2001: 196). Since the state and employers first took on the unions in the labor relations realm (Freeman 1990; Freeman and Pelletier 1990), the British and American unions have not been very effective in lobbying against retrenchment efforts by the Reagan or Thatcher governments (Pierson 1994). In the case of Japan, unions at the workplace level are well organized and maintain cooperative relations with employers (Shirai 1983), but at the national level they have only limited access to political decision-making (Knoke et al. 1996). Quite in contrast to its neighbor, Ireland's unions have gained from regular social concertation with government and employers since the late 1980s (O'Donnell and O'Reardon 2000) and have been less affected by membership decline (Freeman and Pelletier 1990; Roche 1997). Social partnership has spread from the collective bargaining arenas to the social policy arena; thus Ireland is a case of departure from the voluntarist path of long-term decline in union power.

In comparison to the unions under voluntarist labor relations, the well-organized Swedish and Danish unions were much better placed to lobby for welfare-state expansion and—later—against welfare retrenchment (Esping-Andersen 1985). Swedish and Danish unions organize more than 80 percent of all workers and they have not suffered from significant membership loss, thanks to institutional union securities and the selective membership incentive of union-run unemployment insurance in particular (Ebbinghaus and Visser 1999; Rothstein 1992). Scandinavian unions are not only well organized at the central level; they are also strong at workplace level, assuming both local bargaining and representative functions (Hancké 1993; Kjellberg 1983). However, the dominance of the blue-collar unions and their historically strong links to the Social Democratic party (with long spells in office) weakened over time (Ebbinghaus 1995), while employers have retreated from centralized bargaining since the 1980s (Kjellberg 1998; Scheuer 1998; Swenson and Pontusson 2000). While Scandinavian union movements still had considerable organizational power and political influence in the 1970s, their power base has been slowly eroding since the 1980s. Intra-Nordic differences play a role in early exit policies; under Danish occupational union structure, general unions play a strong role in defending the interests of the less-skilled blue-collar workers hit by restructuring, while Swedish sectoral unions tend to be more prone to support integration and activation policies for older workers.

Continental European unions have been much weaker in terms of union membership than Scandinavian unions—they have also suffered from considerable membership decline (Ebbinghaus and Visser 2000). However, they can rely on more institutionalized support than American or British unions (Traxler 1999). In particular, collective bargaining coverage is larger than union membership due to better-organized employer associations and legal extension of collective agreements by the state (Calmfors et al. 2001). In contrast to the Nordic countries, Continental European unions are weaker at the workplace level either due to dual representation or through rival political unionism. Statutory works councils in Germany and the Netherlands are independent institutions with circumscribed codetermination rights and duties, in particular a strike and bargaining ban (Rogers and Streeck 1995). In France and Italy, politically split union movements compete and relations with employers are more conflictual at both national and workplace levels (Goetschy 1998; Regalia and Regini 1998). In addition, given the political strike traditions and the individual (economic and political) strike right (Edwards and Hyman 1994), the politically divided Italian and French union movements have been able to mobilize against retrenchment plans (Ebbinghaus and Hassel 2000). Furthermore, pensioners are a well-represented group among Italian unions—half of all members have retired (Chiarini 1999). Moreover, Continental European unions, together with the employers, play an institutionalized role as social partners in the self-administration of social insurance and labor market administrations (Crouch 2001; Ebbinghaus 2004).

The more direct impact of workplace representatives or local unionists on early retirement practice results from its position in dismissal procedures. Unions have a long tradition of enforcing seniority rules in mass redundancy ('last-in, first-out') that protect those with longer service and/ or older workers, following the interests of their aged membership (Wolf, Kohli, and Künemund 1994) and as the means to protect the workplace representatives (Golden 1997). Most prominently, American unions have enforced seniority rules through collective bargaining, filling the void of legal employment regulations, though this increases the incentives for employers to avoid unionization (Freeman and Medoff 1984). In Japan, the employers' commitment to lifelong employment provides an equivalent to legal employment protection. Employment protection legislation in the 1960s and 1970s provided additional support for seniority rules in Germany and Sweden, initially bargained by unions. The German works council legislation (1972) and Swedish collective agreements included workplace representatives in dismissal notification and social plan negotiation processes: workplace representatives or local unions play an important role in codetermining restructuring policies in Nordic countries and Continental Europe.

Union-enforced seniority rules, however, reinforce the push toward early exit, instead of retaining older workers as initially intended. If older workers are well protected, employers are less willing to hire them and seek ways to circumvent employment protection. When mass layoffs are necessary and early retirement plans are available, firms may seek the consent of workers and their representatives to use early retirement pathways for restructuring.[16] As discussed in Chapter 5, the unemployment bridging pathway and special preretirement programs in the 1980s enabled firms to restructure with workplace representatives' consent, but increasingly against the explicit criticism of national unions and employer associations of such externalization policies. Yet employers, independently of union or worker pressure for early exit, were also interested in circumventing older workers' employment protection and controlling their (early) exit—using mandatory retirement rules, firm-provided early retirement plans, and available public pathways.

6.3.2 *Employment Protection as Push Factor*

Employment protection and anti-age discrimination regulations, whether legislated or collectively agreed, constrain the hiring and firing of older workers (Buechtemann 1993b; Buechtemann and Walwei 1996). Commonly, employment protection laws not only make dismissal contingent on procedural rules and substantial grounds, but they also often provide for severance pay based on age or years of employment. These *seniority*

---

[16] For instance, the German unions in the coal and steel sector were the first to agree to employer dismissal of those workers at age 59 who could rely on the combined pathways of long-term unemployment benefits for one year and a preretirement pension for the old-age unemployed at 60 (Jacobs, Kohli, and Rein 1991b). In the United States, unions pressed employers for early retirement options for workers with long tenure '30 and out': early retirement after thirty years of service (Sass 1997: 231).

rules protect older workers or those who have long served the firm. While protecting the *insiders*—the long-term employed core workforce—from dismissal, age-specific employment protection rules can have the opposite effect for *outsiders*—those seeking employment—since employers will be reluctant to hire older people for fear of the costs of future dismissal. Employment protection based on the length of service would be less of a deterrent, unless the waiting period is relatively short. Smaller firms are often exempted from seniority employment protection and they should therefore be more likely to hire older workers. For example, small Japanese firms provide employment opportunities (at lower wages and with less protection) to older workers who have been forced to retire from larger firms (Kimura et al. 1994).

The length of notice prior to dismissal is age-specific in Sweden and in the Netherlands, while the other European countries stipulate dismissal conditions only by length of service and thus only indirectly protect older workers. The length of notice in Sweden is two months for those under 30, rising to six months for those aged 45 and older. Dutch workers over the age of 45 have two weeks notice, instead of one, per year of service, up to 26 weeks (Ehrenberg and Jakubson 1993: 203–5). Germany used to have rules that were more favorable for white-collar employees (six months after 12 years), but the Conservative government harmonized these rules on a medium level, thereby improving the situation for blue-collar workers, who used to have only three months notice after 20 years. Of the European countries, the shortest period is stipulated in France (two months after two years) and the United Kingdom (about three months after twelve years). American employers are free to hire and fire at will and there are no age- or service-related rules at the federal level, though the 1988 WARN Act introduced a two-month notice in cases of plant closure (Ehrenberg and Jakubson 1993). Despite the lack of statutory protection in Japan, courts have enforced the obligation for employers to prove just cause in cases of both redundancy and individual dismissal. While large Japanese firms have traditionally promised their regular employees employment tenure (*shushin koyo*) until mandatory retirement (*teinen*), part-time and temporary workers (often women) and those working in small firms are not covered by these—civil servant-like—exchanges of company loyalty in return for tenure (Kimura et al. 1994).

Disincentives for combining work and pensions as well as the regulation of mandatory retirement enforced by employers are important for older workers' retirement decision-making. In some systems, in order not to lose full public benefits, workers may be forced to quit working when drawing public pensions or preretirement benefits (Blöndal and Scarpetta 1998; Gruber and Wise 1999*b*). Most early retirement schemes and full disability pensions require withdrawal from work or at least have earnings tests, but even some normal public pensions impose such rules (French and, until the 1999 reform, Swedish pensions). Public pensions' earnings rules that cut benefits depending on other income 'can be considered a form of mandatory retirement "through the backdoor" ' (Casey 1997: 17), since they are a disincentive to continue working beyond the statutory retirement age. The earnings rule was removed from the British flat-rate public pension in 1989, while the United States lowered the reduction factor (finally abolishing it in 2000), and Japan has increased the earnings cap. To prevent abuse, disability insurance, early flexible retirement, and gradual (part-time) pensions have elaborate rules on reducing benefits according to income. The British, the American, and the Japanese disability schemes require strict standards, limiting part-time income or recognizing solely 'full disability' and thus full withdrawal from work. Only recently has the United States allowed the transitional combination of disability benefits with work (O'Day and Berkowitz 2001).

In the absence of enough pull from public exit pathways, American firms relied on push through employment contracts that stipulated *mandatory retirement* (Lazear 1979). However, the United States Congress legislated the Anti-Discrimination in Employment Act in 1967, initially raising the mandatory retirement age to 65, and increasing it to 70 under the Carter administration in 1978, but finally abolishing such rules altogether under the Reagan administration in 1983 (Sheppard 1991: 278). These policies to lift or abolish mandatory retirement, however, were less motivated by antidiscrimination concerns than by an effort to increase the retirement age and thus improve the public pension schemes. As a substitute for mandatory retirement, US firms use (early) retirement and window plans to induce older workers to retire voluntarily, a consequence not intended by the lawmakers of the antidiscrimination act.

The Japanese mandatory retirement must be seen in the context of a firm's internal labor market and responsibility to provide income opportunities after forced retirement (Evans 1991; Kimura et al. 1994). Larger Japanese firms rely on mandatory retirement to respond to their long-term employment guarantee, age-related career trajectories, and seniority pay structure, all of which make older workers more expensive. Japanese employers terminate seniority pay increases around age 50, and enforce mandatory retirement around age 60. In return for lifelong loyalty, large firms provide considerable lump sum severance pay and occupational pensions, or they may reemploy workers within their company network. Some retirees find reemployment in small firms or on farms; in other cases they become self-employed, using their lump sum severance pay as a business investment. As a result, older workers are overproportionally employed in smaller firms (Kimura et al. 1994: 250). This early retirement practice relies on a web of social customs and public policies which allows larger firms to maintain their employment tenure system (Dore 1997).

In several steps, the Japanese government has attempted to increase old-age employment and to raise mandatory retirement practice in firms. It used subsidies, announced intervention early, legislated the 1986 Employment Act, reformed pensions, and finally banned mandatory retirement before age 60 (in 1994) (Kimura and Oka 2001; Kimura et al. 1994). As in the United States, the rise in mandatory retirement age is largely motivated by concerns about the long-term sustainability of pension systems in a rapidly aging society (Endo and Katayama 1998). However, the financial and economic crisis since the 1990s, and aging, have put further pressure on the government to raise the pension and mandatory retirement age (Endo and Katayama 1998; Kimura and Oka 2001); but this threatens to undermine these reemployment practices that are closely tied to Japan's production system (Watanabe 2000). Indeed, we need to look more closely at the varieties of production systems and corporate governance to understand further institutional push factors.

6.3.3 Production Systems as Push Factors

The main claim of the Varieties of Capitalism approach is that modern advanced economies differ in their national production systems, economic governance, and labor relations; thus a firm's production strategy is embedded in a web of supporting social institutions (Hall and Soskice 2001b; Hollingsworth and Boyer 1997a; Soskice 1999). Certainly, there are considerable differences between firms, sectors, and regions within a national economy (Crouch et al. 2001; Hollingsworth, Schmitter, and Streeck 1994), yet the institutional environment is to a large degree shaped by nation-specific regulations, economywide standards, and societal norms set by nation-state legislation, collective agreements, national traditions, state-regulated sectors, and leading national champions. For this macro-comparative study, I only discuss the main differences in national economic systems. Drawing on the established ideal-typical bipolar models in the Varieties of Capitalism literature (see Chapter 3), I confront these with the findings on early exit trajectories.[17] I ask whether and to what extent the specific employment strategies of firms that are embedded in particular types of production systems, corporate governance, and labor relations, explain cross-national differences in early retirement practice at the macro level.

In 'Fordist' *mass production* factories, the production approach is *task-centered* (Marsden 1999), workers have low or general skills and turnover is relatively high, with employers less committed to employment tenure (Crouch, Finegold, and Sako 1999). Thus, a sudden decline in market share and long-term technological changes may cause these firms to shed the less productive and inadequately skilled older workers first. This production model has been prevalent in LMEs (Soskice 1999) of the United States, the United Kingdom, and Ireland. Given the institutional affinity between LME and the liberal-residual welfare state, these firms have limited possibilities to use public pathways to adjust their workforces and externalize these costs onto the welfare state (see Figure 6.1).[18] However, American, British, and Irish firms have used occupational pension, severance pay, and window plans to 'downsize' their older workforces.

Given a largely unregulated flexible labor market, Fordist firms can more easily shed older workers, but they are also more willing to hire older workers. Thus, dismissed older workers without sufficient or with no pre-retirement income frequently work in postcareer 'bridging jobs' at lower wages (Doeringer 1990). This secondary labor market reinforces the advantages of wage and employment flexibility in LMEs. As a consequence of the market-driven push and limited pull, early exit from work has been less pervasive and its trajectory largely follows the cyclical unemployment wave.

The ideal-typical converse model entails a *high-quality and high-skill production* strategy by firms that relies on internal labor markets with a relatively skilled workforce, high-wage structure, and internal labor markets

[17] Since production methods vary across firms and sectors within a country, selected case studies of firms' early retirement policies based on extensive field research (Naschold and de Vroom 1994) provide a rich data source. Such case studies investigate in detail whether firms with different production systems within a national economy vary in their management of human resources and early retirement policies. I base my analysis here on the results of these country studies (Germany, Sweden, the Netherlands, United States, and Japan), and the general comparative findings on national patterns (de Vroom and Naschold 1994; Jacobs and Rein 1994; Naschold, de Vroom, and Casey 1994*a*).

[18] As shown in Chapter 5, early public pensions are not available or actuarially reduced (except for women in the United Kingdom), disability pensions are restricted to medical criteria only, unemployment benefits are short-term, and special preretirement schemes are exceptional (only the United Kingdom during the 1980s).

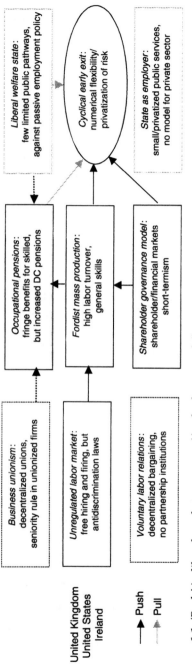

Figure 6.1 'Push' in liberal market economy (Anglophone model)

(Soskice 1999; Streeck 1992). Since function-centered skills and production methods prevail (Marsden 1999), vocational dual training systems (Germany) or firm-provided multitask training (Japan) play important supporting roles (Crouch, Finegold, and Sasko 1999; Culpepper and Finegold 1999). If sudden market changes occur, these firms tend to hoard labor by cutting back on overtime and working time, instead of resorting to mass dismissal (Mosley 1998; Mosley and Kruppe 1996). They also respond to technological change by retraining workers in new production methods, though works councils play an important role in the adaptation process (Streeck 1987a). In fact, promises of lifelong employment provide an incentive for workers to invest in firm-specific skills and cooperative employment relations (Estevez-Abe, Iversen, and Soskice 2001; Soskice 1999).[19] Germany is a prime example of this specialized quality production strategy (Streeck 1992), but firms in other CMEs, such as Sweden and Denmark, the Netherlands, and—to a lesser degree—France and Italy have also shared in the skill-oriented internal labor market model.

Externalization of early retirement costs (see Figure 6.2) through public exit pathways has been used by these skill-intensive production firms not only to restructure their workforces to changing demand but also to maintain seniority pay and career paths for their highly skilled workforces (Naschold, de Vroom, and Casey 1994). In Germany, early retirement has been widely used to adjust workforces and maintain the internal labor market model, though larger firms have been more able to use existing regulations, negotiate with works councils, and top up pension or unemployment benefits with occupational pension and social plans (Auer and Speckesser 1998; Naschold et al. 1994). Similarly, larger Dutch firms in both the industrial and service sectors have used externalization strategies to restructure their (male) workforces, relying on their own or collectively negotiated occupational pension plans, while small firms and female workers tended to use public disability and unemployment pathways on an individual basis and beyond the control of employers (Trommel and de Vroom 1994).

---

[19] Each production system requires a particular skill profile, ranging from firm-specific to industry-specific (or occupational) to general skills, and these skill profiles are reinforced by employment protection and unemployment insurance (Estevez-Abe, Iversen, and Soskice 2001). The more firm-specific, less transportable these skills are, the more employment security, seniority rules, and lifelong employment promises are needed. Favorable unemployment benefits that guarantee sufficient replacement and time to search for an appropriate new job play a role for those with industry-specific skills, while those with firm-specific skills need employment security with a given employer, especially when changing to a new job and retraining by a new firm remains unlikely.

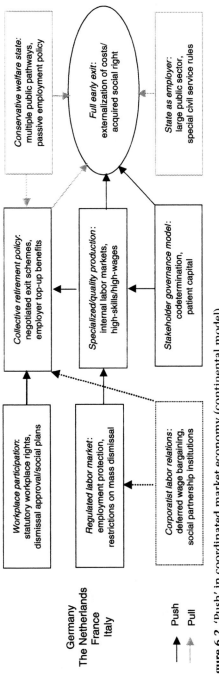

Figure 6.2 'Push' in coordinated market economy (continental model)

In the Latin European countries with more contentious labor relations (France and Italy), *circumventing mass dismissal* by using early retirement was very common among private and public employers. Restructuring occurred unevenly given the disparate economic structure: the large state-owned sector and Fordist mass production factories used early retirement for downsizing (Gray 1996), but also the considerable small and medium-sized firm sector, commonly concentrated in particular regions, with less capacity to use early retirement to externalize costs (Gray 2001). Given the lower importance of high-skill production, it is less maintenance of the internal labor market than preservation of peaceful labor relations that pushes larger private firms and public employers to use early retirement as a socially acceptable restructuring strategy. In France during the 1970s, private and (semi-)public employers were able to dismiss older workers and restructure with the help of the early retirement unemployment allowances administered by the social partners. Since the 1980s, employers have come under more pressure, as the state intervened by lowering the retirement age, regulating exit through negotiated job replacement conditions in 'solidarity contracts', and by pressing the social partners to reform their unemployment funds (Guillemard 1991; Jolivet 2002). Similarly, in Italy the public redundancy program (CIG) has provided opportunities for Italian firms to 'park' older workers, circumvent stringent employment protections, and avoid industrial conflict over mass dismissal (Samek Lodovici 2000*b*). In an effort to flexibilize wages and employment, Italian firms have sought to replace older well-protected 'insiders' by younger less-protected 'outsiders' since the 1980s (Contini and Rapiti 1999). At the same time, unions have defended seniority pensions, which gained in importance over the 1990s, as a social right of older workers (Regini and Regalia 1997).

Scandinavian firms more closely followed the high-quality production model of Continental Europe, but *integration* of older workers in the labor market remained comparatively higher. Swedish firms have been more successful in integrating older workers than Danish firms that used early retirement more extensively in the 1970s and 1980s (Olofsson and Petersson 1994; Petersen 1989), though the 1990s brought a reversal between the two countries in pursuing activation policies (Hansen 2002; Wadensjö 2002). Although some Swedish firms have used early retirement options to shed older workers, with the consent of workplace unions, the larger emphasis on retraining, reassignment, and part-time work has led to a much lower level of early retirement and to a higher degree of *internalization* of costs (Olofsson and Petersson 1994; Wadensjö 2002). Production methods that use job rotation as well as active labor market policies that relocate workers have helped to maintain higher employment levels among older workers—at least prior to the unemployment crisis of the early 1990s. Moreover, as long as the Swedish welfare state provided generous partial pensions, a gradual transition from work to retirement helped integrate older workers longer than in other countries, though these generous programs have been phased out. Neighboring Denmark tended more toward the externalization strategy (Hansen 2002; Petersen 1989). Given its larger small- and medium-sized firm sector, a relatively flexible labor market (with high turnover), and an occupationally fragmented union movement, early exit from work became common with rising unemployment since the 1980s, particularly among older women and less-skilled older male workers. In fact, it was the Danish unskilled worker unions, for men and women, which pushed for preretirement pay as part of the union-run unemployment funds as early as the late 1970s.

Similar to Sweden, Japan is also a case of *internalization* (Naschold, de Vroom, and Casey 1994), though it is more the outcome of particular firm-based production systems and social customs (Kimura et al. 1994) than the result of active labor market policy advanced by government and unions. In order to gain flexibility, Japanese firms rely on function-centered production methods and internal labor markets in which workers are trained to perform multiple tasks (Marsden 1999). Although these firms provide 'lifelong employment tenure', they enforce mandatory retirement, originally as early as age 55 in the 1970s and later at age 60 (Kimura et al. 1994). However, they often reemploy their 'retired' workers with temporary contracts (at lower wages) and often send them on redeployment to subsidiaries and suppliers within the company group (*keiretsu*)[20], which helps to improve information flows between the main firm and suppliers (Dore 1997). Thus, the paradox of the Japanese labor market (Evans 1991)—early mandatory retirement and high-old-age activity levels—can be explained by the particular practice of forced early exit from career-jobs of the internal labor market and various social practices that provide those older workers with employment in the secondary labor market.

The public and private early exit pathways are *institutional complementarities* to the particular tenure employment system. In LMEs, Fordist mass production firms with low-skill profiles use early retirement to achieve numerical flexibility and increase productivity, relying on 'buying' general skills on the external market but at the cost of high turnover. If public

---

[20] A group of companies with cross-shareholdings (Estevez-Abe 2001).

pathways are insufficient, firms will either be willing to pay the price of downsizing via private early retirement plans (thus internalizing the costs) or be capable of shedding labor at low costs (thus shifting the burden onto older dismissed workers). In CMEs, particularly in Continental Europe, high-quality production firms with skilled workforces do not use early retirement primarily as a means to downsize or to restructure in difficult times, but to maintain lifelong employment, seniority pay, and career trajectories irrespective of the business cycle. When public pathways or collectively negotiated schemes are available, larger companies with internal labor markets use early retirement and thus externalize the adaptation costs. Only in exceptional cases, such as Sweden and Japan, are some of these costs internalized by firms, with older workers remaining at least partially active longer, due to particular public policies and social practices.

The dilemma of the skill-intensive production regime is that the more employers rely on seniority wages and employment tenure, the more they are interested in shedding older workers when seniority pay, career trajectories, and employment protection reach their (perceived) age-related limits (Casey 1997). Moreover, high-inactivity rates in preretirement age and high early retirement costs put additional pressure on social expenditure, which subsequently leads, via elevated social contributions, to increased nonwage labor costs that in turn put additional pressure on firms to shed labor (Esping-Andersen 1996c; Scharpf 2001). However, as we have seen, not all high-skill production systems with internal labor markets rely on early exit from work. Although the Swedish and Japanese firms have been under similar pressure to Continental European firms, they have found solutions to keep older workers active longer. The Swedish part-time pension and Japanese reemployment strategies allow gradual transitions from work to retirement, longer retention or sharing of experience within or among firms, and lower expenditures on early retirement programs. However, it remains an open question whether these 'best practices' could be adapted to the particular circumstances of Continental Europe. The welfare retrenchment and the end of full employment in the 1990s have already called the success stories of Sweden and Japan into question.

6.3.4 *Corporate and Financial Governance as Push Factors*

Institutional differences in corporate and financial governance also have repercussions for human resources management and employment strategies (Dore 2000; Jackson and Vitols 2001). Anglophone LMEs rely on capital markets that impose short-term horizons and on antitrust policies that foster competitive interfirm relations (Soskice 1999). Publicly listed companies are under more pressure to respond to sudden declines in demand or profitability by downsizing employment, flattening corporate hierarchies, and selling off unprofitable units. Moreover, firms seek 'hostile' takeovers to boost profits, partly by economies of scale through merger and partly by selling off assets after a takeover. The new parent company may choose not to honor the long-term employment and future pension commitments of the acquired company.[21]

Private pension funds also add to the pressure to downsize. With the exception of Employee Stock Ownership Plans in the United States, trusts are only allowed to reinvest 10 percent in the United States and 5 percent in the United Kingdom into the sponsoring company (Turner and Watanabe 1995: 101). In both the United States and the United Kingdom, the new human resource strategies and the lucrative returns from capital led to a shift from DB to DC schemes. Thus, employers no longer underwrite promised benefits for lifelong service; instead, employees will individually enjoy the returns and bear the risks of financial market developments (Turner 1996). At the same time, individual DC schemes, the American '401(k)' plans (since 1982) and the British private 'opt-out' pension (since 1988), have gained popularity, reinforcing the quest for higher capital market returns and the importance of personal savings for old age. Thus, pension trust funds have gained an increasingly important role in the financial system (Dore 2000; Jackson and Vitols 2001). This has reinforced the pressure on listed companies to produce substantial quarterly profits, thereby amplifying the downsizing forces.

In the CMEs, stable ties between firms and banks have reinforced the long-term commitment to employment stability and corporate welfare benefits. Although short-term financial market pressure has mounted in recent years, CMEs (Germany and Japan in particular) still maintain a long-term investment perspective, given more stable shareholders and the larger role of general banks (Hall and Soskice 2001b; Soskice 1999). Until recently hostile takeovers have been relatively unknown and mergers have been part of market expansion or diversification strategies, less motivated by short-term profits achieved through asset capitalization and economies of scale by downsizing. In both Germany and Japan, a

---

[21] Thus American firms can liquidate pension fund surpluses: 'although Congress made pension trusts irrevocable, it allowed sponsors to recapture the assets of terminated plans that remained after the satisfaction of all plan liabilities' (Sass 1997: 283–4 fn. 29).

considerable portion of postwar occupational pension commitments is reinvested into the firm or group via book reserves.[22]

The Dutch pension funds, while holding the most per capita assets in the late 1980s, invested—with employer–employee consent—less than 20 percent in equities, half of it on foreign stock markets (Turner and Watanabe 1995: 104–5). The French mandatory occupational pension is pay-as-you-go and has only small reserve funds (Reynaud 1996). The Swedish collective supplementary schemes are only partially funded (recently also the blue-collar scheme), while the public ATP scheme invested in public housing. The 1999 pension reform, which merged the basic and earnings-related public pensions, has introduced partial funding (2.5 percent of wages are invested). Hence, with the partial exception of Japanese and Dutch pension funds, occupational pensions have not relied on stock market investments but rather on secure investments, PAYG or book reserves, the latter two financing methods requiring long-term stability and trust.

Recent private pension reforms will increase the importance of funded pensions in Continental Europe and Nordic countries; nevertheless, this will be a gradual transition. Further shifts toward DC and funded pensions as a result of demographic challenges may in the long run undermine the institutionalized systems, and changes in financial and corporate governance may reinforce declines in employer commitments toward their lifelong employees. Thus, at a time when welfare states seek to shift costs from public PAYG pension systems to private-funded systems, employers are ever more reluctant to enter new corporate welfare obligations. In these cases, DC and individual savings plans will also become more dominant; thus DCs will just become a further part of the wage bill or even an individual's savings decision. The long-term commitments of employee and employer enshrined in this production system would thus be increasingly undermined.

6.4 Can the Varieties of Capitalism Explain Early Exit Regimes?

The analysis of production-related *pull* through exit pathways indicated the interest of employers in using early retirement. Particularly in welfare

[22] In 1990–91, less than 10 percent of occupational plans but about 60 percent of accumulated pension funds were book reserves in Germany; thus large firms, in particular, reinvest their tax-exempt pension commitments (Turner and Watanabe 1995: 96–7). 'The popularity of book reserve plans in Japan, in spite of their unfavorable tax treatment, indicates the high value that firms appear to place on the availability of this form of corporate financing' (Turner and Watanabe 1995: 57). However, Japanese multiemployer plans and smaller firms commonly set up employee pension funds and tax-qualified pension plans, respectively; half of the assets in both cases can be invested on the stock market.

systems where public pathways have been less available, the social partners or firms were willing to (co)finance their own early retirement schemes. For employers, occupational pensions would not only provide a means to bind (skilled) workers to the firm, they might also be used to induce and control retirement. However, employers in LMEs have increasingly retreated from DB pensions and 'window' plans, while continuing to downsize. In the other countries, occupational pensions have gained in importance in recent decades, partly as a consequence of reforms toward privatization. This provides a new opportunity space for unions to negotiate occupational pensions, which in turn would lead to increased internalization of retirement costs by wage negotiations. The comparative analysis has shown the importance of analyzing the public–private mix for a better understanding of the pull factors, also correcting the view that early retirement is solely a consequence of public policy. Voluntary plans sponsored by employers or collectively negotiated by the social partners provide considerable pathways to early exit from work.

Adopting a production-related *push* perspective complements the often one-sided pull perspective of early retirement. Political economy interpretations of labor shedding commonly claim structural push factors. Certainly, the overall trend toward early retirement can partly be explained by long-term structural push in the economy: deindustrialization, the growth to limits of the public sector, the older workforce's outdated skill structure, and increased unemployment. However, none of these factors, not even the industrial mix thesis, can explain *cross-national* variations in early exit trajectories in any systematic way. Instead of universal structural push factors, there seem to be mediating institutional 'filters' that translate structural push into particular regime-dependent adaptation strategies.

The analysis of the interaction of production-related employment strategies and corporate governance turns out differently in early exit from work policies (see Table 6.8). Certainly, all private firms experience the need to restructure their workforces in order to adapt to technological change and competitive pressure. They also have come under pressure to downsize in order to meet declines in demand and profitability. However, I argue that the downsizing pressure is stronger but also more cyclical in Fordist mass production firms under LMEs, whereas the need for restructuring seems to be more inherent in high-quality production systems with internal labor markets, highly skilled workforces, and seniority wage systems. The push to shed older workers is indeed more cyclical in LMEs, while it is more long-term and structural in CMEs (see Table 6.8).

Table 6.8. Varieties of Capitalism and early exit patterns

Early exit trend	Full exit (externalized)	Partial exit (internalized)	Cyclical exit (individualized)
High and very early	France Italy		
High	Germany Netherlands		
Moderate (? high)	(Denmark)		United Kingdom
Moderate		*Partial pension:* Sweden	United States
Low	(CME)	*Reemployment:* Japan	Ireland (LME)

Notes: See Table 4.8 for exit trends; CME: coordinated market economy, LME: liberal market economy.

In CMEs, high-quality production firms have sought to shed those older workers with lower skills and lower productivity, as a means to allow skill-enhancement and plant restructuring, while keeping their pledge to maintain employment tenure and seniority wages—which are crucial for their internal labor markets with skilled core workforces. The availability of public pathways has helped to externalize the costs of such restructuring, particularly in Continental Europe. However, firms or the social partners were also willing to set up their own scheme if public pathways were insufficient or cut back. I claim that the production-related push factor is salient enough for firms to use early retirement even if there is not enough pull from public programs. This is confirmed by the tendency of larger Japanese firms to maintain their employment tenure system by enforcing mandatory retirement on older workers, while at the same time offering them reemployment opportunities with partial income compensation (in the absence of public pathways allowing a full exit). Swedish firms have, at times, been able to continue integrating older workers thanks to part-time work, though this depended on generous partial pensions and the support of active labor market policies.

In contrast, American, British, and Irish firms in LMEs are hard pressed to downsize to achieve higher dividends required by the stock market and, particularly, after (unfriendly) mergers. Ironically, the workers' pension funds, as institutional investors, have reinforced such financial market pressure. Initially, Anglophone firms were willing to pay occupational pensions in order to attract and retain skilled blue-collar workers and white-collar employees. They later applied these schemes to use early retirement for restructuring and downsizing, and they are now seeking to relieve themselves of the burden of DB plans and instead offer portable DC plans as mere fringe benefits to a mobile and flexible workforce. Increased privatization of protection and market-driven push will force more and more older dismissed workers into lower-paid 'bridge jobs' in the secondary labor market until and even partly after retirement.

The third institutional variable and the 'missing link' between the protection-related pull and production-related push are differences in *partnership relations*. The bargaining partners play an important mediating role not only in social policymaking and implementation but also in the bargaining and workplace arenas. In LMEs, Fordist mass-producing firms used downsizing to adapt to economic exigencies, while unionists at workplace level lacked legal employment protection or statutory dismissal procedures. Employers only offer window early exit plans when a union is strong enough to enforce seniority rules and management is committed to maintaining good employment relations. In contrast, in CMEs, management and labor respond to restructuring pressure by using early exit from career-jobs as a socially acceptable solution to the high-seniority wage problem and in order to maintain the internal labor market pledge. Both unions and workplace representatives have a preference for early retirement over other restructuring measures since early exit helps protect the prime-age core workforce and high-wage system.

While the early retirement practices of Continental European firms rely heavily on consensual externalization by the social partners, Japanese and Swedish firms partially internalize the costs of keeping older workers employed (Naschold and de Vroom 1994). Whether externalization or internalization prevails is partly a consequence of the availability of public pathways and active policies. Yet it also depends on the social partners' strategies. For instance, Danish union leaders, especially of the general union, were far more inclined to use early exit from work as a labor-shedding strategy than their Swedish colleagues in industrial unions. Although the Swedish and Danish unions were both directly involved in the administration of occupational pensions and unemployment insurance, the Swedish unions adopted a more integrative strategy toward older workers, while the Danish unions pushed for union-run preretirement programs and defended early exit from work against the retrenchment efforts of the 1990s.

In Continental Europe, employers and unions have been willing to 'collude' to foster early retirement for the sake of upholding employment protection and seniority pay. Management was interested in maintaining good relations at the workplace by allowing older workers to retire on favorable conditions. Employer associations and unions at national or sectoral level were willing to bargain over collective early retirement schemes that would complement, if not supplement, public pathways. However, as early retirement becomes an acquired social right, defended by unions, and controlled less and less by management, employers grow increasingly critical. Moreover, the externalization of costs by management–labor collusion has pushed up social expenditures for both public and private schemes, which in turn increase payroll and general taxes that have a negative impact on competitiveness and, subsequently, on labor demand.

The social partners' collusion in using the public exit pathways for firm restructuring policies produces formidable obstacles to reform. Yet the analysis of production-related push indicates that even if public pathways are cut back further or closed in future, a reversal in early exit trends will be highly dependent on the production-related push factors. The (re-)integration of older workers would require a move toward integration of older workers through continued training efforts by employers, increased part-time job opportunities in firms, higher job mobility of older workers, and active labor market policies for older workers. Moreover, the collective bargaining partners and legislators would need to adapt age-related wage systems and employment protections in order to limit the push factors. To compensate for income loss through lower wages or part-time work, partial pension schemes as in Sweden or wage subsidies as in Japan could be a complementary policy on the protection side. Yet as discussed in Chapter 7, the reversal of early exit policies has largely focused on cutting back on protection-related pull rather than on innovative activation policies that could effectively deal with the production-related push factors.

Part III

Reform Obstacles and Opportunities

Chapter 7

Exit from Early Retirement: Paradigm Shifts, Policy Reversals, and Reform Obstacles

Early exit from work has become a widespread social practice—paid for by modern welfare systems. Since the 1970s, the massive use of myriad early retirement provisions has driven up social expenditures, lowered payroll and general taxes, and increased nonwage labor costs. Despite their justification as creating employment opportunities for young job-seekers, these passive labor market policies, enabling early retirement for increasing numbers of people, have not reduced youth unemployment. Indeed, the countries with the most extensive use of early exit, France and Italy, also suffer the highest levels of youth unemployment (Samek Lodovici 2000a). Once thought of as a partial cure for the modern ills of large-scale redundancy and mass unemployment, early exit today is publicly criticized as the wrong medicine (OECD 2000). The early exit route sought to reduce the supply of labor and thereby lower unemployment. Instead, it became a very costly passive labor market policy resulting in insufficient use, if not active disregard, of human capital and expertise (Herberttson and Orszag 2001; OECD 1995b, 1998c). Particularly in Continental Europe, early retirement has expanded significantly over the last three decades, contributing directly to the high social expenditures of these 'welfare states without work' (Esping-Andersen 1996b).

In this chapter, I focus on *policy reversal*, that is, attempts to control the increasingly costly early exit routes and shift toward policies better attuned to an 'active aging society' (OECD 2000). These efforts must be contextualized in broader welfare-state reforms: not merely is the retrenchment at issue, but the recalibration of social policies to international economic pressure, public spending limits, and socio-demographic challenges

(Pierson 2001*b*, 2001*a*). Early retirement is a policy area at the nexus of several social insurance programs that are all affected by ongoing reform efforts: old-age pensions, disability and sickness benefits, and labor market policies. The golden years of welfare-state expansion, until the early 1970s, are long over, with social policymaking experiencing a paradigm shift to welfare retrenchment and restructuring (Pierson 2001*b*).

Three pressing problems require reform, all of which have consequences for early exit from work: (*a*) the future sustainability of pensions, (*b*) the high nonwage labor costs, and (*c*) the need to increase activity rates (Bonoli and Sarfati 2002). Responding to these challenges, governments seek to reverse early exit trends with the help of five policy instruments discussed later: (1) postponing statutory retirement, (2) reforming disability insurance, (3) closing special preretirement schemes, (4) 'activating' older workers, and (5) fostering gradual retirement. For each of these measures a general trend in policy reversal is observable but important cross-national differences remain in problem pressure, timing and scope of reform efforts as well as in success of their implementation. Before outlining the policy problems and paradigm shift, I examine the reversal in these policy areas. In the concluding sections, I review cross-national variations in problem load, policy initiatives, and reform capacities. Thus, the analysis in this chapter focuses on the evolution of policy changes targeted to reverse the post-1970s early exit trends.

7.1 Paradigm Shifts in Early Exit Policies

Since the 1980s, all OECD welfare states experience often significant cost pressure due to early retirement programs and other preretirement pathways. National governments, employer associations, and policy experts now criticize the extensive reliance on early exit as a labor-shedding strategy. International organizations ranging from the OECD to the European Commission have put the financial implications of providing pensions and health care for an increasingly aging society high on their agendas (EU-Com. 1998, 1999*a*; OECD 1995*a*, 1998*c*, 2000). Such organizations as the OECD and European Union have often led these reform debates with international studies on current and future problems, comparative 'benchmarking', specific policy recommendations, and dissemination of 'best practices'. The *epistemic communities* (Haas 1992) of experts brought together by international organizations have played a conspicuous role in shifting the perception of the causes of and cures for the welfare-state crisis (for a critical view on the World Bank, ILO, and European Union see Ney 2000). While national public office holders may have worried less about the problems of future governments in sustaining pension benefits beyond 2000, they did recognize an opportunity to move the political alliances toward a reform coalition.

The 1994 OECD's Job Study was among the first major efforts in international policy learning, prescribing further deregulation of labor markets as the solution for Europe's employment problems, while the European Union approach remained more multifaceted (Casey 2004). Within the European Union, the Open Method of Coordination (OMC) has become a deliberate coordination strategy that seeks to influence national policy-making by setting targets, through benchmarking by peer review and via learning from best practices (Goetschy 2003). Following the Lisbon process to make the European Union 'the most competitive and dynamic knowledge-driven economy by 2010', the Stockholm Council in March 2001 set the intermediate target to increase the employment rate of people aged 55–64 to 50 percent by 2010 (EIRO: EU0104208F). In addition, the Barcelona target of March 2002 seeks to postpone withdrawal from the labor force by five years. Both the OECD and the European Union propose to abolish disincentives to work through preretirement options and policies to increase activity rates for older workers. Three major challenges provide the rationale for welfare-state reforms in general and a reversal in early exit policies in particular.

(1) *Demographic shifts and public pension sustainability.* Due to higher life expectancies, low birth rates, and large elderly cohorts, all OECD countries face the problems that have grown typical of aging societies (Bosworth and Burtless 1998a, OECD 1998c, 2000; Wadensjö 2002). Old-age-dependency ratios will increase due to demographic shifts: fewer and fewer people of working age will have to support more and more people in retirement (Bosworth and Burtless 1998b). The share of the elderly in comparison to the working-age population has grown since the 1960s—with the exception of Ireland, which stagnated, and Japan, which grew rapidly from a low level. Sweden has the highest dependency ratio, followed by France, Germany, the United Kingdom, and Denmark. In contrast, the ratio grew slowly in the Netherlands and the United States. In addition, the duration of old-age 'non-activity' has grown continuously due to ever longer life expectancies and earlier retirements.

As a consequence of these demographic changes, but also due to more generous benefits, all welfare states experienced substantial increases in the overall costs of old-age and disability pensions over the last four decades (see Figure 7.1). However, Continental European welfare states have significantly higher costs than the Scandinavian and British welfare states, which come second, while Ireland, the United States, and Japan make up a third 'low spender' cluster, due in part to more favorable age-dependency ratios. In the future, the demographic 'time bomb' of an ever older citizenry will put PAYG pension systems with DB under even more pressure (Bosworth and Burtless 1998*b*). Therefore, international organizations and national policy experts recommend a shift toward (funded) DC schemes (OECD 2000). They also advocate measures to postpone entry into retirement, which promise the double benefit of decreasing the number of pensioners and increasing the number of active people who pay social contributions. At the European Union level, since the Lisbon European Council in March 2000, long-term sustainability of pensions has become part of the European Union strategy (EU-Com. 2001), though financial and social aims (represented in two different ministerial committees) often conflict in the new OMC on pension policy (De Deken 2003), leading to rather general policy recommendations.

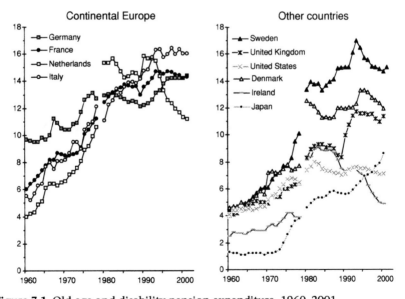

Figure 7.1 Old-age and disability pension expenditure, 1960–2001

Notes: Old-age, survivor, and disability pension expenditure (%GDP); not strictly comparable before and after 1980; incl. mandatory private benefits since 1980.

Sources: 1960–79: OECD (1988, Table C.1); 1980–2001: OECD (2004).

(2) *Increasing labor costs due to rising social expenditures.* In addition to sustainability, inactivity in working age prior to age 65 is seen as a major cause for the high level of social expenditures, in particular social assistance, disability pensions, and unemployment benefits. Since the late 1970s, governments have undertaken welfare retrenchment efforts to control costs: cutting back on social benefits, tightening eligibility criteria, and pushing costs onto private actors (Brown 1988; Giersch 1997; Gilbert 2001; Pierson 1994). Generous social transfers are also criticized for their negative impact on the reservation wage: Workers are less willing to accept a job when working wages are hardly more than social benefits. Early retirement benefits without actuarial deductions are seen as disincentives to work (Blöndal and Scarpetta 1998; Gruber and Wise 1999a). Moreover, in systems with payroll or social contributions, high social expenditures have put particular pressure on nonwage labor costs, thereby pricing even more workers out of employment. In particular, the conservative welfare states are suffering from the 'continental dilemma' (Scharpf 2001): More and more inactive people become dependent on welfare financed through social contributions and general taxes that have to be paid by fewer and fewer actively employed people. Therefore, cost-saving measures in social security are advocated by governments and employers as necessary steps to reduce nonwage labor costs and thus boost employment growth.

(3) *The vicious circle of passive labor market policy.* Early retirement was often defended as opening up new employment opportunities for young people and alleviating unemployment, thus using passive labor market policy to 'better' redistribute available work (Kohli and Rein 1991). However, the labor market effect was rather small due to opportunistic reemployment by firms when early retirement was made conditional on job replacement. As a result, firms did not necessarily create additional jobs for younger workers. Moreover, the job allocation processes for young people and the job profiles of older workers hardly match (Sackmann 1998, 2001). Increased use of early retirement did reinforce expectations of early exit, thus further reducing the time span for a firm to achieve returns on the investment of retraining older workers (Casey 1997). The long-term unemployment benefits for older workers, which were motivated as a social measure due to their lower chances of finding employment, created an unintended 'perverse effect' (Boudon 1977). In other words, the availability of exit pathways fostered the dismissal of older workers by employers, often with the consent of workplace representatives. As skill shortages already exist in some areas and will expand in the future, labor market

experts now advocate activation and integration measures that help retain older workers in employment (Bonoli and Sarfati 2002; Walwei and Werner 2001). The often solely rhetorical political goal of 'lifelong learning' is of particular relevance (Tuijnman and Schömann 1996). More broadly, 'employability' has been a major aim as part of the European Employment Strategy (Goetschy 1999) and will be crucial to meet the European Union's targeted higher employment rates. Changes in age-related hiring, training, and firing policies of firms as well as coordinated adaptation of seniority-related wage scales by collective bargaining partners and less age-sensitive employment regulation by legislators would be needed to improve older workers' (re)employment opportunities, thereby diminishing the 'push' factors toward early exit from work.

7.1.1 Raising the Statutory Retirement Age

Thus, a major paradigm shift has occurred in current public debate, in widespread policy recommendations, and in some legislative measures: to raise the nominal retirement age for public pensions. Several welfare states have granted women the right to draw their public pensions earlier, either generally (by five years in Italy, the United Kingdom, and Japan) or under certain conditions or during earlier periods (France, Germany, and Denmark). Yet in all these countries, except Italy and France, the age limits for women are being equalized with those of their male colleagues (see Table 7.1) due to legislative action. Since women's life expectancies exceed men's, on average by several years, women receive pension payments for a longer period (Davis 1998: 37). Given fewer years of employment due to family-related career interruptions, earlier exit may also lead to lower pensions for women living in systems with earnings-related contributions, thus increasing gender income inequality in old age (Allmendinger 1994).

Following rulings by the European Court of Justice on equal treatment in public and private pensions, every European Union country must phase out gender differences in pension ages (Pierson and Leibfried 1995). The United Kingdom will gradually increase women's retirement age from age 60 to 65 over the decade from 2010 till 2020. Decided by parliament in 1989, Germany's 1992 Pension Reform raised the preretirement option for women with interrupted working careers but 15 years of contributions from age 60 to 65 by 2012. While the phasing-out window has been changed to 2000–4, a flexible pension with actuarial reductions is granted to those women born prior to 1952. France remains the only country that

Table 7.1. Reforms of statutory pension age and seniority/flexible pensions

Country	Reform	Statutory pension age		Seniority or flexible pensions
		Men	Women	
Germany	1989* 1996** 2002***	65	65 (normal) 60 (minimum) –2012: →65* 2000–4: →65**	Seniority: 63 (35+y.) –2002: →65*
Netherlands		65	=	1991 actuarial component 63–67 (+/–)
France	1993*	1982: 65>60 (#37.5 y.)	=	Private sector pensions*: 1994–2002: #37.5 →40 y.
Italy	1992* 1995** 1997*** 2004****	Self-empl.: 65; employees: 60 →65 by 2001*	Self-empl.: 60; employees: 55 →60 by 2001*	Entry 1992– benefits: all #* Entry 1979–: DB→DC by 2013; flexible pensions (57–65); seniority: 57+ by 2008**
				Public/private sector harmonization: seniority 57+ #35y. by 2004*** (40y. by 2008****)
Sweden	1981* 1999**	1976: 67→65	=	1976: partial 60–65, Cuts in benefits*, 61**– Flexible pension** (2003–): 61–64: –0.7%p.m.; deferrable 65–70: + 0.5%p.m. **→ new pension (NDC), partly funded (DC)
Denmark	1998*	67	=	Partial 60–67/**65 (10y. 2nd tier)
	1999**	2004: →65**		Deferrable** –70 1999*: new funded OP
United Kingdom	1993/95* 2003**	65	60 2010–20 →65*	Deferrable by 5 y. (+ 7.5%) Pension credit** (means-tested) 60 (2010–20: →65)
Ireland		1977–: 66 (65 earnings test)	=	No early, no deferrable pension (public service 2004–: cost- neutral early pension)
United States	1983*	65	=	62–65/67* (–6.7% p.a.)
		2002–27 →67*		Deferrable –69: (+4% p.a.) 1984: mandatory retirement ban
Japan	1986* 1994** 1999***	basic 1st tier: 65* 2001–13: → 65** 2nd tier: 60 2001–9** (flat-rate) → 65 2013–25*** → 65	1st: = 65* 2nd: 55 1993–2000 →60* (b. 1928+) 2006–14 → 65** 2018–30 → 65***	Deferrable: –70 (66–70 +12% → +88%), 1998**: mandatory retirement (*teinen*) not before 60

Notes: = Same rules as for men; # contribution years; → phased-in change.

Sources: Compiled from OECD (1995a, 1995b); Kohli et al. (1991); Delsen and Reday-Mulvey (1996a); MISSOC (2003); SSA/ISSA (2003, 2004a, 2004b).

equalized retirement ages for both men and women at the lower pension age of 60, resulting from the Socialists' 1982 reform (Guillemard 1991). Yet in 1993, the contribution period for a normal pension was increased for both men and women working in the private sector (see later). Even though Italy has not yet narrowed the five-year age gap in favor of women—as stipulated by European Union law—in the 1990s it did increase the retirement age by five years for both men and women for cost-saving reasons (see later). Responding to Japanese society's rapid aging and increased labor force participation of women, a 1986 reform phased in higher retirement ages for the receipt of public pensions from age 55 to 60 over the period 1993 to 2000 (Clark 1991: 44).

Postponement of statutory retirement for both men *and* women has been more important for rolling back the trend toward early exit. In order to avoid a social security deficit in the future, the United States was the first country to legislate a rise in the 'normal' retirement age (as early as 1983; phased in over several decades).[1] In 1986, the United States Congress made it unlawful to stipulate a mandatory retirement age in employment contracts, although Congress had already extended the age limit to 70 in 1978 (Hutchens 1994: 418). The German 1992 Pension Reform, reached by all-party consensus in 1989, foresaw a gradual increase not only for female retirement, but also for the seniority pension, popular among male workers (from age 63 to 65 by 2002), and the pension for unemployed older workers (age 60). A highly contested reform in 1996 phased out the long-term pension for the unemployed by 2002; it is now being replaced by a flexible pension for those born after 1937. In Italy, the 1995 Dini pension reform also raised the 'minimum' retirement age step by step from 53 to 54 until 1998, and then to 57 by 2004, although the public sector was granted a later start on reaching the new minimum age. The reform entailed slower harmonization of favorable public with private sector rules and an exemption for older cohorts of blue-collar workers and those with long working lives. This compromise helped the unions to earn their members' approval (Baccaro 2002; Regini and Regalia 1997).

While banning mandatory retirement before age 60 by 1998, Japan's lawmakers also decided, in 1994, to increase the (earnings-related) second-tier public pension age from 60 to 65 for both men and women, yet with a faster timeframe for men (2001–9) than women (2006–14) (Estienne and Murakami 2000). However, the pension can be drawn at age 60 (with

---

[1] The 1983 amendment on raising the statutory retirement age (from age 65 to 66 by 2009 and to 67 by 2025) was expected to remove one-third of the projected actuarial deficit in 2027. Later efforts by Congress to further increase the retirement age failed (Chen 1996: 171–2).

actuarial reduction of the basic pension but full earnings-related portion) in order to supplement lower income from mandatory retirement and subsequent lower paid reemployment, a common practice in many larger firms (Takayama 1996).[2] In March 2000, the Japanese parliament passed a bill to phase in the age of 65 for the earnings-related pension benefits from 2013 until 2025 for men and with a delay of five years for women (2018–30), though an actuarially reduced early pension (−0.5 percent p.a.) can be drawn from age 60 onwards.

Except in Japan, the statutory retirement age was already relatively high (age 65 or higher) in countries with Beveridge basic pension schemes: Sweden, Denmark, Britain (except for women), Ireland, and the Netherlands. Sweden's dramatic economic and financial problems in the early 1990s soon spurred the country to make major social policy changes within a relatively short time span (Hort 2001; Stephens 1996). Sweden's 1992 crisis pact, supported by both the government and the Social Democratic opposition, had foreseen an increase in the normal retirement age by one year, but this plan was later rescinded (Wadensjö 2000b). During the 1990s, the mandatory retirement age was raised to 67 (making it impossible for collective agreements to impose age 65) and the flexible pension age was increased from 60 to 61, while other exit options (via disability pensions for the unemployed) were closed down at the beginning of the crisis. In neighboring Denmark, official pension age remained 67 until the mid-2000s, but the Danes actually retire at age 61 on average, thanks to 'anticipated' disability pensions and special preretirement pay (Hansen 2002). A multiparty 1999 budget settlement, contested by unions and employers, lowered the normal retirement age to 65 as of 2004 and reduced entitlements accordingly in order to induce postponement of exit until the—now more realistic—statutory pension age. In addition, workers receive a premium from the preretirement fund if they continue to work until age 65.

Except for Britain's future long-term change in retirement age for women, the main pension reforms of 1988 and 1995 fostered supplementary individual pensions, while cutting back on the state-earnings-related pension scheme (Bonoli 2000; Lynes 1997). While the firm-sponsored occupational pension funds are largely DB plans that often facilitate early retirement, the new private individual pensions are DC plans, which entail actuarial deductions for early drawing. The Irish basic pension provides no early exit option (but also no deferrable pension), contributory pension is

---

[2] The basic pension's earnings test does not include part-time work (less than 33 hours) or the substantial company bonuses. These 'loopholes' in pension and tax rules allow companies to reemploy their 'retired' workers at lower cost (Takayama 1996: 141–5).

paid at age 66 or with an earnings test at age 65 (and means-tested non-contributory pension at age 66). Only occupational pensions, such as the public service pensions, provide preretirement options (since 2004 with cost-neutral actuarial reduction). Finally, the Dutch basic pension, paid from age 65 onwards to residents, was not altered, as it provided no early exit pathway in contrast to the private preretirement VUT schemes.

While all countries engaged in limiting disincentives to work and brought their statutory pension age up to 65, the French government has not been able to increase the minimum age because 'the French are very much wedded to the idea of official retirement at the age of 60. This entitlement is in many ways a symbol of social progress, something the French have fought for through long years and that was granted them with the advent of a socialist government in 1981' (Reday-Mulvey 1996: 50–1). Yet, de facto, the 1993 Balladur-Veil pension reform extended the minimum contribution period from 37.5 to 40 years, so that 'even if retirement at 60 years is now an established right, many... will have to work well beyond that age in order to clock-up the requisite 40 contribution years' (Reday-Mulvey 1996: 53). However, efforts to impose the same rules on public employees under the Juppé government in 1995 failed due to the strikes mobilized by public sector unions (Bonoli 2000; Bozec and Mays 2000; Vail 1999).

All countries with retirement age below 65 have thus decided to increase normal retirement age gradually, or at least to postpone exit by requiring longer contribution periods or by lowering benefits through actuarial deductions. With the exception of Italy, all countries that had gender gaps in the past have decided to equalize pension ages; all but France chose to raise the female retirement age to that of men. These measures were primarily motivated by concerns about long-term pension sustainability and social security costs in light of currently unfavorable demographic shifts, but they also were meant to increase activity levels. Indeed, every year that a pension is postponed brings additional contributions and delays benefit payments, at least if older workers do not become unemployed or need social assistance.

Political resistance to changes was particularly strong in countries with pay-as-you-go earnings-related contributory systems (Myles and Pierson 2001). The general strikes over the state-imposed welfare retrenchment plans of the Berlusconi government in Italy in 1994 and the Juppé government a year later in France indicate how much veto power unions could still marshall to block such reforms (Ebbinghaus and Hassel 2000). By contrast, the later reforms that the Italian governments negotiated with the main unions demonstrated the importance of social concertation for bringing about and implementing welfare reforms (Regini and Regalia 1997). The French government under Balladur was more successful in 1993 than its successor because it phased in changes and consulted the unions (Bonoli 2000). Moreover, since the private sector unions are much weaker than in the public sector, they had less veto power to oppose the government's reform (Natali and Rhodes 2004).

The German reforms were also gradually phased in; in particular the consensual 1992 Pension Reform had a long transition period, whereas the 1996/97 efforts that anticipated the phased-in reform led to strong criticism by unions and the Social Democrats (Hinrichs 2000b). In general, phased-in reforms tend to limit the impact on older cohorts, which have already paid into the old system for a long period and thus have the strong expectation of receiving the same (early) pensions as colleagues who had recently retired. An immediate shutdown of an exit pathway would cause serious concerns among those older workers with the most concrete expectations to retire early, while younger cohorts may well be less worried about the small additional burden of subsidizing a longer phasing out of seniority rights. Buying the consent of older workers via gradual transitions, exemption rules, and *Vertrauensschutz* (fidelity clauses) for older cohorts has been common in nearly all reform processes of Bismarckian pay-as-you-go pension systems, particularly in Germany, Italy, and France. Yet raising the official retirement age and making early drawing more costly do not necessarily lead to a decline in early exit rates, since much depends on the potential use of other second best alternative pathways.

7.1.2 *Reforming Disability Insurance*

The use of disability programs for early exit from work became notorious as the 'Dutch disease' during the 1980s (Aarts, Burkhauser, and de Jong 1996a), leading subsequently to major reforms throughout Europe (Prinz 2003; Reinhard, Kruse, and von Maydell 1998). Disability transfers were most widespread in the Netherlands (used by 15.2 percent of the working-age population in 1990), followed at a considerable distance by Sweden (7.8 percent), the United Kingdom (6.8 percent), Germany (5.5 percent), and the United States (4.3 percent) (Aarts, Burkhauser, and de Jong 1996b: 4). There is an overall correlation between the 'generosity index' of disability benefits (the net wage replacement rate, see Blöndal and Scarpetta 1998) and disability claims of older people in the early 1990s (see Table 7.2). The 'generous' Dutch and Swedish benefits are paid to 30 percent of Dutch and 25 percent of Swedish older people (age 55–64),

Table 7.2. Replacement rate and recipients of disability benefits

	Replacement rate (1995)	Male recipients (% male LF) 15–64	Recipients (1990) (in % of age group)				
			Total 55–64	Males 55–59	60–64	Females 55–59	60–64
Germany	0.44	5.5	14.0	14.1	21.7	8.0	13.1
Netherlands	0.70	15.2	30.3	25.8	29.1	40.2	48.5
France	0.25	—	—	—	—	—	—
Italy	0.36	—	10.3	8.7	14.9	6.7	11.5
Sweden	0.70	7.8	25.4	16.0	34.3	18.8	32.2
Denmark	0.39	—	15.4	11.2	19.5	12.4	18.8
United Kingdom	0.28	6.8	9.1	11.8	19.1	4.5	1.9
United States	0.45	4.3	6.6	7.4	10.7	3.7	5.1
Japan	0.25	—	—	—	—	—	—

Notes: Sweden: 1989; Germany, Italy: Population for 1989 used; Italy: employees only; LF: labor force.

Sources: Generosity index (weighted by average replacement rate): OECD 1998: Table III.1 p. 48; Male % LF: Aarts, Burk hauser and de Jong (1996b): Table 1.1, pp. 4–5; Recipients: OECD 1995 (No. 16): Table 4.6, pp. 80–1; and own calculations.

while Britain's (but also France's and Japan's) relatively frugal benefits and tighter eligibility rules led to fewer people seeking disability insurance. Yet there are more complicated patterns in disability claims and awards than an incentive-led 'pull' model suggests. In countries with basic pensions without retirement options (in the Netherlands, Sweden, and Denmark), the disability pensions became a quasi-early exit scheme. In Bismarckian pension systems (Germany, Italy, and France), the disability pathway also played a notable role. But in the liberal-residual welfare systems (the United States, the United Kingdom, and Japan), the lower benefits are less of an incentive and the lack of labor market considerations reduces responsiveness to 'push' factors, in particular high unemployment rates.

The Dutch reform process, which influenced policy debates in other countries, is a telling example of the scope and urgency of the problem of cutting back on early exit via disability programs (Aarts, Burkhauser, and de Jong 1996a). Dutch retrenchment was already underway by 1976, when the universalization of benefits to ever larger sections of the population required some cost-saving measures. However, within a decade further contentious retrenchment policies were implemented—against union protest.[3] Yet the cumbersome consensus-driven process and its

---

[3] Labor market considerations, introduced in 1967 and relaxed in 1973, were more strictly applied after 1978. Even though union protests had blocked a center-left proposal a year earlier, the new center-right coalition was able to reduce replacement rates in 1983. The average net replacement rate dropped from 87 percent in 1980 to 72 percent in 1985, leading

piecemeal cost-saving measures failed to bring the system under control. Conflicts ensued such that 'by 1986 employer organizations and right-wing political parties were arguing that previous reforms had been too small and too late in light of deteriorating economic conditions', while 'trade unions and left-wing political parties criticized the first series of cost containment proposals for being inequitable' (Aarts and de Jong 1996*b*: 51). The 1987 Social Welfare Reforms were the first substantial policy reversal, aimed not only at reducing welfare expenditures but also at harmonizing disability pensions with long-term unemployment benefits as well as abolishing gender inequalities. While the government had expected the reform to cut disability transfers by half, the measures brought a very small reduction (10 percent). Subsequently, Prime Minister Lubbers called the Netherlands a 'sick country', and the new center-left government declared the fight against absenteeism and disability dependence their top priority (Visser and Hemerijck 1997). Ultimately, only state intervention in self-administration and political compromises were able to alter the rules, at least for younger entrants.[4] In addition to making changes in eligibility and benefits, the government shifted the burden of sick pay costs onto employers who could now underwrite private insurance (Aarts and de Jong 1996*b*: 63–5). Even though these measures were successful in reducing the rate of new awards and decreasing absenteeism, private employer insurance filled some of the replacement gap left by the state scheme. In fact, the employers' 'stated interest in reducing labor cost was outweighed by their desire to maintain a generous exit option for their redundant workers' (Aarts and de Jong 1996*b*: 64). The 1990s reform thus proved less capable of foreclosing this exit route altogether, but it did succeed in reducing long-term disability among younger cohorts. After take-up rates of partial pensions increased again in the late 1990s, the Donner Commission proposed in 2001 to introduce further obligations on employer and employee sides (de Jong 2003*b*).

Swedish disability insurance served as a major exit route for older workers: One out of three Swedish men and women (age 60–64) used this

to a decrease in disability payments from 22 new awards per 1,000 employed in 1975 to 16 per 1,000 in 1985 (Aarts and de Jong 1996*a*: 40, Table 2.6). Nevertheless, the number of disability benefits, overall costs, and the incidence rate of new awards increased again in the late 1980s.

[4] When the tripartite Social Economic Council was unable to come up with a stringent reform proposal, the cabinet abandoned consensus-seeking and presented its own proposal (Visser and Hemerijck 1997). The reform proposals of 1991 and 1992 made eligibility standards more stringent and planned lower benefits for younger recipients. After fierce resistance, a political compromise left acquired seniority entitlements untouched, requiring only awards to beneficiaries under age 50 to be reevaluated.

scheme and it was the second step following unemployment according to the '58.3 rule'. Employers and local unionists often colluded in using this pathway: 'Since individual firms and their employees did not bear the direct costs, they were free to push older workers permanently out of the labor force without bearing any of the burden of their actions' (Wadensjö and Palmer 1996). As a consequence, the unemployment–disability pathway raised overall social expenditures and lowered the '*de facto* pension age' (Wadensjö and Palmer 1996). In the late 1980s, the Swedish government banned workplace agreements using the '58.3 rule' to circumvent employment protection laws, but early retirement still accounted for about half of all disability benefits, although one-third of disability pensioners were working part-time. With dramatically rising unemployment and the fiscal crisis of the early 1990s, the government closed the disability pension for older jobless unemployed workers (age 60–64) as early as 1991. Consequently, unemployment among older workers increased considerably (Wadensjö 2002). The rate of disability pensioners remained very high in the older age groups during the late 1990s; more than every third woman (and nearly every third man) aged 60–64 and every fifth woman (every sixth man) aged 55–59 received a disability pension, while the abolition of the 'elderly rule' in 1997 has led to a substantial decline in new take-up rates (Kruse 2003: 378–9).

Also in Denmark, the very generous rules of the tax-financed Danish disability insurance (*førtidspension* or literally preretirement pension) were used as a major exit pathway, particularly by women with interrupted work careers who could not claim the unemployment preretirement benefit (Jensen 2003). In the mid-1990s, a policy change occurred toward activation measures provided for unemployed recipients, including subsidized jobs such as flexi-jobs and soft jobs that allow disabled workers to work. As of 2003, working incapacity, not loss of employability, is being applied as the key labor market criterion for disability pensions.

German disability insurance was less 'generous' and not as common: only every fifth older man (age 60–64) and every sixth German woman received disability benefits in the late 1980s (Frick and Sadowski 1996). Moreover, the 1984 Budget Act reduced benefits and raised the minimum contribution period (which affected women with interrupted working careers in particular), thereby limiting the program's further growth. Nevertheless, the German disability program allowed preretirement pensions for severely disabled older workers with 35 contribution years (constituting about one-fourth of all paid disability benefits in 1990). In addition, due to the labor market considerations in disability pensions, 'increasingly, labor market problems have been shifted to the disability pension system' (Frick and Sadowski 1996: 121), although the individual risks of disability and unemployment are not close substitutes (Riphahn 1997).

After unification, the Conservative-Liberal government decided in 1996 to phase out the disability preretirement program more rapidly than stipulated by the 1992 Pension Reform. Nevertheless, the subsequent Social-Democratic–Green government reinstalled a more gradual phase-out timeframe in 1999, though benefits will be actuarially reduced. A break with past disability pension policy occurred in 2000/1, when the former distinction between occupational disability (*Berufsunfähigkeit*) and work incapacity (*Erwerbsunfähigkeit*) was abolished and merged into a single work disability test, while the special pension for severely disabled people (*Schwerbehinderte*) with a functional disability of at least 50 percent was maintained (Viebrok 2003: 203–5). With this pension reform, the seniority pension age was raised from 63 to 65 by 2001, the unemployment pension from 60 to 65 over five years by 2001, the pension for the severely disabled from 60 to 63 between by 2003. The extended 32-month unemployment pathway (for age 57+) was first planned to expire in 2001 but then prolonged until 2006 in order to exempt older unemployed workers from the harsh Hartz reforms of unemployment and social assistance policies. The reform of general disability pensions will have a long-term impact on those born in 1961 or later, as it requires an incapacity to work longer than six hours per day.

For many Italians, the disability program was the only early retirement option during the postwar period, though it did not necessarily provide generous benefits. It became widespread once the eligibility criteria were relaxed in 1970/1, particularly since the disability pension awards provided ample possibilities for 'particularistic-clientelistic' practices: it was 'used as a surrogate for unemployment benefits in the southern regions as well as privileged currency for the *voto di scambio* (i.e. the exchange of preference votes for semilegal or outright illegal concessions of benefits or other "favors")' (Ferrera 2001: 165). After a further wave of disability claims in the early 1980s, a more stringent criterion of 'capacity to work' was introduced in 1984, leading to a decline in take-up (OECD 1995a).[5]

---

[5] About five million Italians (50 percent private sector, 20 percent public sector, and 30 percent self-employed) were on disability pensions, 7 percent of Italians aged 55–59 and 13 percent of Italians aged 60–64 in 1995, compared to 12 and 4 percent ten years earlier (OECD 1995a: Table 5.2; SZW 1997: Table 3–4). In 1990, four million Italians were receiving 'disability' benefits; of which 1.7 million (or 40 percent of the recipients) were self-employed, and only one million (or one-quarter of all recipients) were in the age group 55–64 (OECD 1995b:

After several changes in the 1980s, some 'loopholes' in disability programs were closed in 1995. From 2002, the new pension reform formula will calculate benefits based on lifetime contributions and life expectancy at retirement. As a consequence of the reforms since 1984, the rate of disability pensioners in relation to the labor force dropped considerably, from 15.8 percent in 1980 to 2.9 percent in 1998 (Baldacci and De Santis 2003: 241).

Compared to other Continental European welfare states, France stands out due to its low take-up rate since disability benefits are relatively meager: just 30 percent of former salary for 'partial', and 50 percent for 'full' incapacity to work (Palier 1997: 92).[6] Older French people have instead mainly used other preretirement benefits such as unemployment and early pensions. Similarly, Japan's disability benefits are relatively low and hardly used as bridging devices for early retirement.

The liberal welfare states (the United States and the United Kingdom) have been rather restrictive in granting disability pensions. The two existing US disability pensions—Social Security Disability Insurance (SSDI, 1956) and Supplemental Security Income (SSI, 1972)—were subject to retrenchment efforts relatively early. In 1977, the Carter administration used 'moral suasion' to tighten eligibility decisions by state agencies. The Reagan administration used the 1980 reform passed by the Democratic-led Congress to reduce benefits, tighten control, reevaluate past decisions, and increase work incentives (Sheppard 1991: 278). But in 1984, under public pressure, Congress reversed this reform, making it difficult to remove anyone already on the disability rolls.[7] The recession of the early 1990s brought with it a new wave of applicants.

In the United Kingdom, the Conservative Major government in 1992 abolished the earning-related disability insurance, kept flat-rate benefits, and introduced new living and working allowances based on self-assessment rather than means testing. Despite the intention of retrenchment, these British reforms led to considerable increases in disability expenditures in the 1990s. The United States and the United Kingdom

136–7). Disability insurance provides benefits for three years after just five years of contributions, and for unlimited pensions after twelve years of contributions.

[6] In the 1980s less than 40,000 'disabled' and less than 85,000 'inapt' men and women were held eligible for disability insurance—out of around 400,000 to 500,000 retired persons (Guillemard 1991: 143–4, Table 5.8).

[7] The new practice led to half a million removals, most of which led (in turn) to a wave of appeals, a subsequent ruling by Social Administration Court judges in 1981, a press campaign about the dire consequences in individual cases, and massive complaints by state governors in 1983 (Berkowitz and Burkhauser 1996).

do not recognize 'commensurate' employment as a criterion in disability awards and have been reluctant to allow for partial work incapacity—out of fear that disability benefits might be abused. Both the American and British disability systems actually produce the strongest disincentives to seek work as they have stringent earnings tests, yet disability benefits are kept relatively low in order to maintain strong incentives to work.

7.1.3 *Closing Special Early Retirement Programs*

Almost all eight European countries set up special preretirement programs or at least some special unemployment benefits during the high-unemployment period (Mirkin 1987). Yet fairly soon governments realized that the costs of these relatively generous schemes were going to continue; expenditures surged as mass unemployment persisted into the 1980s. Interestingly, the special programs that were set up as temporary explicit early retirement measures were easier to close down than exit options in general schemes. Britain's JRS is an example of the unplanned rise, ad hoc changes, and final shutdown of such a program (Laczko and Phillipson 1991*a*, 1991*b*). The new Conservative government, committed to welfare retrenchment, made several stop-and-go changes to the scheme inherited from the previous Labour government.[8] When the employment situation improved, the government finally closed this costly but relatively limited program by 1989.

In Germany, it was the Conservative-Liberal Kohl government that closed its own temporary preretirement (*Vorruhestand*) program after only four years (in 1988), despite calls to prolong it, especially by moderate unions. The intention of the 1984 Preretirement Law was to combine changes that shifted the costs incurred by dismissal onto employers and foster instead the use of collectively bargained preretirement programs, with subsidies for job replacement, under the new scheme. The reform was a political compromise between economic and social interests in the Conservative-Liberal coalition (Mares 2001*b*). Not only did the government deem it too costly but also employers thought it too expensive and they wanted more control over their workers' retirement decision (Jacobs, Kohli, and Rein 1991*b*: 209–10). The preretirement pension was replaced

---

[8] The conservatives raised the age limit in 1980 and then lowered it slightly in 1982, only to raise it again in 1984. The JRS part-time option was closed down in 1986, and finally JRS was completely closed off to new entrants in 1989, after some 250,000 people had benefited from it (80 percent of the beneficiaries were men) for one or more years (Laczko and Phillipson 1991*b*: 228).

by a part-time scheme in 1989 that proved very unpopular with firms and workers. Yet closing down the special *Vorruhestand* program did not put an end to early exit from work, given the multiple other pathways. Unification made ad hoc preretirement schemes even more indispensable: The government used special early exit rules to smooth the East German transition from a former socialist planned to a market economy in a socially acceptable way (Börsch-Supan and Schmidt 2001; Ernst 1995).[9]

After preretirement benefits paid by the unemployment funds increased rapidly in the late 1970s, the French state sought to regain control by implementing a double strategy of lowering the overall pension age to 60 and regulating publicly financed preretirement schemes that were based on state–firm 'solidarity' contracts with stringent job replacement conditions (Guillemard 1991). After transitory measures, the French government closed all special state-financed preretirement schemes except the FNE redundancy allocation for which it raised employer contributions and the minimum age (from 55 to 57) in 1984. The largest share of early exit before statutory retirement at age 60 is now financed through the social partners' unemployment scheme, which filled in the gap left by the more restrictive state-run FNE schemes.[10]

Denmark's voluntary preretirement pay (*efterløn*) was promoted by the unions, especially the unskilled workers' unions and more recently by unions of white-collar and professional employees (Hansen 2002; von Nordheim Nielsen 1991). The preretirement pay of the union-administered unemployment funds provided a major pathway to early exit (ages 60–66) throughout the 1980s and 1990s (NOSOSKO 1998). During the 1990s unemployment crisis, a 'transition' preretirement bridge was introduced in 1992 for those aged 55–59 and in 1994 for those aged 50–59 (Hansen 2002). Thus, at least in theory, 'the system did make it possible for an unemployed worker to live on public benefits for approximately 25 years before the official retirement age, during seven of these years as early retired' (Hansen 2002: 177). A turnaround in 1996 closed the pre-60 transition benefits for new entrants. As part of the 1999 reform package,

---

[9] Even before unification, the East German government granted preretirement benefits to men (at age 60) and women (at age 55). Thereafter, these were replaced by a special preretirement benefit (65 percent of net earnings) paid by the unemployment insurance. About 850,000 East Germans were beneficiaries in 1993, but over the next five years all recipients were transferred to the pension scheme upon reaching 60 years of age (Schmähl, George, and Oswald 1996).

[10] After restrictions on collective dismissal and the use of the 'solidarity contracts' in the 1990s, the number of new entrants to the scheme plummeted from 58,000 in 1993 to 8,000 in 2000 and in total only 12 percent of the half million workers who exited early received FNE benefits in 2000 (Jolivet 2002: 258).

contributions to unemployment insurance and early retirement pay were separated and conditions tightened. Joining the preretirement scheme is now completely voluntary and independent from unemployment insurance, with the flexible pension benefits now requiring 25 years of contributions. The popularity of the voluntary preretirement scheme and the vested interests of trade unions made plans to abolish it politically unfeasible. Before the 1999 elections, the Social Democratic government even had to pledge a constitutional guarantee for the new (flexible) preretirement benefits for older workers aged 60 and with 25 years of unemployment insurance contributions (EIRO: DK9902111N). The state has, belatedly, intervened to stem the tide of such expensive labor reduction policies, though it was forced to make concessions to the unions, particularly the strong general workers' union (SiD) with its more than 300,000 members (Ebbinghaus and Visser 2000).

The Dutch preretirement scheme (VUT), negotiated by the social partners, expanded rapidly during the 1980s as the government tightened public disability insurance criteria (de Vroom and Blomsma 1991; Trommel and de Vroom 1994). The popularity of PAYG-financed branch-level collective schemes led to rising costs, higher contributions, as well as problems of moral hazard and free-riding since larger firms could shed older workers, but all employers within a sector would share the costs. A reform of the system proved difficult in light of the need for bipartite consensus and the system's fragmentation into various branch agreements.[11] Following the December 1997 tripartite agreement on state pension reform and changes in government tax policy (Rein and Turner 2001: 133), VUT has become an issue in collective bargaining rounds: A number of recent agreements envisage a transition to a more flexible preretirement program with lower benefits and costs (EIRO: NL9809194F), lowering the incentives for early retirement in the future. Following major controversy, the social partners and government concluded a social agreement in November 2004 on early retirement and disability pension insurance (EIRO: NL0411102F): The government will end its provision of tax incentives for early retirement, while fostering a 'long-term leave' wage fund that could provide up to three years of leave and tax incentives for occupational pensions for workers aged 63 or older (after 40 years of contributions).

---

[11] The VUT contributions have increased considerably, from 0.6 percent of the private sector wage bill in 1981 to 2.4 percent in 1992; in the public sector, the increase was even more dramatic, from 0.4 to 6.8 percent (OECD 1995*b*: 185).

The Italian preretirement scheme as part of the CIGS redundancy fund became particularly widespread in the industrial North-West (50 percent of cases): in 1998, 180,000 workers were on preretirement, of which 120,000 were in the manufacturing industry and 50,000 in steel (OECD 1995a: Table 5.4). In 1989, the government introduced copayments by firms (50 percent in the North, 25 percent in the South), which dampened take-up. The tightening of preretirement redundancy benefits did not reduce early exit, leading instead to mere substitution by alternative pathways. Seniority pensions increased in the 1990s as many blue-collar workers of the cohorts born after 1940 reached the required 35 contribution years before statutory pension age 60 (nearly every fifth new pensioner received such seniority pensions in 2001) (Paulli and Tagliabue 2002: 287). The seniority pension arrangement was the most contested issue in the government–union negotiations over pension reform in 1995 and 1997, with the final compromise entailing a *grandfather clause* that exempts older workers from radical reforms (Baccaro 2002; Natali and Rhodes 2004; Regini and Regalia 1997). After years of controversy, the Italian parliament in 2004 empowered the Berlusconi government to advance the timeframe on seniority pensions from 2008 onwards and require the transfer of all end-of-service allowances into closed (negotiated) or open (individualized) pension funds (EIRO: IT0309203F).

With the exception of Ireland and Sweden, all European welfare states advanced special preretirement programs at some time and they had some involvement of the social partners, except the British JRS. These explicit early retirement programs led firms to externalize their restructuring costs, shifting them onto the national (as in France) or sectoral wage bill (as in the Netherlands), or onto the occupational unemployment funds (as in Denmark). When preretirement schemes were negotiated, wage moderation could be traded against financing early exit benefits—in an exchange benefiting both (restructuring) firms and (older) workers. However, where the state had to underwrite deficits or subsidize benefits, as in the case of the French unemployment scheme and German *Vorruhestand*, governments could not remain indifferent to irresponsible behavior, though they had limited scope to regulate and control the social partners' behavior at different levels or across the whole economy. By the late 1990s, all special preretirement schemes had been closed entirely (British and German schemes already in the 1980s), their eligibility considerably tightened (e.g. French FNE schemes), or the transition toward pre-funded flexible schemes was underway (Denmark and the Netherlands). A major exception is the French social partners' efforts to counteract the government's retrenchment measures: they negotiated new preretirement pay as part of the unemployment scheme in 1995 and renewed it in 1998 (EIRO: FR9901150F; Jolivet 2002).

7.1.4 *From Long-Term Unemployment to Activation Policies*

The unemployment pathway provides early exit options in systems with generous long-term unemployment benefits and special rules for older workers. For jobless older workers who had not yet reached preretirement pension age and those without eligibility for disability pensions, unemployment benefits were the only public program available. In fact, the unemployment rates and especially the long-term unemployment rates for older working age groups were relatively high, particularly before the minimum age, in comparison to other age-related early exit pathways, commonly before age 60. Because older workers had a low chance of reemployment, long-term unemployment benefits or preretirement bridges were introduced for older workers. At the same time, they were no longer required to search for jobs, but they were often unable to receive retraining. Moreover, where unemployment benefits provided a high-wage replacement (as in Continental and Nordic Europe), employers under pressure to restructure would seek to dismiss older workers at the age when they could draw long-term unemployment benefits until they could claim preretirement pensions. In order to circumvent employment protection in these countries, employers need the voluntary agreement of workers and their representatives. The German '59er' (later '57er') rule (Naschold et al. 1994), the Dutch 57.5 rule (Trommel and de Vroom 1994), and the Swedish 58.3 rule (Olofsson and Petersson 1994) for long-term unemployment benefits combined with preretirement options from age 60 all had a similar effect: they led to opportunistic dismissal by employers, often with implicit or explicit consent by workplace representatives. Further, the special preretirement schemes sponsored by the unemployment insurance funds in France (ARPE) and Denmark (*efterløn*) as well as the redundancy scheme (CIGS) in Italy were functional equivalents of these unemployment bridges.

Given the shorter-term and lower benefits of liberal-residual welfare states (Bison and Esping-Andersen 2000), the unemployment pathway was relatively less salient. Exceptions are the British JRS in the 1980s as well as special means-tested unemployment benefits for older workers in Ireland and Japan, which provided benefits for longer than one year prior to pension age. Although unemployment benefits were retrenched during the 1980s, these were targeted more at younger and prime-age workers (Daly 1997; Gilbert 2001). In the 1990s, a shift from passive to more active labor market policies occurred (see Table 7.3), though governments and particularly the labor market parties only slowly reoriented policies toward unemployed older workers, embracing activation policies such as anti-age-discrimination as well as retraining and wage subsidies for older workers (Jespen, Foden, and Hutsebaut 2002*a*).

The United States and Britain abolished mandatory retirement and banned age discrimination. In the United States, the 1982 ban on mandatory retirement in private employment contracts was a measure that paralleled Congress' effort to gradually extend retirement age. Under the Conservative government in Britain, efforts at age-related activation policies remained largely limited to information campaigns against age discrimination during the 1990s. The New Labour government promoted a non-statutory Code of Practice for Age Diversity, and extended its 'New Deal' program to older workers ('50 plus' in 2000), providing employment credits to 35,000 workers during its first year (Walker 2002: 421–2).

Although unemployment was less of an issue in Japan, it did become a problem among older workers in the 1990s. The unemployment insurance fund paid wage subsidies for workers threatened by dismissal as of 1974. From 1995, a 'top-up' wage subsidy for 'semi-unemployed' older workers aged 60–64 with age-related low earnings was added (Kaneko 1998).

Table 7.3. Unemployment rate and labor market policy expenditure

	Unemployment rate (UR)*			Unemployment > 1 year		UR** 55–64	overrep.	1993/94		1999/2001	
	1993	2000	Δ%	1994	2000	2000	2000	LMP	A(%)	LMP	A(%)
Germany	7.9	8.1	+2.5	44.3	53.1	13.5	1.8	3.89	35.2	3.12	39.4
Netherlands	6.6	2.8	−57.6	49.4	33.4	1.9	0.8	4.69	29.9	3.65	43.0
France	11.7	9.5	−18.8	38.3	43.6	7.9	0.9	3.40	37.6	3.12	43.6
Italy	10.2	10.5	+2.9	61.5	60.9	4.7	0.5	3.04	61.8	0.65	—
Denmark	10.2	4.7	−53.9	32.1	20.0	4.0	1.0	6.96	26.1	7.47	60.4
Sweden	9.1	5.9	−35.2	17.3	22.8	6.1	1.2	5.73	51.8	2.72	50.7
United Kingdom	10.5	5.5	−47.6	45.4	19.0	4.4	1.0	2.17	26.3	0.95	38.9
Ireland	15.6	4.2	−73.1	64.3	47.5	2.5	0.6	4.51	35.0	—	—
United States	6.9	4.0	−42.0	12.2	5.3	2.5	0.8	0.64	32.8	0.38	39.5
Japan	2.5	4.7	+88.0	17.5	17.1	5.6	1.4	0.39	23.1	0.82	34.1
OECD	8.0	6.4	−20.0	35.2	33.0	5.5	1.0	—	—	—	—

Notes: *Standardized unemployment rate; Δ%: relative change over time %; unemp. > 1 year: long-term unemployment (over one year); **UR: unemployment rate age 55–64; overrep.: overrepresentation UR 55–64/UR 25–54; LMP: labor market policy (% GDP); A(%): active labor market policy (% LMP).

Sources: OECD (1998*a*, 2001*b*): Appendix.

Long-standing efforts by Japanese governments to persuade and later mandate employers to increase mandatory retirement (*teinen*) were most important: the 1986 Older Workers Promotion Act demanded that firms set their *teinen* age at 60, though only a 1994 amendment made it compulsory, as of 1998 (Kimura and Oka 2001). The government also helped induce Japanese employers to reemploy older workers on temporary contracts or use secondment to related firms, a feature that became a *beneficial constraint* (Streeck 1997*a*) for Japan's coordinated production system (Dore 1997; Watanabe 2000).

Sweden traditionally spent the most on active labor market policy compared to the other OECD countries (Janoski 1994), and older workers were not excluded from retraining and other active labor market policies as they were in most other countries (Wadensjö 2002). Until the late 1980s, unemployment rates were comparatively low overall and for older workers too, but a dramatic increase in the early 1990s led to major pressure on the Swedish welfare state (Jochem 1998, 2000). With the closing down of the disability pension option for older unemployed persons aged 60–64 in 1991 and the abolition of labor market considerations in disability pensions in 1997, these two common exit pathways were foreclosed (Wadensjö 2002).[12] Nevertheless, unemployment among older workers remained at a medium level in the early 2000s (see Figure 7.2), even after overall unemployment declined in the late 1990s. It remains to be seen whether current efforts to integrate older workers will be as successful as they were during the full employment era before the 1990s.

In contrast to Sweden, Denmark's unemployment rate (see Figure 7.2) was already considerable in the early 1980s, and peaked again during the mid-1990s, while active labor market policies were historically less important (Benner and Vad 2000; Jochem 2000). Helped by a move toward activation measures—targeted especially at young job-seekers—since the mid-1990s, the overall unemployment rate declined (Björklund 2000), although older workers' joblessness remained high. In 1998, the new government introduced reforms that cut payments to 91 percent of unemployment benefit for the short-term unemployed (EIRO: DK9812197F). Reform of the preretirement scheme, the abolition of the very early exit scheme in 1996, and changes in preretirement pay (*efterløn*) seem not to decrease take-up of regular unemployment benefits among

---

[12] The government granted a temporary offer of early exit compensation (for long-term unemployed age 60+) in 1997, leading to a 'one-off reduction in long-term unemployment among older workers' (Wadensjö 2002). Early that year, a public job creation program for older workers was also set up as a temporary measure (until 2001).

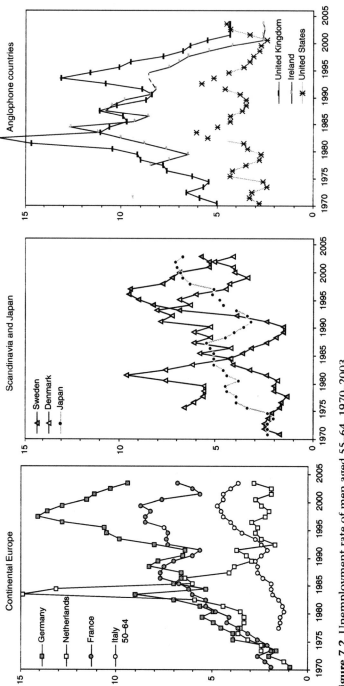

Figure 7.2 Unemployment rate of men aged 55–64, 1970–2003

Notes: Unemployment rate (%) for men aged 55–64 (except Italy: aged 50–64)

Sources: OECD *Labour Force Statistics 1970–2004*.

older workers—unless their employment chances improve.[13] Following its shift toward active labor market policy in the mid-1990s, the Danish government seeks to promote *'Seniorpolitik'* (senior policies) that aim to change personnel policies of firms with respect to retaining older workers (Hansen 2002).

Since 1957, the German pension system had granted early pensions to the long-term unemployed at age 60 and, since 1987, additional unemployment benefits for 32 months, allowing workers to leave at age 57 years and 4 months. The unemployment rate for the age group 55–59 was very high throughout the 1980s and 1990s as employers and works councils agreed to use the '59er' (later '57er') rule to shed workers in return for firm-paid severance packages (Rosenow and Naschold 1994). In order to curtail the combination of long-term unemployment benefits and subsequent preretirement pensions, the Conservative-Liberal government introduced a rule change in 1982 that sought to force firms that dismiss older workers to cover the additional unemployment benefit costs. However, the rule change 'was not effective because it was immediately challenged in the courts' (Jacobs, Kohli, and Rein 1991*b*: 203), demanding a costly and cumbersome review of individual cases. In 1993, the Conservative government reintroduced the fine for dismissal at age 58, though there were several exceptions for smaller firms and those in economic distress. In fact, by the late 1990s, this pathway was again popular under the aggravated labor market conditions, particularly following unification (see Figure 7.2).[14]

Pension reform was back on the political agenda in the mid-1990s, when the controversial 1999 Reform, enacted in 1997 by the Kohl government, stipulated a rapid phasing out. Yet the new Social Democratic-Green government reversed it in 1999 and reinstated the 1992 Reform with its longer phasing-out periods. With the exception of workers born before 1952, jobless workers (aged 60 and older) receive only a flexible pension with actuarial deductions as of 2002, but the age limit will be raised stepwise to the statutory retirement age of 65 by 2012. Part-time and flexible pensions, negotiated by collective agreements, do provide some alternative, though the costs for employers will be higher (paying half of the wages

---

[13] The duration of Danish unemployment benefits was cut from seven years to four years in 2000 for everyone under age 60, and for those older unemployed to 2.5 years, though the latter group now has access to activation measures similar to those introduced for younger workers in 1994 (Hansen 2002: 184–5).

[14] More than half of new male pensioners in East Germany and more than a quarter of new male pensioners in the West took the unemployment pathway, while women instead drew on the early pension at age 60 (VDR 2002).

and making up for the actuarial reductions). While these reforms have focused on 'pull' factors thus far, activation policies have been called for in recent years (Clemens 2001), such as in the declaration of the tripartite talks in March 2001, yet few policy initiatives have been formulated and implemented. One exception is the '50 plus' program for older engineers' employability (Naegele 2002). Proposals for new labor market reforms devised by the independent Hartz Commission prior to the 2002 elections proposed the waiver of active job-search for unemployed older workers, contradicting the overall retrenchment goals. The enacted Hartz reforms limit unemployment insurance benefits for workers aged 55 or older to 18 months instead of previously 32 months (but postponed until 2008), followed by a new means-tested scheme for the long-term unemployed and previous social assistance claimants.

Like its Rhenish neighbor, the Netherlands has many older workers in the age group 55–59 who face a high unemployment risk—that is just prior to the availability of preretirement VUT plans (aged 60+). Since 1982, older workers aged 55 or over are not required to search actively for a job and unemployment benefits for long-term insured can last from age 57.5 through 65. Thus, the '57.5' rule led to the same opportunistic dismissal policies by employers as it did in Germany and Sweden. While cuts in unemployment benefits occurred throughout the 1980s and 1990s (Gorter 2000), no change has occurred in the rules for the older unemployed. Active labor market policies that became part of the Dutch turnaround from high unemployment were aimed primarily at younger job-seekers, with age 45 set as the barrier for placement by the Public Employment Service. Nevertheless, given the increasingly tight labor market situation since the 1990s, there were more calls for policy change and increased training efforts were also directed at older workers (Delsen 2002).

France stands out as a country with a number of sequential and parallel preretirement plans financed by the unemployment funds that are managed by the social partners (Guillemard 1991). 'As a result of increasing competition since 1972 from the guaranteed-income schemes managed by the Unemployment Compensations Fund, the retirement system had been losing its power to regulate definitive exit' (Guillemard 1991: 143). As the state had to increase its subsidies, the social partners 'became aware that the Unemployment Fund's financial difficulties would be blamed on the new early exit pathways. They decided to curtail preretirement arrangements and decisions were made about sharing costs with the state' (Guillemard 1991: 150) in a 1984 agreement. Moreover, the new Socialist government lowered the public pension scheme's retirement age to 60, relieving the unemployment fund, which was capable of financing pre-60 exits from work. Once the conditions for the state's solidarity schemes for workers before age 60 were tightened during the 1990s, the social partners negotiated a new scheme of the unemployment fund ('early retirement for new jobs', ARPE) in 1995, followed by further steps.[15] Alternatively, older workers might be covered by regular unemployment insurance, under the DRE rules; they do not have to actively seek work. By the end of the 1990s, about half a million older people were on early retirement or DRE unemployment benefits in France. Although employers have had to pay a fee when dismissing older workers aged 50 and over since 1987 (since 1992 the fee varies by age), it had little positive effect, even compelling employers to dismiss workers younger than 50, while resisting the hiring of older workers (Jolivet 2002: 259). In terms of active labor market policies, such as the CES wage subsidies for employment of problem groups, older workers have hardly profited.

The situation in Italy contrasts markedly with that in France: unemployment insurance, active labor market policies, and employment services are insufficient. The CIGS redundancy schemes, which were used in the past to circumvent dismissal, functioned as quasi-preretirement schemes for older workers. Restrictions in the early 1990s made it more difficult to remain on CIGS lists until early retirement. Nevertheless, reactivation of older redundant workers has been rather low (Samek Lodovici 2000*b*). Recent efforts by the right-wing government to deregulate the labor market, especially the employment protection rules under the 1970 Workers' Statute, caused widespread protest and strikes in spring 2002 (Ebbinghaus 2003). An agreement in summer 2002 struck between the government and two union centers (though CGIL opposed it) further negotiated reforms on labor market policies (EIRO: IT0207104F). Thus far, without a functioning employment service and unemployment insurance, reform of employment regulation and a change in the CIGS 'mobility lists' seem rather difficult to achieve, particularly given the unions' defense of the rights acquired during the industrial conflicts of the late 1960s (Gualmini 1998).

In nearly all countries, reforms of unemployment pathways met considerable resistance. The special preretirement pensions for the older

---

[15] *Allocation de remplacement pour l'emploi* (ARPE) was established by a union–employer agreement in 1994. It pays preretirement pensions to workers with 40 years of unemployment insurance contributions, provided that their employer would hire a new employee. In addition, the social partners set up a compensation fund (ACA) for older unemployed workers (below 60) in 1997; preretirement allowances for five years under collective agreements within the scope of the 35-hour-week legislation and with reduced social contributions (first in the automobile industry 1999); and the 2001 agreement on special exceptions to the new PARE activation measures for those already on ACA unemployment benefits (Jolivet 2002).

unemployed as part of the German old-age insurance and the Swedish disability scheme could be phased out or even closed down since they were obviously serving a different (passive labor market) purpose than initially intended. Although the Danish government was able to eliminate transitory preretirement pay (aged 50+) within a few years due to its enormous long-term costs for the union-led unemployment funds, it was much more difficult to reform the long established *efterløn*, the preretirement pay (aged 60–66), particularly since the unskilled workers unions defended this 'acquired right' of their 'own' PAYG scheme. The French case shows that state-led reforms may lead to counteraction by the social partners: the bargaining partners negotiated preretirement schemes in order to make up for cutbacks of the state-controlled exit pathway. In Italy, too, limits on redundancy schemes in the 1990s did not reduce early exit, as the cohorts of older workers met seniority pension conditions more easily. Reducing preretirement options for the long-term unemployed may simply lead to substitution with second best alternatives. Moreover, welfare retrenchment in other schemes has neither stopped labor shedding nor has it improved older workers' reemployment chances. Thus, unemployment in old age has increased during difficult labor market situations. Cutting back unemployment benefits has not led to a decrease in old-age unemployment, since older workers still have fewer employment chances. Instead, it may have increased poverty among older unemployed people. The move from passive to active labor market policies—a crucial paradigm shift—has gradually begun to be embraced by governments, employers, unions, and society in general (Walker 2000). Coordination of the social actors at national and workplace levels is necessary to overcome age-related biases in hiring, firing, wage scales, retraining, and activation policies.

7.1.5 *Gradual Retirement and Part-Time Work*

The OECD recommends gradual and part-time pensions not only to reverse the trend of costly pension expenditure but also to promote the shift toward an *active society* (OECD 2000). The prime example has been the Swedish part-time scheme (Wadensjö 1996), set up in 1976, which achieved a take-up rate of 20 percent of the eligible workforce (aged 60–64) in the early 1980s. However, the bourgeois government cut the compensation rate to 50 percent in 1981, which led to a near 50 percent drop in the take-up rate (Delsen 1996c: 58). After the return to power of the Social Democrats in 1987, the replacement rate was raised again to

65 percent, boosting take-up, particularly among women. Moreover, with closure of the alternative unemployment pathway in 1991, the partial pension regained wide use: one-quarter of the eligible older population drew this kind of early partial pension (Delsen 1996c: 58). Closing one alternative had led to an instrument substitution, provoking a response from the Social Democratic government in 1995: It increased the starting age for partial pensions by a year (from age 60 to 61, as of 1996) and cut the replacement rate to 55 percent (Wadensjö 1996). A further decline was expected by 2000 as a result of the phasing out of partial retirement in favor of the less generous part-time 'semi-pension' program.[16] In contrast to the general reorientation toward gradual transitions in other OECD countries, Sweden has largely given up its successful but expensive partial pension scheme.

Denmark introduced a partial preretirement scheme only in 1987, a decade after Sweden (Delsen 1996c). It gave dependent workers and the self-employed over age 60 an allowance (similar to unemployment benefits) proportional to the working hours cut, but the new program had less impact than expected.[17] In the late 1990s, less than 3 percent of men (and less than 1 percent of women) aged 60–66 were on partial pensions (*delpension*) (NOSOSKO 1998: 129). Danish unions and employer associations had long been reluctant to embrace gradual pensions, but in 1995 a new part-time scheme (*delefterløn*) that is relatively generous was introduced as part of voluntary unemployment insurance (Delsen 1996c: 60).

Similarly, the German Pension Reform of 1992, which created new rules for gradual retirement by allowing part-time jobs to be combined with partial pensions, failed due to limited financial incentives and restrictive conditions.[18] New part-time pension schemes, enacted on the initiative of the social partners in 1996, are complemented by collective agreements that cover part of the pension cuts and guarantee at least 85 percent of net wages (EIRO: DE9708224F). But contrary to the law's intention of a

---

[16] So far, the part-time preretirement pension has been relatively unpopular since it entails actuarial reductions (before age 65). In 1993, less than 2,200 men and 500 women were taking part in it compared to about 30,000 men and 19,000 women in the partial pension scheme prior to the reform (Wadensjö 1996: 33).

[17] In 1991, there were only 6,000 beneficiaries per year (Delsen 1996c: 56). Indeed, 'because of the high net compensation rate (between 63 and 75 percent), there is little financial incentive to choose partial rather than full early retirement; and the reduction in working time results in a loss of future supplementary pension entitlements' (Delsen 1996c: 60).

[18] Until age 65, there was an earnings limit for early pensions and part-time pensioners had to pay income tax and higher social security contributions; thus, net earnings for the half pensions (90 percent of average wages) and two-third pensions (83 percent) were close to what they were for full pensions (84 percent) (Schmähl, George, and Oswald 1996: 78).

gradual transition, the five years' part-time work and partial pension arrangement are used mainly to finance two consecutive periods—one of full-time work and the other of full retirement (called the *Blockmodell*), thus de facto allowing full exit from work at age 62.5 (Barkholdt 2001). Nevertheless, the shift from early exit via the pension system to the collectively negotiated part-time arrangements brought an increased role for the social partners, more control for management, and an internalization of a large share of the exit costs by the firms.

The French government also had limited success in institutionalizing gradual pensions. The partial pension law of 1988 had little impact, as it allowed a 60-year-old worker to engage in part-time work while receiving a partial pension (Reday-Mulvey 1996: 54). A new law in 1992 simplified gradual retirement (now 55+). It allowed working time to vary between 40 and 50 percent, and abandoned strict replacement requirements in favor of either financial contributions or a recruitment guarantee from the employer. Since the 1990s, some collective agreements between the social partners provide options for working-time reductions (Reday-Mulvey 1996: 55–6). Yet gradual pensions *à la française* rely largely on state subsidies, negotiated deals with the social partners, and complicated requirements. As a result, mostly large firms take advantage of the program, while most French people still assume a ' "zero sum game" of shortening work-life at both ends of the life-cycle' (Reday-Mulvey 1996: 67). Moreover, as long as there are attractive full exit options via the state-controlled solidarity scheme as in the 1980s or the social partners' preretirement pay as in the 1990s, a gradual transition does not seem very attractive to workers or employers. Part-time employment is only slightly higher for workers aged 55–59, but considerable in the age group 60–64 (20 percent among men, 40 percent among women in 1999): primarily for those who were unable to retire at statutory pension age 60 due to insufficient contribution records (Jolivet 2002: 250).

Prospects for gradual retirement in the United Kingdom are also limited due to the traditional 'culture of early exit in British industry' and 'little enthusiasm among employers for later or phased retirement' (Taylor and Walker 1996: 108). Yet there are signs of a paradigm shift: 'In recent years government policy on older workers has changed from one of encouraging their early retirement to one of trying to increase the supply of older workers and of encouraging employers to utilize this source of labor' (Taylor and Walker 1996: 94). The common DB occupational pension plans usually require full exit, while the public basic pension starts for men at age 65 and for women at age 60. The earnings rule was abolished in

1989, helping older workers to combine their basic pensions with part-time work (Taylor and Walker 1996: 95). Similarly, in the United States, the combination of gradual retirement was supported neither by public pension policy, which enforced earnings limits, nor by employers' DB plans, which often ruled out part-time work since occupational pensions were set up as a way to induce workers to full exit after mandatory retirement had been banned. The public pensions earnings test was relaxed in 1978 and again in 1990, though only for those aged 65 and older (OECD 1995a).

The Japanese practice of mandatory dismissal (*teinen*) and reemployment (*shukko*) of older workers, together with relatively low-pension benefits, functions as a quasi-partial pension program (Kimura et al. 1994). Japanese workers who meet the earnings test receive small state pensions beginning at age 60 and thus draw on low-wage supplements (often with shortened working time due to reemployment).[19] Thus, in Japan gradual retirement has become a common practice but will likely run into increasing difficulties in the future.

Generally, public policies to support gradual retirement have been late and relatively modest in encouraging workers to engage in part-time work and postpone their full retirement (Delsen, Hutsebaut, and Reissert 1999; Delsen and Reday-Mulvey 1996b). Retrenchment policies led Swedish governments to cut back on gradual retirement and even replace its once successful scheme that was often taken as a model by other countries. As with the Swedish cutbacks, the relative failure of the Danish, Dutch, French, and German partial pension initiatives results partly from insufficient financial incentives (Delsen 1996c). Final salary DB rules of public pensions as well as the tax treatment of combined income from work and pensions may act as deterrents (Latulippe and Turner 2000). A major obstacle to gradual retirement is also the 'crowding out' by more generous alternatives of full early exit routes. Finally, the decision to combine part-time work with a partial pension is not a choice made exclusively by the worker; it also depends on the employer's willingness to provide part-time employment (Taylor and Walker 1998). Although it may be beneficial to retain older retired workers, especially those with long experience and special skills, many industrial firms are reluctant to reorganize work for part-time jobs, particularly in the case of shift work and with unskilled or semiskilled workers. 'Although overall there has been a relative bottoming out of the fall of employment rates for older workers', a comparative study

---

[19] In the mid-1990s, about half of all older working men aged 60–64 (about 30 percent of the age group) were working and receiving a pension; this was true for nearly all older working men aged 65–59 (nearly 50 percent of the age group) (OECD 2001a: 36).

on gradual retirement concludes: 'where not securely articulated into company policies, public policies have not yet necessarily produced the expected results' (Delsen and Reday-Mulvey 1996*b*: 11).

7.2   Learning the Lessons of Policy Reversal

7.2.1   *Reversing Exit Pathways*

Due to the demographic challenges to pension sustainability, high social expenditures, and low activity rates, governments have sought to reverse early exit trends since the 1980s. However, policy reversal has entailed a protracted process of social learning, piecemeal policymaking, and insufficient implementation (see Table 7.4). As much as early exit from work was an *unintended* consequence of social rights used for different purposes under the challenging labor market conditions since the mid-1970s (see Chapter 5), governments were slow to recognize the negative effects—and even slower to intervene. When social expenditures increased rapidly in the late 1970s, governments largely relied on a 'muddling through' approach: They started to cut benefits and to expand means testing, particularly in unemployment, disability, and social assistance programs (Morris 1988), but due to large electoral stakes, they remained reluctant to cut back pensions substantially (Pierson 1997). Nevertheless, since the 1980s, the debate on the future sustainability of pension systems has continuously gained in importance as welfare states face rising old-age pension expenditures, falling employment rates among older workers, and mounting old-age dependency. Given diverse exit pathways, governments seeking policy reversal had to tackle several policy areas simultaneously in order to bring early exit from work under control. Reviewing the single reform efforts in the different policy areas, we can detect some general policy-specific trends and problems inherent in policy reversals (see Table 7.4).

(1) *Reversing pension pathways.* Reversing the use of particular *pension* pathways became part of the larger pension reform issue. The first policy decision to raise statutory pension age occurred in liberal-residual welfare states, even though they actually faced less pressing old-age dependency problems and lower expenditures than other types of regimes (see Figure 7.1). During the Reagan and Thatcher era, 'welfare retrenchment' came onto the agenda (Pierson 1994), but due to the popularity of old-age pensions, an increase in statutory pension age could only be phased in

Table 7.4. Reversing pathways to early exit

Pathway	Right	Conditions	Control mechanism	Policy reversal	Reform problems
Pension	Citizenship right/social right (deferred wage; social consideration)	Age/contribution years; special groups (women); seniority (contribution years)	*State:* rules; *firm:* top up pensions; *worker:* voluntary	Raising age limit/contribution years; actuarial reductions; shift to DC-funded benefits; increased privatization	Difficult to reform (acquired right), particularly in PAYG systems; increasing old-age poverty
Disability	Social right for (partially) impaired/age-specific labor market consideration	Medical criteria; labor market criteria; part-time work; income tests	*State:* rules, award; *firm:* liability, sick pay; *worker:* impairment, voluntary application	Cuts in benefits; tighter eligibility rules; relaxed earning limits; governance reform	Difficult to reform when social partners play role; substitution effect: shift to unemployment
Special preretirement	Temporary measure to alleviate labor market	Particular groups/sectors; replacement condition; redundancy	*State:* rules, subsidy; *firm:* cofinancing, plan; *worker:* voluntary	Closing down; tighter conditions; more cofinancing by firm	Intervention difficult in non-state schemes; rise in unemployment
Unemployment	Benefits for long-term unemployed	Contributions/means-tested; voluntary/involuntary; no job search	*State:* rules, fines; *firm:* dismissal; *unions:* social plans; *worker:* in/voluntary	Cuts in benefits; shorter duration; ending of age-specific rules	Opposition by unions; substitution effect: shift to social assistance
Activation policies	Integration of unemployed/older workers	Age limit for training, job subsidies, sheltered jobs; mandatory retirement; age discrimination	*State:* rules, subsidies; *firm:* hiring & firing; *unions:* cooperation; *worker:* voluntary	Ending age limits to activation measures; *anti-*age discrimination laws; lifelong training	Dependent on change in hiring, firing, training and workplaces; cooperation of firms and unions
Gradual retirement	Gradual transition from work to retirement	Stringent part-time rules; earning limits; working hour limits	*State:* rules, subsidies; *unions:* agreement; *firm:* part-time job; *worker:* voluntary	Extending partial retirement; subsidies to firms; collective agreements	Dependent on part-time jobs in firms; adaptation of workplace

over the long term for men and women in the United States and for women in the United Kingdom, starting more than a decade after the legislative decision. Of more immediate importance for reducing disincentives to work were efforts to induce further privatization of pensions (Davis 1997; Hacker 2002) and cuts in the state earnings-related pension in Britain (Blundell and Johnson 1999). As in the United States, Japan increased mandatory retirement rules and in the near future will increase the pension age to 65, but the government made concessions to the unions by retaining the 'work-in' partial pension as a subsidy to the reduced wages paid to older workers (Estienne and Murakami 2000).

In the Netherlands and Denmark, the Beveridge-type basic pension scheme provided no early exit pathway (in contrast to the rapidly expanding disability scheme). It remained largely unaltered, except for the lowering of pension age in Denmark as of 2004. Sweden's major pension reform in the 1990s was primarily undertaken to address concerns about long-term sustainability, not work disincentives, although the actuarially reduced flexible pension will gain in importance for future Swedish pensioners due to the closing of several other pathways, including the partial pension. The introduction of notional DC benefits in the Swedish public pension and DC benefits in some occupational pensions will, in the long run, provide further incentives to continue working.

In Continental Europe, the pressure for pension reform was more acute given rapidly rising old-age dependency ratios, inactivity rates, and pension costs. Cutting back seniority pensions and increasing pension age caused political and social conflicts at times, for example, the Kohl government's reforms in 1996/97, Berlusconi's 1994 pension reform plan, and particularly Juppé's ill-fated 1995 pension reform bill (Ebbinghaus and Hassel 2000). In contrast, the German 1992 Pension Reform was based on a broad interparty consensus, including the social partners (Nullmeier and Rüb 1993), although it phased out most public exit pathways of the old-age and disability pension system over ten to twenty years. In order to make reforms more acceptable to trade unions and the public, *grandfather* rules and hidden changes (by raising contribution years) were applied by the Dini and Prodi governments for the Italian pension reforms of 1995 and 1997 and by the Balladur government for the French private sector pension reform of 1993 (Natali and Rhodes 2004; Taylor-Gooby 1999). Since these pension pathways were based on mature PAYG systems, they turned out to be more resistant to radical change than tax-financed benefits (Myles and Pierson 2001). Governments of Continental European welfare states found it difficult to impose reforms not only for electoral reasons but also because union movements defended the status quo (Brugiavini et al. 2001; Schludi 2001).

More recently, governments have sought to change pension systems not by radically transforming PAYG into funded schemes, but by adding privatized DC schemes on top of the public systems—a strategy that leads to institutional layering (Thelen 2002). The Swedish 1998 Pension Reform, the growth of negotiated occupational pensions in Denmark since the 1990s, the German *Riester* reform enacted in 2001, and the British Stakeholder Pension in 2001 introduced such new funded pension elements. Such *privatization* provides unions with some opportunities to offer pension funds or even negotiate the terms under collective bargaining agreements, provided they are strong enough and employers are willing to negotiate such deferred wage deals (Ebbinghaus 2003). Also the Italian pension reform of 1997 (reinforced by a proxy law in 2004) fostered the conversion of end-of-service into occupational pension funds, giving rise to a number of collective agreements. Similarly, in the Netherlands, the transformation of the PAYG preretirement plans (VUT) to funded flexible pensions will dampen early exit from work (Rein and Turner 2001). However, these new institutional layers that increase the actuarial reductions for early retirement will only have a long-term, gradual impact on early exit patterns of current and future generations.

(2) *Reversing the disability pathway.* A more politically charged and complex reform problem has been the reversal of use of disability pensions as an early exit pathway. Some changes in eligibility rules already occurred during the 1980s, for example, in Italy after the increased clientelist use of disability pensions (Ascoli 1988) and in Germany when contribution period requirements were extended (Frick and Sadowski 1996). Given the comparatively high take-up rate of disability pensions in the Netherlands, not only for older but particularly for younger people, major retrenchment efforts occurred during the late 1980s, causing the largest demonstration in Dutch history (Aarts and de Jong 1996*b*). The cuts in benefits and the review of disability awards did not bring the hoped-for activation, and older workers were partly exempted from these measures. Moreover, the social partners' own special retirement scheme made up for the cuts in benefits and thus retrenchment led only to instrument substitution. Dutch government then tried more systemic reforms, such as changing the governance structure, cost-shifting onto employers to induce changes in the work environment, and reducing disability awards for nonmedical reasons (Visser and Hemerijck 1997). Also in Sweden this

pathway gained major importance. In an unprecedented ad hoc intervention during a fiscal crisis, Sweden abolished its labor market disability pension in 1991, though this may have led to an increase in unemployment pensions (Wadensjö and Palmer 1996). The Dutch and Swedish *systemic* reforms in disability pensions had a considerable impact on cutting expenditures that went beyond the impact of improved labor market conditions.[20]

In the other countries, disability expenditures remained largely stagnant at a lower level than in the Netherlands or Sweden, although these increased noticeably in the United Kingdom during the early 1990s. But 'pull'-oriented reforms of disability pension rules need to be balanced by measures against economic and social *push* factors. Otherwise, people with impairments may suffer from increased income loss and unemployment risks. Hence, more active measures are needed to help older disabled workers to find suitable work, induce employers to hire and retain them, and mandate accessibility and adaptation of workplaces (Delsen 1996*a*; Kuptsch and Zeitzer 2001).

(3) *Reversing the special preretirement pathway.* More than their governments, the French, Dutch, and Danish social partners promoted special preretirement programs from the 1970s onwards; these schemes still existed in the 1990s, despite some transformation. Several governments also introduced special state-run preretirement programs (France, Britain, Germany, and Italy) and tied them to job replacement conditions in order to directly alleviate difficult labor market situations. In contrast to the exit pathways based on general social rights, these special preretirement programs were more easily closed down or eligibility further restricted to reach labor market goals, at least when they were state-run and financed. In the late 1980s, the Conservative governments closed their special schemes in Germany (*Vorruhestand*) and Britain (JRS) and stop-and-go interventions. The French Socialist government supplanted the social partners' unemployment bridging pension by lowering statutory pension age to 60 and introducing state–firm 'solidarity' contracts with job replacement conditions in the early 1980s, though the unemployment funds were subsequently used to finance exit before age 60, particularly since the mid-1990s. Moreover, the special preretirement schemes initiated by unions or social partners in Denmark (*efterløn*) and the Netherlands (VUT)

---

[20] Disability pension costs (in percentage of GDP) were cut back considerably from 6.9 percent in 1990 to 4.1 percent in 2001 in the Netherlands and from 5.7 percent in 1989 to 4.5 percent in 1997 in Sweden, though increasing again thereafter (OECD 2001*c*).

remained largely 'untouchable' by state intervention until the late 1990s, when the governments induced their transformation into flexible pension schemes (Delsen 2002; Hansen 2002). The French scheme run by the social partners remains the only preretirement scheme that has been largely insulated from state intervention, but French employers have recently called for a reform of social policy governance. Hence, state intervention was most likely where schemes had been set up as explicit temporary labor market measures. It was more difficult to change those schemes run by the social partners and financed by PAYG funds.

(4) *Reversing the unemployment pathway.* Most recently, a paradigm shift occurred in labor market policy: from passive to active labor market policy (Jespen, Foden, and Hutsebaut 2002*b*). In most welfare states, unemployment among older workers grew as a pressing problem from the 1970s. Particularly high unemployment rates among older men aged 55–64 existed in the Netherlands and Germany in the early 1980s, in postunification Germany, in France since the 1980s, in Britain and Ireland during the 1980s and early 1990s, and in Sweden and Denmark during the 1990s (see Figure 7.2). In some of these cases, alternative exit pathways relieved unemployment rolls, such as through VUT preretirement in the Netherlands since the mid-1980s. During the late 1990s, improvements in the overall labor market situation and activation policies led to considerable declines in old-age unemployment in Denmark, Sweden, Britain, and Ireland. Costs of labor market policies have declined substantially in Denmark, Sweden, and the United Kingdom over the 1990s due to overall labor market improvements (see Table 7.3).

While some of the initial activation policies in the early 1990s were aimed at young job-seekers, long-term unemployed or social assistance claimants, the new orientation increasingly extends to older workers. For social reasons, older unemployed workers were granted an exemption from the active job-seeking rule, which often kept them out of unemployment statistics—an important political tool for governments. Older workers were also excluded from active labor market policies, paralleling the reluctance of employers to retrain older workers shortly before their expected (early) retirement. However, it is precisely these *socially expected durations* (Merton {1984}) that are a major obstacle to the employability of older workers. Employers' commonly held view that older workers are less productive and flexible is a self-fulfilling prophecy: Expecting older workers to retire early, employers are reluctant to hire and provide them with training, which in turn feeds the employer's view that older workers are less productive. At the same time, older workers are afraid to change jobs and seek early retirement as a safe way out instead of facing prospective unemployment. Of all policy reversals, the change toward activation is therefore the most difficult and gradual undertaking. It poses major challenges to policy change since it entails not only cutting benefit incentives by law, but also altering long-held expectations and personnel practices (Clemens 2001). Here, more than in any other policy area, the cooperation of the social partners in the national bargaining arena as well as management–labor relations in the workplace will be crucial.

(5) *Fostering the partial pension pathway.* Interactions between public policy, collective bargaining, and firm-level employment policies are decisive for gradual pension policies. The success of partial (or gradual) pensions vis-à-vis alternative pathways depends on their relative generosity, as the variable success of the Swedish partial pension strategy indicates (Wadensjö 1996). The gradual pension helped Sweden attain a high-employment rate, a large share of part-time work in old age, and retain older workers longer than in most other European welfare states. However, the once successful policy was replaced in 2001 by a less attractive part-time flexible pension model (Wadensjö 2002). Japan has retained its work-in pension for older workers, which has helped to maintain the highest activity level of all countries. In several European countries, the potential for 'progressive retirement' has been acknowledged (EIRO: TN0109184S). In most cases, these gradual pension arrangements require implementation through collective bargaining (Denmark, Germany, and the Netherlands), state–firm agreements (France), or individual agreements (France, Denmark, and Sweden). Much depends on employers' willingness to provide part-time work and undertake the necessary reorganization of work. The case of the *'Blockmodell'* of German part-time pensions shows that employers, workers, and their representatives may 'collude' in using it for full early exit, thereby undermining the intention of gradual retirement as a smooth transition from work to retirement that prolongs employment (Barkholdt 2001).

7.2.2 The Obstacles to Policy Reversal

In general, reform efforts to reverse early exit have been highly contingent, given the multiple pathways and multilevel actor configurations. Indeed, the recent reform efforts have shown mixed results because of

cost-shifting, policy substitution, and counteraction by the social partners. Endeavors to reverse early retirement remain difficult in the face of
entrenched acquired rights, potential 'instrument substitution' (Casey
1989) due to multiple pathways, and the long-held expectations about
seniority wages and employment protections. A comparison of the reform
record thus far provides some clues as to the institutional obstacles and
conditions for policy change. Given vested interests in social rights, actually changing national pension policies has proven relatively difficult,
even in countries with conservative governments committed to welfare
retrenchment as in the United States under Reagan and the United Kingdom under Thatcher (Pierson 1994). A turnaround in Continental Europe
has proven even more difficult, given PAYG financing and 'earned' social
insurance rights (Myles and Pierson 2001). While the benefits of reversal
remain diffuse and prospective, the costs of change will be more clearly
concentrated and immediate (Pierson 2001*b*).

Closing down early exit options will most clearly affect older workers
who expect to retire early as well as firms under acute pressure to shed
labor. Many exit pathways are seen as acquired social rights by workers and
defended by their unions, thus reformers advancing policy reversal face
deeply entrenched vested interests (Ebbinghaus and Hassel 2000; Natali
and Rhodes 2004). Older workers, employers, and workplace representatives of such firms may well be more vocal in defending the acquired rights
than the larger group of people who might gain from (but are largely
unaware of) the future employment effects of planned reforms. Social
learning (Hall 1993) occurred slowly as governments increasingly faced
the unintended consequences of expanded social rights and were disap-
pointed by the costs of ad hoc labor-shedding measures. The high costs
seemed unjustified given the meager results on reducing unemployment,
and they became part of the employment problem (Scharpf 2001).

In addition to problems of entrenched pension politics, efforts to reverse
early exit face other challenges. Given that there are multiple pathways for
early exit, providing alternative early exit pathways, and multiple actors at
national and workplace levels, narrowing or closing one exit pathway may
merely lead to an instrument substitution (Casey 1989), as workers or
firms chose another exit pathway. For instance, if the labor market consideration for disability pensions is abolished but the labor market situation of people with impairments does not improve, the rolls of long-term
unemployed increase. Thus, instead of reducing early exit from work and
cutting expenses, costs would merely be shifted from one public program
to another, while early exit from work continues. A public–public cost

shift (Casey 1989), that is private actors (employers and workers) cofinancing early retirement, can lead to some savings due to lower benefits (less favorable replacement conditions) or tightened eligibility criteria, but these effects are highly contingent on other available, highly regime-specific 'second best' alternatives.

Where such cost-shifting occurs, the control and financing of early exit changes from state to private actors. Certainly, with a shift from public to private schemes, the public expenditure will decline as private actors (employers or individuals) take on the burden of financing early exit. Yet early exit from work may continue regardless. Even when firms do share in the costs by topping up reduced public benefits or by being forced to contribute due to public costs incurred, early retirement may remain an attractive personnel strategy to buy out older workers instead of dismissing workers of prime age who are, on average, more highly skilled. In fact, employers are in favor of controlling early exit and thus would be willing to cofinance early retirement if they would gain control over who benefits from early exit (Mares 2001b). In cases in which the internalization of costs by firms is considerable, management may seek preventive measures to retain older workers, which would then lower rates of early exit from work (Naschold, de Vroom, and Casey 1994). On the other hand, when employers do not share the costs but continue to discriminate on the basis of age in hiring and firing, then the risk of unemployment and poverty will be borne by older workers alone—unless public welfare programs such as social assistance intervene. As long as economic push factors continue to be strong, it remains difficult to reverse early exit merely by reducing the pull-incentives, i.e. cutting public benefits. Thus, active policies are needed to complement pull-oriented policies in order to reverse the push factors as well (Jespen, Foden, and Hutsebaut 2002b; Martin 1998; Walwei and Werner 2001).

7.2.3 Cross-National Reform Patterns

The timing and scope of reforms vary depending on the specific welfare regime's institutional legacies, problem constellations, and opportunities for change (Hemerijck and Schludi 2000; Scharpf 2000). Reform processes, therefore, show considerable cross-national variations by regime constellation (see Table 7.5). Due to massive labor shedding, policy reversal with respect to early exit was most pressing in the Continental European welfare states (Esping-Andersen 1996c). Yet a U-turn proved most difficult in the face of entrenched acquired rights defended by unions, employers'

Table 7.5. Typology of exit patterns and policy reversal

Regime	Early exit	Exit pathways	Employment regime	Policy reversal
Center Germany Netherlands	High	Multiple pathways: public and private, but externalization of costs	Labor shedding, intergenerational solidarity	Closing/phasing out of public programs; shifting costs onto private actors; scope for collective agreements
Latin Europe France Italy	High/early	Early (seniority) pension, 'bridging' unemployment	Labor shedding, intergenerational solidarity	Phasing out, more state intervention; seniority rights are contentious issue; responsible social partner needed for concertation
Anglophone United Kingdom Ireland United States	Medium	Narrow pathways: individual cost sharing	Flexible labor market, but antidiscrimination laws	Increase incentives to work longer; shift toward DC in private funds
Scandinavian Sweden Denmark	Medium–low	Partial pathways: partial or flexible pension	Full employment aim and (re)integration policies	Ending of generous routes due to financial constraints; activation measures
Asian Japan	Low	Incomplete pathway: reemployment; in-work pension	Mandatory retirement, but reemployment norm	Gradual rise in pension age due to demographics

interests in continuing to externalize the costs of economic restructuring in a peaceful way, and governments' electoral concerns about the short-term consequences for unemployment rates. Moreover, these Continental regimes had institutionalized multiple alternative pathways; thus policy change in one area could not guarantee effectiveness due to instrument substitution and mere cost-shifting (Casey 1989). Indeed, closing down special preretirement programs or introducing partial pensions did not bring about hoped-for changes in activity levels so long as other attractive alternatives for early exit were available to older workers and restructuring firms.

Moreover, the unions, by and large representing the membership interests of the more senior workers aged 45 and above, had some veto power in the bargaining arena and in social administration (Ebbinghaus 2002). Particularly in the countries with contentious labor relations, France and Italy, worker mobilization against the reform project was successful—most prominently in the case of the Juppé and the Berlusconi pension reforms in 1995 and 1994 respectively (Ebbinghaus and Hassel 2000). In Germany and the Netherlands, social partnership relations were more consensual, particularly at the workplace level, given statutory works councils with codetermination rights and more indirect workplace access for unions. Moreover, the social partners also had institutionalized influence in social insurance administration and even in self-regulation of schemes they negotiated. When governments actually succeeded in cutting back on replacement rates for public benefits programs, the social partners (or employers on their own) frequently filled in the gaps between the reduced public benefits and former net wages. Although this infrequently altered the early exit trend, such privatization nevertheless entails a public–private cost shift and thus internalization of exit costs by the actors, the firms, or individuals. In the long run, this internalization could lead to a paradigm shift toward more integrative age-related policies of firms, but privatization also carries with it the potential danger of increased poverty for unemployed, insufficiently insured older workers.

To overcome the social partners' potential capacity to block policymaking and implementation, governments may seek to work with the social partners to find solutions. The major concession that governments have used to strike deals is a gradual phasing in instead of imposing radical, immediate changes. Given the high proportion of older workers and pensioners in union membership, *grandfather* rules make concerted reforms more palatable to union members. Several major reforms were undertaken in the 1990s, most notably the German 1992 Pension Reform, the Dutch disability and governance reforms, the Italian Dini and Prodi pension reforms, and the French private sector pension and recent governance reforms. However, the most difficult policy change for all four Continental European countries is the paradigm shift toward activation: retaining, reemploying, and retraining older workers instead of using early retirement to eliminate them from the workplace. Thus, it is no longer correct to characterize the Continental European welfare states *in toto* as a 'frozen landscape' (Esping-Andersen 1996c). With the exception of France, we do see stabilization and, recently, even slight declines in early exit from work among older workers. However, it is too early to judge whether these declines are due to improved labor market situations or whether they represent a sustainable trend responding to reforms undertaken in the late 1990s.

By the early 1990s, surging public expenditure and rising unemployment undermined the Scandinavian model of full employment and large-scale public sector employment. Within a few years, Sweden departed from its generous disability and gradual retirement programs, while the Danish government sought to intervene in its disability and preretirement schemes. Radical reforms were accomplished more rapidly in crisis-ridden Sweden in the early 1990s since the use of disability for passive policies was 'out of sync' with its long tradition of activation policies. In Denmark, the trade unions, particularly those for unskilled workers, defended the preretirement schemes, given the higher unemployment risks of older unskilled workers and their lower job protection (Estevez-Abe, Iversen, and Soskice 2001). Although Sweden had a long tradition of active labor market policy, the reform of the gradual pensions will make the integration strategy more difficult. Denmark, which has used passive labor market policy more extensively, has recently embraced activation policies for older workers as part of its reorientation. Reforms since the 1990s have led to a recent turnaround in early exit among older workers, particularly among older Swedish men and Danish women. The reforms and improved labor market situations have led to a notable decline in expenditures for disability and old-age pensions (see Figure 7.3).

Policy reversal in the liberal-residual welfare states was largely driven by long-term concerns about demographic trends and welfare-state disincentives to work (Bosworth and Burtless 1998b; King and Wood 1999). Since early retirement was less a pressing structural problem than a cyclical phenomenon, it was subsumed under more general reforms that privatized welfare costs and increased incentives to work. However, early exit from work continued, as the push factors remained important: Employers bought out older workers with occupational welfare benefits or firms reverted to mass dismissal during economic recessions. Increasingly, as pension privatization moves away from DB schemes, the risks of income loss and unemployment have been shifted onto the shoulders of older workers. The United Kingdom and Ireland saw declines in early exit from work, particularly among women, as the labor market situation improved since the late 1980s and unemployment among older workers declined over the 1990s. Otherwise, early retirement remains a rather cyclical and less pressing problem than on the Continent.

Finally, the Japanese welfare state has taken steps to confront its public programs' long-term liabilities, given its rapidly aging population (Endo and Katayama 1998). In the past, the 'lifelong employment system' for (male) workers in large firms was built on mandatory retirement in return

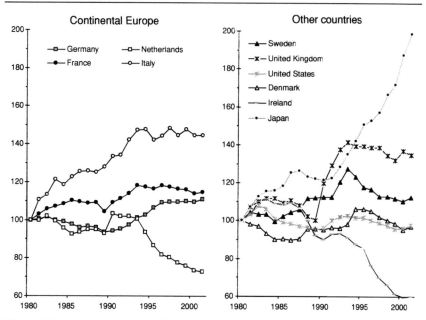

Figure 7.3 Development in old-age and disability pension expenditure since 1980

Notes: Index 1980 = 100; public and mandatory private expenditure on old-age, survivor, and disability pensions (% GDP).

Sources: OECD (2001c, 2004).

for social norms of reemployment, opportunities for secondary employment, and partial pensions. Nevertheless, in contrast to the United States and the United Kingdom, Japan's pension reforms have thus far been based on a social consensus with the unions and an employer commitment to the employment tenure system. However, this system has come under increasing pressure in recent years and employers have become more critical (Grønning 1998). These traditions may also increasingly clash with expanding female labor force participation, intensified labor market dualism, and unprecedented unemployment levels. In fact, Japan has witnessed an increase in early exit for both men and women and has come ever closer to American levels, while older people who do work rely to a large degree on partial pensions (combining work and benefits) as was the case in Sweden thus far.

Measured by the European Union 2010 target set by the Stockholm Council, how close have the European welfare states, the United States, and Japan come to achieving an employment rate of 50 percent for workers aged 55–64? Over a decade (see Figure 7.4), the activity rate has indeed improved for the EU-15 (excluding the new member countries): The total employment rate increased from 36.7 percent (for men: 47.5, for women: 24.7) in 1994 to 42.5 percent (for men: 52.2, for women: 33.2) in 2004. Increased labor force participation by older women in particular drove the overall rate (see Figure 7.4). Continental Europe especially lags behind the target. Germany and the Netherlands currently exceed the target only for men (more than every second older man is working), while female employment rates are still considerably lower (only every third woman aged 55–64 is employed), though the Dutch reforms; and employment 'miracle' have led to a considerable improvement compared to the mid-1990s. The Latin welfare states, France and Italy, still range lowest despite various reforms, even employment rates are only at 41–2 percent for older male workers, not to speak of the still particularly low Italian female employment rate of 20 percent in 2004.

Both the record of and hopes for an active society have always looked much brighter in the Scandinavian countries, with both Sweden and Denmark exceeding the targets, except for Danish women in the 1990s. While Sweden has gradually improved its European record, Denmark has made more advances in bringing female employment up. Similarly, both the United Kingdom and Ireland with high and increasing male employment rates show considerable advances in female employment participation (the United Kingdom with 47 percent has narrowed the gap with the United States model and Ireland with 34 percent is close to the Continental model). The United States has improved its already relatively high employment rate, ranging now from 66 percent for men to 55 percent for women, thus showing the same range as Denmark, but still falling below Sweden. Japan's employment rate is particularly high for men (78 percent), but female employment remains stagnant just below the European Union target line. The Continental European welfare states and in particular the Catholic societies still have a long way to go to meet the European Union targets.

While policymakers in all ten countries followed international agencies' policy recommendations in accepting the need to reverse earlier exit policies, they still find it very difficult to change course by implementing 'best practices' from abroad. Given the entrenched character of acquired social rights and the continued availability of multiple pathways, social compromises are needed to overcome the social partners' blocking power and ensure that some reforms can be implemented. Reform will be difficult as long as a social coalition exists that supports early exit, between firms that strive to externalize their restructuring costs and circumvent

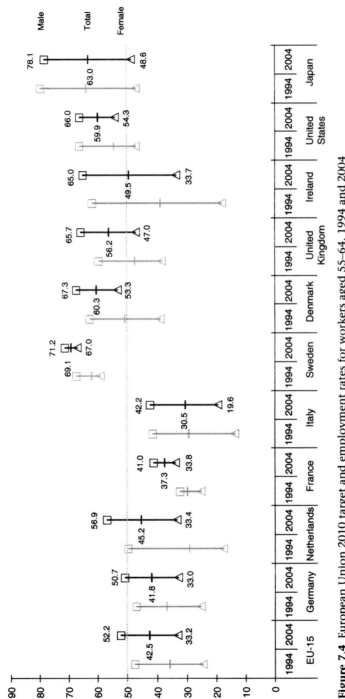

Figure 7.4 European Union 2010 target and employment rates for workers aged 55–64, 1994 and 2004

Notes: European Union target for 2010: 50 percent total employment rate for workers aged 55–64.

Sources: Eurostat (2005), United States, and Japanese labor force data.

seniority employment protection, and workers who perceive early retirement as an acquired social right given long working lives, substantial contributions, and lacking job opportunities for older unemployed people. Public policy needs to bring the social partners into reform consensus, since a reversal requires extensive cooperation at several levels (from the national bargaining arena to the workplace) and needs coordinated changes across different public, bipartite, and voluntary policies in order to avoid further instrument substitution and mere cost-shifting from one scheme to another.

Chapter 8

Conclusion: From Path Dependence to Path Departure?

Early exit from work is a significant trend common to all advanced economies since the 1970s. Consequently, the costly practice of early retirement, in terms of both higher social expenditure and lower employment activity, poses a major challenge to today's welfare states. Yet we find considerable cross-national differences both in early exit trajectories and in recent reform efforts: These provide us with a rich source for exploring the impact of variations in institutional settings and specific social policies. Therefore, this study was conceptualized as a comparative-historical analysis of a diverse set of ten countries, from various parts of Europe to Japan and the United States. The approach was encompassing, taking into account the interaction between protection, production, and partnership factors. Instead of focusing only on individual workers' early retirement decisions or solely on firms' labor-shedding strategies, I stress the importance of the *institutional environments* in which these individual and corporate actors are embedded. To do so, the analysis focused on cross-national variations resulting from national regime specificities in the early exit triangle of protection, production, and partnership.

Following the protection-related *pull* thesis, the comparative findings support the claims that welfare regimes not only shape the incentives that encourage older workers to quit working early, but also considerably affect firms' opportunities to externalize restructuring costs via early retirement. The regime-specific variations of available (public and private) exit pathways explain a significant part of overall cross-national variations in early withdrawal from work, although the social partners or firms sponsor many bridges from work to statutory retirement. The production-related *push* thesis helped to explain why the social partners or firms provide their own exit pathways and why they engage in labor-shedding strategies. Variations in economic governance and production systems account for the ways in which firms shed older workers, from market-driven cyclical downsizing to systemic restructuring that aims to maintain internal labor markets.

While both pull and push factors are necessary, neither alone is sufficient to explain the empirically demonstrated cross-national variations in early exit regimes. Throughout this study, I underlined the central role that the social partners play in shaping, maintaining, and reforming early exit policies. Employers and worker representatives at both national and workplace levels are crucial actors *mediating* between pull and push, finding responses to and altering the protection-related incentives and production-related exigencies. The encompassing approach combined protection-oriented pull *and* production-oriented push perspectives, but extended these arguments with the partnership-oriented analysis—the missing link in so many one-sided and thus less than satisfactory accounts of early retirement.

Today, early retirement ranks among the most urgent topics in welfare reform debates, with policy proposals that range from welfare benefit retrenchment to changing employers' attitudes. Prior to any policy recommendations, it is indispensable to seek to understand the causes for the rise of early exit from work and the serious difficulties countries face in reversing early retirement policies. Therefore, the approach applied here systematically compared the development of early exit from work across ten Western advanced economies with specific institutional configurations to identify both the obstacles to and the opportunities for policy reversal. Two sets of questions provided the foundation for the study's two empirical parts:

- Why did the early exit from work phenomenon spread much more widely in some countries than others? How can we explain considerable *cross-national differences* in the timing and scope of early retirement over the past three decades?

- Why is the *reversal* of early exit from work so difficult? What are the obstacles to reform and under what conditions is change more likely?

This concluding chapter reviews the findings from the theoretical and empirical analyses before discussing the broader consequences for future research and the implications for public policy.

8.1 Early Exit Regimes Compared

8.1.1 *The Actors' Interests*

Chapter 2 examined the main actors' interests at both workplace and national levels. On the one hand, labor supply-oriented explanations of early retirement focus on individual workers' preference for leisure over work, given the financial incentives for public preretirement benefits. Yet not all early retirement decisions by older workers are based on financial gains. There is a multitude of individual social and health-related reasons (such as age-related impairment or chronic illness) as well as firm-induced factors (such as involuntary dismissal) for early exit. The incentive-pull thesis fails to explain why early exit occurs even when no generous benefits are available (i.e. in liberal welfare states) or when push factors prevail (e.g. during economic downturns). On the other hand, the labor demand push perspective stresses the pressure that leads firms to shed older workers via mandatory or early retirement. Here, it is workplace representatives who defend the interests of senior and prime-aged workers, playing a key role in shifting firms' preferences to induce older workers to retire early instead of dismissing the core middle-aged workforce. Both micro-level accounts of pull and push factors, however, take the institutional environment as given and focus on explaining rational decisions by older workers or firms (management and workplace representatives) under given incentives and constraints. These micro-level approaches fail to account for why and how public pathways have become an acquired social right. Nor do they convincingly show how social partners' interests have shaped early retirement policies in the policymaking arena and in collective bargaining. A long-term institutional perspective is needed to account for these path-dependent processes.

Moreover, when we examine the macro-level interest constellations, we find that the three main social actors—the state, employers, and labor representatives—may share similar interests in promoting early exit from work. There are in fact many opportunities for 'collusion' among diverse groupings of social actors, often at the expense of a third party or the public at large. I analyzed six main reasons why actors pursue early retirement:

- Labor unions and allied governing parties share an interest in *advancing social rights* for political reasons, i.e. following the interests of their core membership and electoral constituency respectively.

- As a response to mass unemployment, labor unions and governing parties jointly support early exit as a means of *reducing labor supply* and bringing younger job-seekers into work.

- Both employers and the state have an interest in *'buying' social peace* in times of high unemployment and rapid economic restructuring, facilitating firm downsizing, or restructuring without causing labor conflicts.

- For employers and the state, early retirement benefits *serve as side payments* in corporatist income policies, helping unions to agree on wage moderation in exchange for a deferred social wage (i.e. the right to retire earlier).

- Firms and unions are both interested in *controlling early exit*, though for different reasons: Management wishes to control exit as part of its personnel strategy, while unionists seek to negotiate early exit as a right for their long-standing union members.

- Management and worker representatives have joint interests in *externalizing costs* of labor shedding onto public schemes (or private *inter-firm schemes*).

Without the institutional contexts in which these social actors' interests are embedded, this brief review of the possible points of 'collusion' between social actors remains abstract. However, a satisfactory explanation requires the cross-national analysis of the variable configurations of protection, production, and partnership institutions and their interactions. Understanding these institutional affinities and complementarities is a prerequisite for deriving hypotheses on particular regime-specific interests and on the social partners' and the state's opportunities to foster or restrict early exit from work.

8.1.2 *Protection, Production, and Partnership Institutions*

Thus, in Chapter 3, I examined cross-national variations in protection, production, and partnership institutions, adopting a comparative regime approach. By *regime* I mean the systemic hanging together of institutional arrangements and their environmental embeddedness that shapes actors' incentives and opportunities. In the case of early retirement, it is not sufficient to focus on a single pathway—such as pension insurance—since there are often other social transfer programs, which provide alternatives or substitutes. Only when we look at the 'menu' that these pathways offer and the interactions between them, can we understand how a particular welfare regime may foster or restrict early exit. This approach enables comparison by providing ideal-type 'regimes' as analytical dimensions for mapping real-world cross-national variations. Moreover, assuming the interaction between protection, production, and partnership institutions, I explored their possible institutional affinities, following Weber's concept of *Wahlverwandtschaften*.

To analyze cross-national variations in the *pull* factor, I adopt and adapt for this study Esping-Andersen's established welfare regime typology (1990, 1999): *universalist* Scandinavian welfare states, which guarantee income security, full employment, and social services to all citizens; *conservative* Continental European social insurance states, which provide income maintenance through passive social transfers and which are largely financed by employers and workers; and *liberal-residual* welfare societies in the Anglo-American world (but also Japan), which offer only basic security and rely on voluntary efforts, particularly private firm-based occupational welfare. One can detect considerable interaction of protection and production issues when observing the public–private mix between state and firm-level welfare policies (Rein and Wadensjö 1997b; Shalev 1996) and the different degrees of 'decommodification' (Esping-Andersen 1990), or redistributive policies. We would expect liberal-residual welfare societies to provide the least public support for early retirement, the Continental social insurance states to offer ample opportunities for the social partners to use passive social transfer, and the universalist welfare states to be most committed to maintaining full employment without granting special rights to particular groups.

For the comparative analysis of *push* factors, I have drawn on the recent contributions in political economy that map the varieties of capitalism (Albert 1991; Amable 2005; Crouch and Streeck 1997; Ebbinghaus and Manow 2001a; Hall and Soskice 2001a; Hollingsworth and Boyer 1997b; Streeck and Yamamura 2001). The basic model juxtaposes Anglophone *liberal* market economies (LMEs) and the *coordinated* market economies (CMEs) of Germany, its Rhenish neighbors, Scandinavia, and Japan. These two ideal-typical 'models' entail different institutional features with respect to (*a*) financial and corporate governance, (*b*) the production system, (*c*) training and skill profiles, (*d*) labor market regulation, and (*e*) management–labor relations. Thus, we expect LMEs to adapt to cyclical market pressures through numerical flexibility, using early retirement plans as a downsizing strategy, whereas CMEs would tend toward using early exit from work as a response to the systemic problems of a high-wage or high-skill production system.

Finally, to map the impact of *partnership* institutions, I utilize comparative studies in industrial relations (Crouch 1993; Ebbinghaus and Visser 1997) that differentiate between voluntarist, contentious, and cooperative state–society relations. The *voluntarist* tradition is found in Anglophone economies, *contentious* labor relations have been a problem particularly in southern Europe, and *cooperative* labor relations are present in the remaining countries, though in different arenas (centralized cooperation in Scandinavia, sector-wide cooperation on the Continent, and firm-level cooperation in Japan). In the case of early retirement, national social partnership and workplace relations shape the reconciliation between economic exigencies and social demands. Moreover, the bargaining partners vary in their level of involvement in social policymaking and self-administration. Given regime-specific partnership traditions, we expect that voluntarist labor relations would only lead to local or limited defense of seniority rights, institutionalized cooperative labor relations would provide possibilities for political exchange between social partners, and contentious labor relations would lead to particularistic defense of seniority interests provoking labor conflicts.

Mapping the institutional affinities between protection, production, and partnership, we found some overlap, but without a perfect fit: no simple regime explanation fits all cases of early exit trends and the problems of national policy reversal. The pull thesis works well for the Continental welfare states with massive early retirement and liberal welfare states with less high levels, but the well-developed Swedish and Danish welfare states have much higher activity levels. On the other hand, the push thesis is in line with the cyclical nature of early exit in LMEs and the structural high level of labor shedding via early retirement in CMEs of Continental Europe, yet Japan combines similar internal labor markets with high activity levels. Neither a protection-oriented approach focusing on welfare regimes only nor the production-oriented thesis concentrating on varieties of capitalism can explain cross-national variations in early exit policies alone. Instead, welfare regimes and production systems provide intricate 'institutional complementarities' (Aoki 2001; Milgrom and Roberts 1994) that can alter the effects of labor demand and labor supply respectively. Thus, early retirement policies are not merely politics *against* markets (Esping-Andersen 1985), imposing social rights on markets, they can also be politics *for* markets, providing production-enhancing functions. Taking these regime typologies and working hypotheses into account, I explored their validity in the empirical analysis of early exit trajectories (Part Two) and policy reversal (Part Three).

8.1.3 *Early Exit Trajectories*

Before I untangle the respective impact of pull and push factors in more detail, it is necessary to specify again the explanandum described in Chapter 4. When we speak of retirement, we commonly refer to both the final withdrawal from work *and* the time period of receiving an old-age pension. The institutionalization of a 'normal' statutory age as full withdrawal from work was largely a consequence of the postwar expansion of public pensions. As a result, fewer and fewer people remained active beyond age 65, although in societies with significant agricultural workforces and commonplace self-employment, this trend occurred later, in particular in Japan. Early retirement, measured in this study as the decline in gainful employment before age 65, already started in the 1960s, that is, before the onset of mass unemployment. While the general trend can be easily observed among older men, inconsistent trends in female employment rates due to cohort effects mask the true extent of early exit.

Informed by a life course perspective, I calculated cohort-adjusted *exit rates* (see Appendix Note), enabling comparisons across time, countries, and gender. Early exit from work increased most dramatically in Continental Europe since the 1970s, though Italy already had a considerable level of low employment before age 65 in the 1960s. Although all four Continental European countries examined here have relatively high exit rates among older people (aged 60–64), France and Italy have higher rates of very early exit from work (before age 60) than do Germany and the Netherlands. The Scandinavian welfare states, the Anglophone market economies, and Japan have much lower levels of early exit. Sweden and the United States have moderate levels of early exit, while Japan and Ireland show particularly reduced levels. A more medium level of early exit can be found in the United Kingdom for women (and for men during the 1980s) as well as in Denmark for women (less so for men). Of all ten countries, Japan and Sweden have the highest employment rates in the age group 55–64, despite increasing unemployment in the 1990s that challenged these successful models.

Time-series analyses on the trend toward early exit in Continental Europe show a classic S-curve *diffusion* process, starting slowly in the 1960s, accelerating during the late 1970s, and reaching saturation in the 1990s. In the other countries, the trend tends to *fluctuate* with unemployment after an initial rise in the late 1970s, with levels remaining significantly below those in Continental Europe. The high-exit Continental European countries experienced long-term expansion of early retirement, as it became an acquired social right. In contrast, in the LMEs, early exit from work follows a more cyclical pattern, driven by market forces, and rising in the Scandinavian welfare states and Japan with the belated end of full employment.

8.1.4 *The Protection-Pull Thesis*

As discussed in Chapter 5, there is substantial evidence for the pull thesis of welfare regime-induced early exit patterns. With a few significant exceptions, the more generous welfare states tend to have higher levels of early exit from work. The Continental European welfare states have provided a multitude of early exit pathways, ranging from early statutory retirement, flexible seniority pensions with generous benefits, special early retirement programs, and long-term unemployment 'bridging pensions', to disability pensions with labor market considerations. In comparison, the liberal-residual welfare societies provide fewer and more restricted early retirement opportunities: late statutory retirement (except for women in the United Kingdom), actuarial reductions for flexible early pensions, restricted special retirement programs (if at all), short-term and low unemployment benefits, and meager disability pensions with strict medical criteria. However, there is also evidence that contradicts the pull thesis: Although the Scandinavian welfare states had relatively comprehensive, generous, and accessible pathways during the 1970s and 1980s, they did not experience the same level of early exit from work as did the states of Continental Europe. Moreover, in the United States and the United Kingdom, despite quite limited public pathways, early exit has occurred in several waves. As a result, we need to go beyond the mere pull thesis and look at the interaction between protection and production.

From a comparative perspective, we find expected differences between the three welfare regimes and early exit from work patterns (see Table 8.1):

- *Continental conservative welfare states* provide multiple, generous pathways and have the highest early exit level. Early retirement has become a quasi-social right.

- *Scandinavian universal welfare states* not only provide multiple pathways but also aim at activation through partial pensions and an inclusive strategy. They had lower levels of early exit, partially due to part-time work.

- *Liberal-residual welfare regimes* have lower early exit patterns due to fewer available public pathways. Occupational welfare plans provided

Table 8.1. Early exit from work and regime configurations

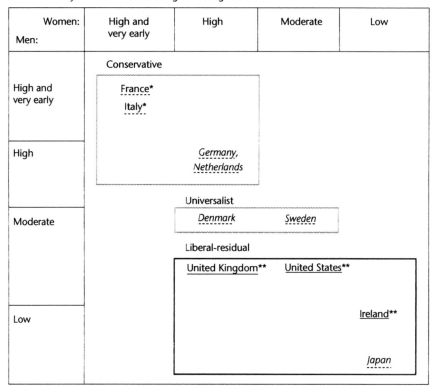

Women: Men:	High and very early	High	Moderate	Low
High and very early	Conservative France* Italy*			
High		Germany, Netherlands		
Moderate		Universalist Denmark	Sweden	
Low		Liberal-residual United Kingdom**	United States**	Ireland** Japan

Notes: Welfare regimes:—conservative;—universalist; — liberal-residual; production system (underlined): liberal market economy; nonliberal market economy; labor relations: *cooperative;* *contentious; **voluntarist.

by firms play a larger role and early exit is more market-induced. As a consequence, individuals increasingly must bear the risks of unemployment and poverty.

There is a correlation between the availability of public pathways and the overall exit trajectories, with the partial exception of Denmark and the United Kingdom. These two countries have traditionally had higher levels of early exit, particularly during the 1980s and among women, brought about by special preretirement schemes and the earlier pension age for women in the United Kingdom and social criteria in 'anticipatory' disability pensions in Denmark.

Different interpretations of the political and social forces behind the expansion of early retirement abound. In the historical-comparative sequence analysis, I cast serious doubt on functionalist claims that early retirement came about because it served the interests of governments and unions to reduce labor supply. Instead, the first exit pathways were opened up before the post-1973 mass unemployment crisis and largely motivated by social concerns and the expansion of social rights. Many public exit pathways were not devised as explicit early retirement policies; instead early exit from work was the *unintended* consequence of policies for other purposes. However, the social partners had an interest in using these available pathways and governments were late in changing course. In fact, the special preretirement schemes, set up by governments after the second oil crisis in order to control the increasingly used existing exit pathways, were meant to partially shift costs onto firms and induce job replacement.

In contrast to their governments, the social partners played a more active role in bringing about new pathways to 'buffer' workers from restructuring, to reduce labor supply, and to 'make room' for younger jobseekers. They were involved in devising preretirement programs in France, the Netherlands, and Denmark. Only the German and Italian social partners were not directly involved in setting up preretirement policies; nevertheless, they were involved in the self-administration of social insurance and defended the status quo. In the LMEs and Japan, it was the firms themselves that used occupational benefits and flexible labor markets (or in Japan secondary labor markets) to adjust their workforces. Thus, to the degree that the pull thesis depends on different partnership traditions and occupational welfare provided by social partners or firms, it was necessary to consider also the push factors. Under what conditions do firms foster and rely on early exit from work?

8.1.5 *The Production-Push Thesis*

The protection-oriented pull thesis does not explain why the social partners played such an active role in bringing about and using early exit; we thus need to turn to the production-related *push* factors. In Chapter 6, I discussed the willingness of employees to cofinance early exit from work in all countries, but particularly in liberal-residual welfare regimes that lack generous public pathways. Most of the larger British, Irish, American, and Japanese employers (in both private and public sectors) provide favorable early occupational pensions, topping up of flexible pensions or special 'window' plans. However, these employer-led pathways remain limited to larger (often unionized) companies, and firms have increasingly retreated from DB pensions and long-term employment commitments.

Private occupational pensions play less of a role than the publicly provided early exit pathways in the Continental European and Scandinavian welfare states, because social partners run schemes beyond the firm.

Among the push factors that explain the trend toward early exit from work are structural changes: deindustrialization and the growth to limits of public employment. However, these general shifts cannot explain the cross-national variations in early exit trajectories in a systematic way, although the particular expansion and stagnation of the public sector in Denmark and Sweden provide one reason for the specific Nordic pattern. An empirical test of the thesis that labor shedding was concentrated in declining industries produces very mixed results at best, and furthermore, it cannot account for the large cross-national differences (Jacobs, Kohli, and Rein 1991c). Although some special early retirement schemes were introduced to facilitate industrial restructuring, early exit from work has become a much broader social right, common across nearly all private industry and public-service sectors. However, the analysis of age-related skill levels shows that older workforces tend to be less skilled, and that those with lower skills have been shed at a higher rate than others.

Although all firms seem to have an interest in using early exit, there are differences according to the particular partnership traditions, labor market regulations, production strategies, and economic governance structures. Taking the ideal-typical production models, we can derive two different sets of push forces. Under LMEs (Britain, Ireland, the United States), Fordist mass production tends to rely more heavily on general skills, while hiring and firing is largely unregulated. As labor turnover is more common, employers use occupational pensions to retain skilled workers. Furthermore, in unionized firms, unions defend seniority rights ('last in, first out' rules) and employers thus have to buy out older workers with 'golden handshakes'. Given liberal corporate and financial governance, short-termism puts additional pressure on these firms to be numerically flexible during downturns. Therefore, early exit patterns in LMEs tend to be *cyclical*, as some companies used firm-sponsored early retirement plans to downsize during economic downturns, while others shed older workers in largely unregulated labor markets, pushing the risks of finding work (or income support) onto individuals.

Quite in contrast, CMEs tend to have firms with specialized or functionally flexible production methods, requiring industry or company-specific skills and well-developed vocational training (Estevez-Abe, Iversen, and Soskice 2001). Labor rights are more institutionalized: Employment is highly regulated, collectively negotiated wages tend to be high and more egalitarian, and workers have codecision rights, particularly in employment matters. Corporate governance follows a stakeholder model that gives some codecision rights to worker representatives at company level. Furthermore, financial and corporate governance has thus far consistently provided long-term patient capital. Therefore, during economic downturns, companies could hoard skilled workers, instead of downsizing immediately. However, given the seniority wage system and the need for costly skill upgrading, employers seek to induce timely retirement in order to enhance efficiency and maintain internal labor markets. Given the institutionalized workers' rights and more favorable public benefits, early retirement is a socially acceptable means for restructuring; it is likely to receive the support of workers and workplace representatives.

Nevertheless, neither early exit practice is in equilibrium. They follow either a downward or an upward spiral. In the case of the *shareholder* model in LMEs, financial market pressure has increasingly pushed companies to withdraw from their commitment to DB pensions. Moreover, unions have lost in bargaining power and can hardly enforce seniority rights. Thus, the burden of continued downsizing is placed on individuals, and this cost has been amplified by retrenchment in liberal welfare states. On the other hand, the *stakeholder* employment model in CMEs has led to a self-defeating, self-reinforcing spiral of early exit from work. Unions are still strong enough to defend social rights, welfare states still provide public exit pathways that allow externalization of costs, and employers themselves find labor shedding of older workers the easiest way to maintain the internal labor market. Employers' belief in the diminished productivity of older workers leads to the self-fulfilling prophecy about the 'socially expected duration' (Merton {1984} 1996) of ever shorter employment tenure: Older workers are less productive; therefore, they are shed earlier, but because employers expect workers to retire early, they stop investing in training at earlier stages, and thus older workers have obsolete skills, which indeed make them less productive.

However, the country case studies show two exceptions to the vicious circle of the internal labor market model: Sweden and Japan maintained higher levels of activity in older age groups, at least prior to the 1990s. In Sweden, the combination of partial pensions and part-time work allowed firms to retain older workers and their expertise. The Swedish work integration strategy has been highly contingent on the generosity of the public benefits, the willingness of employers to reorganize work, the support of local unions at workplace level, and activation policies by public employment agencies. In fact, this model came under severe pressure with the end of full employment in the 1990s and the fiscal crisis of the Swedish welfare state, which cut back on partial pension benefits. In recent years, the gradually phased-in pension reforms and future skill shortage may once again lead to a return to the prolonged working life model (Wadensjö 2002).

A very different social practice is at the heart of the Japanese partial exit model. Larger firms enforce mandatory retirement around age 60, but they provide reemployment at a lower wage or 'secondment' to smaller supplier firms. In addition, firm-sponsored benefits are provided as income supplements to the lower earnings, until public pension age. This model also came under pressure in the 1990s, as Japanese employers were more reluctant to fulfill their 'social responsibility' and the pension reforms gradually postponed pensions to cope with the country's rapidly aging population. The importance of a long working life remains, but it may entail further segmentation into a primary core workforce ('company men') and a secondary labor market made up of women, older men, and the unemployed (Brinton 1998).

The analysis of push factors complements and fine-tunes the analysis of protection-induced pull factors. The basic claim of the Varieties of Capitalism (Hall and Soskice 2001*a*) approach seems to be valid: The interactions of the different institutional arrangements pose specific incentive structures and follow different institutional logics at firm level. Firms in LMEs are more likely to suffer cyclical downsizing pressure, and early exit from work remains a partly internalized firm strategy or individualized risk of unemployment and poverty in old age. In contrast, firms in CMEs face the contingencies of seniority wage, high skill, highly regulated, and cooperative workplace relations. They seek to buy out older workers in a socially acceptable way, supported by multiple possibilities for externalizing these restructuring costs (Naschold and de Vroom 1994). The analysis of economic push factors also suggests that a reversal in early exit trends cannot be achieved merely by cutting back on public pathways. As long as firms are compelled to downsize or restructure, labor shedding will continue—a particular challenge to public policy that seeks to reverse the trends of early exit from work.

8.1.6 Reversing Early Exit from Work

Given escalating social expenditures, declining activity rates, and unfavorable demographic shifts, international organizations and national experts call for changes in welfare-state policies. More and more, the political actors see early retirement as an increasingly costly passive labor market policy, which has not lowered overall or youth unemployment, but rather contributes to pricing out labor through high nonwage labor costs. From the OECD and European Union to national policy communities, a paradigm shift has occurred. Political actors argue for the reversal of early exit policies with reference to three challenges to contemporary welfare states:

- *demographic* changes toward an aging society undermine the *sustainability* of old-age public pensions, particularly PAYG systems;
- *high social expenditures* for inactive people increase *labor costs* and thus drive even more people out of work; and
- *passive labor market policies* that merely seek to redistribute work do not solve the employment problem, instead *activation* policies that enhance employability are needed.

Reversing the course of early exit from work involves a plethora of measures, given the multitude of existing pathways and the interactions between pull and push factors. Although the challenges to welfare states are widely acknowledged, reformers face fundamental problems in reversing early exit policies due to the multitude of existing pathways and multiple actor constellations. Retrenchment in one pathway may lead to 'instrument substitution' (Casey 1989) as actors seek the next best alternative. Closing down a pathway may also merely shift costs between public programs or between public and private actors. By and large, the retrenchment strategy would then reduce neither early exit nor overall costs. Furthermore, 'privatization' entails reducing the work disincentives and increasing internalization of costs by the actors themselves (firms and older workers). In addition, tightening of rules by the 'principal' can also fail due to insufficient implementation through the 'agent', particularly where social partners self-administer or even self-regulate programs. Moreover, cutbacks on public benefits have also run into the problem that the social partners have compensated the income gap, annulling such reforms' incentive to work effects.

Reversing early exit will entail more than altering the protection-induced pull, it would also require the lowering of production-related push. Thus, changes in employer, workplace, and bargaining policies with respect to hiring, training, part-time jobs, and firing are necessary to retain (or reintegrate) older workers in employment. Employer's willingness to facilitate the adaptation of working conditions to be more accessible given the capabilities and needs of older workers will also be necessary. Changing the long-held expectations of employers, works councilors, and workers will require coordinated information campaigns by state agencies and associations.

Realization of the need for policy change has taken several decades since the first mass use of early exit pathways in the late 1970s. Governments were late in recognizing the largely unintended consequences of early exit options and their diffusion as a widespread social practice pursued by the social partners. The first retrenchment efforts attempted to cut welfare benefits or tighten eligibility criteria without any major systemic change. Five major reform policy measures (reviewed in Chapter 7) include: (1) raising statutory-pension age; (2) recalibrating disability pensions; (3) closing special early exit programs; (4) shifting from passive to active labor market policies; and (5) fostering gradual pensions and extended part-time work.

(1) Increasingly, concerns about the long-term sustainability of pensions and the declining activity rates led to reforms of statutory old-age *pensions*, though the changes were mainly phased in over long periods. Moreover, the reform of seniority pensions and the raising of retirement age were contentious issues. While mass protest arose in some cases, other reforms were based on interparty consensus and social concertation with the social partners (Ebbinghaus and Hassel 2000). To the degree that public pensions were mature PAYG systems, the public and the unions saw these early exit pathways as acquired social rights (Myles and Pierson 2001). Only gradual systemic changes were possible, with concessions to the social partners. Nevertheless, the gradual introduction of privately funded DC pensions in several of these countries is a change that will reduce incentives to retire early as actuarial principles gain importance in the future.

(2) Reforms of the *disability* pathway have been more difficult. The 'Dutch disease' (Aarts, Burkhauser, and de Jong 1996*a*), the use of disability pensions for early exit, has been particularly problematic in the Netherlands, and to a lesser degree in Denmark and Sweden. A sequence of Dutch retrenchment efforts proved only partially successful until the entire governance structure of social insurance administration was remodeled. But if labor shedding is not reversed, the elimination of labor market considerations in disability pension programs, as in the Netherlands and Sweden, will increase unemployment rolls. However, changes in employers' workplace environments and safety policies could reduce early exit from work due to health-related problems.

(3) Governments were able to close special *preretirement* schemes more quickly than preretirement options under pay-as-you-go old-age pension systems. Yet those special schemes set up by the social partners proved more resistant. Thus, the British and German Conservative governments could shut down these state schemes in the 1980s, while the French, Dutch, and Danish collective schemes had a much longer life.

(4) The pull–push interaction proves important in the case of *partial pensions* that aim at a gradual (but postponed) transition toward retirement (Delsen and Reday-Mulvey 1996a; Laczko 1988; Latulippe and Turner 2000). Despite its past successes, Sweden's recent reform has abolished the generous partial pensions, while countries in Continental Europe along with Denmark and Japan seek to foster progressive retirement. Thus far, they have had limited success due to more attractive alternatives and all actors' reluctance to embrace part-time work. The German use of a 'block model' is an example that shows how easily the intention of partial pensions as gradual withdrawal can be undermined: The part-time pension becomes a quasi-early retirement scheme with the bargaining partners' consent (Barkholdt 2001).

(5) Most recently, the shift from passive labor market policies toward *activation* measures has been advocated (Clemens 2001; Jespen, Foden, and Hutsebaut 2002a). Age discrimination in hiring, training, and dismissal policy is deeply ingrained and even policymakers seem reluctant to invest in the retraining of older workers. But public policy has some means to induce employers and workers to change their expectations and behavior in the short term, such as through disseminating information about 'best practices'. Within the European Union, activation policy and employability are now propagated as part of the European Employment Strategy that also seeks to coordinate national labor market policies with the social partners (Goetschy 1999, 2000).

Although we can find 'sequential policy learning' over time from policy failures and past policies' negative effects (Hemerijck and Schludi 2000; Hemerijck and van Kersbergen 1999), there are cross-national variations due to the specific problem constellations. Given the very different exit patterns across countries, the problem load varies greatly between welfare regimes (see Table 8.2). The Continental European welfare states have multiple entrenched public pathways and social partners have some veto power in policy formation and implementation. Policy reversal has thus been rather late and contentious at times, particularly in France and Italy. In Germany and the Netherlands, consensual reforms have been

Table 8.2. Policy reversals across welfare-state regimes and labor relations

Exit problem load	Phasing-in compromise but occasional conflict	Late phasing-in/ activation policy	Early phasing-in/ privatization
High and very early	*Conservative* WS *Contentious* LR France, Italy		
High	*Conservative* WS *Consensual* LR Germany, Netherlands		
Female: high; *Men: moderate*		*Universalist* WS *Corporatist* LR Denmark	*Liberal* WS *Voluntarist* LR United Kingdom
Moderate		Sweden	United States
Low *(but future problem)*		*Residual* WS *Cooperative* LR Japan	(*social pacts*) Ireland

Notes: See Table 4.8 for exit trends; WS: welfare-state regime; LR: labor relations.

attempted in the past, though some more recent reform efforts have met opposition. In universalist Scandinavia, while public old-age and disability pension programs remain the domain of the political actors, unions and employers have an institutionalized role in the area of employment policy, which has facilitated more active labor market policies. The difficulties faced by liberal-residual welfare states due to early retirement have been less severe. Nevertheless, the United States and Britain have also embarked on reforms of their public pension systems and the trend toward increased private pensions will add further pressure to work longer. Not only does the problem load vary across countries, but so do opportunity structures for reforms due to variations in social partnership traditions.

8.2 Going Beyond Path Dependence

8.2.1 Unintended Consequences and Path Dependence

This study of rising early exit from work as a widespread social practice and the difficulties of reversing these trends provides insights contributing to the development of institutional theory (see also Ebbinghaus 2005*a*). Historical institutionalism has thus far been largely concerned with path dependence, institutional inertia, and entrenched interests (Pierson 2000*a*, 2000*b*), while the theory of institutional change, which could account for path departure, requires advancement (Clemens and Cook

1999; Thelen 1999, 2002). Moreover, rational actor accounts of the politics of social policy tend to stress the pre-strategic interests of micro-level actors (individuals, employers, and unions) in preferring particular public policies and their strategic interactions in the political game, using available veto points (Anderson, Immergut, and Schulze 2006; Immergut 1991; Levi 2000; Mares 2003). Instead, I contend that while micro-level actors may well have interests in particular public policies, this cannot explain the existence of these policies—unless the social partners themselves were involved or the government deliberately aimed to serve these actors' interests.

The comparative-historical account showed that it was partly due to *unintended consequences* of public benefits set up for social purposes that older workers and social partners could adjust the workforce in a socially acceptable way, adapting to economic changes. In contrast to many functionalist accounts, we should not assume that an institution's benefits must be the reason for its origin: Although the social partners have used the available exit pathways for their purposes, they were not always instrumental in enacting them. Many public policies that provided major exit pathways predated the rise in early exit or were set up specifically with other intentions. Nevertheless, in a minority of cases, the establishment of specific preretirement options can be linked to policies promoted or even negotiated by social partners. Whether intended or not, exit pathways were *used* by the social partners to serve their interests. Thus, following Stinchcombe, we should separate two explanations: (*a*) the circumstances that explain the *origin* of an institution and (*b*) the subsequent process of its *self-reproduction* (Stinchcombe 1968: 102–3). Not all exit pathways were planned as such, but once available they provided a strong incentive for older workers, employers, and workplace representatives to adapt their strategies and expectations about the usefulness of early exit.

However, analysis of this social practice's self-reproduction would not provide a sufficient account if it did not also show why those affected by the externalities of the social partners' collusion were unable to end it. We need to explain why governments did not (or only insufficiently and belatedly) intervene once they realized the unintended consequences of public policies designed for other purposes. Initially, governments committed benign neglect since they believed that early exit would temporarily relieve difficult labor market situations. When they discovered early exit's actual costs, they sought to intervene, but faced the problems of policy reversal. In fact, governments attempted to regulate early exit or to even close down exit pathways only after a considerable time lag following the rise of early exit from work. However, given the multiple pathways and the constellation of multilevel actors, policy reversal is very difficult: There may well be substitution effects as actors search for 'second-best alternatives'; changes may only shift costs between programs; reducing the pull incentives will hardly change the production-related push factors; and the social partners may be able to block or counteract welfare retrenchment.

The explanation of the diffusion and persistence of early exit as a widespread social practice exemplifies the theory of path-dependent *feedback* mechanism (Pierson 2000*a*). On the basis of the economic theory of *increasing returns* (Arthur 1994: 112–13), Paul Pierson distinguishes four processes that account for institutional inertia: (*a*) large setup costs, (*b*) learning effects, (*c*) coordination effects, and (*d*) adaptive expectations (Pierson 2000*b*: 76–7). In my account, *social expectations* shared by the social actors have been crucial in perpetuating early exit practices (see Figure 8.1). Two actor constellations in and across workplaces have promoted the proliferation of this 'social innovation': (i) older workers (and

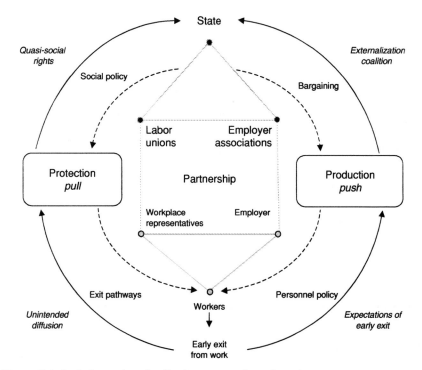

Figure 8.1 Path-dependent feedback processes in early retirement

workplace representatives) support early exits and (ii) the employers (and workplace representatives) use it for their own purposes. As early as the 1930s, sociologist Robert K. Merton indicated several social mechanisms for such *unintended* consequences as a result of diffusion processes (Merton 1936). His well-known example describes how just the rumor of bankruptcy can lead to a self-fulfilling prophecy: as panicked depositors withdraw their funds, the bank indeed falls into insolvency. Moreover, Merton also pointed out the impact of social comparison (with peers) and social expectations, as social mechanisms that have large-scale consequences (Merton 1967). Both processes help to explain the expansion of early retirement and the subsequent difficulties of reversing its course, particularly in Continental Europe (Ebbinghaus 2000). While there are welfare-related 'pull' factors that affect labor supply (the increasing probability of workers deciding to withdraw from work early), there are also 'push' factors that account for labor demand problems, especially the tendency of firms to release older workers.

On the 'pull' side, public policies provided (often unintended) pathways to early retirement (Kohli et al. 1991). Disability rules, for instance, were increasingly used over time to release older workers from work. Moreover, many arrangements set up for particular circumstances became generalized through peer comparisons and public expectations to all sectors and conditions: Early retirement programs that had started in particular sectors became a quasi-social right for all. In fact, once a particular cohort had retired early, the following cohorts claimed the right to do the same. This holds true particularly in PAYG systems, where workers perceive that they have already paid into a scheme, that their former colleagues were allowed to take early retirement, and that they will have thus earned the same right when they reach the same age. However, this originally unintended diffusion of early exit has had the perverse effect of necessitating increases in welfare-state expenditures and social security contributions, leading to further pressure on labor markets (Esping-Andersen 1996c). Historically, once the quasi-social right was firmly entrenched, it became very difficult for governments to reverse such policies, or even control the ongoing early exit regimes, not least because there are also 'push' factors at work. This self-reinforcing diffusion process of a quasi-social right of early withdrawal, in which programs largely intended for other purposes are generalized, exemplifies the diffusion-like path-dependent processes (Ebbinghaus 2005a).

On the 'push' side, employers (or personnel departments) also have good reasons to collude with worker representatives in releasing older workers during a phase of downsizing and/or to maintain a high-skill internal labor market (Ebbinghaus 2001). This is particularly the case when public policies provide opportunities to offload the costs and early retirement benefits are socially acceptable to workplace representatives. Yet there is also a mechanism of deterministic path dependence at work that leads to unintended consequences. Employers defend early retirement by suggesting that older workers are less productive, although empirical evidence has not confirmed this belief (Casey 1997). Regardless of true productivity rates, once employers assume that workers will exit early, they stop investing in continuing education or retraining measures for workers as their supposed early retirement age approaches. This leads to an ever earlier outdating of older workers' skill profiles, which then serves as proof of their lower productivity, a genuine self-fulfilling prophecy. Reversing early exit trends would therefore also require the adjustment of firm-level actors' expectations. Thus, the largely unfounded belief of employers about older workers' age-related productivity—in combination with firms' use of early retirement for socially accepted restructuring—leads to a self-reinforcing, self-fulfilling prophecy with long-term negative effects on welfare states.

Social partners select the appropriate repertoire of strategies from the potential pathways provided by the welfare regime and under the pressure of the particular production system. This cross-national comparison shows that social actors have not used identical pathways to achieve early exit. There are indeed culturally specific *functional alternatives*. Most strikingly, the Japanese mandatory exit from career jobs does not lead to exit from work as it does in other countries, due to employers' commitment to offer reemployment opportunities. Social partners play an important role in selecting, if not actually devising, appropriate social practices for their specific needs. The *institutional complementarities* have been conceptualized as functionally reinforcing institutions in the Varieties of Capitalism approach (Aoki 2001; Hall and Soskice 2001a; Milgrom and Roberts 1994). However, they are not an 'automatic' consequence of institutional affinities between protection and production regimes, evolving instead from social practices adapted by the social partners at national and workplace levels under given opportunity structures and constraints.

The literature on institutional complementarities has largely focused on *beneficial constraints* (Streeck 1997a), such as the advantages of vocational training programs supported by chambers of commerce and handicrafts. There are also institutional complementarities in the case of early retirement. For instance, generous public pathways in Germany have supported the high-skill and high-wage production model: German firms can use publicly funded early retirement options to restructure in a socially and employment acceptable way and thus maintain their seniority wage and employment tenure system. However, in contrast to 'beneficial constraints', there are severe long-term, aggregate *perverse effects* from this labor-shedding strategy—in both the protection and production spheres. Early retirement has contributed to a vicious circle of welfare state unsustainability. The increasing popularity of early exit as a labor-shedding strategy leads to high social expenditures that drive up non-wage labor costs. This in turn forces firms to shed even more workers through early retirement. This 'welfare-without-work' problem is particularly prominent in Continental welfare states (Esping-Andersen 1996c; Scharpf 2001).

8.2.2 Toward Institutional Change and Path Departure

Given these negative externalities of early exit, we expect that the social actors, in particular governments, would step in. However, state intervention occurred belatedly, met major obstacles, and rarely led to a systemic change. Thus, the second research question asked: Why is policy reversal so difficult and under which conditions is change possible? Esping-Andersen's important study *Three Worlds of Welfare Capitalism* (Esping-Andersen 1990) assumes that long-term historical political forces shape welfare regimes, specifically the redistributive principles and institutional mix of social policies. At critical junctures in the formation of welfare states, new political alliances led to systemic reforms of certain policies adopted to deal with the new social risks arising in industrial societies (Flora and Alber 1981). Other societal options at a critical juncture were not taken—they became 'suppressed historical alternatives' (Moore 1978), thus foreclosing a particular developmental path taken by other nations. For example, the road toward universal citizenship pensions was foreclosed in Germany through the institutionalization of social insurance for workers under Bismarck in 1889 and again after World War II, when the Adenauer government's pension reform of 1957 introduced a full PAYG system.

For Esping-Andersen, societal forces and historical legacies have led to entrenched regimes or frozen institutional landscapes from which they can hardly escape, even when they result in perverse effects. Most crucially, the Continental European welfare states (Esping-Andersen 1996c; Scharpf 2001) are locked into the 'welfare state without work' problem. They suffer the Continental dilemma: as passive labor market policies are used to take workers out of work to alleviate labor market disequilibria, the higher are the social security costs, which in turn lead to higher labor costs and thus yet more pressure to shed labor. Although smaller *parametric* reforms have been implemented in an attempt to shift the costs of social security between different insurance systems, these reforms have not changed the status quo.

Arguments in favor of path persistence in pension policy emphasize the difficulties of altering a PAYG system due to the double-payer problem, as the current working generation would have to pay for the acquired rights of pensioners and save for their own future pensions (Pierson 1997). Because the benefits of a system change would be diffused and can only be received in the future, welfare retrenchment would lead to immediate and concentrated cuts—a change in social policy that is politically difficult to achieve, particularly given the *blame avoidance* of office-seeking politicians (Myles and Pierson 2001). The PAYG principle in social insurance is certainly a strong self-reinforcing process, resembling the path dependence theorem of economic theory, which assumes strong institutional inertia (see Ebbinghaus 2005*a*).

Nevertheless, several welfare states that were said to be frozen landscapes (Esping-Andersen 1996*c*) have been able to substantially reform (Hinrichs 2000*a*; Palier 2000; Reynaud 2000; Taylor-Gooby 1999). The analysis of reform policies to reverse the early exit from work trends (see Chapter 7) indicates some processes that could lead to institutional *change*. Indeed, it is this second conception of path dependence, which does not assume institutional inertia, that seems most attuned to studying institutional change of welfare states (Ebbinghaus 2005*a*). Some welfare states have been able to make up for missed opportunities and reintroduce 'suppressed historical alternatives' in particular situations of crisis and then expand upon them. The Dutch pension system introduced a basic pension system after World War II, after emergency measures had temporarily prepared the ground and private occupational pensions had in the mean time filled the void of earnings-related supplements (Haverland 2001). Those pension systems that already enjoyed institutional arrangements, like a private second-tier, would not have to introduce such a scheme from scratch but could use these '*dormant*' historical alternatives to start a gradual process of transforming an old-age security system from public toward private provisions.

Moreover, minor gradual changes in the past might lead to a long-term gradual transformation, increasing the share of private pensions through a steady reduction in benefits from the PAYG public system. Gradual changes might thus lead to long-term systemic *recalibration* of a system; these may also be more acceptable politically, not least because the changes are at first unobservable or too complicated to understand (Myles and Pierson 2001). Grandfathering rules that exempt current pensioners from retrenchment at the expense of future beneficiaries have been a common device in welfare reforms negotiated by governments with trade unions, as the core union membership is exempted or less affected by changes (Brugiavini et al. 2001; Ebbinghaus and Hassel 2000). Hence, there does exist a large variety of intermediate changes (*path departure*) between the extreme cases of status quo maintenance (*path stabilization*) claimed by political scientists and radical system change (*path switching*) often advocated by economists (see Figure 8.2).

In the comparative-historical analysis of policy reversal concerning early exit from work presented in this book, the following general strategies were observed in ongoing policy reversal:

- *Systemic* change remains largely limited to special public preretirement programs that are exclusively tax-financed or not yet mature PAYG systems.

- *Parametric* changes, such as altering benefit indexation from wages to inflation, occurred relatively often, since their long-term effects remain largely concealed.

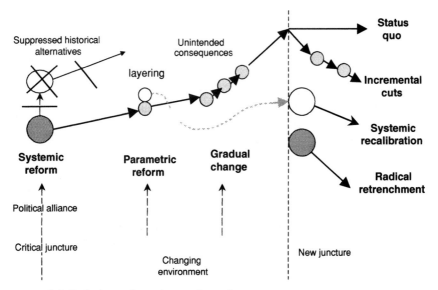

Figure 8.2 Path dependence in pension reform processes

- *Phased-in* changes, such as the raising of statutory retirement age over time and exempting current older age cohorts from immediate cuts, reduce opposition, and are common in systems with consensual policymaking.
- *Institutional layering* occurred through the introduction of new elements (such as second-tier private pensions) without changing the entrenched core, but with the long-term prospect of a gradual shift in balance between old and new institutions.
- *Shifting costs* from public to private actors can lead to a higher internalization of early exit costs by the social actors, though it could also lead to an individualization of poverty risk, if firms continue to shed older workers.
- *Governance* reforms that bring a new division of responsibilities between the state and the social partners can reinstill social responsibility, especially if negative externalities and the outsiders' interests are taken into account.

The contingent nature of policy reversal indicates that institutional change is a rather slow and often contradictory process. Historical-institutionalist studies of welfare retrenchment emphasize the largely political obstacles to systemic reform and the piecemeal pace of institutional change (Pierson 1994, 2001c). Complementing that research, this comparative analysis reveals the highly contingent nature of institutional change due to the complex interactions between the institutional spheres of protection and production, as well as multilevel actor constellations with locked-in social expectations that foster the social practice of early exit from work. Not only for political reasons but also for practical reasons, reversing this entrenched practice of early exit from work can only be achieved through coordinated reforms that take into account the interaction between protection and production, as well as bring the social partners into a reform coalition.

8.3 Policy Implications for Aging Societies

On the basis of the findings of this comparative-historical study, I will suggest some broad policy recommendations. First, all social actors—the state and social partners—need to reach a *shared understanding* of both policy problems and potential solutions. The negative externalities of widespread early exit practices, while well known, have yet to be commonly accepted by all social partners. Tripartite national institutions and international policy exchanges such as the European Union's OMC in employment, pension, and social inclusion policies provide a forum for policy learning (De Deken 2003; Goetschy 2000; Teague 2001). Government and social partners must agree on the broad aims of reforms such as the future sustainability of welfare policies and increases in employment activity. Social partners have to recognize the negative externalities from the described vicious circles of labor shedding that reinforce the labor cost problem and older workers' outdated skill profiles. Nevertheless, it will not be sufficient for the social partners to embrace a shared understanding of the common problem; this must be brought into the public domain. Successful active aging policies would require substantial turnaround in employer policies and practices in hiring, training, and dismissing older workers (Jespen, Foden, and Hutsebaut, 2002a). Thus, an important strategy for reversing early exit as a social practice will be the change of entrenched social expectations by older workers themselves, management officials, and workplace representatives. Information, deliberation, and persuasion through associational channels could be crucial and more effective than public, state-sponsored campaigns.

Second, governments need to *include the social partners* in reform coalitions. Because changes in early exit policy affect the social partners' key interests, it is difficult and often counter-productive to impose reform without their consent. Social concertation is not only advisable to circumvent reform blockage in the political decision-making arena but also a more realistic approach to avoid implementation problems. A reversal of early exit from work requires changes in the shared policy space that go beyond the reach of public policy. As exemplified in countries such as France and the Netherlands, the social partners have used their own collective schemes to finance early retirement if public policy fails to provide sufficient early exit opportunities. Moreover, in the implementation phase, the social partners can also undermine policy changes from above, whether well intentioned or not. Policymakers need to recognize that early retirement is a policy area that lies at the interface of public policy, collective bargaining, and firm-level labor relations.

Third, reforms to reverse early exit have to be *coordinated across policy arenas* and should take into account both push and pull factors. This comparative analysis has shown that neither pull-protection nor push-production factors singly account for early exit regimes, but that there are intricate institutional complementarities. Therefore, one-sided policy changes that address only the protection side or only aim to intervene on the production side are doomed to failure. As long as firms continue to shed older workers, a cut in benefits will only place the burden of adaptation onto the shoulders of the social partners or on the individual worker alone. For too long, public policymakers have focused on welfare retrenchment, largely for budgetary reasons. Only belatedly have they realized that narrowing exit pathways requires complementary policies to reintegrate and retain older workers in employment. The success of partial pension policies, for instance, remains contingent on employers' willingness to provide part-time jobs to older workers. Similarly, (re)integrating disabled workers usually entails inexpensive but crucial adaptations of workplaces. Hence, all social actors that affect social and employment policy should be included in social concertation: not only would the legitimacy of coordinated reforms increase, but also the deliberation required to design adequate policy solutions could take into account the diverse pull and push pressures.

Fourth, the *governance structures* may need to be reformed to reinforce social responsibility. Thus far, the social partners' collusion of interests at national and workplace levels has fostered the social practice of early exit from work. In order to evade past externalization coalitions, the governance of social and employment policy and the coordination with the collective bargaining realm should be reformed. On the one hand, it may be necessary to reallocate responsibilities. When social partners have the capacity to block reforms due to veto power in social administration but are not responsible for their actions' consequences, responsibility needs to be reorganized to overcome externalization opportunities. On the other hand, the social concertation process should be opened up to other groups and more general interests. It would be advisable not only to bring in the 'outsiders,' such as the unemployed, but also to have independent (or state) representatives in partnership institutions. Given the key role played by the social partners in early exit policies and practices thus far, such a reform project could only work if social concertation succeeds in bringing the social partners to assume their 'social responsibility' and internalize a larger part of the considerable social costs of early exit policies.

A reversal in early exit from work would thus entail a veritable paradigm shift in policymaking from passive to active labor market policies and from the common practice of externalization of adaptation costs onto public schemes to an internalization of such costs by the firms. Rapidly aging populations will make such foresight and action necessary if pension and other welfare programs are to be sustained, but active aging and lifelong learning will also be necessary for labor market reasons. Experts predict a shortage of skilled labor among young workers and an aging workforce in the future; therefore, it will become increasingly important to devise strategies to retain older, experienced workers and adapt working conditions appropriately. In the future, we may expect a better-educated workforce with higher levels of female labor force participation in older age groups, which may well increase activation levels. On the other hand, increased part-time, flexible, and interrupted careers, reduced future pension benefits, and less social transfers for older workers will also entail increased risks of unemployment or poverty in older age. The challenge to governments and social partners will be to adapt the current protection, production, and partnership institutions to foster a more sustainable work–life balance in aging societies.

Appendix Note

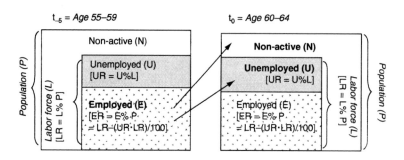

Absolute 'exit' rate for age group 60–64 (cf. cohort 5 years ago):

$$\longrightarrow \quad EX^{60-64}_{t_0} \;=\; ER^{60-64}_{t_0} \;-\; ER^{55-59}_{t_{-5}}$$

Relative 'exit' rate for age group 60–64 (cf. cohort 5 years ago):

$$\longrightarrow \quad EX^{60-64}_{t_0}\% \;=\; (ER^{60-64}_{t_0} \;-\; ER^{55-59}_{t_{-5}}) \;/\; ER^{55-59}_{t_{-5}} \cdot 100$$

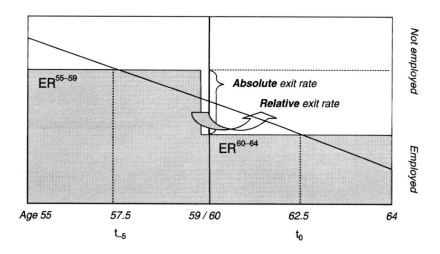

References

Aarts, L. J. M., Burkhauser, R. V., and de Jong, P. R. (eds.) (1996). *Curing the Dutch Disease: An International Perspective on Disability Policy Reform*. Aldershot: Avebury.
—— —— —— (1996*b*). 'Introduction and Overview', in L. J. M. Aarts, R. V. Burkhauser, and P. R. de Jong (eds.), *Curing the Dutch Disease*. Aldershot: Avebury, pp. 1–19.
—— and de Jong, P. R. (1993). 'Early Retirement of Older Male Workers under the Dutch Social Security Disability Insurance Programme', in A. B. Atkinson and M. Rein (eds.), *Age, Work and Social Security*. New York: St. Martin's Press, pp. 20–50.
—— —— (1996*a*). 'The Dutch Disability Program and How it Grew', in L. J. M. Aarts, R. V. Burkhauser, and P. R. de Jong (eds.), *Curing the Dutch Disease: An International Perspective on Disability Policy Reform*. Aldershot: Avebury, pp. 21–46.
—— —— (1996*b*). 'Evaluating the 1987 and 1993 Social Welfare Reforms: From Disappointment to Potential Success', in L. J. M. Aarts, R. V. Burkhauser and P. R. de Jong (eds.), *Curing the Dutch Disease*. Aldershot: Avebury, pp. 47–69.
Adema, W. (1999). 'Net Public Social Expenditure', *OECD Labour Market and Social Policy Occasional Papers*, 39.
Alber, J. (1982). *Vom Armenhaus zum Wohlfahrtsstaat: Analysen zur Entwicklung der Sozialversicherung in Westeuropa*. Frankfurt: Campus.
Albert, M. (1991). *Capitalisme contre Capitalisme*. Paris: Le Seuil.
Allmendinger, J. (1994). *Lebensverlauf und Sozialpolitik: Die Ungleichheit von Mann und Frau und ihr öffentlicher Ertrag*. Frankfurt: Campus.
—— and Hinz, T. (1998). 'Occupational Careers under Different Welfare Regimes: West Germany, Great Britain and Sweden', in L. Leisering and R. Walker (eds.), *The Dynamics of Modern Society: Poverty, Policy and Welfare*. Bristol: Policy Press, University of Bristol.
Amable, B. (2005). *Les Cinq Capitalismes. Diversité des systèmes économiques et sociaux dans la mondialisation*. Paris: Seuil.
Anderson, K. M. and Meyer, T. (2003). 'Social Democracy, Unions, and Pension Politics in Germany and Sweden'. *Journal of Public Policy*, 23/1: 23–54.
—— Immergut, E. M. and Schulze, I. (eds.) (2006). *Oxford Handbook of West European Pension Politics*. Oxford: Oxford University Press, forthcoming.
Aoki, M. (2001). *Towards a Comparative Institutional Analysis*. Cambridge, MA: MIT Press.

apRoberts, L. and Turner, J. (1997). 'Enterprise and the State: Interactions in the Provision of Employees' Retirement Income in the United States', in M. Rein and E. Wadensjö (eds.), *Enterprise and the Welfare State*. Cheltenham: Edward Elgar, pp. 352–79.

Arthur, W. B. (1994). *Increasing Returns and Path Dependence in the Economy*. Ann Arbor, MI: University of Michigan Press.

Ascoli, U. (1988). 'The Italian Welfare State in the 1980s: Less State and More Market?' in R. Morris (ed.), *Testing the Limits of Social Welfare: International Perspectives on Policy Changes in Nine Countries*. Hanover, CT: University Press of New England, pp. 165–92.

Ashford, D. E. (1991). 'Advantages of Complexity: Social Insurance in France', in J. S. Ambler (ed.), *The French Welfare State: Surviving Social and Ideological Change*. New York: New York University Press, pp. 32–57.

Atchley, R. C. (1982). 'Retirement as a Social Institution'. *Annual Review of Sociology*, 8: 263–87.

Auer, P. and Speckesser, S. (1998). 'Labour Markets and Organisational Change: Future Working Structures for an Ageing Work Force'. *Journal of Management and Governance*, 1/2: 177–206.

Baccaro, L. (2002). 'Negotiating the Italian Pension Reform with the Unions: Lessons for Corporatist Theory'. *Industrial and Labor Relations Review*, 55/3: 413–31.

Baldacci, E. and De Santis, G. (2003). 'Disability Pensions in Italy: The Law and the Numbers', in C. Prinz (ed.), *European Disability Pension Policies*. Aldershot: Ashgate, pp. 225–52.

Baldwin, P. (1990). *The Politics of Social Solidarity: Class Bases of the European Welfare States 1875–1975*. Cambridge: Cambridge University Press.

Baltes, P. B. (1997). 'On the Incomplete Architecture of Human Ontogeny: Selection, Optimization, and Compensation as Foundation of Developmental Theory'. *American Psychologist*, 52/4: 366–80.

Barkholdt, C. (2001). 'Rentenzugang und Altersteilzeit', in C. Barkholdt (ed.), *Prekärer Übergang in den Ruhestand. Handlungsbedarf aus arbeitsmarktpolitischer, rentenrechtlicher und betrieblicher Perspektive*. Wiesbaden: Westdeutscher Verlag, pp. 149–75.

Batstone, E., Boraston, I., and Frenkel, S. (1977). *Shop Stewards in Action: The Organization of Workplace Conflict and Accommodation*. Oxford: Blackwell.

Behrendt, C. (2000). 'Private Pensions—A Viable Alternative? Their Distributive Effects in a Comparative Perspective', *International Social Security Review*, 53/3: 3–26.

Benner, M. and Vad, T. B. (2000). 'Sweden and Denmark: Defending the Welfare State', in F. W. Scharpf and V. Schmidt (eds.), *Welfare and Work in the Open Economy*, Vol. II. Oxford: Oxford University Press, pp. 399–466.

Berger, S. and Compston, H. (eds.) (2002). *Policy Concertation and Social Partnership in Western Europe: Lessons for the 21st Century.* New York: Berghahn Books.

Berkowitz, E. D. and Burkhauser, R. V. (1996). 'A United States Perspective on Disability Programs', in L. J. M. Aarts, R. V. Burkhauser, and P. R. de Jong (eds.), *Curing the Dutch Disease.* Aldershot: Avebury, pp. 71–91.

Bertelsmann Stiftung and BDA (eds.) (2005). *Beschäftigungschancen für ältere Arbeitnehmer: internationaler Vergleich und Handlungsempfehlungen.* Gütersloh: Verlag Bertelsmann Stiftung.

Berthold, N. and Hank, R. (1999). *Bündnis für Arbeit: Korporatismus statt Wettbewerb.* Tübingen: Mohr Siebeck.

Bison, I. and Esping-Andersen, G. (2000). 'Unemployment, Welfare Regime, and Income Packaging', in D. Gallie and S. Paugam (eds.), *Welfare Regimes and the Experience of Unemployment in Europe.* New York: Oxford University Press, pp. 69–86.

Bispinck, R. (1997). 'The Chequered History of the Alliance for Jobs', in G. Fajertag and P. Pochet (eds.), *Social Pacts in Europe.* Brussels: ETUI, pp. 63–78.

—— (2002). 'Tarifpolitischer Jahresbericht 2001: Moderate Lohnabschlüsse plus "Altersvorsorge" '. *WSI Mitteilungen*, 55/2: 67–76.

Björklund, A. (2000). 'Going Different Ways: Labour Market Policy in Denmark and Sweden', in G. Esping-Andersen and M. Regini (eds.), *Why Deregulate Labour Markets?* Oxford: Oxford University Press, pp. 148–80.

Blanchet, D. and Pelé, L.-P. (1999). 'Social Security and Retirement in France', in J. Gruber and D. A. Wise (eds.), *Social Security and Retirement around the World.* Chicago, IL: University of Chicago Press, pp. 101–33.

Blomsma, M. and Jansweijer, R. (1997). 'The Netherlands: Growing Importance of Private Sector Arrangements', in M. Rein and E. Wadensjö (eds.), *Enterprise and the Welfare State.* Cheltenham: Edward Elgar, pp. 220–65.

Blöndal, S. and Scarpetta, S. (1998). 'The Retirement Decision in OECD Countries', *OECD Economic Working Papers*, No. 202.

Blossfeld, H.-P., Buchholz, S., and Hofäcker, D. (eds.) (2006). *Globalization, Uncertainty and Late Careers in Society.* London: Routledge (forthcoming).

Blundell, R. and Johnson, P. (1999). 'Pensions and Retirement in the United Kingdom', in J. Gruber and D. A. Wise (eds.), *Social Security and Retirement around the World.* Chicago, IL: University of Chicago Press, pp. 403–35.

Boeri, T. Brugiavini, A., and Maignan, C. (2001). 'Early Retirement: Reasons and Consequences', in T. Boeri, A. Börsch-Supan, A. Brugiavini, R. Disney, A. Kapteyn, and F. Peracchi (eds.), *Pensions: More Information, Less Ideology.* Boston/Dordrecht: Kluwer, pp. 29–53.

Bonoli, G. (2000). *The Politics of Pension Reform: Institutions and Policy Change in Western Europe.* Cambridge: Cambridge University Press.

—— (2003). 'Social Policy through Labour Markets: Understanding National Differences in the Provision of Economic Security to Wage-Earners'. *Comparative Political Studies*, 36/9: 1007–30.

References

Bonoli, G. and Sarfati, H. (2002). 'Conclusions: The Policy Implications of a Changing Labour Market–Social Protection Relationship', in H. Sarfati and G. Bonoli (eds.), *Labour Market and Social Protection Reforms in International Perspective: Parallel or Converging Tracks?* Aldershot: Ashgate, pp. 453–86.

Börsch-Supan, A., Brugiavini, A., Jürgens, H., Mackenbach, J., Siegrist, J., and Weber, G. (2005). *Health, Ageing and Retirement in Europe—First Results from the Survey of Health, Ageing and Retirement in Europe.* Mannheim: MEA, University of Mannheim.

—— and Schmidt, P. (2001). 'Early Retirement in East and West Germany', in R. Riphahn, D. J. Snower, and K. F. Zimmermann (eds.), *Employment Policy in Transition: The Lessons of German Integration for the Labor Market.* Heidelberg: Springer, pp. 83–102.

—— and Schnabel, R. (1999). 'Social Security and Retirement in Germany', in J. Gruber and D. A. Wise (eds.), *Social Security and Retirement around the World.* Chicago, IL: University of Chicago Press, pp. 135–80.

Bosworth, B. and Burtless, G. (eds.) (1998*a*). *Aging Societies: The Global Dimension.* Washington, DC: Brookings Institution.

—— —— (1998*b*). 'Population Aging and Economic Performance', in B. Bosworth and G. Burtless (eds.), *Aging Societies. The Global Dimension.* Washington, DC: Brookings Institution, pp. 1–32.

Boudon, R. (1977). *Effets pervers et ordre social.* Paris: Presse Universitaire de France.

Bound, J. and Burkhauser, R. V. (1999). 'Economic Analysis of Transfer Programs Targeted on People with Disabilities', in O. Ashenfelter and D. Card (eds.), *Handbook of Labor Economics*, Vol. 3C. Amsterdam: Elsevier, pp. 3417–528.

Bovens, M., 't Hart, P., and Peters, B. G. (eds.) (2001). *Success and Failure in Public Governance: A Comparative Analysis.* Cheltenham: Edward Elgar.

Bozec, G. and Mays, C. (2000). 'The Pension Reform Process in France'. *Innovation*, 13/4: 373–88.

Brinton, M. C. (1993). *Women and the Economic Miracle. Gender and Work in Postwar Japan.* Berkeley, CA: University of California Press.

—— (1998). 'Institutional Embeddedness in Japanese Labor Markets', in M. C. Brinton and V. Nee (eds.), *The New Institutionalism in Sociology.* New York: Russell Sage Foundation, pp. 181–207.

Brown, M. K. (ed.) (1988). *Remaking the Welfare State: Retrenchment and Social Policy in America and Europe.* Philadelphia, PA: Temple University Press.

Brugiavini, A. (1999). 'Social Security and Retirement in Italy', in J. Gruber and D. A. Wise (eds.), *Social Security and Retirement around the World.* Chicago, IL: University of Chicago Press, pp. 181–237.

—— Ebbinghaus, B., Freeman, R., Garibaldi, P., Holmund, B., Schludi, M., and Verdier, T. (2001). 'Part II: What Do Unions Do to the Welfare States?' in T. Boeri, A. Brugiavini, and L. Calmfors (eds.), *The Role of Unions in the Twenty-First Century: A Report to the Fondazione Rodolfo Debenedetti.* Oxford: Oxford University Press, pp. 157–277.

Buechtemann, C. F. (ed.) (1993a). *Employment Security and Labor Market Behavior: Interdisciplinary Approaches and International Evidence*. Ithaca, NY: ILR Press.

—— (1993b). 'Introduction: Employment Security and Labor Market Behavior', in C. F. Buechtemann (ed.), *Employment Security and Labor Market Behavior*. Ithaca, NY: ILR Press, pp. 1–66.

—— and Walwei, U. (1996). 'Employment Security and Dismissal Protection', in G. Schmid, J. O'Reilly, and K. Schömann (eds.), *International Handbook of Labour Market Policy and Evaluation*. Cheltenham: Edward Elgar, pp. 652–92.

Calmfors, L., Booth, A., Burda, M., Checchi, D., Naylor, R., and Visser, J. (2001). 'Part I: The Future of Collective Bargaining in Europe', in T. Boeri, A. Brugiavini, and L. Calmfors (eds.), *The Role of Unions in the Twenty-First Century: A Report to the Fondazione Rodolfo Debenedetti*. Oxford: Oxford University Press, pp. 1–134.

Card, D. and Freeman, R. B. (1993). 'Small Differences that Matter: Canada vs. the United States', in R. B. Freeman (ed.), *Working under Different Rules*. New York: Russell Sage, pp. 189–222.

Carlsson, B. (1995). 'Developments in the Swedish Early Retirement Scheme: The Drive Against High Welfare Expenditure and Ill-health'. *Journal of Social Policy*, 24/2: 193–217.

Casey, B. (1989). 'Early Retirement: The Problem of "Instrument Substitution" and "Cost Shifting" and their Implications for Restructuring the Process of Retirement', in W. Schmähl (ed.), *Redefining the Process of Retirement: An International Perspective*. Berlin: Springer-Verlag, pp. 133–50.

—— (1992). 'Redundancy and Early Retirement: The Interaction of Public and Private Policy in Britain, Germany and the USA'. *British Journal of Industrial Relations*, 30/3: 425–43.

—— (1996). 'Exit Options from the Labour Force', in G. Schmid, J. O'Reilly, and K. Schömann (eds.), *International Handbook of Labour Market Policy and Evaluation*. Cheltenham: Edward Elgar, pp. 379–401.

—— (1997). *Incentives and Disincentives to Early and Late Retirement*, ILO Conference, Geneva, Sept. 1997.

—— (2004). 'The OECD Jobs Strategy and the European Employment Strategy: Two Views of the Labour Market and the Welfare State'. *European Journal of Industrial Relations*, 10: 329–52.

—— and Bruche, G. (1983). *Work or Retirement? Labor Market and Social Policy for Older Workers in France, Great Britain, the Netherlands, Sweden and the USA*. Aldershot: Gower.

—— and Laczko, F. (1989). 'Early Retired or Long-Term Unemployed? The Situation of Non-working Men Aged 55–64 from 1979 to 1986'. *Work, Employment & Society*, 3/4: 509–26.

—— and Wood, S. (1994). 'Great Britain: Firm Policy, State Policy and the Employment and Unemployment of Older Workers', in F. Naschold and B. de Vroom (eds.), *Regulating Employment and Welfare*. Berlin: W. de Gruyter, pp. 363–94.

References

Castles, F. G. and Mitchell, D. (1993). 'Worlds of Welfare and Families of Nations', in F. G. Castles (ed.), *Families of Nations: Patterns of Public Policy in Western Democracies*. Aldershot: Dartmouth, pp. 93–128.

Chen, Y.-P. (1996). 'Gradual Retirement in the United States: Macro Issues and Policies', in L. Delsen and G. Reday-Mulvey (eds.), *Gradual Retirement in the OECD Countries*. Aldershot: Dartmouth, pp. 164–85.

Chiarini, B. (1999). 'The Composition of Union Membership: The Role of Pensioners in Italy'. *British Journal of Industrial Relations*, 37/4: 577–600.

Clark, R. L. (1991). *Retirement Systems in Japan*. Homewood, IL: Irwin.

—— and Anker, R. (1993). 'Cross-national Analysis of Labor Force Participation of Older Men and Women'. *Econmic Development and Cultural Change*, 41/3: 489–512.

—— York, E. A., and Anker, R. (1999). 'Economic Development and Labor Force Participation of Older Persons'. *Population Research and Policy Review*, 18/5: 411–32.

Clasen, J. (2005). *Reforming European Welfare States: Germany and the United Kingdom Compared*. Oxford: Oxford University Press.

Clayton, R. and Pontusson, J. (1998). 'Welfare-State Retrenchment Revisited: Entitlement Cuts, Public Sector Restructuring, and Inegalitarian Trends in Advanced Capitalist Societies'. *World Politics*, 51/1: 67–98.

Clemens, E. S. and Cook, J. M. (1999). 'Politics and Institutionalism: Explaining Durability and Change'. *Annual Review of Sociology*, 25: 441–66.

Clemens, W. (2001). *Ältere Arbeitnehmer im sozialen Wandel. Von der verschmähten zur gefragten Humanressource?* Opladen: Leske & Budrich.

Cochrane, A. and Clarke, J. (eds.) (1993). *Comparing Welfare States: Britain in International Context*. London: Sage.

Compston, H. (ed.) (1997). *The New Politics of Unemployment: Radical Policy Initiatives in Western Europe*. London: Routledge.

Contini, B. and Rapiti, F. M. (1999). ' "Young in, Old out" Revisited: New Patterns of Employment Replacement in the Italian Economy'. *International Review of Applied Economics*, 13/3: 395–415.

Crouch, C. (1986). 'Sharing Public Space: States and Organized Interests in Western Europe', in J. A. Hall (ed.), *States in History*. Oxford: B. Blackwell, pp. 177–210.

—— (1993). *Industrial Relations and European State Traditions*. Oxford: Clarendon Press.

—— (1999). 'Employment, Industrial Relations and Social Policy: New Life in an Old Connection'. *Social Policy & Administration*, 33/4: 437–57.

—— (2001). 'Welfare State Regimes and Industrial Relations Systems: The Questionable Role of Path Dependency Theory', in B. Ebbinghaus and P. Manow (eds.), *Comparing Welfare Capitalism*. London: Routledge, pp. 105–24.

Crouch, C., Finegold, D., and Sako, M. (1999). *Are Skills the Answer? The Political Economy of Skill Creation in Advanced Industrial Countries*. Oxford: Oxford University Press.

—— le Galès, P., Trigilia, C., and Voelzkow, H. (eds.) (2001). *Local Production Systems in Europe: Rise or Demise?* Oxford: Oxford University Press.

Crouch, C. and Pizzorno, A. (eds.) (1978). *The Resurgence of Class Conflict in Western Europe since 1968* (2 vols.). London: Macmillan.

—— and Streeck, W. (eds.) (1997). *Political Economy of Modern Capitalism: Mapping Convergence and Diversity.* London: Sage.

Culpepper, P. and Finegold, D. (eds.) (1999). *The German Skill Machine.* New York: Berghahn Books.

Daly, M. (1997). 'Welfare States under Pressure: Cash Benefits in European Welfare States over the Last Ten Years'. *Journal of European Social Policy,* 7/2: 129–46.

—— (2000). 'A Fine Balance: Women's Labor Market Participation in International Comparison', in F. W. Scharpf and V. Schmidt (eds.), *Welfare and Work in the Open Economy,* Vol. II. Oxford: Oxford University Press, pp. 467–510.

Davis, E. P. (1995). *Pension Funds, Retirement-Income Security, and Capital Markets: An International Perspective.* Oxford: Clarendon Press.

—— (1997). 'Private Pensions in OECD Countries—The United Kingdom', *OECD Labour Market and Social Policy Occasional Papers,* 21.

—— (1998). 'Population Aging and Retirement Income Provision in the European Union', in B. Bosworth and G. Burtless (eds.), *Aging Societies. The Global Dimension.* Washington, DC: Brookings Institution, pp. 33–110.

De Deken, J. (2003). 'The Role of Benchmarking and the Open Method of Coordination in the Transformation of European Welfare States: The Case of Old-Age Pensions and Labour Market Reform', *ESPAnet Conference,* Copenhagen.

de Jong, P. R. (2003*a*). 'Disability and Disability Insurance', in C. Prinz (ed.), *European Disability Pension Policies.* Aldershot: Ashgate, pp. 77–106.

—— (2003*b*). 'The Dutch Disability Experience', in C. Prinz (ed.), *European Disability Pension Policies.* Aldershot. Ashgate, pp. 253–76.

de Vroom, B. and Blomsma, M. (1991). 'The Netherlands: An Extreme Case', in M. Kohli, M. Rein, A.-M. Guillemard, and H. van Gunsteren (eds.), *Time for Retirement.* New York: Cambridge University Press, pp. 97–126.

—— and Naschold, F. (1994). 'The Dialectics of Work and Welfare', in F. Naschold and B. de Vroom (eds.), *Regulating Employment and Welfare.* Berlin: W. de Gruyter, pp. 1–18.

Delsen, L. (1996*a*). 'Employment Opportunities for the Disabled', in G. Schmid, J. O'Reilly, and K. Schömann (eds.), *International Handbook of Labour Market Policy and Evaluation.* Cheltenham: Edward Elgar, pp. 520–50.

—— (1996*b*). 'Gradual Retirement in the Netherlands', in L. Delsen and G. Reday-Mulvey (eds.), *Gradual Retirement in the OECD Countries.* Aldershot: Dartmouth, pp. 111–32.

—— (1996*c*). 'Gradual Retirement: Lessons from the Nordic Countries and the Netherlands'. *European Journal of Industrial Relations,* 2/1: 55–67.

—— (2002). 'Active Strategies for Older Workers in the Netherlands', in M. Jespen, D. Foden and M. Hutsebaut (eds.), *Active Strategies for Older Workers.* Brussels: ETUI, pp. 299–344.

References

Delsen, L. Hutsebaut, M., and Reissert, B. (1999). 'From Early to Phased Retirement in the European Union', in J.-Y. Boulin and R. Hoffmann (eds.), *New Paths in Working Time Policy*. Brussels: ETUI, pp. 183–211.

—— and Reday-Mulvey, G. (eds.) (1996a). *Gradual Retirement in the OECD Countries: Macro and Micro Issues and Policies*. Aldershot: Dartmouth.

—— —— (1996b). 'Macro Issues and Policies', in L. Delsen and G. Reday-Mulvey (eds.), *Gradual Retirement in the OECD Countries*. Aldershot: Dartmouth, pp. 3–12.

Di Biase, R., Gandiglio, A., Cozzolino, M., and Proto, G. (1997). 'The Retirement Provisions Mix in Italy: The Dominant Role of the Public System', in M. Rein and E. Wadensjö (eds.), *Enterprise and the Welfare State*. Cheltenham: Edward Elgar, pp. 149–94.

Diamond, P. and Gruber, J. (1999). 'Social Security and Retirement in the United States', in J. Gruber and D. A. Wise (eds.), *Social Security and Retirement around the World*. Chicago: University of Chicago Press, pp. 437–73.

Doeringer, P. B. (ed.) (1990). *Bridges to Retirement: Older Workers in a Changing Labor Market*. Ithaca, NY: ILR Press.

Dogan, M. and Pelassy, D. (1990). *How to Compare Nations: Strategies in Comparative Politics*. London: Chatham House.

Dore, R. (1997). 'The Distinctiveness of Japan', in C. Crouch and W. Streeck (eds.), *Political Economy of Modern Capitalism*. London: Sage, pp. 19–32.

—— (2000). *Stock Market Capitalism: Welfare Capitalism. Japan and Germany versus the Anglo-Saxons*. Oxford: Oxford University Press.

Dudley, G. and Richardson, J. (2001). 'Managing Decline: Governing National Steel Production under Economic Adversity', in M. Bovens, P. 't Hart, and B. G. Peters (eds.), *Success and Failure in Public Governances*. Cheltenham: Edward Elgar, pp. 33–44.

Ebbinghaus, B. (1995). 'The Siamese Twins: Citizenship Rights, Cleavage Formation, and Party-Union Relations', in C. Tilly (ed.), *Citizenship, Identity and Social History (International Review of Social History*, Supplement 3). Cambridge: Cambridge University Press, pp. 51–89.

—— (1999). 'Does a European Social Model Exist and Can it Survive?' in G. Huemer, M. Mesch, and F. Traxler (eds.), *The Role of Employer Associations and Labour Unions in the EMU: Institutional Requirements for European Economic Policies*. Aldershot: Ashgate, pp. 1–26.

—— (2000). 'Any Way out of "Exit from Work"? Reversing the Entrenched Pathways of Early Retirement', in F. W. Scharpf and V. Schmidt (eds.), *Welfare and Work in the Open Economy*, Vol. II. Oxford: Oxford University Press, pp. 511–33.

—— (2001). 'When Labour and Capital Collude: The Political Economy of Early Retirement in Europe, Japan and the USA', in B. Ebbinghaus and P. Manow (eds.), *Comparing Welfare Capitalism*. London: Routledge, pp. 76–101.

—— (2002). 'Trade Unions' Changing Role: Membership Erosion, Organisational Reform, and Social Partnership in Europe'. *Industrial Relations Journal*, 33/5: 465–83.

—— (2003). 'Ever Larger Unions: Organisational Restructuring and its Impact on Union Confederations'. *Industrial Relations Journal*, 34/5: 446–60.

Ebbinghaus, B. (2004). *Reforming Welfare States and Social Partnership in Europe: Variations in Social Governance and Institutional Change*, ISA-RC19 Conference 'Welfare State Restructuring'. Paris, 2–4 Sep. 2004.

—— (2005*a*). 'Can Path Dependence Explain Institutional Change? Two Approaches Applied to Welfare State Reform', *MPIfG Discussion Paper*, 05/02.

—— (2005*b*). 'When Less is More: Selection Problems in Large-N and Small-N Cross-National Comparison'. *International Sociology*, 20/2: 133–52.

—— and Hassel, A. (2000). 'Striking Deals: Concertation in the Reform of Continental European Welfare States'. *Journal of European Public Policy*, 7/1: 44–62.

—— and Kittel, B. (2005). 'European Rigidity vs. American Flexibility? The Institutional Adaptability of Collective Bargaining'. *Work and Occupations*, 32/2: 163–95.

—— and Kraus, P. A. (1997). 'Die variable Geometrie der Subsidiarität: Zur Problematik territorialer und funktionaler Integration in Europa', in T. König, E. Rieger, and H. Schmitt (eds.), *Europäische Institutionenpolitik*. Frankfurt: Campus, pp. 335–58.

—— and Manow, P. (2001*a*). 'Introduction: Studying Varieties of Welfare Capitalism', in B. Ebbinghaus and P. Manow (eds.), *Comparing Welfare Capitalism*. London, New York: Routledge, pp. 1–24.

—— —— (eds) (2001*b*). *Comparing Welfare Capitalism: Social Policy and Political Economy in Europe, Japan and the USA*. London, New York: Routledge.

—— and Visser, J. (1997). 'Der Wandel der Arbeitsbeziehungen im westeuropäischen Vergleich', in S. Hradil and S. Immerfall (eds.), *Die westeuropäischen Gesellschaften im Vergleich*. Opladen: Leske & Budrich, pp. 333–75.

—— —— (1999). 'When Institutions Matter: Union Growth and Decline in Western Europe, 1950–1995'. *European Sociological Review*, 15/2: 1–24.

—— —— (2000). *Trade Unions in Western Europe since 1945* (Handbook and CD-ROM). London: Palgrave/Macmillan.

Edwards, P. K., Hall, M., Hyman, R., Marginson, P., Sisson, K., Waddington, J., and Winchester, D. (1998). 'Great Britain: From Partial Collectivism to Neo-liberalism to Where?' in A. Ferner and R. Hyman (eds.), *Changing Industrial Relations in Europe*. Oxford: Blackwell, pp. 1–54.

—— and Hyman, R. (1994). 'Strikes and Industrial Conflict: Peace in Europe?' in R. Hyman and A. Ferner (eds.), *New Frontiers in European Industrial Relations*. Oxford: Blackwell, pp. 250–80.

Eghigian, G. (2000). *Making Security Social: Disability, Insurance, and the Birth of the Social Entitlement State in Germany*. Ann Arbor, MI: University of Michigan Press.

Ehrenberg, R. G. and Jakubson, G. H. (1993). 'Introduction: Employment Security and Labor Market Behavior', in C. F. Buechtemann (ed.), *Employment Security and Labor Market Behavior*. Ithaca, NY: ILR Press, pp. 200–14.

EIRO (document number). *European Industrial Relations Online*. Dublin: Dublin Foundation [www.eiro.eurofound.ie].

References

Endo, Y. and Katayama, E. (1998). 'Population Aging and Japanese Economic Performance', in B. Bosworth and G. Burtless (eds.), *Aging Societies: The Global Dimension*. Washington, DC: Brookings Institution, pp. 240–66.

Ernst, J. (1995). *Frühverrentung in Ostdeutschland*. Frankfurt: Peter Lang.

Esping-Andersen, G. (1985). *Politics Against Markets: The Social Democratic Road to Power*. Princeton, NJ: Princeton University Press.

—— (1987). 'Institutional Accomodation to Full Employment: A Comparison of Policy Regimes', in H. Keman, H. Paloheimo, and P. F. Whiteley (eds.), *Coping with Economic Crisis*. London: Sage, pp. 83–110.

—— (1990). *Three Worlds of Welfare Capitalism*. Princeton, NJ: Princeton University Press.

—— (1992). 'The Emerging Realignment between Labour Movements and Welfare States', in M. Regini (ed.), *The Future of Labour Movements*. London: Sage, pp. 133–59.

—— (1993). 'The Comparative Macro-Sociology of Welfare States', in L. Moreno (ed.), *Social Exchange and Welfare Development*. Madrid: CSIC, pp. 123–36.

—— (1996a). 'Conclusion: Occupational Welfare in the Social Policy Nexus', in M. Shalev (ed.), *The Privatization of Social Policy?* London: Macmillan, pp. 327–38.

—— (ed.) (1996b). *Welfare States in Transition: National Adaptations in Global Economies*. London: Sage.

—— (1996c). 'Welfare States without Work: The Impasse of Labour Shedding and Familialism in Continental European Social Policy', in G. Esping-Andersen (ed.), *Welfare States in Transition: National Adaptations in Global Economies*. London: Sage, pp. 66–87.

—— (1997). 'Hybrid or Unique? The Japanese Welfare State between Europe and America'. *Journal of European Social Policy*, 7/3: 179–89.

—— (1999). *Social Foundations of Postindustrial Economies*. Oxford: Oxford University Press.

—— and Korpi, W. (1984). 'Social Policy as Class Politics in Post-War Capitalism: Scandinavia, Austria and Germany', in J. H. Goldthorpe (ed.), *Order and Conflict in Contemporary Capitalism*. Oxford: Clarendon Press, pp. 179–208.

—— and Regini, M. (eds.) (2000). *Why Deregulate Labour Markets?* Oxford: Oxford University Press.

—— and Sonnberger, H. (1991). 'The Demographics of Age in Labor-Market Management', in J. Myles and J. Quadagno (eds.), *States, Labor Markets, and the Future of Old-Age Policy*. Philadelphia, PA: Temple University Press, pp. 227–49.

—— and van Kersbergen, K. (1992). 'Contemporary Research on Social Democracy'. *Annual Review of Sociology*, 18: 187–208.

Estevez-Abe, M. (2001). 'The Forgotten Link: The Financial Regulation of Japanese Funds in Comparative Perspective', in B. Ebbinghaus and P. Manow (eds.), *Comparing Welfare Capitalism*. London: Routledge, pp. 190–214.

—— Iversen, T., and Soskice, D. (2001). 'Social Protection and the Formation of Skills: A Reinterpretation of the Welfare State', in P. A. Hall and D. Soskice (eds.), *Varieties of Capitalism*. New York: Oxford University Press, pp. 145–83.

Estienne, J.-F. and Murakami, K. (2000). 'The Japanese Experience of Review and Reform of Public Pension Schemes', in E. Reynaud (ed.), *Social Dialogue and Pension Reform*. Geneva: International Labour Office, pp. 49–66.

EU-Com. (1998). *Modernising and Improving Social Protection in the European Union. Communication from the Commission*. Brussels: EU Commission.

—— (1999a). *Towards a Europe for All Ages: Promoting Prosperity and Intergenerational Solidarity*, COM(1999) 221 final. Brussels: EU Commission.

—— (1999b). *Towards a Single Market for Supplementary Pensions*, COM (1999) 134 final. Brussels: EU Commission.

—— (2001). *Supporting National Strategies for Safe and Sustainable Pensions through an Integrated Approach*, COM(2001) 362 final. Brussels: EU Commission.

Eurostat (2005). *European Labour Force Surveys 1973–2004*. Luxembourg: Eurostat (NewCronos database).

Evans, R., Jr. (1991). 'The Puzzle of Early Retirement and Permanent Layoffs in Japanese Labor Market'. *Journal of Asian Economics*, 2/2: 301–7.

Fajertag, G. and Pochet, P. (eds.) (2000). *Social Pacts in Europe: New Dynamics*. Brussels: ETUI.

Ferner, A., Keep, E., and Waddington, J. (1997). 'Industrial Restructuring and EU-wide Social Measures: Broader Lessons of the ECSC Experience'. *Journal of European Public Policy*, 4/1: 56–72.

Ferrera, M. (1984). *Il Welfare State in Italia. Sviluppo e crisi in prospettiva comparata*. Bologna: Il Mulino.

—— (1996). 'The "Southern Model" of Welfare in Social Europe'. *Journal of European Social Policy*, 6/1: 17–37.

—— (2001). 'Targeting Welfare in a "Soft" State: Italy's Winding Road to Selectivity', in N. Gilbert (ed.), *Targeting Social Benefits: International Perspectives and Trends*. New Brunswick, NJ: Transaction Publishers, pp. 157–86.

—— and Gualmini, E. (2000). 'Italy: Rescue from Without?' in F. W. Scharpf and V. Schmidt (eds.), *Welfare and Work in the Open Economy*, Vol. II. Oxford: Oxford University Press, pp. 351–98.

Flora, P. (1986a). 'Introduction', in P. Flora (ed.), *Growth to Limits: The Western European Welfare States Since World War II*. Vol. I. Berlin: W. de Gruyter, pp. xii–xxxvi.

—— (ed.) (1986b). *Growth to Limits: The Western European Welfare States Since World War II*, Volume IV: 'Appendix'. Berlin: W. de Gruyter.

—— and Alber, J. (1981). 'Modernization, Democratization, and the Development of Welfare States in Western Europe', in P. Flora and A. J. Heidenheimer (eds.), *The Development of Welfare States in Europe and America*. New Brunswick, NJ: Transaction Books, pp. 37–80.

—— and Heidenheimer, A. J. (eds.) (1981). *The Development of Welfare States in Europe and America*. New Brunswick, NJ: Transaction Books.

Fox, A. (1985). *History and Heritage. The Social Origins of the British Industrial Relations System*. London: G. Allen & Unwin.

References

Freeman, R. (1990). 'On the Divergence of Unionism among Developed Countries', in R. Brunetta and C. Dell'Aringa (eds.), *Labour Relations and Economic Performance*. London: Macmillan, pp. 304–22.

—— (1993). 'How Labor Fares in Advanced Economies', in R. B. Freeman (ed.), *Working under Different Rules*. New York: Russell Sage, pp. 1–28.

—— and Medoff, J. L. (1984). *What Do Unions Do?* New York: Basic Books.

—— and Pelletier, J. (1990). 'The Impact of Industrial Relations Legislation on British Union Density'. *British Journal of Industrial Relations*, 28/2: 141–64.

Frick, B. and Sadowski, D. (1996). 'A German Perspective on Disability Policy', in L. J. M. Aarts, R. V. Burkhauser, and P. R. de Jong (eds.), *Curing the Dutch Disease*. Aldershot: Avebury, pp. 117–31.

Gauron, A. (ed.) (2000). *Formation tout au long de la vie*. Paris: La Documentation française.

Gern, K.-J. (1998). 'Recent Developments in Old-Age Pension Systems: An International Overview', *Kiel Working Papers, 863*.

Giersch, H. (ed.) (1997). *Reforming the Welfare State*. Heidelberg: Springer.

Gilbert, N. (ed.) (2001). *Targeting Social Benefits. International Perspectives and Trends*. New Brunswick, NJ: Transaction Publishers.

Gillin, C. T. and Klassen, T. R. (1995). 'Age Discrimination and Early Retirement Policies: A Comparison of Labor Market Regulation in Canada and the United States'. *Journal of Aging & Social Policy*, 7/1: 85–102.

Goetschy, J. (1998). 'France: The Limits of Reform', in A. Ferner and R. Hyman (eds.), *Changing Industrial Relations in Europe*. Oxford: Blackwell, 355–94.

—— (1999). 'The European Employment Strategy: Genesis and Development'. *European Journal of Industrial Relations*, 5/2: 117–37.

—— (2000). 'The European Employment Strategy from Amsterdam to Stockholm: Has it Reached its Cruising Speed?' *Industrial Relations Journal*, 32/5: 401–18.

—— (2003). 'The European Employment Strategy, Multi-level Governance, and Policy Coordination: Past, Present and Future', in J. Zeitlin and D. Trubek (eds.), *Governing Work and Welfare in a New Economy*. Oxford: Oxford University Press, pp. 59–87.

Golden, M. A. (1997). *Heroic Defeats: The Politics of Job Loss*. New York: Cambridge University Press.

—— Wallerstein, M., and Lange, P. (1999). 'Postwar Trade-Union Organization and Industrial Relations in Twelve Countries', in H. Kitschelt, P. Lange, G. Marks, and J. Stephens (eds.), *Continuity and Change in Contemporary Capitalism*. New York: Cambridge University Press, pp. 194–230.

Goldthorpe, J. H. (2001). 'Causation, Statistics, and Sociology'. *European Sociological Review*, 17/1: 1–20.

Goodin, R. E., Headey, B., Muffels, R., and Dirven, H.-J. (1999). *The Real Worlds of Welfare Capitalism*. Cambridge: Cambridge University Press.

—— and Rein, M. (2001). 'Regimes on Pillars: Alternative Welfare State Logics and Dynamics'. *Public Administration*, 79/4: 769–801.

Gorter, C. (2000). 'The Dutch Miracle?' in G. Esping-Andersen and M. Regini (eds.), *Why Deregulate Labour Markets?* Oxford: Oxford University Press, pp. 181–211.

Gould, A. (1993). *Capitalist Welfare Systems: A Comparison of Japan, Britain and Sweden*. London: Longman.

Graebner, W. (1980). *A History of Retirement: The Meaning and Function of an American Institution, 1885–1978*. New Haven, CT: Yale University Press.

Gray, D. (1996). 'How Unemployable are Displaced Manufacturing Workers? An Analysis of Adjustment Costs and Supplemental Adjustment Assistance Benefits in France'. *European Journal of Political Economy*, 12: 685–708.

Gray, D. M. (2001). 'An Application of the 'Insider-Outsider' Hypothesis: Categorial Adjustment Assistance Programs in France'. *European Journal of Political Economy*, 17/1: 139–56.

Green-Pedersen, C. and Lindbom, A. (2002). *Politics within Paths: The Trajectories of Danish and Swedish Pension Systems*, ECPR Joint Sessions. Turin, 22–27 March 2002.

Grønning, T. (1998). 'Whither the Japanese Employment System? The Position of the Japan Employers' Federation'. *Industrial Relations Journal*, 29/4: 295–303.

Gruber, J. and Wise, D. A. (eds.) (1999a). *Social Security and Retirement around the World*. Chicago, IL: University of Chicago Press.

—— —— (1999b). 'Introduction and Summary', in J. Gruber and D. A. Wise (eds.), *Social Security and Retirement around the World*. Chicago, IL: University of Chicago Press, pp. 1–35.

Gualmini, E. (1998). *La politica del lavoro*. Bologna: Il Mulino.

Guillemard, A.-M. (1991). 'France: Massive Exit through Unemployment', in M. Kohli, M. Rein, A.-M. Guillemard, and H. van Gunsteren (eds.), *Time for Retirement*. New York: Cambridge University Press, pp. 127–80.

—— (2003). *L'âge de l'emploi. Les sociétés à l'épreuve du vieillissement*. Paris: Amand Colin.

—— and Rein, M. (1993). 'Comparative Patterns of Retirement: Recent Trends in Developed Societies'. *Annual Review of Sociology*, 19: 469–503.

—— and van Gunsteren, H. (1991). 'Pathways and their Prospects: A Comparative Interpretation of the Meaning of Early Exit', in M. Kohli, M. Rein, A.-M. Guillemard, and H. van Gunsteren (eds.), *Time for Retirement*. New York: Cambridge University Press, pp. 362–87.

Haas, E. B. (1990). *When Knowledge is Power: Three Models of Change in International Organizations*. Berkeley, CA: University of California Press.

Haas, P. M. (1992). 'Introduction: Epistemic Communities and International Policy Coordination'. *International Organizations*, 46/1: 1–35.

Hacker, J. S. (2002). *The Divided Welfare State: The Battle over Public and Private Social Benefits in the United States*. Cambridge: Cambridge University Press.

—— (2005). 'Policy Drift: The Hidden Politics of US Welfare State Retrenchment', in W. Streeck and K. Thelen (eds.), *Beyond Continuity. Institutional Change in Advanced Political Economies*. Oxford: Oxford University Press, pp. 40–82.

Hall, P. A. (1997). 'The Role of Interests, Institutions, and Ideas in the Comparative Political Economy of the Industrialized Nations', in M. I. Lichbach and A. S. Zuckerman (eds.), *Comparative Politics: Rationality, Culture, and Structure*. New York: Cambridge University Press, pp. 174–207.

—— and Gingerich, D. W. (2004). 'Varieties of Capitalism and Institutional Complementarities in the Macroeconomy: An Empirical Analysis', *MPIfG Discussion Paper*, 04/5.

—— and Soskice, D. (eds.) (2001*a*). *Varieties of Capitalism: The Institutional Foundations of Comparative Advantage*. New York: Oxford University Press.

—— —— (2001*b*). 'An Introduction to Varieties of Capitalism', in P. A. Hall and D. Soskice (eds.), *Varieties of Capitalism*. New York: Oxford University Press, pp. 1–68.

—— and Taylor, R. C. R. (1996). 'Political Science and the Three New Institutionalisms'. *Political Studies*, 44: 936–57.

Hancké, B. (1993). 'Trade Union Membership in Europe, 1960–1990: Rediscovering Local Unions'. *British Journal of Industrial Relations*, 31/4: 593–613.

Hansen, H. (2002). 'Active Strategies for Older Workers in Denmark', in M. Jespen, D. Foden, and M. Hutsebaut (eds.), *Active Strategies for Older Workers*. Brussels: ETUI, pp. 171–205.

Hassel, A. and Ebbinghaus, B. (2000). 'From Means to Ends: Linking Wage Moderation and Social Policy Reform', in G. Fajertag and P. Pochet (eds.), *Social Pacts in Europe: New Dynamics*. Brussels: ETUI, pp. 61–84.

Haverland, M. (2001). 'Another Dutch Miracle? Explaining Dutch and German Pension Trajectories'. *Journal of European Social Policy*, 11/4: 308–23.

Heclo, H. (1974). *Modern Social Politics in Britain and Sweden: From Relief to Income Maintenance*. New Haven, CT: Yale University Press.

Heinelt, H. (1991). *Frühverrentung als politischer Prozeß*. Wiesbaden: DUV.

Hemerijck, A. and Manow, P. (2001). 'The Experience of Negotiated Reforms in the Dutch and German Welfare States', in B. Ebbinghaus and P. Manow (eds.), *Comparing Welfare Capitalism*. London: Routledge, pp. 217–38.

—— and Schludi, M. (2000). 'Sequences of Policy Failures and Effective Policy Responses', in F. W. Scharpf and V. Schmidt (eds.), *Welfare and Work in the Open Economy*, Vol. I. Oxford: Oxford University Press, pp. 125–228.

—— and van Kersbergen, K. (1999). 'Negotiated Policy Change: Towards a Theory of Institutional Learning in Tightly Coupled Welfare States', in D. Braun and A. Busch (eds.), *Public Policy and Political Ideas*. Cheltenham: Edward Elgar, pp. 168–85.

Herberttson, T. T. and Orszag, J. M. (2001). 'The Costs of Early Retirement in the OECD', *Institute of Economic Study, University of Iceland, Working Paper*, 2001/02.

Hinrichs, K. (2000*a*). 'Elephants on the Move: Patterns of Public Pension Reform in OECD Countries'. *European Review*, 8/3: 353–78.

—— (2000*b*). 'Von der Rentenversicherungs- zur Alterssicherungspolitik: Formen und Reformprobleme', in K. Hinrichs, H. Kitschelt, and H. Wiesenthal (eds.), *Kontingenz und Krise*. Frankfurt: Campus, pp. 291–317.

Hohnerlein, E.-M. (1998). 'Italien', in H.-J. Reinhard, J. Kruse, and B. B. von Maydell (eds.), *Invaliditätssicherung im Rechtsvergleich*. Baden-Baden: Nomos, pp. 231–313.

Hollingsworth, J. R. and Boyer, R. (1997a). 'Coordination of Economic Actors and Social Systems of Production', in J. R. Hollingsworth and R. Boyer (eds.), *Contemporary Capitalism: The Embeddedness of Institutions*. New York: Cambridge University Press, pp. 1–47.

—— —— (1997b). *Contemporary Capitalism*. New York: Cambridge University Press.

—— Schmitter, P. C., and Streeck, W. (eds.) (1994). *Governing Capitalist Economies: Performance and Control of Economic Sectors*. New York: Oxford University Press.

Hort, S. (2001). 'From a Generous to a Stingy Welfare State? Sweden's Approach to Targeting', in N. Gilbert (ed.), *Targeting Social Benefits: International Perspectives and Trends*. New Brunswick, NJ: Transaction Publishers, pp. 187–210.

Howell, C. (1992). *Regulating Labor. The State and Industrial Relations Reform in Postwar France*. Princeton, NJ: Princeton University Press.

Huber, E., Ragin, C., and Stephens, J. D. (1993). 'Social Democracy, Christian Democracy, Constitutional Structure, and the Welfare State'. *American Journal of Sociology*, 99/3: 711–49.

—— and Stephens, J. D. (1998). 'Internationalization and the Social Democratic Model: Crisis and Future Prospects'. *Comparative Political Studies*, 31/3: 353–97.

—— —— (2001a). 'Welfare State and Production Regimes in the Era of Retrenchment', in P. Pierson (ed.), *The New Politics of the Welfare State*. New York: Oxford University Press, pp. 107–45.

—— —— (2001b). *Development and Crisis of the Welfare State: Parties and Policies in Global Markets*. Chicago, IL: University of Chicago Press.

Hughes, G. (1994). *Private Pensions in OECD Countries: Ireland*. Paris: OECD.

—— and Nolan, B. (1996). 'Pension Plans and Labor Market Structure: Evidence from Ireland', in E. Reynaud, L. apRoberts, B. Davies, and G. Hughes (eds.), *International Perspectives on Supplementary Pensions*. Westport, CT: Quorum, pp. 168–84.

—— and Stewart, J. (eds.) (1999). *The Role of the State in Pension Provision: Employer, Regulator, Provider*. Deventer: Kluwer.

—— —— (eds.) (2000). *Pensions in the European Union: Adapting to Economic and Social Change*. Boston, MA: Kluwer.

Hutchens, R. (1994). 'The United States: Employer Policies for Discouraging Work by Older People', in F. Naschold and B. de Vroom (eds.), *Regulating Employment and Welfare*. Berlin: W. de Gruyter, pp. 395–431.

—— (1999). 'Social Security Benefits and Employer Behavior: Evaluating Social Security Early Retirement Benefits as a Form of Unemployment Insurance'. *International Economic Review*, 40/3: 659–78.

ILO (1980–89). *Cost of Social Security*. Geneva: ILO (various issues).

—— (2000). 'Income Security and Social Protection in a Changing World'. *World Labour Report*, 2000.

Immergut, E. M. (1991). 'Institutions, Veto Points, and Policy Results: A Comparative Analysis of Health Care'. *Journal of Public Policy*, 10/4: 391–416.

Inkeles, A. (1974). 'The Emerging Social Structure of the World'. *World Politics*, 27/4: 467–95.

Inkeles, A. and Usui, C. (1989). 'Retirement Patterns in Cross-National Perspective', in D. I. Kertzer and K. W. Schaie (eds.), *Age Structuring in Comparative Perspective*. Hillsdale, NJ: L. Erlbaum, pp. 227–61.

Iversen, T. and Cusack, T. (2000). 'The Causes of Welfare State Expansion: Deindustrialization or Globalization?' *World Politics*, 52/April: 313–49.

Jackson, G. and Vitols, S. (2001). 'Between Financial Committment, Market Liquidity and Corporate Governance: Occupational Pensions in Britain, Germany, Japan and the USA', in B. Ebbinghaus and P. Manow (eds.), *Comparing Welfare Capitalism*. London: Routledge, pp. 171–89.

Jacobi, O., Keller, B., and Müller-Jentsch, W. (1998). 'Germany: Facing New Challenges', in A. Ferner and R. Hyman (eds.), *Changing Industrial Relations in Europe*. Oxford: Blackwell, pp. 190–238.

Jacobs, K., Kohli, M., and Rein, M. (1991a). 'The Evolution of Early Exit: A Comparative Analysis of Labor Force Participation Patterns', in M. Kohli, M. Rein, A.-M. Guillemard, and H. van Gunsteren (eds.), *Time for Retirement*. New York: Cambridge University Press, pp. 36–66.

—— —— —— (1991b). 'Germany: The Diversity of Pathways', in M. Kohli, M. Rein, A.-M. Guillemard, and H. van Gunsteren (eds.), *Time for Retirement*. New York: Cambridge University Press, pp. 181–221.

—— —— —— (1991c). 'Testing the Industry-Mix Hypothesis of Early Exit', in M. Kohli, M. Rein, A.-M. Guillemard, and H. van Gunsteren (eds.), *Time for Retirement*. New York: Cambridge University Press, pp. 67–96.

—— and Rein, M. (1994). 'Early Retirement: Stability, Reversal, or Redefinition', in F. Naschold and B. de Vroom (eds.), *Regulating Employment and Welfare*. Berlin: W. de Gruyter, pp. 19–49.

Janoski, T. (1994). 'Direct State Intervention in the Labour Market', in T. Janoski and A. M. Hicks (eds.), *The Comparative Political Economy of the Welfare State*. New York: Cambridge University Press, pp. 54–92.

JAP-LFS (2001). *Japanese Labor Force Survey 2001*. Tokyo: Statistics Bureau of Japan [www.stat.go.jp].

Jefferys, S. (1995). 'European Industrial Relations and Welfare States'. *European Journal of Industrial Relations*, 1/3: 317–40.

Jensen, P. H. (2003). 'Disability Pensions: Trends and Policies in Denmark', in C. Prinz (ed.), *European Disability Pension Policies*. Aldershot: Ashgate, pp. 139–64.

Jespen, M., Foden, D., and Hutsebaut, M. (eds.) (2002a). *Active Strategies for Older Workers*. Brussels: ETUI.

—— —— —— (2002b). 'Active Strategies for Older Workers in the European Union: A Comparative Analysis of Recent Experiences', in M. Jespen, D. Foden, and M. Hutsebaut (eds.), *Active Strategies for Older Workers*. Brussels: ETUI, pp. 437–60.

Jochem, S. (1998). *Die skandinavischen Wege in die Arbeitslosigkeit: Kontinuität und Wandel der nordischen Beschäftigungspolitik im internationalen Vergleich.* Opladen: Leske & Budrich.

—— (2000). 'Nordic Labour Market Policies in Transition'. *West European Politics,* 23/3: 115–38.

Johnson, R. (2001). 'Why the "Average Age of Retirement" is a Misleading Measure of Labor Supply'. *Monthly Labor Review,* 124/12: 38–40.

Jolivet, A. (2002). 'Active Strategies for Older Workers in France', in M. Jespen, D. Foden, and M. Hutsebaut (eds.), *Active Strategies for Older Workers.* Brussels: ETUI, pp. 245–74.

Kaneko, Y. (1998). 'The Employment Policy for Aged Workers and the Financing of Unemployment Insurance'. *Review of Population and Social Policy,* 7: 45–60.

Kangas, O. and Palme, J. (1992). 'The Private–Public Mix in Pension Policy', in J. E. Kolberg (ed.), *The Study of Welfare State Regimes.* Armonk, NY: M. E. Sharpe, pp. 199–237.

—— —— (1996). 'The Development of Occupational Pensions in Finland and Sweden: Class Politics and Institutional Feedbacks', in M. Shalev (ed.), *The Privatization of Social Policy?* London: Macmillan, pp. 211–40.

Kapteyn, A. and de Vos, K. (1999). 'Social Security and Retirement in the Netherlands', in J. Gruber and D. A. Wise (eds.), *Social Security and Retirement around the World.* Chicago, IL: University of Chicago Press, pp. 269–303.

Katzenstein, P. J. (1985). *Small States in World Markets: Industrial Policy in Europe.* Ithaca, NY: Cornell University Press.

Katznelson, I. and Hanagan, M. P. (eds.) (1991). *The Working-Class and the Welfare State.* Champaign, IL: University of Illinois Press.

Kii, T. (1991). 'Retirement in Japan', in J. Myles and J. Quadagno (eds.), *States, Labor Markets, and the Future of Old-Age Policy.* Philadelphia, PA: Temple University Press, pp. 268–89.

Kimura, T. and Oka, M. (2001). 'Japan's Current Policy Focus on Longer Employment for Older People', in V. W. Marshall, W. R. Heinz, H. Krüger, and A. Verma (eds.), *Restructuring Work and the Life Course.* Toronto: University of Toronto Press.

—— Takagi, I., Oka, M., and Omori, M. (1994). 'Japan: Shukko, Teinen and Reemployment', in F. Naschold and B. de Vroom (eds.), *Regulating Employment and Welfare.* Berlin: W. de Gruyter, pp. 247–307.

Kimura, Y. (1997). 'The Role of the Japanese Company in Compensating Income Loss after Retirement', in M. Rein and E. Wadensjö (eds.), *Enterprise and the Welfare State.* Cheltenham: Edward Elgar, pp. 195–219.

King, D. and Wood, S. (1999). 'The Political Economy of Neoliberalism: Britain and the United States in the 1990s', in H. Kitschelt, P. Lange, G. Marks, and J. Stephens (eds.), *Continuity and Change in Contemporary Capitalism.* New York: Cambridge University Press, pp. 371–97.

Kitschelt, H., Lange, P., Marks, G., and Stephens, J. (1999). 'Convergence and Divergence in Advanced Capitalist Democracies', in H. Kitschelt, P. Lange,

G. Marks, and J. Stephens (eds.), *Continuity and Change in Contemporary Capitalism*. New York: Cambridge University Press, pp. 427–60.

Kittel, B. (1999). 'Sense and Sensitivity in Pooled Analysis of Political Data'. *European Journal of Political Research*, 35: 225–53.

Kjellberg, A. (1983). *Facklig oranisering i tolv länder*. Lund: Arkiv.

—— (1992). 'Sweden: Can the Model Survive?' in A. Ferner and R. Hyman (eds.), *Industrial Relations in the New Europe*. Oxford: Blackwell, pp. 88–142.

—— (1998). 'Sweden: Restoring the Model?' in A. Ferner and R. Hyman (eds.), *Changing Industrial Relations in Europe*. Oxford: Blackwell, pp. 74–117.

Klammer, U. (1997). *Alterssicherung in Italien: Eine institutionelle, theoretische und empirische Analyse*. Berlin: Duncker & Humblot.

Knoke, D., Pappi, F. U., Broadbent, J., and Tsujinaka, Y. (1996). *Comparing Policy Networks: Labor Politics in the U.S., Germany, and Japan*. New York: Cambridge University Press.

Knuth, M. and Kalina, T. (2001). *Unemployment as a Transition From Employment to Retirement in West Germany*. Gelsenkirchen: Institut Arbeit und Technik.

Kochan, T. A., Katz, H. C., and McKersie, R. B. (1994). *The Transformation of American Industrial Relations*. Ithaca, NY: ILR Press.

Kohl, J. (1993). 'Der Wohlfahrtsstaat in vergleichender Perspektive: Anmerkungen zu Esping-Andersens "The Three Worlds of Welfare Capitalism" '. *Zeitschrift für Sozialreform*, 39/2: 67–82.

—— (2000). 'Der Sozialstaat: Die deutsche Version des Wohlfahrtsstaates—Überlegungen zu seiner typologischen Verortung', in S. Leibfried and U. Wagschal (eds.), *Der deutsche Sozialstaat: Bilanzen, Reformen, Perspektiven*. Frankfurt: Campus, pp. 115–52.

Kohli, M. (1985). 'Die Institutionalisierung des Lebensverlaufs: Historische Befunde und theoretische Argumente'. *Kölner Zeitschrift für Soziologie und Sozialpsychologie*, 37/1: 1–29.

—— (1986). 'Social Organization and Subjective Construction of the Life Course', in A. B. Sørensen (ed.), *Human Development and the Life Course: Multidisciplinary Perspectives*. Hillsdale, NJ: Lawrence Erlbaum, pp. 271–92.

—— (1987). 'Retirement and the Moral Economy: A Historical Interpretation of the German Case'. *Journal of Ageing Studies*, 1/1: 125–44.

—— and Rein, M. (1991). 'The Changing Balance of Work and Retirement', in M. Kohli, M. Rein, A.-M. Guillemard, and H. van Gunsteren (eds.), *Time for Retirement*. New York: Cambridge University Press, pp. 1–35.

—— —— Guillemard, A.-M., and van Gunsteren, H. (eds.) (1991). *Time for Retirement: Comparative Studies on Early Exit from the Labor Force*. New York: Cambridge University Press.

Kolberg, J. E. (ed.) (1992). *The Study of Welfare State Regimes*. Armonk, NY: M. E. Sharpe.

—— and Esping-Andersen, G. (1991). 'Welfare States and Employment Regimes', in J. E. Kolberg (ed.), *The Welfare State as Employer*. Armonk, NY: M. E. Sharpe, pp. 3–35.

Korpi, W. (1983). *The Democratic Class Struggle*. London: Routledge & Kegan Paul.

—— (1995). 'The Development of Social Citizenship in France since 1930: Comparative Perspectives', in B. Palier (ed.), *Comparing Social Welfare Systems in Europe: Vol. 1. Oxford Conference: France–United Kingdom*. Paris: MIRE, pp. 9–47.

—— (2001). 'Contentious Institutions: An Augmented Rational-Action Analysis of the Origins and Path Dependency of Welfare State Institutions in Western Countries'. *Rationality and Society*, 13/2: 235–83.

—— and Palme, J. (1998). 'The Paradox of Redistribution and Strategies of Equality: Welfare State Institutions, Inequality, and Poverty in the Western Countries'. *American Sociological Review*, 1998/63: 661–87.

—— and Shalev, M. (1980). 'Strikes, Power, and Politics in Western Nations, 1900–1976'. *Political Power and Social Theory*, 1: 301–34.

Kruse, A. (2003). 'Social Security and Disability in Sweden', in C. Prinz (ed.), *European Disability Pension Policies*. Aldershot: Ashgate, pp. 369–92.

Kuptsch, C. and Zeitzer, I. (2001). 'Public Disability Programs under New Complex Pressures', in D. D. Hoskins, D. Dobbernack, and C. Kuptsch (eds.), *Social Security at the Dawn of the 21st Century: Topical Issues and New Approaches*. New Brunswick, NJ: Transaction Publishers, pp. 205–30.

Kvist, J. (1999). 'Welfare Reform in the Nordic Countries in the 1990s: Using Fuzzy-Set Theory to Access Conformity to Ideal Types'. *Journal of European Social Policy*, 9/3: 231–52.

Laczko, F. (1988). 'Partial Retirement: An Alternative to Early Retirement? A Comparison of Phased Retirement Schemes in the United Kingdom, France and Scandinavia'. *International Social Security Review*: 147–69.

—— and Phillipson, C. (1991*a*). *Changing Work and Retirement: Social Policy and the Older Worker*. Milton Keynes: Open University.

—— —— (1991*b*). 'Great Britain: The Contradictions of Early Exit', in M. Kohli, M. Rein, A.-M. Guillemard, and H. van Gunsteren (eds.), *Time for Retirement*. New York: Cambridge University Press, pp. 222–51.

Lane, C. (1995). *Industry and Society in Europe: Stability and Change in Britain, Germany and France*. Aldershot: Edward Elgar.

Lange, P. (1984). 'Unions, Workers and Wage Regulation: The Rational Bases of Consent', in J. H. Goldthorpe (ed.), *Order and Conflict in Contemporary Capitalism*. Oxford: Clarendon Press, pp. 98–123.

—— and Meadwell, H. (1991). 'Typologies of Democratic Systems: From Political Inputs to Political Economy', in H. J. Wiarda (ed.), *New Directions in Comparative Politics*. Boulder, CO: Westview, pp. 82–117.

Lash, S. and Urry, J. (1987). *The End of Organized Capitalism*. Cambridge: Polity Press.

Latulippe, D. (1996). 'Effective Retirement Age and the Duration of Retirement in the Industrial Countries between 1950 and 1990'. *ILO Issues in Social Protection, Discussion Paper 2*, Geneva: ILO.

—— and Turner, J. A. (2000). 'Partial Retirement and Pension Policy in Industrialized Countries'. *Industrial Labour Review*, 139/2: 179–95.

References

Lazear, E. P. (1979). 'Why is there Mandatory Retirement?' *Journal of Political Economy*, 87/6: 1261–84.

—— (1986). 'Retirement from the Labor Force', in O. Ashenfelter and R. Layard (eds.), *Handbook of Labor Economics*. Amsterdam: Elsevier, pp. 305–53.

—— (1990). 'Pensions and Deferred Benefits as Strategic Compensation'. *Industrial Relations*, 29/2: 263–80.

Lehmbruch, G. and Schmitter, P. C. (eds.) (1982). *Patterns of Corporatist Policy-Making*. London: Sage.

Leibfried, S. (1994). 'Sozialstaat oder Wohlfahrtsgesellschaft: Thesen zu einem japanisch-deutschen Sozialpolitikvergleich'. *Soziale Welt*, 45/4: 389–410.

Levi, M. (2000). 'The Economic Turn in Comparative Politics'. *Comparative Political Studies*, 33/6/7: 822–44.

Levy, J. D. (2000). 'France: Directing Adjustment?' in F. W. Scharpf and V. Schmidt (eds.), *Welfare and Work in the Open Economy*, Vol. II. Oxford: Oxford University Press, pp. 308–50.

Lieberson, S. (1991). 'Small N's and Big Conclusions: An Examination of the Reasoning in Comparative Studies Based on a Small Number of Cases'. *Social Forces*, 70/2: 307–20.

—— (1994). 'More on the Uneasy Case for Using Mill-Type Methods in Small-N Comparative Studies'. *Social Forces*, 72/4: 1225–37.

Lonsdale, S. and Aylward, M. (1996). 'A United Kingdom Perspective on Disability Policy', in L. J. M. Aarts, R. V. Burkhauser, and P. R. de Jong (eds.), *Curing the Dutch Disease*. Aldershot: Avebury, pp. 93–115.

Lumsdaine, R. L. and Mitchell, O. S. (1999). 'New Development in the Economic Analysis of Retirement', in O. Ashenfelter and D. Card (eds.), *Handbook of Labor Economics*, Vol. 3C. Amsterdam: Elsevier, pp. 3261–307.

Lutjens, E. (1996). 'Supplementary Pensions in the Netherlands', in E. Reynaud, L. apRoberts, B. Davies, and G. Hughes (eds.), *International Perspectives on Supplementary Pensions*. Westport, CT: Quorum, pp. 16–23.

Lynch, J. (2001). 'The Age-Orientation of Social Policy Regimes in OECD Countries'. *Journal of Social Policy*, 30/3: 411–36.

Lynes, T. (1997). 'The British Case', in M. Rein and E. Wadensjö (eds.), *Enterprise and the Welfare State*. Cheltenham: Edward Elgar, pp. 309–51.

Mahoney, J. (2003). 'Strategies of Causal Assessment in Comparative Historical Analysis', in J. Mahoney and D. Rueschemeyer (eds.), *Comparative Historical Analysis in the Social Sciences*. New York: Cambridge University Press, pp. 337–72.

Manow, P. (1997). 'Social Insurance and the German Political Economy', *MPIfG Disscussion Paper*, 2/97.

—— and Seils, E. (2000). 'Adjusting Badly: The German Welfare State, Structural Change and the Open Economy', in F. W. Scharpf and V. Schmidt (eds.), *Welfare and Work in the Open Economy*, Vol. II. Oxford: Oxford University Press, pp. 264–307.

Mares, I. (2001*a*). 'Firms and the Welfare State: When, Why and How Does Social Policy Matter to Employers', in P. A. Hall and D. Soskice (eds.), *Varieties of Capitalism*. New York: Oxford University Press, pp. 184–212.

—— (2001*b*). 'Enterprise Reorganization and Social Insurance Reform: The Development of Early Retirement in France and Germany'. *Governance*, 14/3: 295–317.

—— (2003). *The Politics of Social Risk. Business and Welfare State Development*. New York: Cambridge University Press.

Marsden, D. (1999). *A Theory of Employment Systems: Micro-Foundations of Societal Diversity*. Oxford: Oxford University Press.

Marshall, T. H. (1950). *Citizenship and Social Class. The Marshall Lectures*. Cambridge: Cambridge University Press.

Martin, C. J. (2000). *Stuck in Neutral: Business and the Politics of Human Capital Investment Policy*. Princeton, NJ: Princeton University Press.

Martin, J. P. (1998). 'What Works Among Active Labour Market Policies: Evidence from OECD Countries' Experiences', *OECD Labour Market and Social Policy Occasional Papers*, 35.

Maruo, N. (1986). 'The Development of the Welfare Mix in Japan', in R. Rose and R. Shiratori (eds.), *The Welfare State: East and West*. New York: Oxford University Press, pp. 64–79.

Mayer, K. U. and Müller, W. (1986). 'The State and the Structure of the Life Course', in A. B. Sørensen (ed.), *Human Development and the Life Course: Multidisciplinary Perspectives*. Hillsdale, NJ: Lawrence Erlbaum, pp. 217–45.

—— and Schoepflin, U. (1989). 'The State and the Life Course'. *Annual Review of Sociology*, 15: 187–209.

Mayntz, R. and Nedelmann, B. (1987). 'Eigendynamische soziale Prozesse'. *Kölner Zeitschrift für Soziologie und Sozialpsychologie*, 39: 648–68.

Merton, R. K. (1936). 'The Unanticipated Consequences of Purposive Social Action'. *American Sociological Review*, 1/6: 894–904.

—— (1967). *On Theoretical Sociology. Five Essays, Old and New*. New York: Free Press.

—— {1984}. 'Socially Expected Durations: A Case Study of Concept Formation in Sociology', in P. Sztompka (ed.), *Robert K. Merton: On Social Structure and Science*. Chicago, IL: University of Chicago Press, 1996, pp. 162–9.

Milgrom, P. and Roberts, J. (1994). 'Complementarities and Systems: Understanding Japanese Economic Organization'. *Estudios Economicos*, 9: 3–42.

MIRE (ed.) (1997). *Comparing Social Welfare Systems in Southern Europe*, Vol. III. *Florence Conference: Southern Europe*. Paris: MIRE.

Mirkin, B. A. (1987). 'Early Retirement as a Labor Force Policy: An International Overview'. *Monthly Labor Review*, 110/3: 19–33.

MISSOC (1998–2003) *Mutual Information System on Social Protection in the European Union* Brussles: European Commission. [www.europa.eu.int]

Moore, B., Jr. (1978). *Injustice. The Social Bases of Obedience and Revolt*. New York: M. E. Sharpe.

Morin, M.-L. and Vicens, C. (2001). 'Redundancy, Business Flexibility and Workers' Security: Findings of a Comparative European Survey'. *Industrial Labour Review*, 140/1: 45–67.

Morris, R. (1988). 'Changing Patterns of Public Social Welfare Policy in Nine Countries, 1975–1986: Predicting Future Trends', in R. Morris (ed.), *Testing the Limits of Social Welfare: International Perspectives on Policy Changes in Nine Countries*. Hanover, CT: University Press of New England, pp. 1–38.

Mosley, H. (1998). 'Short-Time Work Schemes in France, Germany, Italy and Spain: From Cyclical to Structural Intervention', in P. Auer (ed.), *Employment Policies in Focus: Labour Markets and Labour Market Policy in Europe and Beyond—International Experiences*. Berlin: IAS/MISEP, pp. 172–87.

—— and Kruppe, T. (1996). 'Employment Stabilization through Short-time Work', in G. Schmid, J. O'Reilly, and K. Schömann (eds.), *International Handbook of Labour Market Policy and Evaluation*. Cheltenham: Edward Elgar, pp. 594–622.

Myles, J. (1983). 'Comparative Public Policies for the Elderly: Framework and Resources for Analysis', in A.-M. Guillemard (ed.), *Old Age and the Welfare State*. London: Sage, pp. 19–44.

—— (1989). *Old Age in the Welfare State: The Political Economy of Public Pensions*, 2nd edn. Lawrence: University Press of Kansas.

—— and Pierson, P. (2001). 'The Comparative Political Economy of Pension Reform', in P. Pierson (ed.), *The New Politics of the Welfare State*. New York: Oxford University Press, pp. 305–33.

Naegele, G. (2002). 'Active Strategies for Older Workers in Germany', in M. Jespen, D. Foden, and M. Hutsebaut (eds.), *Active Strategies for Older Workers*. Brussels: ETUI, pp. 207–43.

—— and Walker, A. (2002). *Ageing and Social Policy: Towards an Agenda for Policy Learning Between Britain and Germany*. London: Anglo-German Foundation.

Naschold, F. and de Vroom, B. (eds.) (1994). *Regulating Employment and Welfare: Company and National Policies of Labour Force Participation at the End of Worklife in Industrial Countries*. Berlin: W. de Gruyter.

—— —— and Casey, B. (1994). 'Regulating Employment and Retirement: An International Comparison between Firms and Countries', in F. Naschold and B. de Vroom (eds.), *Regulating Employment and Welfare*. Berlin: W. de Gruyter, pp. 433–89.

—— Oppen, M., Peinemann, H., and Rosenow, J. (1994). 'Germany: The Concerted Transition from Work to Welfare', in F. Naschold and B. de Vroom (eds.), *Regulating Employment and Welfare*. Berlin: W. de Gruyter, pp. 117–82.

Natali, D. and Rhodes, M. (2004). 'Trade-offs and Veto Players: Reforming Pensions in France and Italy'. *French Politics*, 2: 1–23.

Ney, S. (2000). 'Are You Sitting Comfortably … Then We'll Begin: Three Gripping Policy Stories about Pension Reform'. *Innovation*, 13/4: 341–71.

NOSOSKO (1998). *Förtida utträde från arbetslivet 1987–1996: En jämförelse mellan de nordiska länderna*. Copenhagen: Nordisk Socialstatistisk Komité.

NOSOSKO (2000). *Social Protection in the Nordic Countries 1998: Scope, Expenditure and Financing*. Copenhagen: Nordisk Socialstatistisk Komité.

Nullmeier, F. and Rüb, F. W. (1993). *Die Transformation der Sozialpolitik*. Frankfurt: Campus.

Obinger, H. and Wagschal, U. (1998). 'Drei Welten des Wohlfahrtsstaates? Das Stratifizierungskonzept in der Clusteranalytischen Überprüfung', in S. Lessenich and I. Ostner (eds.), *Welten des Wohlfahrtskapitalismus*. Frankfurt: Campus, pp. 109–35.

O'Day, B. and Berkowitz, M. (2001). 'Disablity Benefit Programs: Can We Improve the Return-to-Work Record?' in G. L. Albrecht, K. D. Seelman, and M. Bury (eds.), *Handbook of Disability Studies*. Thousand Oaks, CA: Sage, pp. 633–41.

O'Donnell, R. and O'Reardon, C. (2000). 'Social Partnership in Ireland's Economic Transformation', in G. Fajertag and P. Pochet (eds.), *Social Pacts in Europe: New Dynamics*. Brussels: ETUI, pp. 237–56.

OCED (1963). *Manpower Statistics, 1950–62*. Paris: OECD.

—— (1985–2004). *Labour Force Statistics 1963/83–1983/2003*. Paris: OECD (various years).

—— (1988). *Reforming Public Pensions*. Paris: OECD.

—— (1992). 'Private Pensions and Public Policy', *OECD Social Policy Studies*, 9.

—— (1995*a*). *The Labour Market and Older Workers*. Paris: OECD.

—— (1995*b*). *The Transition from Work to Retirement*. Paris: OECD.

—— (1998*a*). *Employment Outlook 1998*. Paris: OECD.

—— (1998*b*). *Financial Market Trends*. No. 69. Paris: OECD.

—— (1998*c*). *Maintaining Prosperity in an Ageing Society*. Paris: OECD.

—— (1998*d*). 'Workforce Ageing in OECD Countries', in *Employment Outlook 1998*. Paris: OECD, pp. 123–51.

—— (1999). *Statistical Compendium*. Paris: OECD.

—— (2000). *Reforms for an Ageing Society*. Paris: OECD.

—— (2001*a*). *Ageing and Income: Financial Resources and Retirement in 9 OECD Countries*. Paris: OECD.

—— (2001*b*). *Employment Outlook 2001*. Paris: OECD.

—— (2001*c*). *Social Expenditure Database 1980–1998 (SOCX)*. Paris: OECD.

—— (2004). *Social Expenditure Database 1980–2001 (SOCX)*. Paris: OECD.

Olofsson, G. and Petersson, J. (1994). 'Sweden: Policy Dilemmas of the Changing Age Structure in a "Work Society" ', in F. Naschold and B. de Vroom (eds.), *Regulating Employment and Welfare*. Berlin: W. de Gruyter, pp. 183–245.

O'Loughlin, A. (1999). 'Social Policy and Older People in Ireland', in S. Quin, P. Kennedy, A. O'Donnell, and G. Kiely (eds.), *Contemporary Irish Social Policy*. Dublin: University College Dublin, pp. 221–42.

Olson, M. (1965). *The Logic of Collective Action: Public Goods and the Theory of Groups*, 2nd edn. Cambridge, MA: Harvard University Press.

—— (1982). *The Rise and Decline of Nations*. New Haven, CT / London: Yale University Press.

References

Oswald, C. (2001). *Das Ausscheiden aus dem Erwerbsleben in Deutschland und Großbritannien: Eine empirische Untersuchung mit Paneldaten.* Frankfurt: Peter Lang.

Øverbye, E. (1997). 'Retirement from the Labour Force: A Multiple Choice Exercise? Pre-Retirement in the Nordic Countries in a European Context', in A. Bosco and M. Hutsebaut (eds.), *Social Protection in Europe: Facing up to Changes and Challenges.* Brussels: ETUI, pp. 139–55.

Paci, M. (1989). 'Public and Private in the Italian Welfare System', in P. Lange and M. Regini (eds.), *State, Market, and Social Regulation: New Perspectives on Italy.* Cambridge: Cambridge University Press, pp. 217–34.

Palier, B. (1997). 'A 'Liberal' Dynamic in the Transformation of the French Social Welfare System', in J. Clasen (ed.), *Social Insurance in Europe.* Bristol: Policy Press, pp. 84–106.

—— (2000). ' "Defrosting" the French Welfare State'. *West European Politics,* 23/2: 113–36.

—— and Bonoli, G. (1995). 'Entre Bismarck et Beveridge: "Crises" de la Sécurité Sociale et Politique(s)'. *Revue française de science politique,* 4/45: 668–99.

Palme, M. and Svensson, I. (1999). 'Social Security, Occupational Pensions, and Retirement in Sweden', in J. Gruber and D. A. Wise (eds.), *Social Security and Retirement around the World.* Chicago, IL: University of Chicago Press, pp. 355–402.

Pampel, F. C. and Weiss, J. A. (1983). 'Economic Development, Pension Policies, and the Labor Force Participation of Aged Males: A Cross-National, Longitudinal Approach'. *American Journal of Sociology,* 89/2: 350–72.

—— and Williamson, J. B. (1989). *Age, Class, Politics, and the Welfare State.* New York: Cambridge University Press.

Paulli, A. and Tagliabue, M. (2002). 'Active Strategies for Older Workers in Italy', in M. Jespen, D. Foden, and M. Hutsebaut (eds.), *Active Strategies for Older Workers.* Brussels: ETUI, pp. 275–98.

Pemperton, H. E. (1936). 'The Curve of Culture Diffusion Rate'. *American Sociological Review,* 1/4: 547–56.

Petersen, J. H. (1989). 'The Process of Retirement in Denmark: Trends, Public Discussion and Institutional Framework', in W. Schmähl (ed.), *Redefining the Process of Retirement: An International Perspective.* Berlin: Springer, pp. 63–81.

Pfeffer, J. and Salancik, G. R. (1978). *The External Control of Organizations. A Resource Dependence Perspective.* New York: Harper & Row.

Pierson, P. (1993). 'When Effect Becomes Cause: Policy Feedback and Political Change'. *World Politics,* 45/4: 595–628.

—— (1994). *Dismantling the Welfare State? Reagan, Thatcher, and the Politics of Retrenchment.* New York: Cambridge University Press.

—— (1997). 'The Politics of Pension Reform', in K. G. Banting and R. Boadway (eds.), *Reform of Retirement Income Policy.* Kingston/Ontario: School of Policy Studies, pp. 273–93.

—— (2000a). 'Increasing Returns, Path Dependence, and the Study of Politics'. *American Political Science Review,* 94/2: 251–67.

Pierson, P. (2000*b*). 'Not Just What, but When: Timing and Sequence in Political Processes'. *Studies of American Political Development*, 14/Spring: 72–92.

—— (2001*a*). 'Post-industrial Pressures on the Mature Welfare States', in P. Pierson (ed.), *The New Politics of the Welfare State*. New York: Oxford University Press, pp. 80–104.

—— (2001*b*). 'Coping with Permanent Austerity: Welfare State Restructuring in Affluent Democracies', in P. Pierson (ed.), *The New Politics of the Welfare State*. New York: Oxford University Press, pp. 410–56.

—— (ed.) (2001*c*). *The New Politics of the Welfare State*. New York: Oxford University Press.

—— and Leibfried, S. (1995). 'Multitiered Institutions and the Making of Social Policy', in S. Leibfried and P. Pierson (eds.), *European Social Policy: Between Fragmentation and Integration*. Washington, DC: Brookings Institution, pp. 1–40.

Pizzorno, A. (1978). 'Political Exchange and Collective Identity in Industrial Conflict', in C. Crouch and A. Pizzorno (eds.), *The Resurgence of Class Conflict in Western Europe since 1968*, Vol. II: 'Comparative Analyses'. London: Macmillan, pp. 277–98.

Polanyi, K. (1944). *The Great Transformation: The Political and Economic Origins of our Time*. Boston, MA: Beacon Press.

Pontusson, J. (1997). 'Between Neo-Liberalism and the German Model: Swedish Capitalism in Transition', in C. Crouch and W. Streeck (eds.), *Political Economy of Modern Capitalism*. London: Sage, pp. 55–70.

Prinz, C. (ed.) (2003). *European Disability Pension Policies: 11 Country Trends 1970–2002*. Aldershot: Ashgate.

Przeworski, A. and Teune, H. (1970). *The Logic of Comparative Social Inquiry*. New York: Wiley.

Quadagno, J. (1987). 'Theories of the Welfare State'. *Annual Review of Sociology*, 13: 109–28.

Quin, S., Kennedy, P., O'Donnell, A., and Kiely, G. (eds.) (1999). *Contemporary Irish Social Policy*. Dublin: University College Dublin.

Quinn, J. and Burkhauser, R. V. (1990). 'Work and Retirement', in R. H. Binstock and L. K. George (eds.), *Handbook of Aging and the Social Sciences*, 3rd edn. New York: Academic Press, pp. 307–27.

Ragin, C. C. (1987). *The Comparative Method: Moving Beyond Qualitative and Quantitative Strategies*. Berkeley, CA: University of California Press.

—— (2000). *Fuzzy-Set Social Science*. Chicago, IL: University of Chicago Press.

—— and Becker, H. S. (eds.) (1992). *What is a Case? Exploring the Foundations of Social Inquiry*. Cambridge: Cambridge University Press.

Reday-Mulvey, G. (1996). 'Gradual Retirement in France', in L. Delsen and G. Reday-Mulvey (eds.), *Gradual Retirement in the OECD Countries*. Aldershot: Dartmouth, pp. 45–68.

Regalia, I. and Regini, M. (1998). 'Italy: The Dual Character of Industrial Relations', in A. Ferner and R. Hyman (eds.), *Changing Industrial Relations in Europe*. Oxford: Blackwell, pp. 459–503.

Regini, M. and Regalia, I. (1997). 'Employers, Unions and the State: The Resurgence of Concertation in Italy?' *West European Politics*, 20/1: 210–30.

Rein, M. (1996). 'Is America Exceptional? The Role of Occupational Welfare in the United States and the European Community', in M. Shalev (ed.), *The Privatization of Social Policy?* London: Macmillan, pp. 27–43.

—— and Rainwater, L. (eds.) (1986*a*). 'The Public/Private Mix', in M. Rein and L. Rainwater (eds.), *Public/Private Interplay in Social Protection: A Comparative Study*. Armonk, NY: M. E. Sharpe, pp. 3–24.

—— —— (1986*b*). *Public/Private Interplay in Social Protection: A Comparative Study*. Armonk, NY: M. E. Sharpe.

—— and Turner, J. A. (2001). 'Public–Private Interactions: Mandatory Pensions in Australia, the Netherlands and Switzerland'. *Review of Population and Social Policy*, 10: 107–53.

—— and Wadensjö, E. (1997*a*). 'The Emerging Role of Enterprise in Social Policy', in M. Rein and E. Wadensjö (eds.), *Enterprise and the Welfare State*. Cheltenham: Edward Elgar, pp. 1–32.

—— —— (eds.) (1997*b*). *Enterprise and the Welfare State*. Cheltenham: Edward Elgar.

Reinhard, H.-J., Kruse, J., and von Maydell, B. B. (eds.) (1998). *Invaliditätssicherung im Rechtsvergleich*. Baden-Baden: Nomos.

Reynaud, E. (1996). 'Financing Models for Pay-As-You-Go Systems', in E. Reynaud, L. apRoberts, B. Davies, and G. Hughes (eds.), *International Perspectives on Supplementary Pensions*. Westport, CT: Quorum, pp. 71–81.

—— (1997*a*). 'France: A National and Contractual Second Tier', in M. Rein and E. Wadensjö (eds.), *Enterprise and the Welfare State*. Cheltenham: Edward Elgar, pp. 65–98.

—— (1997*b*). 'Private Pensions in OECD Countries: France', *OECD Labour Market and Social Policy Occasional Papers*, 30.

—— (ed.) (2000). *Social Dialogue and Pension Reform: United Kingdom, United States, Germany, Japan, Sweden, Italy, Spain*. Geneva: International Labour Office.

—— apRoberts, L., Davies, B., and Hughes, G. (eds.) (1996). *International Perspectives on Supplementary Pensions*. Westport, CT: Quorum.

Rhodes, M. (ed.) (1996). *Southern European Welfare States*. London: Frank Cass.

—— (2001) 'The Political Economy of Social Pacts: "Competitive Corporatism" and European Welfare Reform', in P. Pierson (ed.), *The New Politics of the Welfare State*. New York: Oxford University Press, pp. 165–94.

Rieger, E. (1991). 'Strategien der Institutionenbildung. Über die Bedeutung von Wahlverwandtschaften im Prozeß der Entstehung des Wohlfahrtsstaates'. *Journal für Sozialforschung*: 157–75.

—— (1998). 'Soziologische Theorie und Sozialpolitik im entwickelten Wohlfahrtsstaat', in S. Lessenich and I. Ostner (eds.), *Welten des Wohlfahrtskapitalismus: Der Sozialstaat in vergleichender Perspektive*. Frankfurt: Campus, pp. 59–89.

Riphahn, R. (1997). 'Disability, Retirement and Unemployment—Substitute Pathways for Labour Force Exit? An Empirical Test for the Case of Germany'. *Applied Economics*, 29/5: 551–61.

Roche, W. K. (1997). 'Between Regime Fragmentation and Realignment: Irish Industrial Relations in the 1990s'. *Industrial Relations Journal*, 29/2: 112–25.

Rogers, J. and Streeck, W. (eds.) (1995). *Works Councils: Consultation, Representation, and Cooperation in Industrial Relations*. Chicago, IL: University of Chicago Press.

Rokkan, S. (1980). 'Eine Familie von Modellen für die vergleichende Geschichte Europas'. *Zeitschrift für Soziologie*, 9/2: 118–28.

—— (1999). *State Formation, Nation-Building and Mass Politics in Europe. The Theory of Stein Rokkan* (ed. by P. Flora, S. Kuhnle, and D. Urwin). Oxford: Oxford University Press.

Rose, R. (1985). 'The Significance of Public Employment', in R. Rose (ed.), *Public Employment in Western Nations*. Cambridge: Cambridge University Press, pp. 1–53.

—— and Urwin, D. (1969). 'Social Cohesion, Political Parties and Strains in Regimes'. *Comparative Political Studies*, 2/1: 7–67.

Rosenow, J. and Naschold, F. (1994). *Die Regulierung der Altersgrenzen: Strategien von Unternehmen und die Politik des Staates*. Berlin: Sigma.

Rothenbacher, F. (2004). 'The Welfare State of the Civil (or Public) Servants in Europe: A Comparison of the Pension Systems for Civil (or Public) Servants in France, Great Britain, and Germany', *MZES Working Paper*, 74.

Rothstein, B. (1992). 'Labor-market Institutions and Working-class Strength', in S. Steinmo, K. Thelen, and F. Longstreth (eds.), *Structuring Politics: Historical Institutionalism in Comparative Analysis*. New York: Cambridge University Press, pp. 33–56.

Russig, H. (1986). 'Redundancy and the Public/Private Mix', in M. Rein and L. Rainwater (eds.), *Public/Private Interplay in Social Protection: A Comparative Study*. Armonk, NY: M. E. Sharpe, pp. 149–201.

Sackmann, R. (1998). *Konkurrierende Generationen auf dem Arbeitsmarkt: Altersstrukturierung in Arbeitsmarkt und Sozialpolitik*. Opladen: Westdeutscher Verlag.

—— (2001). 'Age and Labour-Market Chances in International Comparison'. *European Sociological Review*, 17/4: 373–87.

Samek Lodovici, M. (2000a). 'The Dynamics of Labour Market Reform in European Countries', in G. Esping-Andersen and M. Regini (eds.), *Why Deregulate Labour Markets?* Oxford: Oxford University Press, pp. 30–65.

—— (2000b). 'Italy: The Long Times of Consensual Re-regulation', in G. Esping-Andersen and M. Regini (eds.), *Why Deregulate Labour Markets?* Oxford: Oxford University Press, pp. 271–306.

Sartori, G. (1994). 'Compare Why and How: Comparing, Miscomparing and the Comparative Method', in M. Dogan and A. Kazancigil (eds.), *Comparing Nations: Concepts, Strategies, Substance*. Oxford: Blackwell, pp. 14–34.

Sass, S. A. (1997). *The Promise of Private Pensions: The First Hundred Years*. Cambridge, MA: Harvard University Press.

Savolainen, J. (1994). 'The Rationality of Drawing Big Conclusions Based on Small Samples in Defense of Mill's Methods'. *Social Forces*, 72/4: 1217–24.

Scarbrough, E. (2000). 'West European Welfare States: The Old Politics of Retrenchment'. *European Journal of Political Research*, 38: 225–59.

—— (2002). *The Political Perils of Privatized Pensions: Stakeholder Pensions in Britain*, ECPR Joint Sessions. Turin, 22–27 March 2002.

Scharpf, F. W. (1991). *Crisis and Choice in European Social Democracy*. Ithaca, NY: Cornell University Press.

—— (1997). *Games Real Actors Play: Actor-Centered Institutionalism in Policy Research*. Boulder, CO: Westview Press.

—— (2000). 'Economic Changes, Vulnerabilities, and Institutional Capabilities', in F. W. Scharpf and V. Schmidt (eds.), *Welfare and Work in the Open Economy*, Vol. I. Oxford: Oxford University Press, pp. 21–124.

—— (2001). 'Employment and the Welfare State: A Continental Dilemma', in B. Ebbinghaus and P. Manow (eds.), *Comparing Welfare Capitalism*. London: Routledge, pp. 270–83.

—— and Schmidt, V. (eds.) (2000). *Welfare and Work in the Open Economy*, 2 vols. Oxford: Oxford University Press.

Scherer, P. (2002). 'Age of Withdrawal from the Labour Force in OECD Countries', *OECD Labour Market and Social Policy Occasional Papers*, 49.

Scheuer, S. (1998). 'Denmark: A Less Regulated Model', in A. Ferner and R. Hyman (eds.), *Changing Industrial Relations in Europe*. Oxford: Blackwell, pp. 146–70.

Schludi, M. (2001). 'The Politics of Pensions in European Social Insurance Countries', *MPIfG Discussion Paper*, 01/11.

—— (2005). *The Reform of Bismarckian Pension Systems: A Comparison of Pension Politics in Austria, France, Germany, Italy and Sweden*. Amsterdam: Amsterdam University Press.

Schmähl, W. (1997). 'The Public–Private Mix in Pension Provision in Germany: The Role of Employer-based Pension Arrangements and the Influence of Public Activties', in M. Rein and E. Wadensjö (eds.), *Enterprise and the Welfare State*. Cheltenham: Edward Elgar, pp. 99–148.

—— and Böhm, S. (1994). 'Occupational Pension Schemes in the Private and Public Sector in the Federal Republic of Germany—An Overview'. *Zentrum für Sozialpolitik, Universität Bremen, Arbeitspapier*, 5.

—— —— (1996). 'Supplementary Pensions in the Federal Republic of Germany', in E. Reynaud, L. apRoberts, B. Davies, and G. Hughes (eds.), *International Perspectives on Supplementary Pensions*. Westport, CT: Quorum, pp. 7–15.

—— George, R., and Oswald, C. (1996). 'Gradual Retirement in Germany', in L. Delsen and G. Reday-Mulvey (eds.), *Gradual Retirement in the OECD Countries*. Aldershot: Dartmouth, pp. 69–93.

Schmidt, V. A. (1996). 'Industrial Policy and Policies of Industry in Advanced Industrialized Nations (Review Article)'. *Comparative Politics*, 28: 225–48.

Schmitter, P. C. (1974). 'Still the Century of Corporatism?' *Revue of Politics*, 36: 85–131.

—— and Lehmbruch, G. (eds.) (1981). *Trends Toward Corporatist Intermediation.* Beverly Hills: Sage.

—— and Streeck, W. {1981}. 'The Organization of Business Interests: Studying the Associative Action of Business in Advanced Industrial Societies', *MPIfG Discussion Paper*, 99/1, 1999.

Schömann, K., Felchtner, S., Mytzek, R., and Schömann, I. (2000). 'Moving Towards Employment Insurance: Unemployment Insurance and Employment Protection in the OECD', *WZB Discussion Papers*, FS-I-00-201. Berlin: Wissenschaftszentrum.

Schwartz, H. (1994). 'Small States in Big Trouble: State Reorganization in Australia, Denmark, New Zealand, and Sweden in the 1980s'. *World Politics*, 46/4: 527–55.

Seeleib-Kaiser, M. and Thränhardt, A. M. (2000). 'Wohlfahrtsgesellschaft statt Wohlfahrtsstaat in Japan: Zwischen westlichen Vorbildern und eigenständigem Modell', in H. Obinger and U. Wagschal (eds.), *Der gezügelte Wohlfahrtsstaat: Sozialpolitik in reichen Industrienationen.* Frankfurt: Campus, pp. 283–328.

Seitan, M. (2001). *The Irish Pension System and Reform*, World Bank Conference. Vienna, April 6–7, 2001.

Sengenberger, W. (1992). 'Intensified Competition, Industrial Restructuring and Industrial Relations'. *Industrial Labour Review*, 131/2: 139–54.

Settersten, R. A. and Mayer, K. U. (1997). 'The Measurement of Age, Age Structure, and the Life Course'. *Annual Review of Sociology*, 23: 233–61.

Shalev, M. (1992). 'The Resurgence of Labour Quiescence', in M. Regini (ed.), *The Future of Labour Movements.* London: Sage, pp. 102–32.

—— (ed.) (1996). *The Privatization of Social Policy? Occupational Welfare and the Welfare State in America, Scandinavia and Japan.* London: Macmillan.

—— (2006). 'Limits of and Alternatives to Multiple Regression in Comparative Research'. *Comparative Social Research*, 25 (forthcoming).

Sheppard, H. L. (1991). 'The United States: The Privatization of Exit', in M. Kohli, M. Rein, A.-M. Guillemard, and H. van Gunsteren (eds.), *Time for Retirement.* New York: Cambridge University Press, pp. 252–83.

Shinkawa, T. and Pempel, T. J. (1996). 'Occupational Welfare and the Japanese Experience', in M. Shalev (ed.), *The Privatization of Social Policy?* London: Macmillan, pp. 280–326.

Shirai, T. (1983). 'A Theory of Enterprise Unionism', in T. Shirai (ed.), *Contemporary Industrial Relations in Japan.* Madison, WI: University of Wisconsin Press, pp. 117–44.

Shorter, E. and Tilly, C. (1974). *Strikes in France 1830–1968.* Cambridge: Cambridge University Press.

Skocpol, T. (1984). 'Emerging Agendas and Recurrent Strategies in Historical Sociology', in T. Skocpol (ed.), *Vision and Method in Historical Sociology.* Cambridge: Cambridge University Press, pp. 356–91.

—— (1992). *Protecting Soldiers and Mothers: The Political Origins of Social Policy in the United States.* Cambridge, MA: Belknap Press.

Sørensen, A. B. (1992). 'Retirement, Individual Performance and Labour Market Structures', in W. J. A. van den Heuvel, R. Illsely, A. Jamieson, and C. P. M. Knipscheer (eds.), *Opportunities and Challenges in an Ageing Society*. Amsterdam: North-Holland, pp. 73–89.

—— (1994). 'Firms, Wages, and Incentives', in N. J. Smelser and R. Swedberg (eds.), *The Handbook of Economic Sociology*. Princeton, NJ: Princeton University, pp. 504–28.

Sorge, A. (1976). 'The Evolution of Industrial Democracy in the Countries of the European Community'. *British Journal of Industrial Relations*, 14/3: 274–94.

Soskice, D. (1991). 'The Institutional Infrastructure for International Competitiveness: A Comparative Analysis of the UK and Germany', in A. B. Atkinson and R. Brunetta (eds.), *Economics for the New Europe*. London: Macmillan, pp. 45–66.

—— (1999). 'Divergent Production Regimes: Coordinated and Uncoordinated Market Economies in the 1980s and 1990s', in H. Kitschelt, P. Lange, G. Marks, and J. Stephens (eds.), *Continuity and Change in Contemporary Capitalism*. New York: Cambridge University Press, pp. 101–34.

SSA (1999). *Social Security Programs Throughout the World, 1999*. Washington, DC: Social Security Administration.

SSA/ISSA (2003). *Social Security Programs Throughout the World: The Americas, 2003*. Washington, DC: Social Security Administration.

—— (2004a). *Social Security Programs Throughout the World: Europe, 2004*. Washington, DC: Social Security Administration.

—— (2004b). *Social Security Programs Throughout the World: Asia and the Pacific, 2004*. Washington, DC: Social Security Administration.

Statistisches Bundesamt (2005). *Mikrozensus* (internal data). Wiesbaden: Statistisches Bundesamt.

Steinmeyer, H.-D. (1996). 'Labor Mobility and Supplementary Pensions', in E. Reynaud, L. apRoberts, B. Davies, and G. Hughes (eds.), *International Perspectives on Supplementary Pensions*. Westport, CT: Quorum, pp. 185–90.

Stephens, J. D. (1979). *The Transition from Capitalism to Socialism*. Urbana, IL: University of Illinois Press.

—— (1996). 'The Scandinavian Welfare States: Achievements, Crisis and Prospects', in G. Esping-Andersen (ed.), *Welfare States in Transition: National Adaptations in Global Economies*. London: Sage, pp. 32–65.

Stinchcombe, A. L. (1965). 'Social Structure and Organizations', in J. G. March (ed.), *Handbook of Organizations*. Chicago, IL: R. McNally, pp. 142–93.

—— (1968). *Constructing Social Theories*. New York: Harcourt, Brace & World.

Stock, J. H. and Wise, D. A. (1990). 'Pensions, the Option Value of Work and Retirement'. *Econometrica*, 58/5: 1151–80.

Streeck, W. (1987a). 'Industrial Relations and Industrial Change: The Restructuring of the World Automobile Industry in the 1970s and 1980s'. *Economic and Industrial Democracy*, 8: 437–62.

Streeck, W. (1987*b*). 'Vielfalt und Interdependenz. Überlegungen zur Rolle von intermediären Organisationen in sich ändernden Umwelten'. *Kölner Zeitschrift für Soziologie und Sozialpsychologie*, 39/3: 471–95.

—— (1992). *Social Institutions and Economic Performance. Studies of Industrial Relations in Advanced Capitalist Economies*. London: Sage.

—— (1995). 'Works Councils in Western Europe: From Consultation to Participation', in J. Rogers and W. Streeck (eds.), *Works Councils: Consultation, Representation, and Cooperation in Industrial Relations*. Chicago: University of Chicago Press, pp. 312–49.

—— (1997*a*). 'Beneficial Constraints: On the Economic Limits of Rational Voluntarism', in J. R. Hollingsworth and R. Boyer (eds.), *Contemporary Capitalism: The Embeddedness of Institutions*. New York: Cambridge University Press, pp. 197–219.

—— (1997*b*). 'German Capitalism: Does it Exist? Can it Survive?' in C. Crouch and W. Streeck (eds.), *Political Economy of Modern Capitalism*. London: Sage, pp. 33–54.

—— (2001). 'Introduction: Explorations into the Origins of Nonliberal Capitalism in Germany and Japan', in W. Streeck and K. Yamamura (eds.), *The Origins of Nonliberal Capitalism*. Ithaca, NY: Cornell University Press, pp. 1–38.

—— and Thelen, K. (2005). 'Introduction: Institutional Change in Advanced Political Economies', in W. Streeck and K. Thelen (eds.), *Beyond Continuity: Institutional Change in Advanced Political Economies*. Oxford: Oxford University Press, pp. 1–39.

—— and Yamamura, K. (eds.) (2001). *The Origins of Nonliberal Capitalism: Germany and Japan in Comparison*. Ithaca, NY: Cornell University Press.

Swedish Labour Force Surveys (2005). *Arbetskrafts undersökningarna 1974–2004*. Stockholm: Statistics Sweden.

Swenson, P. and Pontusson, J. (2000). 'The Swedish Employer Offensive Against Centralized Bargaining', in T. Iversen, J. Pontusson, and D. Soskice (eds.), *Unions, Employers, and Central Banks*. New York: Cambridge University Press, pp. 77–106.

Swenson, P. A. (2002). *Capitalists against Markets: The Making of Labor Markets and Welfare States in the United States and Sweden*. New York: Oxford University Press.

SZW (1997). *Income Benefits for Early Exit from the Labour Market in Eight European Countries: A Comparative Study*. Den Haag: Ministerie van Sociale Zaken en Werkgelegenheid.

Takayama, N. (1996). 'Gradual Retirement in Japan: Macro Issues and Policies', in L.Delsen and G. Reday-Mulvey (eds.), *Gradual Retirement in the OECD Countries*. Aldershot: Dartmouth, pp. 135–63.

Taylor, A. J. (1989). *Trade Unions and Politics. A Comparative Introduction*. London: Macmillan.

Taylor, P. and Walker, A. (1996). 'Gradual Retirement in the United Kingdom', in L.Delsen and G. Reday-Mulvey (eds.), *Gradual Retirement in the OECD Countries*. Aldershot: Dartmouth, pp. 94–110.

—— —— (1998). 'Employers and Older Workers: Attitudes and Employment Practices'. *Ageing and Society*, 18: 641–58.

Taylor-Gooby, P. (1999). 'Policy Change at a Time of Retrenchment: Recent Pension Reform in France, Germany, Italy and the UK'. *Social Policy & Administration*, 33/1: 1–19.

Teague, P. (2001). 'Deliberative Governance and EU Social Policy'. *European Journal of Industrial Relations*, 7/1: 7–26.

Thelen, K. (1999). 'Historical Institutionalism in Comparative Politics'. *Annual Review of Political Science*, 2: 369–404.

—— (2002). 'The Explanatory Power of Historical Institutionalism', in R. Mayntz (ed.), *Akteure–Mechanismen–Modelle: Zur Theoriefähigkeit makro-sozialer Analysen*. Frankfurt: Campus, pp. 91–107.

Tilly, C. (1984). *Big Structures, Large Processes, Huge Comparisons*. New York: Russell Sage.

Titmuss, R. M. {1958}. *Essays on the 'Welfare State'*. London: Allen and Unwin 1976.

—— {1968}. *Commitment to Welfare*. London: Allen and Unwin 1976.

Tolliday, S. and Zeitlin, J. (eds.) (1985). *Shop Floor Bargaining and the State: Historical and Comparative Perspectives*. Cambridge: Cambridge University Press.

Tonge, J. (1997). 'Britain', in H. Compston (ed.), *The New Politics of Unemployment: Radical Policy Initiatives in Western Europe*. London: Routledge, pp. 87–102.

Trampusch, C. (2005). 'Institutional Resettlement: The Case of Early Retirement in Germany', in W. Streeck and K. Thelen (eds.), *Beyond Continuity: Institutional Change in Advanced Political Economies*. Oxford: Oxford University Press, pp. 203–28.

Traxler, F. (1999). 'The State in Industrial Relations: A Cross-national Analysis of Developments and Socioeconomic Effects'. *European Journal of Political Research*, 36: 55–85.

—— Blaschke, S. and Kittel, B. (2001). *National Labour Relations in Internationalized Markets: A Comparative Study of Institutions, Change, and Performance*. Oxford: Oxford University Press.

Trommel, W. and de Vroom, B. (1994). 'The Netherlands: The Loreley-Effect of Early Exit', in F. Naschold and B. de Vroom (eds.), *Regulating Employment and Welfare*. Berlin: W. de Gruyter, pp. 51–115.

Tsoukalis, L. and Ferreira, A. da. S. (1980). 'Management of Industrial Surplus Capacity in the European Community'. *International Organizations*, 34/3: 355–76.

Tuijnman, A. C. and Schömann, K. (1996). 'Life-long Learning and Skill Formation', in G. Schmid, J. O'Reilly, and K. Schömann (eds.), *International Handbook of Labour Market Policy and Evaluation*. Cheltenham: Edward Elgar, pp. 462–88.

Turner, J. A. (1996). 'Risk Bearing in Pension Plans', in E. Reynaud, L. apRoberts, B. Davies, and G. Hughes (eds.), *International Perspectives on Supplementary Pensions*. Westport, CT: Quorum, pp. 82–96.

—— and Watanabe, N. (1995). *Private Pension Policies in Industrialized Countries: A Compartive Analysis*. Kalamazoo, MI: W. E. Upjohn Institute for Employment Research.

US-CPS (2000). *US Current Population Survey 2000*. Washington, DC: US Bureau of the Census [www.bls.census.gov].

Vail, M. I. (1999). 'The Better Part of Valour: The Politics of French Welfare Reform'. *Journal of European Social Policy*, 9/4: 311–29.

van Kersbergen, K. (1995). *Social Capitalism: A Study of Christian Democracy and the Welfare State*. London: Routledge.

van Waarden, F. (1995). 'Government Intervention in Industrial Relations', in J. Van Ruysseveldt, R. Huiskamp, and J. van. Hoof (eds.), *Comparative Industrial and Employment Relations*. London: Sage, pp. 109–33.

VDR (2002). *Rentenversicherung in Zeitreihen*. Berlin: Verband Deutscher Rentenversicherungsträger [www.vdr.de].

Viebrok, H. (2003). 'Disability Pensions in Germany', in C. Prinz (ed.), *European Disability Pension Policies*. Aldershot: Ashgate, pp. 197–224.

Visser, J. (1990). *In Search of Inclusive Unionism*. Deventer: Kluwer.

—— (1998). 'The Netherlands: The Return of Responsive Corporatism', in A. Ferner and R. Hyman (eds.), *Changing Industrial Relations in Europe*. Oxford: Blackwell, pp. 283–314.

—— (2002). 'The First Part-Time Economy in the World: A Model to Be Followed?' *Journal of European Social Policy*, 12/1: 23–42.

—— and Hemerijck, A. (1997). *'A Dutch Miracle': Job Growth, Welfare Reform, and Corporatism in the Netherlands*. Amsterdam: Amsterdam University Press.

von Nordheim Nielsen, F. (1991). 'The Politics of Ageing in Scandinavian Countries', in J. Myles and J. Quadagno (eds.), *States, Labor Markets, and the Future of Old-Age Policy*. Philadelphia, PA: Temple University Press, pp. 127–74.

von Prondynski, F. (1998). 'Ireland: Corporatism Revived', in A. Ferner and R. Hyman (eds.), *Changing Industrial Relations in Europe*. Oxford: Blackwell, pp. 55–73.

von Rhein-Kress, G. (1993). 'Coping with Economic Crisis: Labour Supply as a Policy Instrument', in F. G. Castles (ed.), *Families of Nations: Patterns of Public Policy in Western Democracies*. Aldershot: Dartmouth, pp. 131–78.

Wadensjö, E. (1991). 'Sweden: Partial Exit', in M. Kohli, M. Rein, A.-M. Guillemard, and H. van Gunsteren (eds.), *Time for Retirement*. New York: Cambridge University Press, pp. 284–323.

—— (1996). 'Gradual Retirement in Sweden', in L. Delsen and G. Reday-Mulvey (eds.), *Gradual Retirement in the OECD Countries*. Aldershot: Dartmouth, pp. 25–44.

—— (1997). 'The Welfare Mix in Pension Provisions in Sweden', in M. Rein and E. Wadensjö (eds.), *Enterprise and the Welfare State*. Cheltenham: Edward Elgar, pp. 266–308.

—— (2000a). 'The New Swedish Pension System', in G. Hughes and J. Stewart (eds.), *Pensions in the European Union: Adapting to Economic and Social Change*. Boston, MA: Kluwer, pp. 147–60.

—— (2000b). 'Sweden: Reform of the Public Pension System', in E. Reynaud (ed.), *Social Dialogue and Pension Reform*. Geneva: International Labour Office, pp. 67–80.

References

Wadensjö, E. (2002). 'Active Strategies for Older Workers in Sweden', in M. Jespen, D. Foden, and M. Hutsebaut (eds.), *Active Strategies for Older Workers*. Brussels: ETUI, pp. 381–402.

Wadensjö, E. and Palmer, E. E. (1996). 'Curing the Dutch Disease from a Swedish Perspective', in L. J. M. Aarts, R. V. Burkhauser, and P. R. de Jong (eds.), *Curing the Dutch Disease*. Aldershot: Avebury, pp. 133–55.

Walker, A. (2000). 'Why Active Public Policies Are Needed in Response to the Ageing Workforce', in E. Gabaglio and R. Hoffmann (eds.), *European Trade Union Yearbook 1999*. Brussels: European Trade Union Institute, pp. 341–54.

—— (2002). 'Active Strategies for Older Workers in the UK', in M. Jespen, D. Foden, and M. Hutsebaut (eds.), *Active Strategies for Older Workers*. Brussels: ETUI, pp. 403–35.

Walwei, U. and Werner, H. (2001). 'Employment Problems and Active Labor Market Policies in Industrialized Countries', in D. D. Hoskins, D. Dobbernack, and C. Kuptsch (eds.), *Social Security at the Dawn of the 21st Century*. New Brunswick, NJ: Transaction Publishers, pp. 133–70.

Warr, P. (1994). 'Age and Job Performance', in J. Snel and R. Cremer (eds.), *Work and Ageing: A European Perspective*. London: Taylor & Francis, pp. 309–22.

Watanabe, S. (2000). 'The Japan Model and the Future of Employment and Wage Systems'. *Industrial Labour Review*, 139/3: 307–33.

Weber, M. {1922}. *Wirtschaft und Gesellschaft. Grundriss der Verstehenden Soziologie*. Tübingen: J.C.B. Mohr.

—— (1978). *Economy and Society*, 2 vols. Berkeley, CA: University of California Press.

Weir, M., Orloff, A. S., and Skocpol, T. (eds.) (1988). *The Politics of Social Policy in the United States*. Princeton, NJ: Princeton University Press.

Western, B. (1998). 'Institutions and the Labor Market', in M. C. Brinton and V. Nee (eds.), *The New Institutionalism in Sociology*. New York: Russell Sage Foundation, pp. 224–43.

Whiteside, N. (1995). 'Aiming at Consensus: The Politics of the "Social" and "Industrial" Wage in Britain after the Second World War', in B. Palier (ed.), *Comparing Social Welfare Systems in Europe, Vol. I: Oxford Conference: France—United Kingdom*. Paris: MIRE, pp. 509–33.

Wilensky, H. L. and Lebeaux, C. N. (1958). *Industrial Society and Social Welfare*. New York: Free Press 1965.

Wincott, D. (2001). 'Reassessing the Social Foundations of Welfare (State) Regimes'. *New Political Economy*, 6/3: 409–25.

Wise, D. A. (1993). 'Firm Pension Policy and Early Retirement', in A. B. Atkinson and M. Rein (eds.), *Age, Work and Social Security*. New York: St. Martin's Press, pp. 51–88.

Wolf, J., Kohli, M., and Künemund, H. (eds.) (1994). *Alter und gewerkschaftliche Politik: Auf dem Weg zur Rentnergewerkschaft?* Köln: Bund Verlag.

Wollmann, H. (2000). 'Comparing Institutional Development in Britain and Germany: (Persistent) Divergence or (Progressing) Convergence?' in H. Wollmann and E. Schröter (eds.), *Comparing Public Sector Reform in Britain and Germany: Key Traditions and Trends in Modernisation*. Aldershot: Ashgate, pp. 1–26.

Wright. (ed.) (1994). *Privatization in Western Europe: Pressures, Problems and Paradoxes*. London: Pinter.

Yashiro, N. and Oshio, T. (1999). 'Social Security and Retirement in Japan', in J. Gruber and D. A. Wise (eds.), *Social Security and Retirement around the World*. Chicago, IL: University of Chicago Press, pp. 239–67.

Index